AF674911

The
Religion of the Ṛigveda

H.D. GRISWOLD
Ph.D. (Cornell), D.D. (Union)

MOTILAL BANARSIDASS PUBLISHERS
PRIVATE LIMITED • DELHI

First Edition: Delhi, 1971
Reprint: Delhi, 1999

ISBN: 81-208-0745-6

MOTILAL BANARSIDASS
41 U.A. Bungalow Road, Jawahar Nagar, Delhi 110 007
8 Mahalaxmi Chamber, Warden Road, Mumbai 400 026
120 Royapettah High Road, Mylapore, Chennai 600 004
Sanas Plaza, 1302, Baji Rao Road, Pune 411 002
16 St. Mark's Road, Bangalore 560 001
8 Camac Street, Calcutta 700 017
Ashok Rajpath, Patna 800 004
Chowk, Varanasi 221 001

PRINTED IN INDIA
BY JAINENDRA PRAKASH JAIN AT SHRI JAINENDRA PRESS,
A-45 NARAINA, PHASE I, NEW DELHI 110 028
AND PUBLISHED BY NARENDRA PRAKASH JAIN FOR
MOTILAL BANARSIDASS PUBLISHERS PRIVATE LIMITED,
BUNGALOW ROAD, DELHI 110 007

TO MY WIFE

FOREWORD

Two things have attracted the author to the study of the *Ṛigveda;* first, the living interest which has lured him on ever since he began the study of Vedic in 1889 with Prof. WEBER of Berlin, after previously reading Sanskrit with Prof. MACDONELL of Oxford; and secondly, the fact that he has had the advantage of living nearly thirty years in the Punjab, the very habitat of the Vedic Indians.

The religion of the *Ṛigveda* in the form in which it was professed and practised is, of course, dead, and yet, in a sense, it still lives. As the Old Testament has fulfilled itself in three monotheisms, Judaism, Christianity and Islām, so the *Ṛigveda* has fulfilled itself in the popular polytheism, the philosophic pantheism and the occasional monotheism of India. If it is impossible to understand present-day Hinduism without a knowledge of the *Ṛigveda,* the reverse is also true that it is impossible to understand the *Ṛigveda* without a knowledge of modern Hinduism; for very many of the doctrines and rites of Hinduism point back to the *Ṛigveda* as their fountain-head and as such are survivals of that ancient time.

While it is true that the Ṛigvedic gods have passed into the twilight, yet the *Ṛigveda* itself abides as a permanent source of material for the reconstruction of the ancient religion. As the New Testament reveals the nature of early Christianity, and the Qurān that of early Islām, so does the *Ṛigveda* that of early Vedism. Two things are necessary as an adequate equipment for the reconstruction of Vedic religion — a knowledge of the Ṛigvedic text and a knowledge of the Ṛigvedic land. The writer can claim only a moderate acquaintance with the text of the *Ṛigveda,* in this respect falling short of the linguistic equipment possessed by the great Vedic scholars of the world. On the other hand, the fact of residence in the Punjab for nearly thirty years ought to yield some fruit. For as Palestine is sometimes called 'the fifth Gospel', so the Punjab might well be called 'the fifth Veda'. Its *fauna* and *flora* must be essentially the same to-day as they were 1000 B.C. So with the general look of the land — great rivers threading their way through great plains, and to the north the snow-capped Himālayas. During the lapse of 3000 years the climatic and meteoric conditions which rule to-day can hardly have changed very much, such as the great heat of the pre-monsoon season, the dust storms, the monsoon rains, and the feverish time immediately following the close of the monsoon.

Then as regards the blood of Aryan and Dasyu, the ancient inhabitants of the land, it is found commingled in the present-day population of the Punjab. The Kāshmīrī and Punjabī Brāhmans represent probably the purest Aryan blood; but the whole population, like every other race on the face of the earth, is to be regarded as more or less a mixture. Thus the Vedic antithesis between Aryan and Dasyu has been resolved into a higher synthesis consisting of the blending of the two races. To dwell in living contact, then, with a people whose forebears were Aryans or Dasyus or both is to occupy a certain vantage ground for the study of the earliest literature produced by their ancestors.

Again, the present-day Punjabī, the dialect of the Punjab, is undoubtedly a direct descendant of the earliest

Vedic dialect spoken in these parts[1]. The Punjābī vocabulary is large, and it is highly probable that a critical examination of it on the part of a competent scholar would throw light on some of the obscure words of the *Ṛigveda*. The Ṛigvedic age, then, has projected down to the present time (of course in blended and modified forms) its language, blood and religious conceptions. To be for years in living contact with these survivals of the past is an advantage which the writer has enjoyed for the study of the *Ṛigveda*. Whether he has made good use of his opportunities or not is for the expert reader to judge.

It was in 1909 that the present writer promised to prepare this book for *The Religious Quest of India Series*. He has often been tempted to drop the task as he came to realize more fully its magnitude and difficulty. It has been due to the steady encouragement of Dr. J. N. FARQUHAR, his colleague on the editorial staff, that this work has ever seen the light. An unusually long furlough in the U. S. A. (1919-1920) made possible continuous work at Ithaca, New York, where the writer enjoyed the use of the Cornell University Library. His thanks are due to the Librarian and staff for the many courtesies received. His thanks are also due to A. C. WOOLNER, Esq., M. A., Principal of the Oriental College, Lahore, for looking over several

---

1. *Compare the following list of words in Vedic and Punjābī:—*

Vedic	Punjābī		Vedic	Punjābī	
agni	*agg*	'fire'	*bhrātā*	*bhrā*	'brother'
yajña	*jag*	'sacrifice'	*duhitā*	*dhī*	'daughter'
deva	*de*	'god'	*mātā*	*mā*	'mother'
pitā	*pio*	'father'	*vāyu*	*vā*	'wind'

chapters of the MS. and suggesting many corrections and improvements; also to Prof. Macdonell for permission to quote several of his translations of Ṛigvedic hymns.

As regards the method of transliteration, it is in general that of the JRAS.

CONTENTS

Part *A*. Introduction

Part *B*. Religious Contents of the Ṛigveda.

Part *C*. The Significance and Value of the Ṛigveda.

ABBREVIATIONS USED IN THE NOTES

AJP.	*American Journal of Philology.*
Banerjea, AW.	Banerjea, *Arian Witness,* Calcutta, 1875.
Barth, RI.	Barth, *Religions of India,* (E. Tr.) Boston, 1882.
Bartholomæ, AW.	Bartholomæ, *Altiranisches Wörterbuch,* 1905.
Bergaigne, RV.	Bergaigne, *Religion Védique,* I-III, Paris, 1878-1883.
Bhandarkar CV.	Bhandarkar Commemoration Volume, Poona, 1917.
Bloomfield, AV.	Bloomfield, *Atharva-Veda,* 1899, in Grundriss.
Bloomfield, HAV.	Bloomfield, *Hymns of the Atharva-Veda,* SBE. XLII, 1897.
Bloomfield, RC.	Bloomfield, *Relative Chronology,* in JAOS. 21 (1901).
Bloomfield, RV.	Bloomfield, *Religion of the Veda,* New York, 1908.
Bloomfield, RVR.	Bloomfield, *Ṛig-Veda Repetitions,* in HOS. 1916.
Bloomfield, HL.	Bloomfield, *Hittite Language,* in JAOS. 41 (June 1921).
Bode, *Bokhara.*	de Bode, *Bokhara, its Amír and its People,* London, 1845.
Bohnenberger, AGV.	Bohnenberger, *Der Altindische Gott Varuna,* 1893.
Bradke, DA.	v. Bradke, *Dyāus Asura.*
Brugmann, CGIL.	Brugmann, *Comparative Grammar of the Indo-Germanic Languages,* E Tr., I-IV, 1888.
Brunnhofer, IT.	Brunnhofer, *Iran und Turan.* 1893.
Carnoy, IVO.	Carnoy, *Iranian Views of Origins* in JAOS. 36, p. 307 ff.
Clayton, RV.	Clayton, *Ṛig-Veda and Vedic Religion,* Madras, 1913.
Crooke, PR.	Crooke. *Popular Religion and Folk-Lore of Northern India,* I-II, London, 1896.
Darmesteter, OA.	Darmesteter, *Ormazd et Ahriman,* Paris, 1877.
Deussen, AGP.	Deussen, *Allgemeine Geschichte der Philosophie,* Leipzig, 1894.
ERE.	Hastings, *Encyclopædia of Religion and Ethics,* Edinburgh.
E. Tr.	English Translation.
Farquhar, CH.	Farquhar, *Crown of Hinduism,* London, 1915.
" , MRMI.	" , *Modern Religious Movements in India,* New York, 1915.
" , PH.	Farquhar, Primer of Hinduism, London, 1912.
" , ORLI.	" , *Outline of the Religious Literature of India,* London, 1920.
Feist, KAHI.	Feist, *Kultur, Ausbreitung und Herkunft der Indo-germanen,* 1913.
Geldner, G.	Geldner, *Glossar,* Stuttgart, 1907.

Geldner & Kaegi, SL. Geldner & Kaegi, *Siebenzig Lieder*.
Grassmann, RV. Grassmann, *Ṛig-Veda Uebersetzt*, I-II. Leipzig, 1876-1877.
Griffith, HR. Griffith, *Hymns of the Ṛigveda* 1-II. Benares, 1896.
Griswold, *Brahman*. Griswold, *Brahman: A Study of Indian Philosophy*, New York, 1900.
Griswold, GVR. Griswold, *God Varuṇa in the Ṛig-Veda*, Ithaca, 1910.
Grundriss *Grundriss der Indo-Arischen Philologie und Altertumskunde* (Encyclopædia of Indo-Aryan Research), Strassburg.
Haddon, WP. Haddon, *Wanderings of Peoples*, London, 1911.
Hillebrandt, AI. Hillebrandt, *Alt-Indien*.
" , Brahman. " , Art. *Brahman* in ERE.
" , LR. " , *Lieder des Ṛigveda*, Göttingen, 1913.
" , VM. " , *Vedische Mythologie*, I-III, Breslau, 1891, 1899, 1902.
" , V. & M. Hillebrandt, *Varuṇa und Mitra*, Breslau, 1877.
Hirt, IG. Hirt, *Indogermanen*, I-II, 1905-1907.
Hopkins, ION. Hopkins, *India Old and New*, New York, 1901.
" , HR. " , *History of Religions*, 1918.
" , RI. " , *Religions of India*, Boston, 1898.
HOS. Harvard Oriental Series.
IGI. *Imperial Gazetteer of India*.
IA. *Indian Antiquary*, Bombay.
Jackson, IR. Jackson, *Die Iranische Religion* (in Iranian *Grundriss*).
Jastrow, RBA. Jastrow, *Religion of Babylonia and Assyria*, 1898.
JAOS. *Journal of the American Oriental Society*.
JA. *Journal Asiatique*, Paris.
JRAS. *Journal of the Royal Asiatic Society*.
Keith, IM. Keith, *Indian Mythology*, 1917, in vol. VII of *The Mythology of All Nations*.
Keith, TS. Keith, *Taittiriya Saṅhitā*, I-II, 1914 in HOS.
Kuhn, HFG. Kuhn, *Herabkunft des Feuers und des Göttertranks*, Berlin, 1859.
Lajpat Rai, AS. Lajpat Rai, *Ārya Samāj*, London, 1915.
Ludwig, RV. Ludwig, *Der Rigveda*, I-V, 1876-1883.
Macdonell, HR. Macdonell, *Hymns from the Ṛigveda*, London, 1922.
" , Principles. " , *Principles to be followed in translating the Ṛigveda* (Bhandarkar CV. 1917).
Macdonell, SL. Macdonell, *Sanskrit Literature*, London, 1900.
" , SL. in IGI. " , *Sanskrit Literature* in Imperial Gazetteer of India, 1908, Vol. II.

Macdonell, VM. Macdonell, *Vedic Mythology* in *Grundriss*, Strassburg, 1897.

Macdonell, VRS. Macdonell, *Vedic Reader for Students*, London, 1917.

Macnicol, IT. Macnicol, *Indian Theism*, London, 1915.

Meyer, GA. Meyer, *Geschichte des Altertums*, I^3, 1909.

Moore, HR. Moore, *History of Religions*, I. 1914.

Moulton, EZ. Moulton, *Early Zoroastrianism*, London, 1913.

„ , I. „ , *Iranians* in ERE. VII.

„ , TM. „ , *Treasure of the Magi*, London, 1917.

Mrs. Stevenson, HJ. Mrs. Sinclair Stevenson, *Heart of Jainism*, London, 1915.

„ „ , RT. „ „ „ *Rites of the Twice-Born*, London, 1920.

Muir, OST. Muir, *Original Sanskrit Texts*, London, 1858 ff.

Müller, PR. Max Müller, *Physical Religion*, 1891.

Myriantheus, AAD. Myriantheus, *Die Açvins oder die Arischen Dioskuren*. 1876.

N. T. New Testament.

O. T. Old Testament.

Oldenberg, *Buddha*. Oldenberg, *Buddha*, E. Tr., London, 1882.

„ , LAI. „ , *Die Literatur des Alten Indien*, Berlin, 1903.

„ , LU. „ , *Die Lehre der Upanishaden und die Anfänge des Buddhismus*, Göttingen, 1915.

„ , RV. Oldenberg, *Die Religion des Veda*, Berlin, 1894.

„ , Ṛv. Noten. „ , *Rigveda, Textkritische und Exegetische Noten*, I-II. Berlin, 1909, 1912.

PW. *Sanskrit-Wörterbuch*, Böhtlingk and Roth, St. Petersburg, Vols. I-VII. 1855-1875.

Phillips, TV. Phillips, *Teaching of the Vedas*, London, 1895.

Pischel & Geldner, VS. Pischel und Geldner, *Vedische Studien*, I-III, Stuttgart, 1889, 1897, 1901.

P. D. Śāstrī, DM. Prabhu Dutt Śāstrī, *Doctrine of Māyā*, London, 1911.

Prellwitz, EWGS. Prellwitz, *Etymologisches Wörterbuch der Griechischen Sprache*, Göttingen, 1905.

PSBA. *Proceedings of the Society of Biblical Archæology.*

Ragozin, VI. Ragozin, *Vedic India*, London, 1895.

Rapson, CHI. Rapson, *Cambridge History of India*, Vol. I. Cambridge, 1922.

Roosevelt, WW. Roosevelt, *Winning of the West*, 1889.

SBE. *Sacred Books of the East*, Oxford.

SKT. Sanskrit.

Sāyaṇa. Sāyaṇa, *Commentary on Ṛigveda*, Ed. Max Müller.
Scherman, PH. Scherman, *Philosophische Hymnen*, Strassburg, 1887.
Schrader, AR. Schrader, *Aryan Religion* in ERE, II.
„ , IG. „ , *Die Indogermanen*, 1911.
„ , RIA. „ , *Reallexikon der Indogermanischen Altertumskunde*, 1901.
Schrœder, AR. Schrœder, *Arische-Religion*, Vol. I. Leipzig, 1914.
Soper, RM. Soper, *Religions of Mankind*, 1921.
Spiegel, AP. Spiegel, *Die Arische Periode*, 1887.
Strauss, BV. Strauss, *Bṛihaspati in Veda*, 1905.
Sādhu. Streeter and Appasamy, *The Sādhu*, London, 1921.
SKPAW. *Sitzungsberichte der Königlich-Preussischen Akadamie der Wissenschaften.*
Usener, *Götternamen*. Usener, *Götternamen. Versuch Einer Lehre von der religiösen Begriffsbildung*, 1896.
Vedic Index. Macdonell and Keith, *Vedic Index of Names and Subjects*, London, 1912.
Vend. Vendīdād.
Wallis, CR. Wallis, *Cosmology of the Ṛigveda*. 1887.
Weber, IS. Weber, *Indische Studien*, Berlin.
Whitney & Lanman, AV. Whitney and Lanman, *Atharva-Veda Saṁhitā* in ETr. HOS., Harvard, 1905.
Winternitz, GIL. Winternitz, *Geschichte der Indischen Litteratur*, Leipzig 1904.
Yāska, *Nirukta*. Yaska, *Nirukta*.
ZDMG. *Zeitschrift der deutschen morgenländischen Gesellschaft*, 1847 ff.
Zimmer, AL. Zimmer, *Altindisches Leben*, Berlin, 1879.

THE RELIGION OF THE ṚIGVEDA

PART A.

INTRODUCTION

CHAPTER I.

THE ANTECEDENTS OF THE RIGVEDIC AGE

1. Indo-European Period

a) **The Ṛigveda reflects the life of certain Aryan tribes living in the Punjab. We may think of them as occupying the fertile territory of the northern Punjab extending from the Kābul valley to the Jumna, and also as following the banks of the great rivers some distance southward toward the sea. The most striking features of their home were the mountains on the north and the five (or seven) rivers which rising in the mountains flowed downward through the land. The aboriginal inhabitants were called Dasyus, and the Ṛigveda is dominated throughout by the antithesis between Aryan and Dasyu. The Dasyus of the Punjab were connected ethnologically with other aborigines of India. But who were the Aryans? Unlike the Hebrews, who after their settlement in Palestine retained lively traditions of their escape from Egypt and their journey through the wilderness, the Aryan tribes of the Punjab, although aware of the existence of ancient priests and poets, yet betray no slightest consciousness that they had not always lived in the Punjab. So far as their testimony is concerned, we might think of them as autochthonous. But there are reasons for holding that the Aryan tribes came into India as strangers from the north-west. For we see them pushing their way steadily eastward, and the Ganges river, mentioned only once or twice in the ṚIK, is still before them on their horizon. Then, too, their names for year undergo a significant shift, which can be explained only through change of habitat. When they lived in a** colder climate ten years were called 'ten winters' (*hima*); in the Punjab, where the cold season was like their former autumn (*śarad*), ten years would be 'ten autumns'; and later on in the 'middle land', where the characteristic season is the rains (*varśāṇi*), ten years would be called 'ten rainy seasons'. But there is a still more decisive proof.

b) The greatest linguistic discovery of the nineteenth century and perhaps of all time was the discovery of the Indo-European family of languages[1]. This is hardly less important in the sphere of philology than the discovery of America in the sphere of geography. According to Brugmann's classification there are included within the Indo-European family the following eight major groups: Aryan (including Iranian and Indian), Armenian, Greek, Albanian, Italic, Keltic, Teutonic and Balto-Slavic. These groups cover practically all the languages of Europe except such negligible quantities as Basque, Lapp, Finnish, Hungarian, Turkish, etc. They cover also at least three out of the many language groups of Asia, namely, Armenian, Iranian, and the Aryan languages of India, besides the lately discovered Tocharian, and apparently an element in Hittite.[2] Thus we see that the Vedic Aryans are connected linguistically and possibly racially with Persians, Greeks, Romans, Russians, Germans and English. No longer do they stand battling in the Punjab against the Dasyus, as they are represented in the pages of the Ṛv., while themselves unconnected with the rest of mankind. They represent the vanguard of the Āryan dispersion Indiaward.

c) In order to indicate the nature of the linguistic evidence on which the unity of the Indo-European (IE.) family is based, there is here subjoined a short table of cognate words in some of the more important related languages :—

---

[1] Brugmann, CGIL., Vols. I-IV., 1888; Schrader, RIA., 1901; Feist, KAHI., 1913.

[2] "It (*i. e.* Hittite) seems to contain an injection of I. E. material"—Bloomfield, Hittite Language, JAOS., June, 1921.

Sanskrit	Avestan	Greek	Latin	Gothic	Lithuanian	English
1 pitár	pitar	πατήρ	Pater	fadar		father
2 mātár	mātar	μάτηρ	mater		mote	mother
3 bhrā́tar	bhrātar	φρήτηρ	frāter	brothar	broterelis	brother
4 svásar	xvauhar	ἔορ	soror	swistar	sesu	sister
5 sūnú-s	hunu-s	υἱός		sunus	sūnus	son
6 duhitár	dugedā	θυγάτηρ		dauhtar	dukte	daughter
7 snuṣā		νυός	nurus			(daughter-in-law)
8 śváśuras	xvasurō	ἑχυρός	socer		szesznras	(father-in-law)
9 śvaśrū́s		ἑχυρά	socrus	swaihrō		(mother-in-law)
10 pitṛivyas	tuiryo	πάτρως	patruus			(father's brother)
11 nápāt	napāt		nepōs		nepōtis	nephew
12 vīrá	vīrō		vir	wair	wgras	(man)
13 jánī	jainis	γυνή		qēns		queen
14 pátis	paitis	πόσις	pot-	faths	patis	(master)
15 pátnī	pathnī	πότνια			pati	(mistress)
16 viśpáti	vīs-paiti				wiesz-pats	(clan-lord)
17 dámpati	dangpaiti	δεσπότης	dom-inus			(house-lord)
18 rā́jā			rex	reiks		(king)
19 víś	vīs	οἶκος	vīcus	weihs		(clan)
20 dámas		δόμος	domus			tim(b)er
21 jánas		γένος	genus			kin
22 vidhávā			vidua	widuwō		widow
23 gāús	gaus	βοῦς	bōs			cow
24 úksan	uxṣam			auhsa		ox
25 áśva	aspā	ἵππος	equus	aihwa		(horse)
26 śvā́	spā	κύων	canis	hunds	szu	hound
27 ávis		οἶς	ovis		avis	(sheep)
28 sū-kará	hū	ὗς	sūs			sow
29		πόρκος	porcus		parszas	pork
30 ajá		αἴξ			ozys	(goat)
31 haṁsá		χήν	anser			goose
32 vṛ́ika	vehrko	λύκος	lūpus	wulfs	vilkas	wolf
33 ṛ́ikṣa	arsa	ἄρκτος	ursus			(bear)
34 múṣ		μῦς	mūs			mouse
35 śárdha				hairda		herd

Sanskrit	Avestan	Greek	Latin	Gothic	Lithuanian	English
36 paśú	pasu		pecus	faihu		fee
37 yugám		ζυγόν	jugam	juk	jungas	yoke
38 púr		πόλις			pilis	(city)
39 dvār	dvaṛ	θύρα	fores	daur	durys	door
40 nāús		ναῦς	navis			(ship)
41 yáva	yava	ζεά			javas	(grain)
42		ἅλς	sāl	salt		salt
43 drú	dru	δρῦς		triu		tree
44 sarpís		ἔλφος				salve
45 mádhu	madu	μέθυ			medus	mead
46 bāhú	bāzu	πῆχυς				(arm)
47 dán		ὀδούς	dens	tunþus	dantis	tooth
48 pád		πούς	pēs	fōtus		foot
49 jānu		γόνυ	genu	kniu		knee
50 ūrṇā		λῆνος	lāna	wulla	vilna	wool
51 áyas	ayah		aes	aiz		(metal)
52 dhūmás		θυμός	fumus		dumas	(smoke)
53 an 'to breathe'		ἄνεμος	animus			
54 ájras		ἀγρός	ager	akrs		acre
55 dvāú		δύο	duo	twai		two
56 trayás		τρεῖς	tres	threis	tri	three
57 usás	usah	ἠώς	aurora		auszra	(dawn)[1]
58 agní-s			ignis		ugnis	(fire)
59 śrád		καρδία	cor	hairto	szirdis	heart
60 śatám		ἑ-κατόν	cent-um		szim̃tas	hundred
61 śŕiṅga		κέρας	cornu			horn
62 hímā	zayan	χειμών	hiems		zema	(winter)
63 devá	daevō		deus		devas	(god)
64 Dyāús		Ζεύς	Jupiter			(Jupiter)
65 hutá (?)				guth		god
66 dhāman		θέσις		dōms		doom
67 ágas		ἄγος				(sin)
68 ás			ōs			(mouth)
69 śálā		καλία	cella			hall

[1] Words in parenthesis in the table above give the meaning but are not the etymological equivalents of the series after which they stand.

d) This table of cognate words will show at a glance how closely related the different branches of the IE. family are. These languages must be regarded as only dialectical variations of one original IE. speech. To explain the cause of some of the variations, mention may be made of the consonantal shift which separates the Teutonic tongues from all the other members of the IE. family. The following series of consonants are affected by this shift[1]:—

Labials	bh	b	p	(f)
Dentals	dh	d	t	(th)
Velars	gh	g	k	(h)
Palatals	gh′	g′	k′	(h′)

The law known as 'Grimm's Law'[2] means that wherever bh or its equivalent is found in any other IE. tongue, b will appear in the Teutonic, e. g. Skt. bhrấtar=Eng. brother. As bh shifts to b, so b shifts to p, and p to f. The same rule holds good throughout the other series. In other words, there is a shifting forward in the Teutonic, bh to b, dh to d, gh to g, etc. This shift, by which the Teutonic tongues are placed on a different consonantal level from that of the other cognate tongues, may be compared with a geological fault. Palatalisation takes place in Tocharian by which the dental t becomes ch (c), as Skt. mātar, Toch. mācar. It will be seen that[3] Armenian, Tocharian and old Irish have suffered greater phonetic

---

[1] *Cf.* O.W. Emerson, *History of the English Language*, p. 3 ff.

[2] Jacob Grimm, 1785-1863.

[3] A short list of *Tocharian*, *Armenian* and *Old Irish* equivalents of Sanskrit words is now presented for the sake of completeness of statement:—

Sanskrit	*Tocharian*	*Armenian*	*Old Irish*	*Meaning*
pitár	pācar (A)	hair	athir	father
mātár	mācar	mair	mathir	mother
bhrấtar	pracar	elbair	brathir	brother
svásar	sar	khoir	siur	sister
duhitár	ckācar	dustr		daughter
vīrá	wir		fer	(man)
gấús		kou	bo	cow

decay than Sanskrit, Avestan, Greek, Latin and Lithuanian. The term Indo-European (IE.) indicates that the languages of this great family are found in both Europe and Asia. A more scientific distinction between eastern and western IE. is found in the difference which holds between the Centum-group and the Śatam-group, which difference apparently indicates the existence of dialectical variations within the primitive IE. In the Centum the IE. palatals gh′, g′, k′, h′ appear as stops, while in the Śatam they appear as spirates. Thus the spirate ś (sh) in Skt. Śatam[1] 'hundred' appears as the stop k in the Greek ἑκατον and the Latin centum. The languages of the Centum-division are Hellenic, Italic, Celtic, Teutonic, the Asiatic Tocharian[2] recently discovered in Eastern Turkestān, and possibly an IE. element in the ancient Hittite of Asia Minor. The Śatam-division consists of Balto-Slavic, Albanian, Thracian, Phrygian, Armenian and Indo-Iranian. Some of these languages are not only neighbours geographically, but are also closely allied linguistically. Thus the Indian and the Iranian constitute one group, the Indo-Iranian. In like manner, although to a less extent, Greek is allied to Latin, Latin to Celtic, and Teutonic to Balto-Slavic.

A glance at the table of IE. cognate words[3] will show that they all occur in at least two and many of them in

Sanskrit	*Tocharian*	*Armenian*	*Old Irish*	*Meaning*
śvā́	ku (B)	śun	cu	hound
ṛkṣa		arj	arth	(bear)
dvā́r		durn	dorus	door
	sālyi (B)	al	salann	salt
bāhú	pokem (A)	bazuk		(arm)
dán		atamn	det	tooth
pád	pe (A)	otn		foot
ū́rṇā		gelmn	olan	wool
ās	āś (B)		ā	mouth

[1] p. 4, No. 60.

[2] Vid. Sieg and Siegling, *Tocharisch die Sprache der Indoskythen*, in SKPAW., 1908, XXXIX, and S. Feist, KAHI., pp. 428-431.

[3] pp. 3-4.

six or seven different IE. tongues. Since there is no evidence that these are loan words, we are shut up to the conclusion that, in most cases, they go back to one prehistoric speech, that is to say, the speech of the IE. clans before their separation. Words for cow, brother, foot, heart, etc. are found in the most widely separated branches of the IE. family. Through the study of such words, then, we are able to penetrate to the prehistoric stage of IE. life and culture. Help is also furnished by prehistoric archæology and the study of comparative IE. institutions as seen in the oldest historical sources.

e) In this way, then, we get the following picture[1] of the stage of culture reached by the IE. clans before their separation[2]. The pastoral and agricultural stage had been reached. Animals that had been domesticated were the cow, sheep, dog, horse, and, less certainly, goat and swine (23-30), also the goose (31). Cattle-rearing was the great occupation, and herds of cattle constituted the wealth (35-36). There were draught animals such as oxen (24), as proved by names for cart and yoke (37). Bears and wolves (32-33) are mentioned among wild animals, but not camels, lions or tigers. Clothing consisted of the skins of wild and domestic animals, and of wool (50), which was woven. As regards articles of food, *yava* (41), 'barley', or perhaps in general 'corn', was grown. Evidently the flesh of domestic and wild animals was eaten, since the names of the inner organs of the body, such as the heart (59), would seem to imply the knowledge gained from slaughtered animals. There is no common vocabulary of fishing. Hence we may infer that fish were not used originally as an article of food. The same thing holds true of milk, which apparently, as in China to-day, was not a primitive article of IE. diet. Butter, too, (44) was apparently used

[1] I am much indebted for the following sketch to O. Schrader, *Die-Indo-Germanen*, 1911; Sigmund Feist, *Kultur, Ausbreitung und Herkunft der Indo-Germanen*, 1913, and H. Hirt, *Die Indo-Germanen*, Vols. I-II, 1905-1907.

[2] Reference by number will be made to the table of IE. words on pp. 3-4.

more as a salve or ointment than for food. In the matter of agricultural terminology there is a cleft between eastern and western IE., which would seem to indicate that the western Aryans put more stress on agriculture and the eastern Aryans on the pastoral life. Quite likely physical and climatic conditions were at the basis of this difference. It may be that the non-existence of a primitive word for salt (42) in the Indo-Iranian branch, and its existence in all the rest, fits in with this difference, since salt is more needed for a vegetable than for an animal diet. The general name for tree (43) is common, but there are no special names for fruit trees, indicating that tree culture was not yet practised. The primitive IE. intoxicant was a honey product (45).

Houses (19, 20) were used, which had doors (39), posts and roofs, but were doubtless little better than huts. These houses were probably partially underground, to ward off the cold of winter. There is no mention of any furniture, such as beds, chairs, tables. Mats and skins may have been used to sit on. Because of the joint family system, a house would naturally expand into a clan-village (19). There were also forts (38), or places of refuge in times of danger. Many such prehistoric forts have been discovered. There is a primitive name for field (54), but no evidence of any private property in land. As means of travel, carts[1] and also boats (40) were used. The linguistic evidence, then, indicates that the undivided IE. clans were in a condition of unstable equilibrium between the nomadic and the settled life. There is evidence of some trade in IE. times. The numbers 1-10 and 100 (55-56, 60) are primitive. The cow was the oldest measure of value (23, 36). Judging from later evidence, there were probably customs of hospitality, such as the interchange of gifts between host and guest, which made it possible for the wandering trader to journey in safety. The winter was the northern winter, because of

---

[1] Skt. *anas*, 'cart'; *cf.* Lat. *onus*, 'burden'.

the common words for snow and ice (62). Probably, there were names for only two seasons, winter and summer, the name winter also designating the year. There was the common idea of the month as the measurer of time.

The outlines of the present family system were already in existence (1-11), the father being the head (16-17) and the son's wife being adopted into the clan of her husband. It was the joint family system, the primitive names (1-11) indicating that the family consisted of a man and his wife and children, his brothers and their families, his sons and their families, besides the old people, grandfather and grandmother. From a comparative study of the customs and institutions of the different IE. branches in connection with the linguistic evidence, it is clear that the authority of the head of the family (16-17) was unlimited. He had the power of life and death. Sons were greatly desired as warriors, avengers of blood, performers of funeral rites, and as means for the continuation of the clan. There was, owing to the chronic warfare of the time, usually a dearth of men and a superfluity of women. Hence girl infants as not needed were often exposed. Old people, too, were frequently put out of the way especially in time of need. The joint family coffer was controlled by the head of the family. Primitive IE. marriage was by purchase or capture. The lot of the wife was not easy. She was more or less a beast of burden. Her mother-in-law ruled her with an iron hand. Separate dining of the two sexes was, according to the evidence, a primitive custom. There are traces also among the Scythians, Thracians, Slavs, Germans and Indo-Aryans of 'satī', the custom of a wife voluntarily accompanying her husband in death[1]; also of a distinct prejudice against the second marriage of widows (22). The brother was the guardian of the honour of his sister, and after the death of the father an unmarried sister came under his authority. IE. antiquity was dominated by the idea of the necessity of

[1] Schrader, *Indogermanen*, 97.

marriage. So indispensable was it considered that, according to the evidence, the unmarried dead were sometimes even married ritually to the living, that they might be thus provided for in the life to come[1]. The future comfort of the dead husband was the primitive idea of 'satī'.

The patriarchal family may have been preceded by the so-called 'matriarchate', according to which descent was reckoned from the mother[2]. While the change to the patriarchal system would diminish the independence of women, it would greatly increase the dignity and purity of family life. Whether there was a totemistic stage is disputed. If totemism, as F. B. Jevons thinks, "led to the domestication of plants and animals", and so was "the prime motor of all material progress[3]", then it must be placed considerably anterior to the prehistoric IE. period, which we are studying; for already the pastoral and agricultural stages had been reached. Monogamy was the rule, polygamy the exception. As between different clans, probably exogamy was the custom. There is evidence to indicate joint land possession on the part of the members of a clan. The wife as purchased was the property of her lord and master (14). Hence marriage was later called the lordship *(patitva)* of the husband over the wife. Accordingly there was the double standard of morality. The single family would usually develop into the 'large family' and the clan (19, 21). The 'joint family' goes naturally with agriculture, where much help is needed. There is no evidence of slavery in IE. times. A clan was united together by the bonds of birth, speech and custom. There is no evidence of any formal political union among the various IE. tribes, although they would usually act together in time of war. The earliest federation (namely of the Indo-Iranian tribes) may be inferred from the

---

[1] Schrader, *Totenhochzeit*, 1904.

[2] The so-called 'mutterrecht' was clearly found among the pre-Aryan Etruscans, Picts, and Iberians.

[3] Introduction to the History of Religion, 1896, p. 113.

common name "Ārya". Different clans may have often been different in blood, although the same in language and custom. There were clan-lords or kings (16, 18). The clan-lord was chosen by the clan, the brotherhood acting together in the choice of a head. The term 'Indo-European' is not racial[1], but purely linguistic.

f) It has been truly said that the study of the religion of a people is not to be separated from that of its history and culture[2]. Accordingly IE. religion must now be linked up with IE. culture as described above. There were two lines of development, according to the evidence, the worship of ancestors and the worship of the 'Heavenly Ones' (63)[3]. The worship of ancestors is closely connected with the sense of the solidarity of the family. For primitive man death involved not annihilation but a state of weakness, a kind of shadowy existence. He knew that faintness on the part of the living is removed by food. By parity of reasoning faintness and weakness on the part of the departed must be removed in the same way. Hence the custom of feeding the dead. This must be regarded as at first of the nature of a pious service, not as worship. It is the expression of a family's affection for a departed member, not unmingled also with the fear of a possibly troublesome ghost. That such customs were followed by the IE. clans before their separation is rendered in the highest degree probable by the evidence of prehistoric graves as well as of the funeral rites of the Greeks, Romans, Indians and Lithuanians. The ceremonies included lamentation for the dead, burning (or burial) of the corpse, purification after the funeral, the death-feast, and the feeding of the dead. There were also gifts to the dead,

[1] The clans which spoke primitive Indo-European probably belonged in part at least to the so-called 'Nordic' race. The term "Wiros" might be taken as a convenient name for the speakers of primitive Indo-European. *Cf.* CHI. I. 66 ff.

[2] Harnack quoted by Schrader, ERE. II, 13.

[3] Schrader, *Aryan Religion* in ERE. II. 11-57, and Hirt, *Indogermanen*, II. 485-522.

which were buried or burned with the corpse, gifts of such things as, according to the analogy of this life, would be useful in the life to come, *e. g.* food, weapons, furniture, clothes, domestic animals, and in some cases servants and even wife. After the funeral there was a rigidly appointed service of the dead, food and drink being offered on stated occasions up to six weeks after the death, during which time the spirit of the departed was supposed to hover about. The food and drink were displayed, and the dead was formally invited to the feast and then as formally dismissed. In this way the living were bound to the dead by a long chain of death ceremonies. The inevitable tendency resulting from such pious service was the apotheosis of the dead, they being called by the Greeks "divine uncles" (θεοὶ πατρῷοι), by the Romans "divine parents" (*Di parentes*), by the Indians "divine fathers" (*divāḥ pitaraḥ*), and by the White Russians "sacred grandfathers" (*svjaty dzjady*). The very names which they bear indicate their close relationship with the living. Such ancestors, who, while living, had governed the family and cared for its welfare, would after death naturally become tutelary house deities, like the Roman *Di parentes*. The service and worship of ancestors was one of the foundations of primitive social organization. Relatives were united in ancestor-worship, in the right of inheritance, and in the duty of blood-revenge. A son was necessary to perform the funeral rites of his father. The patriarchal head of a family or clan, while alive, was the human father, but on his death became a divine father. He was the guardian genius of the clan, charged especially with the duty of promoting its fertility. Rites connected with ancestral worship involved expert guidance, in other words, priestly functions. In all primitive societies the head of the family, as the one standing, because of age and experience, in closest communication with the ancestors, is usually priest, shaman or medicine man. Old women as priestesses doubtless shared in similar functions. There were no priests in the technical sense, but there may have been families in which propitiatory and magic rites were handed down from father to son[1].

In addition to the awe and reverence felt toward dead ancestors there was a keen sense of the potency and mystery[2] of natural phenômena. Here again we have the working of analogy. Children and peoples in the childhood stage find it natural to ascribe to inanimate objects the same powers of will and effort which they themselves are conscious of possessing. Accordingly, from a very primitive period, the whole of nature was regarded as an aggregate of animated entities. Each object or phenomenon of nature, such as heaven, earth, sun, wind, lightning, etc., could be named, isolated from the rest, and made into a special object of awe and wonder. Thus to name things was to fixate attention upon them, make them objects of reflection and imagination, and so proceed in the direction of full personification. In this way there was the possibility of as many different special objects of awe as there are different phenomena in the world, an endless number. Usener in his *Götternamen* has assumed a stage anterior to that of personal gods, which he calls the stage of *Sondergötter,* 'special gods', 'departmental gods', holding that 'personal gods' were developed out of these. As proof of his thesis Usener cites the testimony of the Roman *Indigitamenta,* according to which every single fact and process of agriculture was under the direction of a special god, Ceres presiding over growth, Flora over blossoming, Insitor over sowing, etc., and the testimony of the old Prusso-Lithuanian religion, which had a special god for every aspect of cattle-raising. But the evidence thus cited is chronologically late, long after the conception of personal gods had been formed. What can be assumed, however, with practical certainty to be prehistoric is, in the words of Schrader, "the mere capacity and the tendency to form into a divinity every conception in nature or in culture which was of significance for primitive man[3]".

---

[1] Schrader, *Indogermanen,* 146.

[2] *Secretum illud,* Tacitus, *Germania,* Chap. IX. [3] ERE. II. 32.

The two IE. linguistic equations in religion which have successfully run the gauntlet of criticism are the following:—

Skt. *Dyāús Pitár* = Gr. Ζεῦ Πάτερ = Lat. *Ju-piter;* and
Skt. *devá-s* = Lith. *deva-s* = Lat. *deus.*

The reconstruction of the primitive IE. worship of the 'heavenly ones' finds a sure starting point in this material. The *deivos*[1] (*div* 'to shine' and *div* 'sky') were the bright heavenly ones, such as sun, moon, morning star, lightning, wind, dawn, etc. *Dyāus-Zeus-Jupiter,* the sky, was regarded as Father Sky, and his children were the Devas, who appear in the sky. Thus Father Sky and his children the Devas constituted 'the real kernel of the primitive Aryan religion"[2]. Such an interpretation of the sky represents the beginning at once of IE. myth-making and IE. science. The sky, both day and night, remains the same in form. Within its capacious limits come and go the 'heavenly ones', sun, wind, rain, lightning, dawn, etc., playing each his respective part in the ordered life of the clan of the devas. As clan-lord (*viśpati*) of the 'heavenly ones', *Zeus-Dyāus-Diespiter* is supreme. He bends down over the earth and fertilizes it with the rain which is his seed. From this point of view also he is called 'father'.

If the differentia of a 'personal god' is the exerting of influence outside of his own proper sphere, then it is doubtful if the stage of personal gods had then been reached. In fire, dawn, lightning, etc. the primitive IE. peoples adored the mysterious powers, the divine *animæ,* which manifested themselves in the phenomena of the sky, but possibly not as yet any god who was regarded as a person. The IE. period was, accordingly, the period of 'special' or 'departmental' gods, whatever else it may have been. Whether there had already been formed a motley crowd of special gods, out of which the *deivos* had been separated because of their significance for the life at that time, or whether the *deivos* alone had thus been isolated,

---

[1] Assumed prehistoric form. [2] ERE. II. 33.

is a question that we cannot answer. Actually there may have been but few special gods recognized, while multitudes may have been acknowledged as potentially to be discovered. We may compare the 33,000,000 Hindu gods, very few of whom are actually named. If, on the other hand, every *nomen* is a *numen*, and everything named becomes thereby a 'special god', then we have already in the IE. period multitudes of special gods, potentially, if not actually, millions. To illustrate: *janus* as the name of an object means 'door', but as the name of the mysterious potency manifested in the door it means 'he of the door'. So *vesta* means 'hearth' and 'she of the hearth'; *agni* 'fire' and 'he of the fire'; *uṣas* 'dawn' and 'she of the dawn', etc.

The Heavenly ones were worshipped by offerings of food. There was a close resemblance between the feeding of the dead (the divine fathers) and the feeding of the gods. Most probably the feeding of the gods arose from the feeding of the dead. As the dead needed to be strengthened by food, so also did the gods, for example, Agni 'fire' through oblations of ghee. The fireless offering was the more primitive method, according to which food was laid out on a sacrificial litter, to which the gods were invited. The fire-offering came later. Magic, of course, is of immemorial antiquity. It is more or less interwoven with prayer and sacrifice.

g) What is the significance and value of the religious ideas attained by the IE. clans before their dispersion? The primitive tendency to regard all nature as animate was the first step towards a spiritual interpretation of the universe. This reading of the world in terms of human life was the beginning of anthropomorphism, every external object as well as man being regarded as possessing an *anima*. It was only a question of time for the human figure to be added to the human *anima* present in each phenomenon[1].

[1] This tendency toward anthropomorphism is infinitely suggestive, pointing, as it does, toward the conception of God manifesting Himself as man and of man attaining to the image of God.

The custom of feeding dead ancestors was a recognition of life beyond the grave and the worshipping of them as 'divine fathers' was a confession of faith that the departed ones had in some sense or other become "partakers of the divine nature"[1]. Thus through pious memorial gifts the living were closely bound up with the blessed dead, and the memory of the good deeds of the departed was an incentive to practise the same virtues. 'Father Heaven' and his children the 'Heavenly Ones' were conceived after the analogy of an earthly clan-father and his clan[2]. The head of an earthly clan was at once father and lord. By analogy the head of the heavenly clan of the *deivos* must be the same. Thus several religious ideas of fundamental importance are at least dimly adumbrated through the conception of Father[3] Sky and his children the Heavenly Ones, namely: God as heavenly, as light, as father and as lord, and the conception of the world as *ordered.* Surely on that far-off 'bank and shoal of time' the Eternal God had not left Himself without witness. Through their own nature as men gathered into families and clans, through the external world which ever confronted them as an object of curiosity and awe, and through their experiences of fatherhood and lordship, life and death, God spoke to them, as they were able to hear. It all comes home to us very personally, since the people to whom we refer were among the ancestors not only of the Indian and Persian Aryans, but also of most of the peoples of modern Europe and America.

h) The original home of the IE. peoples is unknown. The data bearing upon the problem are linguistic (as found on pp. 3-5), ethnological, that is, the distribution of IE. peoples over the earth, and archæological, the evidence of their migrations and settlements. Besides this there is the more or less indefinite weight to be ascribed to historical

---

[1] 2 Peter, I. 4.

[2] This gives, at least implicitly, the concept of *order*.

[3] It is noteworthy that 'father', an epithet belonging to ancestor-worship, is carried over and applied to the sky.

precedent, such as the migrations that have taken place from Central Asia in historical times, and the settlement by Alexander of Greek colonies in Bactria. The linguistic evidence points clearly to a temperate, if not a cold climate. The earliest conjecture was Central Asia[1], east of the Caspian. A more westerly situation in Southern Russia on the border between Europe and Asia was a later conjecture of scholars[2]. The recent discovery of Tocharian in Eastern Turkestân has tended somewhat to revive the earlier view[3]. The extremely archaic character of Lithuanian speech suggests that the original IE. home may have been not far from Lithuania[4]. The latest hypothesis is that of Professor Giles[5], who thinks that the original habitat or 'area of characterization' of the IE. clans was in Austria-Hungary, the region enclosed by the Carpathians, Erzgebirge, Böhmer Wald, Austrian Alps and Balkans. The fact that Central Asia has been historically a veritable *officina gentium*, or 'hive of the nations', whence have gone forth Scythians, Huns and Turks, renders possible the view that the IE. clans came from the same region. Tocharian, a Centum tongue, is far removed from the other Centum tongues, which are all found in Western Europe. It is possible, then, to hold that Tocharian is a stay-at-home, and that the speakers of the other Centum tongues have all migrated westward. If there was an early connection between the Indo-European and the Ural-Altaic families of languages, as Sweet[6] asserts, then this would suggest some area in Russia as the primitive habitat. The archaic character of Lithuanian does not help much in settling the question; for by parity of reasoning the Punjab might be taken as the original IE. home, because the primitive consonants are

---

[1] "Somewhere in Asia." -- Max Müller.

[2] Schrader, RIA. 878; Meyer, GA. 1[2]. 41.

[3] Meyer, *op. cit.*, 801; Keith, *Indo-Iranians* in Bhandarkar, CV. 91.

[4] Bender, *Princeton Lectures*, No. 8, on *The Aryan Question*, October 1921.

[5] CHI. I. 68.

[6] *History of Language*, London, 1899, p. 112 ff.

best preserved in Sanskrit[1]. The fact that Alexander brought Greeks with him all the way from Macedonia and settled a colony of them in Bactria, while he himself and several of his Græco-Bactrian successors invaded India from Bactria as a base, and the further fact that IE. peoples — Phrygians, Mysians, Bithynians, Hittites (?), Armenians, Persians — stretched in almost a continuous line from the Dardanelles to Bactria, suggest the possibility that the Aryan advance to India may have been through Asia Minor and North Persia[2]. Winckler's notable discovery in 1906 at Boghaz-köi, the old Hittite capital in Asia Minor, of a cuneiform inscription (1400 B.C.) containing the names Indra, Mitra, Varuṇa and Nāsatya, may possibly be interpreted as a landmark of the IE. advance eastward[3]; and, at any rate, it fits in well with Hrozny's[4] interpretation of Hittite as an IE. tongue[5].

It might also be assumed that the IE. clans, being largely in the pastoral stage, roamed over the great 'grassy plain'[6] of Central Europe and Asia, extending perhaps from the Danube and the plains of North Germany through Southern Russia on into Central Asia[7]. This would cover practically all the territory embraced by the previous hypotheses. The pressure of enemies round about would doubtless be even more effective than a circle of mountains to hold a primitive tribe together and give it a unified development. Thus something may be said for each of the above-mentioned hypotheses as to the original home of the IE. people. The whole question must be left as a

---

[1] Icelandic, though the farthest removed from the centre of the Teutonic world, is nevertheless the most archaic of the Teutonic group.

[2] Hopkins, HR. 171; Giles, CHI. I. 70-72.

[3] Giles, *op. cit.* 72.

[4] *Die Sprache der Hettiter*, Leipzig, 1917.

[5] More probably only an IE. loan element. See p. 2, n. 2.

[6] Haddon, WP.

[7] The valleys of the Ural and Volga, Don and Dnieper, and also that of the Danube, would furnish a suitable habitat for the undivided IE. tribes. *Cf.* Meyer, GA. I². 579.

"stimulating and fruitful uncertainty"[1]. That the problem is 'stimulating' is shown by the number of scholars, especially German, who during the last three decades have addressed themselves to its solution.

i) The date of the dispersion of the IE. tribes is also unknown. The only material bearing directly on the problem consists of the dates of IE. migrations, settlements and inscriptions: *e.g.* the appearance of Aryan-speaking bands in connection with the Cassite invasion of Babylonia B.C. 1760[2], and at the same time the earliest reference to the Hittites in history[3]; the Dorian invasions of Greece, B.C. 1500-1100; the Boghaz-köi inscription, B.C. 1400; the date of Zoroaster, B.C. 1000[4]; the founding of Rome, B.C. 753; and the Celtic invasions of Gaul, Spain and Britain, B.C. 800-300. From these figures a later date than B.C. 2000 can hardly be assumed. The period B.C. 3000-2000, with a conventional average of 2500 B.C. may be presented as a reasonable conjecture[5]. The discovery of fire had already taken place; the domestication of animals and plants and the transition from the stone to the metal age were in process.

j) On the basis, then, of evidence drawn from the words common to the IE. tongues, the study of prehistoric graves, the witness of the earliest IE. literature, such as the Ṛigveda, the Homeric poems, Herodotus, Tacitus, etc., as well as from the study of the institutions, customs and folklore of the peoples concerned, there is a very high degree of probability, amounting in most cases to practical certainty, that

---

[1] Quoted by Marcus Dods with reference to the authorship of the anonymous Epistle to the Hebrews, *Expositor's Greek Testament*, IV. 234.

[2] Haddon, WP. 20-21, 25, 27.

[3] Meyer, GA. I[2], 577.

[4] Moulton, TM., 6, 13; Oldenberg, LU. [4] The traditional date is 660 B.C.

[5] Feist, KAHI., postulates B.C. 2500-2000 for the breaking up of the IE. unity. But Hirt, *Indogermanen*, assumes a still later date B.C. 1800-1600. "Need not be placed later than 3000 B.C." — Keith, *Indo-Iranians*, in Bhandarkar, CV. 92.

among the undivided IE. clans the following customs were prevalent: the joint family system organized on a patriarchal basis, the authority of the head of the family being absolute over life and death, polygamy to some extent, especially among leading men, early marriage of girls, prejudice against widow remarriage, exposure of female infants, the frequent going of a wife with her husband in death, or in other words *satī*, feeding of the dead, human sacrifice, especially of captives, worship of ancestral spirits, and the worship of the personified phenomena of nature such as sky, sun, moon, wind, fire, water, lightning, etc. Such were some of the customs which our IE. ancestors practised. In Europe, through the clashing of different types of culture, and especially through the impact of Christianity, these primitive customs have been either greatly modified or done away with altogether. In India, because of her *isolation*[1] through the ages, most of these customs persist intact or even in an exaggerated form. Thus India is a land of archaic survivals.

2. Indo-Iranian Period.

a) The sources of information, as might be expected, are much more abundant than for the IE. period. Ṛigveda and Avesta may both be used as indirect witnesses to what existed before Indian and Iranian separated. For there are a large number of technical religious words in each literature which are only dialectical variants, *e. g. yajña* and *yasna*, 'sacrifice', *ṛita* and *asha*, 'order', *Asura* and *Ahura*, 'Lord', etc., etc. It goes without saying that the existence, for example, of the word *yajña* in the Ṛik and of *yasna* in the Avesta is proof enough that the thing signified originally by both words alike existed in the period before the Indian group broke away from the Iranian. As a matter of fact, Veda and Avesta are so closely related that each is a good commentary on the other. In order to make this clear,

[1] *Cf. Indo-Aryan Thought and Culture* by Prabhaker S. Shilotri, New York, 1913.

there is here subjoined a short list of cognate Vedic and Avestan words of a technically religious character:—

Vedic	Avestan	Meaning	Vedic	Avestan	Meaning
Ásura	Ahura	Spirit, Lord	áhuti	āzūiti	offering
Aryamán	Airyaman	Aryaman	amṛíta	amesha	immortal
Arámati	Ārmaiti	piety	Ā́rya	Airya	Aryan
Apām nápāt	Apām napāṭ	water-child	Indra	Indra (Andra)	Indra
āptyá	āthwya	watery	uṣás	ushah	dawn
ápas	āpo	waters	uśíj	usij	priest
Átharvan	Āthravan	fire-priest	ṛitá	asha	order
āprī́	āfri	Āprī	Gandharvá	Gandarewa	Gandharva
Tritá	Thrita	Trita	miyédha	myazda	sacrificial meal
devá	daēva	god, demon	Yamá	Yima	Yama
drúh	druj	evil spirit	yajñá	yasna	sacrifice
Nárāśáṁsa	Nairyosanghá	Narāśaṁsa	Yajatá	yazata	worshipful
Nā́satyā (u)	Naonhaithya	Dioscuri	yātú	yatu	demon
Púraṁdhi	Purendi	Puraṁdhi	vájra	vazra	bolt
barhís	barezish	litter	Vāyú	vayu	wind
Bhága	Bagha	Bhaga	Vivásvant	Vīvaṅhvant	Vivasvant
bhūtá	būiti	ghost	Vṛitrahán	Verethragna	Vṛitra-slayer
mádhu	madu	mead	sumatí	humata	good thought
mántra	manthra	spell	sūktá	hūkhta	good word
manyú	mainyu	wrath	sóma	haoma	soma
mā́s	māh	moon	svár	hvar	sun
Mitrá	Mithra	Mitra	hótar	zaotar	invoking priest

It requires only a glance at these parallel columns of words to become convinced of the close connection of Vedic and Avestan religion as well as of language. These separate lines of development point back to one undivided Indo-Iranian people, language, culture and religion. Spiegel's *Die Arische Periode* (1887), although it is somewhat out of date, nevertheless shows what can be done through the use of such material in reconstructing the cultural and religious conditions of the undivided Indo-Iranians.

b) The undivided tribes bore one common name which appears in both the Old Persian *Ariya* and the Vedic *Ārya*. This common name points to a union of tribes, the earliest federation of IE. clans of which there is any evidence. Assuming B. C. 3000-2000 as the period within which the dispersion of the IE. clans took place, we may postulate provisionally B. C. 2500-1500 as the period when the Indo-Iranian tribes lived together as one people. Whether they lived all that time in Bactria and the neighbouring regions is unknown. It may be that their line of advance lay through Asia Minor and that the various IE. tribes which settled in that region, Phrygians, Armenians and others were either left behind in their course or followed later in their wake. Be that as it may, one thing is certain that the Indo-Iranian tribes were together for a considerable time and then separated, the Indian branch moving by one or more migrations into the Punjab, and the Iranian branch remaining in Bactria and Persia. As a result, the two linguistic groups, Indian and Iranian, "lie closer together than any other distinct languages in the IE. family"[1]. Before the dispersion of the Indo-Iranian tribes, their habitat in Bactria and still more their line of march eastward from Asia Minor, if they came that way, would have brought them into fairly close contact, by trade and otherwise, with the great centres of Babylonian culture in the Euphrates-Tigris plain. It is possible that the mystical and sacred number seven, which is such a favourite in both Veda and Avesta, as well as in the Hebrew Old Testament, was borrowed from Babylon[2], especially if its origin was due to the observation of astronomical facts such as the seven planets (sun, moon and five planets) or the seven stars of the Great Bear. It is possible, too, as Oldenberg thinks, that there may have been some Babylonian influence upon the development of Indo-Iranian religious and ethical ideas.

c) The two lines of religious development which were found in the IE. period, namely, the worship of ancestors and the worship of the 'heavenly ones', continued throughout the Indo-Iranian period; for they appear in both the

---

[1] Moulton, Art, *Iranians* in ERE., Vol. VII.

[2] So v. Schroeder, *Arische Religion*, I. 427-429.

Ṛv. and the Avesta, especially in the Younger Avesta. The service and worship of the *Pitṛis* in the Ṛv. is paralleled by the similar service and worship of the *Fravashis* in the Avesta [1]. The worship of the 'heavenly ones' also continued through the Indo-Iranian period, for we see it in full bloom in the Ṛv. There was indeed among the Iranians the religious reformation connected with the name of Zoroaster, through which Ahura Mazda, 'the Wise Lord', was made the supreme and sole object of worship, the daevas of the old religion being degraded to the position of demons, or at least to that of angels; but this reformation was followed, as is so often the case, by a counter-reformation, which restored the daēvas to their old position, or at least to the status of angels. If the Boghaz-köi gods, Varuṇa, Mitra, Indra and the Nāsatya (B. C. 1400) were early Iranian deities, as Oldenberg thinks, then they must have preceded the Zoroastrian reformation, since at a later period Varuna drops out altogether, or rather is replaced by the name Ahura Mazda, and the three gods Indra and the two Heavenly Twins are turned into demons. If they were Vedic deities, then their appearance on the Boghaz-köi inscription proves a backward connection at that early age between the Punjab and Asia Minor, and suggests strongly that that was the route which the Indo-Iranian clans followed in reaching their eastern home. If Indo-Iranian or early Iranian deities, then we have Varuṇa as the Heaven God (Ouranos?) and four 'heavenly ones' as his associates, namely, Mitra, Indra and the two Aśvins. The next important outside evidence concerning early Iranian religion is found in the famous passage of Herodotus (I. 131), which reads as follows: "Their custom is to ascend to the highest peaks of the mountains, and to offer sacrifices to Zeus, calling the whole vault of the sky Zeus; and they sacrifice also to sun, moon, earth, fire, water, and winds" [2]. Here we have clearly the old IE. pantheon consisting of

---

[1] See especially *Farvardin Yasht*. [2] Moulton, EZ. 391-392.

the sky-god Dyāus and his children, 'the heavenly ones'. The Yashts prove sufficiently that the Younger Avesta admits of such worship[1].

d) Certain new developments in religion were introduced during the Indo-Iranian period:—

(1) *The conception of 'order'*[2]. This was present at least implicitly in the IE. period, being involved in the cosmic order represented by the rule of Heaven[3] over 'the heavenly ones', and in the social and moral order created by the rule of the clan-father over the clan. It first became explicit, however, during the period represented by the Tel-el-Amarna correspondence (B. C. 1400) in which there occur certain names containing *arta-*, as Artashuvara and Artatama, which remind one of the later Persian names Artaxerxes, Artaphernes, etc. The element *arta* in these names stands for the Avestan *asha* and the Vedic *ṛita.* That carries back the origin of this important conception to at least 1400 B. C. And, as we have seen, its roots run back still further into the IE. period. In both Veda and Avesta *ṛita-asha* is fundamentally important. In the Ṛik it covers the threefold order, cosmic, ritualistic and moral. In the Avesta it runs out into the meanings, right, truth, righteousness, holiness,—all ethical in connotation. Veda and Avesta, then, are witnesses that the conception existed before the breaking up of the Indo-Iranian unity.

(2) *The Ethical conception of God.* A conception like *ṛita-asha* would naturally have its effect upon the idea of God. Scholars practically agree that Varuṇa equals Ahura

---

[1] From the combined testimony of the Boghaz-köi inscription, the Rik and the Younger Avesta, it is clear that among the Indo-Iranian gods were included Varuṇa, Mitra, Soma, Aryaman, Indra, the Aśvins, Vivasvant and Yama. *Cf.* Farquhar, ORLI. 2.

[2] Vedic *ṛita*, Avestan *asha*.

[3] "A people whose worship included the Sky, loftiest of all nature-deities, and those ancestor-gods who are ever the most potent to stir up the feeling of a close bond between religion and conduct, had native material on which to work." Moulton, EZ. 245.

Mazda, that is to say, the ethical god of the Ṛik is regarded as the same in origin as the ethical and supreme god of the Avesta. This means that a movement in the direction of ethical monotheism preceded the Indo-Iranian dispersion. This movement was not originated by the reformation connected with the name of Zoroaster, since that took place after the Indo-Iranian separation, probably as early as 1000 B. C. What the Zoroastrian reformation really did was to take up the earlier reform movement and carry it forward to its logical issue in an ethical monotheism. The Vedic period had nothing corresponding to the Zoroastrian reformation. Hence the Vedic Varuṇa did not rise far above the level of the pre-Zoroastrian Ahura Mazda[1] ethically very great, but not the supreme God.

(3) *Something corresponding to the Iranian Amesha Spentas and the Indian Adityas.* These two groups of gods have, as we shall see, so many points of contact that a common preparation during the undivided Indo-Iranian period for both lines of development seems to be demanded. Father Dyāus was clearly the chief deity of the Indo-Iranian as he had been of the undivided IE. clans. We may think of him as having other names which emphasized various aspects of his nature, such as Asura 'Lord', Varuṇa (or Varena) 'Encompasser', Mitra 'Friend', Aryaman 'True', Bhaga 'Distributor', etc. The mystical number 'seven' may have served as a framework to unite this special group and to isolate it from all the rest. The list of names furnished a plurality associated with Dyāus as his supreme council, but also a plurality in unity, since the various names were all names of Dyāus and served merely to

---

[1] That Ahura Mazda was pre-Zoroastrian in origin has been apparently proved by documentary evidence through Prof. Hommel's discovery of the name *Assara Mazāš* in an Assyrian inscription of the reign of Assur-banipal (B. C. 668-626). The archaic form of the name Assara instead of Ahura (*cf*. Nāsatya, in place of Nāonhaithya in the Boghaz-köi inscription) carries us back before the Iranian consonantal shift from *s* to *h*, doubtless to a period not far removed from that of the Boghaz-köi inscription. See PSBA., 1899, 132, and Moulton, Ez. 31 ff.

express different aspects of his unitary nature. Between this hypothetical scheme and the Amesha Spentas intervened the great cleft of the Zoroastrian reform, which rejected all of these names as unsuitable except the one name Ahura 'Lord', and created substitutes for the rest more in harmony with the spiritual ideas of the Reform. Thus the Amesha Spentas represent a radical change. The Ādityas, on the other hand, continue more closely the old tradition[1].

(4) *Development of demonology*. Both Veda and Avesta are conscious of the forces of physical evil in the world. In both alike sickness, death, impurity, darkness, drought, cold, etc., are ascribed to the action of demons. In this they were only following primitive habits of thought. Corresponding, however, to the ethical spirit of the Avesta is its emphasis on *moral evil* as the work of demons[2]. Such emphasis, too, is not altogether absent from the Ṛv. It looks as if in both Veda and Avesta, but particularly in the Avesta, the conception of an ethical order and of an ethical god had heightened the consciousness of moral evil in the world. The result of the Iranian reform movements was that the earlier Indo-Iranian daēvas were reduced to the status of demons, and so men were classified as either 'worshippers of Mazda' or 'worshippers of the daēvas'. In the words of Darmesteter[3] "Persia took her demons in real earnest"; for she had *Angra Mainyu*, 'enemy spirit' standing over against *Spenta Mainyu* 'holy spirit'. In the Ṛv. this ethical distinction is not so sharply drawn as it is in the Avesta.

(5) *Development of the priesthood*. The common terms for priest, *Atharvan-Āthravan* 'fire-priest', *hotar-zaotar* 'invoking priest', etc., indicate a differentiation of priestly functions in the Indo-Iranian period. Knowledge of such technical functions, we may be sure, had a tendency to be

[1] v. Schrœder, AR. I. 441-444.

[2] *Cf. Angra Mainyu*, 'Enemy Spirit', Druj 'Lie', etc. The sins of pride, unbelief and sodomy are ascribed in Vend. I to the influence of demons.

[3] SBE. IV, p. LXII.

propagated in priestly families[1]. There are many references in the Ṛv. to ancient priestly families, Bhṛigus, Atharvans, etc. Mixed up though they be with mythical and legendary material, there are nevertheless quite likely in many of them historical reminiscences of priestly families reaching back into the dim past, possibly to the time before the separation of the Indo-Iranian clans. Such specialization of function led to great results in India. Priestly technique demanded considerable knowledge—knowledge that could be gained only through division of labour—for its proper exercise. In this way the tradition was naturally set of a learned priestly class made up of different orders of priests. As a result the religious literature of India, so far as it has been aryanized, is the work of the priesthood, and its fundamental conceptions represent largely the thinking of the same dominant community.

---

[1] In the Khordād and Ābān Yashts (IV. 10 and V. 86) there is mention of Āthravans and their pupils, clearly a reference to priestly schools. For example, in the Khordād Yasht, 10, we are told that "a spell may be divulged by an Āthravan to his pupil".

CHAPTER II.

THE RIGVEDIC AGE

1. **Sources.**—The primary source for the Ṛigvedic age is, of course, the *Ṛigveda.* It contains a multitude of allusions to persons and things, mostly however incidental and fugitive. To illustrate from the hymns translated the kind of information thus given, we may note the following allusions: skin of slain beast, V. 85, 1; barley, *yava*, V. 85, 3; dice-playing, II. 12, 4-5; V. 85, 8; VII. 86, 6; X. 34; strong drink, *surā,* VII. 86, 6; cattle-thief, VII. 86, 5; wild beasts, I. 154, 2; II. 33, 11; cattle at pasture, VI. 54, 5-6; chariots, VI. 54, 3; VII. 71, 2; sacrificial posts, IV. 51, 2; desert lands, I. 35, 8; water-skin, V. 83, 7; medicines, II. 33, 2, 4, 7, 12; winter, II. 33, 2; river-crossing, II. 33, 3; III. 33; necklace, II. 33, 10; gold, I. 85, 9; II. 33, 9; bow and arrows, II. 12, 10; II. 33, 10; wolves, X. 127, 6; debt, X. 34, 4, 10; 127, 7; villagers, X. 127, 5; spears, I. 85, 4; wells, I. 85, 10; snakes, II. 12, 3; battle, II. 12, 8; mountains, II. 12, 13; rivers, II. 12, 12; spies, I. 25, 13, etc., etc. By piecing together all such references and allusions a fairly complete picture of Vedic life[1] may be secured. Two indirect sources of information may be singled out for special mention, the similes and metaphors[2] of the Ṛik., and the anthropomorphised picture of the Ṛigvedic gods.

There will be no attempt to give an exhaustive picture of Vedic life. For the purpose in hand it will be sufficient to sketch briefly the geographical, climatic, ethnological and cultural background, which conditioned the religious thinking and practice of the Vedic Aryans. They clearly brought

---

[1] As found in Macdonell and Keith's *Vedic Index of Names and Subjects*, Vols. I-II. London, 1912, and in Zimmer's *Altindische Leben*, Berlin, 1879.

[2] *Gleichnisse und Metaphern im Ṛigveda* by A. Hirzel, Leipzig, 1890; and article in the *Journal of the Punjab Historical Society*, Vol. I. 56 ff. on *Vedic Social Life according to the Similes in the Agni Hymns of the Ṛigveda*, by H. D. Griswold.

with them a large inheritance from the past in addition to what they achieved in their new habitat in India. For, as we have seen, the roots of Vedic life and thought run back into the Indo-Iranian period and even beyond that into the Indo-European period.

2. GEOGRAPHY—Four points of the compass may be mentioned as enclosing the area occupied by the Vedic Indians, viz. the river *Rasā* on the west, and the Ganges on the east, to the north the snowy mountains, and to the south the sea. Since the Avestan form of *Rasā* is *Raṅhā*, and the Rasā is mentioned several times as a river in the extreme north-west of the Vedic territory[1], it is probable that it refers to a real stream, perhaps originally the Araxes or Jaxartes[2]. If this is a correct interpretation, then the name betrays an historical reminiscence of an earlier home to the north of the Hindu Kush. In other passages, however, it is the name of a mythic stream encompassing the atmosphere and the ends of the earth[3] and once called 'Mother Rasā'. With the passage of time and the fading out of the memory of the original Rasā as a real earthly stream, it was quite natural for it to be charged finally with mythical elements. The Ganges (*Gaṅgā*) is directly mentioned only once in the Ṛv.[4], and indirectly once through the epithet (*Gāṅgya*) 'being on the Ganges'[5]. It was on the eastern horizon of the Vedic Indians. On the north were the 'snowy' mountains[6], clearly

---

[1] Ṛv. I. 112, 12; V. 53, 9; X. 75, 6.

[2] So Zimmer, AL. 15-16; Macdonell and Keith, *Vedic Index*, II. 209. It may be that there was a Rasā on the Punjab side of the Hindu Kush. If so, it was doubtless named after the original Bactrian Rasā, a procedure altogether natural.

[3] Ṛv. V. 41, 15; IX. 41, 6; X. 108, 1-2; 121, 4.

[4] X. 75, 5.

[5] VI. 45, 31.

[6] *Ime himavantaḥ*, X. 121, 4.

a reference to the snow-covered Himālayas.[1] To the south was the *Samudra,* literally the 'gathering of waters', which denotes at least the river Indus when it receives the Punjab tributaries, and becomes a sea-like expanse of waters. While there is no definite proof that the Vedic settlements extended to the mouth of the Indus, we may yet regard it as highly probable that the Vedic people had some knowledge of the ocean. The Indian Aryans were a daring and adventurous people. In the winning of the wild West of America from savage beasts and savage aborigines, there were ever intrepid hunters and Indian fighters, like Daniel Boone, who were wont to push into the wilderness far in advance of the regular settlements. So was it doubtless in Vedic days. It is most unlikely, then, that the Indian Aryans were without at least a dim knowledge of the Indian ocean[2].

The region comprehended within these four points, Rasā and Gaṅgā, snowy mountains and sea, is approximately the territory drained by the Indus and its tributaries, extending as far south as to the junction of the main river with its branches, that is, a region corresponding roughly to the present Punjab, North-Western Province and Kabul valley.

Of the Aryan habitat as thus defined the most prominent features were the rivers. The 'seven rivers' *(sapta sindhavaḥ)* of the Aryan country are often mentioned in the Ṛv.[3], either a conventional number like 'the seven churches that are in Asia'[4], or a reference to the five[5] well-known rivers of the Punjab together with the two boundary streams, Sarasvatī and Indus. In at least one passage[6] *sapta sindhavaḥ*

---

[1] On days when the atmosphere is clear (confessedly a rare experience) the snowy Himālayas are plainly visible to one travelling by train on the N. W. Railway line all the way from Sahāranpur to Amritsar, as the present writer knows from experience.

[2] Zimmer, AL. 25; *Vedic Index* II, 431-433.

[3] I. 32, 12; 35, 8; IV. 28, 1, etc.

[4] Rev. I. 4.

[5] Sutlej, Beās, Rāvi, Jhelum and Chenāb.

[6] VIII. 24. 27.

is the designation of the land[1]. We may assume that the Vedic settlements occupied the submontane region, where the water is near the surface, all the way from Kabul to Ambala, and also followed the banks of the rivers some distance toward the sea. The phenomena of mountain, river and sea furnished the Vedic singer with plenty of imagery for describing the drama of the storm. He saw in the sky an aerial ocean. There were cloud mountains which Indra pierced with his bolt, and in which he hollowed out deep beds for the aerial rivers. The special geographical features of the Punjab were not without influence upon the development of the folklore concerning the gods, which comes under the head of mythology.

The rivers of the Punjab furnished natural political boundaries and natural lines of defence. The famous victory of Sudās over the ten kings was won on the banks of the Paruṣṇī[2] (Rāvī). We are reminded that Porus[3] contested Alexander's passage of the Jhelum and that the boundary between Ranjit Singh's territory and British territory was the Sutlej. The Sikh army definitely began hostilities, when it crossed the Sutlej into British territory. In the Vedic age the boundary rivers must have been also the scene of frequent crossings and recrossings in connection with plundering raids[4]. One can imagine, too, that individual Vedic adventurers, of the spirit of Daniel Boone, would frequently cross over a river into the territory of the Dasyus or of a hostile Aryan tribe, and attempt exploits, either winning booty or having to get back to

---

[1] *Cf.* Vend. I. 18; *Hapta Hindu.*

[2] Rv. VII. 18, 8-9. The mention of the Yamunā in v. 19 of the same hymn may possibly be interpreted with Macdonell and Keith (Vedic Index I. 500) as a reference to another victory of Sudās, on the theory that the hymn is a condensed account of more than one victory.

[3] πῶρος *i. e.* the *Paurava* prince.

[4] Such an one as is described in Viśvāmitra's hymn to the rivers Vipāś and Śutudrī (III. 33), in which there is mentioned a village or 'horde' of the Bharatas crossing the rivers in quest of booty (cows).

their own side of the river as speedily as possible by swimming or by boat. Such experiences seem to be presupposed in the following verses:—

And *may we dive* with thee across
All enmities and hostile powers,
As swimmers over water-streams. II. 7, 3; and
Put us across hostilities
As with a boat, thou radiant god,
Expelling evil with thy light.
For welfare carry us across,
As in a boat o'er Sindhu's wave,
Expelling evil with thy light. I. 97. 7-8.

Such similes are very numerous in the Ṛv. In fact, the Vedic experience of being helped across a river to a place of safety, together with later experiences of the same sort, has left almost as deep a mark upon Hindu religious symbolism as the crossing of the Jordan has upon Christian symbolism[1]. The boats used in crossing the Punjab rivers must have been very simple in structure, probably dugouts or rafts. The paddle was apparently used for steering as well as for propulsion.

3. CLIMATE.—The climatic changes experienced by the Vedic Aryans in passing from Bactria into the Punjab were numerous and striking. From a temperate climate[2] they passed into one almost torrid[3]. Winter was a thing of the past. The Punjab cold season was like their former autumn. As earlier they had reckoned the years as so many winters, so now in the Punjab they began to reckon them as so many autumns[4], although the older terminology was still in use[5]. In the distribution of the rainfall there

---

[1] One may compare the line of the Christian *bhajan*; *Kaun kare mohi par?* 'Who will put me across?' In the same hymn *Pār Karaiya* is a divine title.

[2] Unusally cold in winter but pretty hot in summer. *Cf.* de Bode's *Bokhāra*, 56.

[3] During July and August 1922, according to the weather reports in the Pioneer, the hottest places in India were Peshawar, Dera Ismail Khan, Jacobabad, Lahore, Lyallpur, Multan, Fort Sandeman, Sialkot and Rawalpindi, all in the Punjab or the neighbouring regions of the N. W. Frontier and Baluchistan.

[4] Ṛv. II. 27, 10; III. 36, 10., etc.

[5] Ṛv. I. 64, 14; II. 33, 2; V. 54, 15; VI. 48, 8.

were striking differences. In Bactria, as in most temperate climates, rain falls more or less throughout the year[1], alternating with snow in winter; but in the Punjab, with the exception of one or more winter rains (usually in January), no rain ordinarily falls during the rest of the year except in connection with the monsoon, between June and October. The monsoon in the Punjab is often very deficient, although quantities of rain usually fall in the lower Himalayas and flood the Punjab rivers. The 'lūh', or monsoon wind, which is such a characteristic feature of the United Provinces, is hardly felt in the Punjab; but for several months preceding the breaking of the monsoon the Punjab is afflicted with violent dust storms, accompanied by strong wind and not infrequently causing darkness even at midday. The monsoon is followed in September and October by a very feverish and unhealthy season lasting for several weeks. Before the coming of the monsoon rains, the heat is extreme, often as high as 117° in the shade and 170° in the sun. Thus in the Punjab habitat of the Vedic Aryans the drama of the elements had its own special setting, which must have modified to some extent the mythology which the Aryans brought with them from their trans-Himālayan home. The bipartite division of the year into winter and summer[2], six months each, which dates from the IE. period, was broken up in the Vedic age into three seasons, spring *(vasantā)*, summer *(grīṣma)* and autumn *(śarad)*[3]. The Ṛik knows also the winter *(himā)* as a reminiscence from the past; and in the Frog-song[4] the rainy season[5] is mentioned twice.

---

[1] "Thunder storms are not infrequent, especially in spring". De Bode's *Bokhāra*, 47; and "Out of 186 days . . . 68 were overclouded or rainy"—*op. cit.*, 52.

[2] *himā* and *samā*. [3] Ṛv. X. 90, 6. [4] VII. 103, 3, 9.

[5] *Prāvṛis*. The rainy season is mentioned by name only here in the Ṛv., in harmony with the fact that the monsoon in the Punjab tends to be light. When the Aryan tribes reached the United Provinces, the three seasons became five, and 'the rains' (*varṣāḥ*), as the most characteristic season, furnished the name for the year. While there is a distinct difference between the Western and Eastern Punjab as regards the average amount of rainfall, yet the contrast drawn by Keith

4. ARYANS.—The Ṛigveda is dominated throughout by the antithesis between Aryan and Dasyu, the foreign invader and the aboriginal inhabitant of the land. The antecedents and ethnic connections of the Aryan invaders have already been considered. The year 1500 B.C. has been accepted as a provisional date (a mere conventional average) for the entrance of the Aryans into the Punjab. They came either as a single invading host after the manner of Alexander's invasion, or more probably in successive bands covering perhaps several centuries. There are plenty of historical analogies for both types of invasion, but no direct evidence. Hence we are shut up to an imaginative reconstruction of the probable (or possible) course of events, guided by analogy. It is quite probable that there was some trade between Bactria and the Punjab[1] prior to the Aryan invasion, as the date of the invasion in any case was comparatively recent. Aryan traders or adventurers may well have visited the Punjab before that time and carried back a 'report of the land'[2]. As already stated[3], the eighteenth century B.C. was characterised in Western Asia by tribal migrations and conquests. It was marked by the Hittite invasion of Akkad (circa 1760 B.C.), the Hyksos invasion and conquest of Egypt (about 1700 B.C.) and the Kassite overthrow of the First Babylonian Dynasty, in connection with which was the first appearance of the Aryan in history[4]. About this time the Mitāni, whose rulers may have been speakers of Indo-European, settled in northern Mesopotamia and prepared the way for the Boghaz-köi inscription and the Iranian proper names in the *Tel-el-Amarna* correspondence.

While certain IE. tribes were thus settling in Persia

(CHI. I. 79) between the 'thunder and lightning' of the Ambala region and the 'gentle' showers of the rest of the Punjab, seems to the author much overdrawn.

[1] For the modern trade route between Bokhāra and Kābul, see de Bode's Bokhāra.

[2] Compare the fur-traders who did so much for the exploration of North America in the early days. [3] p. 19. [4] Meyer, GA., I², 577-579.

and Mesopotamia, it is altogether probable that other tribes of the same people were beginning to cross the Hindu Kush into the Punjab. The method of invasion was probably a combination of peaceful penetration and armed force. The analogy of early racial expansions[1] makes probable a series of Aryan invasions and settlements in the Punjaḅ rather than one single invasion and conquest of the land. So we may assume tentatively that the Aryan tribes entered the Punjab by incursion after incursion extending over possibly several centuries, it may be from 1700 to 1300 B. C. Probably each invasion was a tribal affair not done rapidly, but after the manner of migratory pastoral peoples[2]: Grierson's distinction[3] between the Aryan languages of the 'Midland' and those of the 'Outland' seems to demand more than one migration to account for it. This is quite apart from the cogency of his theory of the latest Aryan invasion by way of Gilgit and Kashmir. The relative position to one another of the Aryan tribes in India suggests also the same explanation of earlier and later immigrations[4].

There is plenty of evidence in the Ṛv. that the Aryan tribes not only fought against the Dasyus, but also were

---

[1] Compare the numerous waves of Semitic invasion into Palestine, the conquest of Britain by Jute, Angle, Saxon, Dane and Norman, extending over many centuries, and the gradual winning of the wild West of America through the forward pressure of the Scotch-Irish 'backwoodsmen', who were equally good at hunting, fighting and tilling the soil. See Roosevelt, WW. Vol. I.

[2] "We may be certain that the invasions were no mere incursions of armies, but gradual progressive movements of whole tribes." — Rapson, CHI. I. 43.

[3] IGI. I., 1907, Chap. on Languages.

[4] So Macdonell and Keith, Index I. 168-169: "The geographical position of the *Kuru-Pancālas* renders it probable that they were later immigrants into India than the *Kosala-Videhas* or the *Kāsis*, who must have been pushed into their more eastward territories by a new wave of Aryan settlers from the west". So Oldenberg *(Buddha 9)* who speaks of "the first immigrants" and of "a second wave of the great tide of immigration". So also James Kennedy, JRAS., October 1919, p. 510: "The immigrants from Bactria had come at intervals through a long series of years."

frequently at war among themselves, in which case Dasyu allies would probably at times be found on the one side or the other. For example:—

Looking to you and to your friendship, heroes twain,
Forward have gone the broad-ribbed[1] warriors keen for spoil;
Both Dāsa foes and Ārya foes smite and destroy,
With succour help Sudās, O Indra-Varuṇa. VII. 83, 1; and
Thou hast our foemen, Indra, of both races,
O hero, both the Ārya and the Dāsa,
Struck down like forest trees with well-aimed axes;
In fights thou rentest them, most manly warrior. VI. 33, 3[2].

On the hypothesis that the Aryan tribes entered the Punjab at different times, it is easy to see how warfare between tribe and tribe would have been especially easy. The earliest invaders may also have made common cause with the Dasyus against the later Aryan invaders, very much as Anglo-Saxons and Celts combined forces against the Danes. Under these circumstances some clans of Aryan origin doubtless shared with the Dasyus in the degradation which must have befallen them both alike[3].

This, on the whole, seems to be the most reasonable hypothesis of the way in which the Aryans entered India, and it is supported by the weight of expert opinion. Nevertheless, in the light of the numerous armed invasions of the Punjab made by Persians, Macedonians, Scythians, White Huns, Moghuls, etc., it must be left an open question. It is barely conceivable that the Aryan invaders entered practically as a single warrior band, got a foothold in the Punjab, sent off settlements in various directions, which

---

[1] Or 'with broad sabres armed'—Macdonell, H. R. 51.

[2] Cf. also I. 102, 5; III. 32, 14; VI. 22, 10, etc.

[3] Compare *Vedic Index* 265: "It is also probable that the Śūdras came to include men of Aryan race, and that the Vedic period saw the degradation of Aryans to a lower social status. This seems, at any rate, to have been the case with the *Rathakāras*". In this connection it is worth while mentioning that the classes in the Punjab which Risley (*The People of India,* 2nd Ed., edited by Crooke, Calcutta, 1915, pp. 37, 40, 356-359), on the basis of skull-measurement, finds as the purest specimens of Aryan blood, include (*mirabile dictu!*) the despised *Chuhras*.

formed the basis of the different Aryan tribes, and developed dialectic variations in speech.

5. DASYUS.—The Dasyus[1] were clearly the aboriginal inhabitants of the Punjab, in the opinion of Baines[2], ethnologically connected with the Kols. Since, however, the cerebral letters are characteristic of the Dravidian languages, but not of the Indo-European, and are found in the Ṛik but not in the Avesta, we may conclude that speakers of Ḍravidian tongues were found in the Punjab at the time of the Aryan invasions[3]. They differed from the Aryans, in appearance, speech and religion. As contrasted with the white Aryan colour, the Dasyus were dark-skinned. So in the following passage:

In fights hath Indra helped the Aryan worshipper,
Giving a hundred aids in every battle-drive,
In battle-drives that win the light;
Plaguing the lawless gave he up
To Maṇu's folk *the dusky skin:*[4]
Burning, as 'twere, he every greedy foe consumes,
Yea quite consumes the venturesome. I. 130, 8.

Clearly referring to the 'black skin' of the Dasyus is the *Dasa colour* as mentioned in the following stanza:

Who hath made all things in this world unstable,
Humbled *the Dūsa colour*[5] or destroyed it;

---

[1] *Dasyu* and *Dāsa* are words of uncertain origin. Dasyu corresponds with the Iranian *daṅhu*, *daqyu* meaning 'province'. In the Behistun inscription Darius calls himself *Khsāyathiya dahyunām* 'ruler of provinces,' which is the phonetic equivalent of the Vedic *Kṣatriyo Dasyunām* 'ruler of Dasyus' (or enemies). The original meaning, as Zimmer thinks (AL. 110) may have been 'enemy', the development in Iranian giving *daṅhu* the meaning 'province' as the country of conquered enemies. It would be quite natural for the invading Aryans to call their foes in the Punjab by their old name for 'enemy'. The same word in later Persian appears in the form *dih* (pl. *dihāt*) 'village'. There is also a Vedic root *das* 'to waste', which may furnish the derivation. *See Vedic Index* under *Dasyu* and *Dāsa*. It is possible that the words had a more contemptuous connotation than merely 'enemy', something like 'heathen', 'wretch', 'fiend', 'rustic' *(gaṅwār)*.

[2] Ethnography (in Grundriss), 1912, p. 3.

[3] Rapson, CHI. I. 41-42, 49.

[4] *Kṛiṣṇā tvac* 'black skin'. So probably X. 41, 1.

[5] *Dāsa varṇa*.

Who takes the foe's possessions, as a gambler
Stakes of his rival, — he, O men, is Indra. II. 12, 4.

As might be expected, the Aryan colour is also mentioned:

He won the sun, he won the heavenly horses,
Indra obtained the cow that feedeth many;
Won, too, the golden treasure for enjoyment,
The Dasyus smote and helped *the Aryan colour*[1]. III. 34, 9.

The 'white-hued[2]' friends who are mentioned as helping Indra in the conquest of the land are doubtless to be taken as Aryans.

Furthermore, the Dasyus are called in one passage *anāsah*[3] 'noseless,' according to the most probable interpretation, or possibly 'misfeatured.' It is quite likely a reference to the broader and flatter non-Aryan nose of the aborigines. In the same passage occurs another epithet[4] 'of stammering speech', or more probably 'of hostile speech', since it is used of Aryan[5] as well as of Dasyu enemies. The passage may be rendered as follows:

Didst crush the *noseless* Dasyus with thy weapon,
And in their home didst overthrow the *fiend-voiced*[6]. V. 29, 10.

The great difference, however, between Aryan and Dasyu was religious. The Dasyus were given such negative epithets as 'riteless'[7], 'lawless'[8], 'without devotion'[9], 'not sacrificing'[10], 'indifferent to the gods'[11], etc., as in the following:

---

[1] *Ārya varṇa.*

[2] *Svitnya*, I. 100, 18. So Macdonell and Keith, Index I. 356, 6.

[3] Either *an-āsaḥ* 'without face' or *a-nāsaḥ* 'without nose', V. 29, 10. Or possibly *an-āsaḥ* should be interpreted as 'without mouth', that is 'speechless', unable to use the speech of the Aryans. This well illustrates the difficulty of Vedic interpretation. At any rate as applied to the Dasyus it is a term of reproach and contempt.

[4] *Mṛidhra-vācaḥ* V. 29, 10, lit. 'whose voice is hostile'. This may possibly refer to the war-cry of the enemy, which may have been as terrible for the invading Aryan as the war-whoop of the American Indian was for the frontier settler.

[5] Of the Aryan *Pūru* in VII. 18, 13.

[6] *Mṛidhravāc* 'dessen Rede mangelhaft, barbarisch redend' — Geldner, Glossar.

[7] *a-karman*, X. 22, 10. [8] *a-vrata*, I. 51, 8. [9] *a-brahman*, IV. 16, 9; [10] *a-yajvan*, VIII. 70, 11. [11] *a-devayu*, VIII. 70, 11.

Who is no-man, who loves nor god
Nor sacrifice nor Aryan law[1],
Him let his friend[2] the mountain hurl to speedy death,
The mountain hurl the Dasyu down. VIII. 70, 11.

Once more:

Against us is the riteless senseless Dasyu,
Inhuman, keeping alien laws;
Do thou, O slayer of the foe,
This Dasyu's weapon circumvent. X. 22, 8.

Thus Ārya in the thought of the invaders came to be a synonym for 'godly', 'devout', and Dasyu for 'godless' as in I. 51, 8:

Distinguish Aryans from the Dasyus; chastening
The lawless make them subject to the pious man[3].

The only positive information concerning the religious practices of the Dasyus is to be found in two references to what were in all probability phallus-worshippers[4]: 'No phallus-worshipper come near our offering,' VII. 21, 5; and in X. 99, 3 we are told that Indra slew the *śiśna-devāḥ*, when he by craft got the treasure of the hundred-gated fort[5].

The clashing of Aryan and Dasyu on the plains of the Punjab was of distinct significance for the social and religious history of India. The outstanding points of difference, as we have seen, were race, colour and religion. These lines of difference were sharply drawn. The very term 'Dasyu', as opposed to Ārya, meaning as it did 'fiend', came to be applied to the demons, so that there is a very

---

[1] Note the collection of epithets, *anyavrata, amānuṣa, ayajvan, adevayu*.

[2] Here the mountain as opposed to the plain, is called the 'friend' of the Dasyu, presumably because it was his refuge, as Ludwig thinks (RV. III. 1). So the Hebrews occupied the hill country of Palestine (Judges I. 19) and the Britons took refuge in the mountains of Wales and the highlands of Scotland against the victorious Anglo-Saxons.

[3] *Barhismat*, lit. he who has strewn the litter for the gods.

[4] *Śiśna-devāḥ*, 'whose god is a phallus' VII. 21, 5; X. 99, 3.

[5] See Macdonell, VM. 155. Doubtless there is here ascribed to Indra, the war-god of the Vedic Aryans, the exploits which the people accomplished under his inspiration.

frequent ambiguity in the reference of the word, whether to human or to demonic enemies. There was a sharp distinction drawn between the Ārya colour and the Dāsa colour, the Aryans coming from a cold climate being white, and the Dasyus having lived for centuries or millenniums in the hot climate of India being black[1]. This difference in colour was one of the causes that lay at the foundation of caste, for the very name of caste is *varṇa* 'colour'[2]. If the interpretation of *śiśnadevāḥ* as 'phallus-worshippers' is correct, as is most likely, then the contrast between Aryan and Dasyu in the matter of religion was equally great; and so the religious difference was drawn as sharply as the other differences. For the Aryan the conception of the divine fatherhood was embodied in the idea of Father Sky, the bright heavenly one; for the Dasyu the same conception was expressed in the form of *liṅga-worship*. *Śiśnadeva* is a term of reproach and contempt in the Ṛv. But the time came in India, when this same worship became widespread even among the Brāhmans. The despised Dasyus had thus their revenge.

---

[1] It was only in India that the white Aryans encountered a really dark race in ancient times. The clash was marked by what was perhaps the first appearance in history of the "colour line". Of course the Greek, Latin and Celtic Aryans encountered the olive-skinned Mediterranean races, but found no serious difficulty in amalgamation. In modern times the 'colour line' as between white and Negro has been most difficult in America and South Africa. In both regions alike it has been the contrast of white Aryans (Indo-Europeans) and those of dark skin.

[2] "The ultimate cause of the extreme rigidity of the caste system, as compared with the features of any other Aryan society, must probably be sought in the sharp distinction drawn from the beginning between the Ārya and the Śūdra. The contrast which the Vedic Indians felt as existing between themselves and the conquered population, and which probably rested originally on *the difference of colour* between the upper and the lower classes, tended to accentuate the natural distinctions of birth, occupation, and locality, which normally existed among the Aryan Indians, but which among the Aryan peoples never developed into a caste system like that of India .... If there had been no *varṇa*, caste might never have arisen". *Vedic Index* II. 267. 270. But see Ketkar, *History of Caste in India,* Ithaca, 1909, and Vincent Smith, *Oxford History of India,* 1919, pp. 34-43.

6. Conquest of the land.—The early struggle between Aryan and Dasyu must have been as ruthless and bloody as that between invading Jute, Angle and Saxon and the indigenous Celt for the possession of Britain, or between Hebrew and Canaanite for the possession of Palestine, or between backwoodsman and American Indian for the possession of the great plains of the West. The bow was the main weapon of the Veda[1], as is clear from the great battle-hymn VI. 75, in which the bow is the only offensive weapon mentioned. This is a kind of Vedic 'song of the Bow'. It is a fairly late hymn, standing at the very end of the sixth book, and composed apparently of fragments. The following is Griffith's translation, with some changes:—

Weapons of War, VI. 75.

1. Like that of threatening storm-cloud is his visage,
When armour-clad he seeks the lap of battle.
Be thou victorious with unwounded body;
So may the thickness of thine armour shield thee.

2. With Bow let us win kine, with Bow the battle,
With Bow be victors in the sharp encounters.
The Bow does to the foeman what he loves not;
Bow-weaponed may we subjugate all quarters.

3. Close to his ear, as fain to speak, she presseth,
Holding her well-loved friend in her embraces;
Strained on the Bow she whispers like a woman,—
This Bow-string that preserves us in the combat.

4. These meeting, like a woman and her lover,
Bear, mother-like, their child upon their bosom.
May the two Bow-ends, starting swift asunder,
Scatter, in unison, the foes that hate us.

5. With many a son, the sire of many daughters,
He makes a clatter, going down to battle;
Bound on the back, the Quiver, launched in action,
In every fray and struggle is victorious.

---

[1] *Vedic Index*, I. 205. So important was the bow as the supreme weapon of war that later in the Mahābhārata *Dhanurveda* 'the science of the bow' meant the science of war in general.

11. Her tooth a deer-horn, dressed in eagles' feathers,
Bound with cow-hide, launched forth, she flieth onward;
Where warriors rush apart or rush together,
There may the Arrows furnish us protection.

12. O glowing Arrow, pass us by[1],
And let our bodies be as stone;
May Soma intercede for us,
And Aditi protect us well.

14. It compasses the arm with serpent windings,
Defending from the impact of the bow-string;
Knowing well all the ways of the hand-smiter[2],
May it guard manfully the man on every side.

15. Now to the Arrow poison-smeared,
Horn-headed shaft or metal-tipped,
Divine, born of Parjanya's seed,
Be this high adoration given.

16. Loosed from the bowstring fly away,
Thou Arrow, sharpened by our *prayer*[3];
Go forth and fall upon our foes,
And leave not one of them alive.

17. Where flights of hurtling Arrows show
Like locks dishevelled of young boys;
Even there may Brahmanaspati
And Aditi protect us well,
Protect us well through all our days.

18. Thy vital parts with coat of mail I cover,
With immortality King Soma clothe thee;
Varuṇa give enlargement more than ample,
And in thy triumph may the gods be joyful.

19. Whoso would kill us, whether he
Be alien foe or one of us,
May all the gods discomfit him.
Prayer is my dearest coat of mail.

This hymn is addressed to the deified weapons of war. Since the bow occupied the most important position in the Vedic armoury, all its parts are named; bow[4], bowstring[5],

---

[1] Or, Avoid us thou whose flight is straight.

[2] See Oldenberg, RVN. I. 416.

[3] *Brahman*, 'spell'. So v. 19.

[4] *dhanvan*.

[5] *jyā*.

bow-ends[1], quiver[2], arrows[3] and (by implication) hand-guard[4]. Arrow-heads were tipped either with horn or with metal and were sometimes at least smeared with poison. The bowman wore some kind of protecting armour[5], and fought most effectively from the war-chariot[6]. By means of the bow the Vedic Indian won battles and was successful in cattle raids. War-chariots were the artillery of antiquity. Much depended upon the swiftness of the horses and the skill of the charioteer. Hence chariot-racing as a sport was only a practice for the serious business of war[7]. In this hymn there are two references to prayer *(brahman)*, but prayer here is used undoubtedly in the sense of magic incantation or spell[8]. In fact, some if not all of the stanzas of this hymn are probably spells[9], and doubtless they owe their preservation to their apparently successful use in this capacity[10]. Weapons of war and especially the chariot play a large part in the equipment and furnishing of the Vedic gods. Indra the supreme war-god of the Vedic Indians is armed with a club[11], and the gods in general are mounted on chariots. It is probable that the Vedic Aryans offered sacrifice before battle and called on Indra for help[12].

Gradually but surely the Aryans overcame the Dasyus and got possession of the choicest parts of the Punjab. The Dasyus were either killed or reduced to slavery[13], or driven

---

[1] *ārtnī*. [2] *isudhi*. [3] *isu, būna*.

[4] *hastatra* (understood) or perhaps *hastaghna*. [5] *varman*.

[6] *ratha*. [7] Zimmer, AL. 293.

[8] See Hillebrandt (ERE. art. *Brahman*) for the meaning 'magic spell'.

[9] Notably vv. 12, 16, 17, 19. If the Frog-song, VII. 103, is a rain-charm, it is quite reasonable to regard VI. 75 as a battle-charm. As other examples of battle-charms may be mentioned VIII. 70, 10 and X. 22, 8.

[10] We may cite Balak's hiring of Balaam to curse Israel (Numbers XXII. 2-6) as an Old Testament instance of the use in war of hostile spells.

[11] *vajra*.

[12] Zimmer, AL. 294. With this compare the similar custom among the Hebrews, 1 Sam. VII. 9-10, XIII. 9-13.

[13] Rv. VII. 86, 7; VIII. 56, 3; X. 62, 10. The meaning *dāsa* 'slave' is due to the fact that the *Dāsa* class were recruited from the *Dāsa* people.

to take refuge in the mountains[1] and desert places. They probably found the war-chariot difficult to contend with, and so found their natural refuge in the mountains, very much as the Hebrews were able to hold only the hill country of Palestine and not the plains, because of the iron chariots of their enemies[2]. Śambara, the mountain-dwelling[3] son of Kulitara[4] has the appearance of being a Dāsa chieftain, in some passages at least. The famous Divodāsa[5] was the great antagonist of Śambara[6], whom he often defeated. Names of Aryan chieftains, such as *Trasadasyu*[7] 'before whom the Dasyus tremble', and *Dasyave vṛika*[8] 'the wolf for the Dasyus', are reminiscent of the successful struggle.

There is frequent mention of 'forts' or 'strongholds'[9], generally as belonging to the Dāsas, for the Aryans undoubtedly took the offensive and the Dasyus defended themselves in forts as best they could. Probably each Dāsa (as well as Aryan[10]) settlement had its fortified enclosure consisting of earthworks with wooden palisades and a ditch[11], in which the people could find refuge in time of danger, taking with them also their cattle[12]. There seems to be a

---

[1] Rv. VIII. 70, 11 (so Ludwig); II. 12, 11; IV. 30, 14; VI. 26, 5.

[2] Judges I. 19. [3] Rv. II. 12, 11; IV. 30, 14; VI. 26, 5.

[4] IV. 30, 14.

[5] The name is to be interpreted as 'slave of Dyāus' (so Oldenberg RV. 155 note 1) after the analogy of slave of Varuṇa (implied in VII. 86, 7), with which may be compared δοῦλος Ἰησοῦ Χριστοῦ, Rom. I. 1, etc. Divodāsa may have been of Dāsa origin as Hillebrandt thinks (VM. I. 97), but at any rate he was an ally of some of the Aryan tribes, and was clearly regarded by them as practically one of themselves. Perhaps a *convert* from the Dasyus.

[6] I. 112, 14; 130, 7; II. 19; 6, etc.

[7] V. 33, 8; VII. 19, 3, etc. [8] VIII. 51, 2; 55, 1; 56, 1, 2.

[9] *Pur*, I. 53, 7-8; III. 15, 4; IV. 26, 3; 27, 1, etc.

[10] The *pur* 'fort' was Indo-European, see p. 4, No. 38.

[11] See *Vedic Index*, I. 538-540 (under *pur*).

[12] A parallel situation is to be found in the early days when the American backwoodsmen won the region west of the Alleghany mountains from the red Indians. "When a group of families moved out into the wilderness, they built themselves a station or stockade fort, a square palisade of upright logs.......... The families only lived in the fort when there was war with the Indians, and even then not in winter". — Roosevelt, WW. I. 144.

reference to the capture of Dāsa forts in the following as translated by Griffith:

> In the wild joy of Soma I demolished
> Śambara's forts, ninety and nine, together;
> And, utterly, the hundredth habitation,
> When helping Divodāsa Atithigva. IV. 26, 3.

In some passages there is undoubtedly reference to the cloud-forts of the demon-Dasyus, and in others *pur* is used metaphorically as, *e. g.* when Agni is besought to guard his worshipper with 'strongholds of iron'[1].

7. Organization of Society.

a) Vedic Tribes.—There is frequent reference in the Ṛv. to the 'five peoples'[2], a term of somewhat uncertain application. It is found in each book of the Ṛv.[3] and is probably to be taken as a conventional number for the Aryan tribes in the Punjab, just as the number of rivers was conventionally seven[4]. In I. 108, 8 the five names of *Yadus, Turvaśas, Druhyus, Anus* and *Pūrus* are mentioned together. Both Indra and Agni are described as *pañcajanya,* 'belonging to the five peoples'[5]; and there is a reference to them in the hymn to Sarasvatī (VI. 61, 12), as if they were settled on or near that river in the eastern Punjab. From all the evidence it looks as if, in their steady progress eastward[6], the Aryan tribes were stopped for a time in the region of the Sarasvatī and Kurukṣetra, unable to force their way through the masses of aborigines[7] holding the great

---

[1] I. 58, 8.

[2] *pañca-janāḥ, -mānuṣāḥ, -Kṛṣṭayaḥ, -Kṣitayaḥ, -carṣaṇyaḥ.*

[3] *Vedic Index* I. 466 n. 1.

[4] The *Vedic Index* mentions the names of 31 rivers and 66 tribes as occuring in Vedic Literature. Of course, not so many are found in the Ṛv. but at any rate more than five tribes and seven rivers.

[5] V. 32, 11; IX. 66, 20.

[6] The general direction of the Aryan migrations was from cold and poor lands to those warmer and richer. Oldenberg, LAI, 7.

[7] See James Kennedy's theory (The Aryan Invasion of Northern India JRAS. October 1919, p. 513) that what really stopped the Aryan advance was the dense aboriginal population of the Jumna-Ganges valley.

"gateway of India"[1]. There they were crowded together and forced to coalesce, until they grew strong enough to break through the gateway. The region of Kurukṣetra, then, was the area of their fusion; and when they appear later on the upper Jumna and Ganges under the name of *Pañcālas,* there may possibly be a reference in the very name to the "five" tribes from the fusion of which they by hypothesis sprang[2]: At any rate the names of the tribes mentioned in I. 108, 8 had practically ceased to be. While the Aryans were in the Punjab, their divisions were tribal, but when they reached the more thickly populated

---

[1] "It would be difficult to exaggerate the importance to India of the existence of the great desert of Rajputana. The ocean to the south-east and south-west of the peninsula was at most times an ample protection against overseas invasion, until the Europeans rounded the Cape of Good Hope. The vast length of the Himalaya, backed by the desert plateau of Tibet, was an equal defence on the north side. Only to the north-west does India lie relatively open to the incursions of the war-like peoples of Western and Central Asia. It is precisely in that direction that the Indian desert presents a waterless void extending north-eastward from the Rann of Cutch, for some 400 miles, with a breadth of 150 miles. In rear of the desert a minor bulwark is constituted by the Aravalli range. Only between the north-eastern extremity of the desert and the foot of the Himalayas below Simla is there an easy gateway into India.........Delhi stands on the west bank of the Jumna at the northern extremity of the Aravallis, and may truly be called the historical focus of all India; for, as we have seen, it commands the gateway which leads from the Punjab plain to Hindustan, the plain of the Jumna and the Ganges. Here the fate of invasions from India from the north-west has been decided. Some have either never reached this gateway or have failed to force their way through it. The conquest of Darius in the latter part of the sixth century B. C. and of Alexander the Great in the years 327-5 B. C., were not carried beyond the Punjab plain. Such direct influence as they exercised in modifying the character of Indian civilization must therefore have been confined to this region. On the other hand, the invasions which have succeeded in passing the gateway and in effecting a permanent settlement in Hindustan have determined the history of the whole subcontinent. These belong to two groups, the Aryan and the Musalman, distinguished by religion, language, and type of civilization and separated from each other by an interval of probably some two thousand years." Mackinder, CHI. I. 21-3.

[2] *Pañcāla* and *Pañca* "five". Suggested by Professor Weber, IS. I. 202, and Geldner, VS. III. 108 n. 1., but questioned by Macdonell and Keith, Index, I. 469.

basin drained by the Jumna and the Ganges, it was differences of caste that received the emphasis. In the land of the "seven rivers" the population was divided into Aryan and Dasyu, ancient and hereditary foes of each other. In the region of *Madhyadeśa* it was no longer Aryan and Dasyu, but priest, king, subject and serf [1], the Dasyus [2] forming the fourth and servile element in the total population, while the first three orders consisted of 'twice-born' Aryans. This fourfold division of the population which forms the basis of caste undoubtedly had its real beginning in the Ṛigvedic age, reaching its full culmination in the period of the Yajurveda [3].

b) King and Kṣatriyas [4]. The *Kṣatriyas* were the ruling class among the Aryan tribes in the Punjab, and normally each tribe had its chieftain or king. Thus the king was the Kṣatriya *par excellence.* In some cases at least Vedic monarchy was hereditary, for descent can be traced. Undoubtedly the necessities of the war with the Dasyus helped to strengthen the monarchical element, and perhaps even to create it, where it did not exist before [5]. The ruling class and the military class coincided, as they do in every age. The Vedic nobility provided the rulers in times of peace and the military leaders in times of war. *Sudās, Divodāsa* and *Trasadasyu* are names of prominent kings. The highest level was reached by the Vedic nobility in the matter of strength, beauty, wealth and happiness. They were the favoured class. Hence most of the Vedic gods were patterned after the nobility. They were in fact

---

[1] *Brāhmaṇa, Rājanya, Vaiśya* and *Śūdra*, Rv. X. 90. 12, a late hymn.

[2] With the Dasyu tribes that were degraded to the status of Śūdras or virtually serfs, may be compared the similar degradation which overtook the remnants of the early population of Palestine, Hittites, Amorites, Perizzites, Hivites and Jebusites, in the days of Solomon, about 975 B. C. (2 Chron. VIII. 7-8).

[3] See Macdonell and Keith on *Varṇa* (Index II. 247 ff.). See also Rv. VIII. 35, 16-18 for a clear reference to *brahma, kṣatram* and *viśaḥ*.

[4] See *Vedic Index* under *Kṣatriya, Rājan* and *Rājanya*.

[5] So the wars with the Philistines helped to create the monarchy in Israel. 1 Sam. VIII, 5, 19-20.

glorified Kṣatriyas. The Kṣatriya god *par excellence* was Indra.

c) Priesthood. — As we have seen[1], the priesthood was well developed before the Indian and Iranian clans separated. Hence the Aryan chiefs were accompanied into India by priests, who had already a fairly complicated ritual connected with the Soma offering and the fire sacrifice. It is possible that some of the priestly families mentioned in the Ṛik as authors of the 'family books' began their career as priests before entering India. The continuity of the Soma-sacrifice both in Persia and India would seem to demand such an unbroken tradition, and the very term *brāhmaṇa*, 'son of a brahman', indicates the hereditary character of the priesthood. As is usual even in primitive societies, priestly functions were largely in the hands of a special priestly class. Already in the Ṛigvedic age the distinction between ruler and priest[2] was clearly drawn[3]. There were several functions[4] such as recitation of hymns, manual acts of sacrifice, and singing of songs, which required several classes of priests for their proper performance. The oldest list[5] mentions seven different kinds of priests. The chief of the seven priests was the *hotar* or reciting priest. He sang the hymns, and in early times during the creative period of the Ṛv. he composed them also. Apart from the seven priests stood the *purohita*, the domestic chaplain of king or noble. According to the later ritual every king must have a *purohita* who alone could properly officiate for the king[6]. He was the spiritual adviser of the king, and in the nature of things

---

[1] p. 26.

[2] *Kṣatriya* and *brāhmaṇa*.

[3] "Priests and sorcerers everywhere differ from the mass of the population at an earlier period of culture than any of the lay classes". — Landtman, *Priest and Priesthood (Primitive)* in ERE.

[4] Keith, *Priest and Priesthood* (Hindu) in ERE.

[5] Ṛv. II. 1-2, *hotṛi, potṛi, neṣṭri, agnīdh, praśāstri, adhvaryu* and *brahmán*.

[6] The position of Samuel in relation to Saul was quite analogous to that of the *purohita* to the king in ancient India. 1 Samuel XIII. 8-12; XV. 10-35.

tended to become also his adviser in temporal matters[1] Examples of *purohitas* in the Ṛv. are Viśvāmitra[2] and Vasiṣṭha[3] in relation to king Sudās, and Devāpi[4] the purohita of Śantanu. The semi-political[5] as well as religious functions of the purohita[6] undoubtedly contributed to the growing influence of the priesthood.

The nobility and priesthood were closely connected by ties of mutual dependence. The noble was dependent upon the priest for the proper performance of the sacrifice and the priest was dependent upon the noble for his honorarium. The *dakṣiṇa* or sacrificial 'fee' was greatly appreciated by the priests, and many a 'gift-laud'[7] celebrates the generosity, anticipated or realized, of wealthy Kṣatriya patrons. For example, *I. 126, 1-3* is a *Danastuti:*

1. Thoughtfully I present these lively praises
   To Bhāvya dweller by the Sindhu river,
   Who measured out for me a thousand pressings[8],
   The King unconquerable, desiring glory.
2. In one day I received a hundred *niṣkas*[9],
   A hundred gift-steeds from the urgent monarch,
   Of the lord's cows a thousand, I Kakṣivant.
   His fame undying hath he spread to heaven.
3. Dark coloured horses Svanaya's gift, and chariots,
   Ten of them, came to me, filled full of women[10].

---

[1] The Brāhman *purohita* of the Vedic king pointed as an institution in the direction of the Brāhman *mantrin* or prime minister of later times, e. g. Kalhaṇa Paṇḍit in Kashmīr, and the Peshwas of the Marāṭha Kings.

[2] III. 33, 53. [3] VII. 18, 83. [4] X. 98.

[5] "The purohita, the spiritual and temporal aid of the king, his chaplain and chancellor". — Bloomfield AV. in SBE. XLII. p. LXVII.

[6] See *Vedic Index* under *Purohita* and *Ṛitvij*.

[7] *Dānastuti*.

[8] *Sava* (acc. pl., savān) 'pressings of Soma'. But in the *Kauśika Sūtra* the word frequently means 'the formal bestowal of the *dakṣiṇā*.' See Bloomfield, HAV. 414, 528, etc. If in this late *Dānastuti* hymn *sava* has this meaning, then the translation should be: 'Who made to me a thousand gift-bestowals'.

[9] *Niṣka* 'necklace' (*cf*. II. 33, 10). The *niṣka* was used as a kind of currency or measure of value. *Cf*. *Vedic Index* under Niṣka. Vedic *niṣkas* should be discovered in the great mounds of the Punjab.

[10] Or 'with mares to draw them' (Griffith).

There followed after sixty thousand cattle.
Kakṣīvant gained them at the day's conclusion.

According to the above-translated 'gift-laud' the prince Svanaya Bhāvya, who dwelt by the Indus, had apparently been in trouble probably from some Gandhāra tribe (v. 7), and had implored help (v. 2). This the priest Kakṣīvant rendered through his sacrifices, prayers and spells[1]. Hence the magnificent gifts of the king, which the priestly recipient celebrates probably with suitable exaggeration. The gifts include horses, cows, gold ornaments and female slaves (?), but not land[2]. It indicates that there were Aryan tribes still dwelling on the Indus.

Most or all of the material of the Ṛv. is due to the mutual relationship and co-operation of wealthy Kṣatriya patrons and indigent Brāhman priests. In the early creative days of Ṛigvedic literature the *hotar* priests did not merely recite the hymns, but also composed the hymns they recited[3]. We may assume with a high degree of probability that very few hymns in the Ṛik collection were composed except by priests under contract to wealthy patrons to provide the hymns necessary for the solemnizing of the sacrifice. And as the supreme ritual of the Ṛv. was the *Soma* ritual, which gathered up in itself the worship of all the gods, it follows that most of the hymns were composed for the Soma sacrifice. This means that the Ṛigveda is a literary monument of the religious views and practices of the Vedic aristocracy and priesthood alone, the usages of the Vaiśyas and Śūdras being inadequately represented. Along with the 'hieratic' religion of the Ṛv. there were current undoubtedly lower forms of belief, which were later collected in the *Atharvaveda*, practices such as charms and spells, which receive comparatively slight recognition in the Ṛv.[4]

---

[1] Compare Exodus XVII. 8-13, 1 Sam. VII. 5-11.

[2] See *Vedic Index* under *Dakṣiṇā*.

[3] See *Vedic Index* under *Ṛtvij*, and Oldenberg, RV. 380.

[4] While this, on the whole, is true, it must be admitted that recent research has tended to diminish somewhat this difference between *Ṛigveda* and *Atharvaveda*.

There were priestly gods as well as warrior gods. If Indra was conceived after the likeness of the Kṣatriya, Agni and Bṛihaspati are represented as divine priests.

d) Vaiśyas.—Apart from the nobility and the priesthood the rest of the population of Aryan descent was included under the name of Vaiśyas[1], that is, 'commons', 'subjects'. They constituted the agricultural and industrial class. According to the later literature their distinctive sign was the goad of the ploughman, and their subordinate position in relation to the nobility was indicated by their characterization as 'tributary to another', 'to be oppressed at will'[2], etc. The Vaiśyas formed the backbone of the state[3]. Superior to, but resting upon them, were the Brāhman and Kṣatriya communities. Brāhman, Kṣatriya and Vaiśya as Aryan in descent were sharply distinguished from Śūdra. As a class the Vaiśyas seem to have had little to do with the political, religious and intellectual life of the Vedic age. On the whole, like the Śūdras, they were an inarticulate element in the population, with some tendency to fall rather than rise in social standing[4]. Probably their religious practices were largely of an Atharvanic character, consisting of domestic and agricultural charms[5]. The bucolic Pūṣan armed with a goad seems to have been a Vaiśya deity.

e) Śūdras.—The Śūdras[6] as in general people of non-Aryan blood, colour and religion were at the bottom of the social scale in Vedic India. If according to the *Aitareya Brāhmaṇa*[7] the Vaiśya could be 'oppressed at will', the Śūdra could be 'slain at will'. The term *Śūdra* occurs only once in the Ṛv.[8] as the substitute and equivalent for the

---

[1] Rv. X. 90, 12 (only here), but compare VIII. 35, 16-18, where *brahma*, *kṣatram* and *viśaḥ* are mentioned together.

[2] See *Vedic Index* articles *Vaiśya* and *Varṇa*.

[3] *Cf.* the agricultural communities of most modern states.

[4] *Cf.* the *Rathakāras*, 'chariot-makers'.

[5] Bloomfield, HAV. in SBE. XLII. 140-160.

[6] Probably the term *Śūdra* (*cf.* Ptolemy's Σύδροι, VI. 20) was originally the name of a tribe which opposed the Aryan invasion. See *Vedic Index* under Śūdra.

[7] VII. 29, 4. [8] X. 90, 12.

earlier *Dasyu (Dāsa)*. It covers the aboriginal population so far as reduced to a state of subjection to the Aryan. While the Śūdra was separated from the Vaiśya by difference of blood, he was industrially akin to the Vaiśya. The presence of a dark servile class in Vedic society was undoubtedly responsible for the growth of the feeling that manual labour was undignified[1]. This feeling tended to depress the status of Vaiśyas. We know little or nothing about the religious beliefs and practices of the Śūdras except what is suggested by the expression *śiśnadeva*[2]. It is safe to assume that they were Atharvanic in character, consisting of demon-worship, charms and spells. The later religious history of India was conditioned by the interaction of Ārya and Śūdra. If Śūdra religion was aryanised, it is equally true that Aryan religion was śūdraized.

8. Conclusion.—When the Aryan tribes passed the Hindu Kush, they crossed, as it were, their Rubicon[3]. In large measure shut out from the fellowship of their brother Aryans of the West, they were shut in with the aborigines of India in an age-long isolation, never effectively broken until the coming of the later Aryans, namely, the Portuguese, Danish, Dutch, French and English. Classes that ordinarily remain fluid, such as nobility, priesthood and commons, became in India crystalized into castes, because of the addition of the fourth or Śūdra class. Probably it was colour more than anything else, which was responsible for caste[4]. In the clashing of Aryan and Dasyu there must have been much intermingling of blood. There was an ancient as well as a modern Eurasian population[5]. The later philosophical

---

[1] Compare the similar condition of things during the slave-holding days in the Southern States of America, when white labourers were often regarded as 'poor white trash', industrially and even socially akin to the Negroes.

[2] See p. 39.

[3] Oldenberg, LAI. 2.

[4] The problem in America of the relation of 'White' and 'Negro' is very similar. *Cf. Vedic Index*, art *Varṇa*.

[5] There is no reproach involved in this statement. The artistic Greek people are the product of the fusion of northern Aryan tribes with the Mediterranean race. The English people represent a fusion of invading Teutonic tribes with the Celtic inhabitants of Britain: Anglo-Celts they should be called.

and theological systems of India as well as her characteristic attitude of pessimism toward life may be regarded not as pure Aryan, but as Ârya-Dravidian products. The significance of the Ṛigveda is this that its hymns, with negligible exceptions, represent the Aryan as standing in stern antagonism to the Dasyu and all his ways. It is therefore the purest expression on the soil of India of the Aryan spirit[1].

---

[1] *Cf.* Macnicol, IT. 191.

CHAPTER III.

THE RIGVEDIC BOOK

1. **Introductory.**—The *Ṛigveda* is the Vedic book *par excellence.* Chronologically, it is the oldest book in Hindu literature. Theoretically, it is the most sacred, as it heads[1] the list of books which come under *śruti* or 'revelation'. The word *Veda* means knowledge or wisdom[2], and *Ṛig (Ṛik)* is the name for laudatory verse or stanza. Hence the compound word Ṛig-Veda may be translated as 'Verse-Wisdom'[3]. It is the earliest and most sacred wisdom of the Indian Aryans set forth in the form of stanzas which are grouped in hymns. The unit of revelation, as in the Qurān, seems to be the verse.

The *Ṛigveda* is a great collection *(saṁhitā)* of a thousand or more hymns. It is, however, only one out of four collections. For besides the Ṛv., there is the *Sāman* or chant-Veda, the *Yajus* or Veda of sacrificial formulæ, and the *Atharvan* or Veda of 'popular religion'. The four Vedas are not unconnected with one another. Thus all the stanzas of the Sāmaveda except seventy-five are found in the Ṛv. The Yajurveda and the Atharvaveda also have a considerable amount of material in common with the Ṛv. What we really have, then, in the four Vedas is the distribution of the original Vedic material into four *saṁhitās* or 'collections'[4]. The four Vedas are a fourfold presentation of the primitive Veda, in some such way as the four Gospels are a fourfold presentation of the primitive Gospel. By 'primitive Veda' of course is meant the poetic material of the Vedic age before it was collected. Such material

---

[1] In the *Puruṣa Sūkta* (Ṛv. X. 90. 9) the stanzas *(ṛicaḥ)* of the *Ṛik* are mentioned before the verses *(sāmāni)* of the *Sāman*, and the *Yajus*.

[2] Cognates of *Veda* are Gr. οἶδα, Lat. vid-eo, Eng. *wit*.

[3] Hopkins, ION. 23.

[4] Hopkins, ION, 24.

existing in the various Vedic clans and priestly families consisted, as the four historic collections show, of 'a heterogeneous combination of old hymns, charms, philosophical poems, and popular songs, most but not all of which are of religious content'[1]. This primitive Vedic material was in part 'hieratic' or priestly, having to do with the worship of the great gods, such as Agni, Indra, Soma; and in part, popular, consisting of house ceremonies, charms and magic spells[2]. The Ṛigveda, while containing some popular material, especially in the tenth, first and seventh books[3], is pre-eminently a text-book of priestly religion; whereas the Atharvaveda, though containing some priestly material, is very largely a text-book of popular religion.

The process of the formation of the Ṛigveda as a collection of hymns must have been complete by about 800 B. C., and the true date may be still earlier. The complete Ṛik is presupposed in the existing Brāhmaṇas, which, according to the most moderate possible estimate, cannot be dated later than 800 to 600 B. C. The other three Vedas were collected rather later than the Ṛik, but we need not discuss the dates of their formation here. It is, besides, quite probable that long before the fourfold collection was formally made, the Vedic material began to break up into four groups on the basis of religious use. Thus the reference in the *Puruṣa-Sūkta*[4] may be only to an incipient classification of the Vedic material into laudatory verses (ṛicaḥ) used by the *Hotṛi* or invoking priest,

---

[1] Hopkins, ION. 23.

[2] Bloomfield, AV. 2, and *On the Relative Chronology of the Vedic Hymns*, JAOS, 21 (1901) p. 46.

[3] "Considerably more than one half of the RV. stanzas which correspond to the AV. belong to the tenth book of the RV., largely to the last *anuvāka* of that book; about one-sixth to the first book; about one-tenth to the seventh book; about one-eighth to all the other books put together." Bloomfield, AV. 46.

[4] Rv. X. 90.

chants (sāmāni) used by the *Udgātri* or singing priest, and sacrificial formulas (yajus) used by the *Adhvaryu* or officiating priest. The final redaction of the four collections may very well have been only a *de jure* recognition of what had for some time been a *de facto* state of things.

The motive which determined the fourfold collection of the Vedic material was, then, primarily *practical* — to serve the interests of the ritual[1]. Of course, there was in operation at the same time a more theoretical motive, namely, the preservation from change and destruction of the ancient heritage of sacred song.

But though the Ṛigveda as a collection is not to be dated later than 800 B. C., the final settlement of the exact spelling of the text as we have it to-day, did not take place until after the completion of the older Brāhmaṇas, about 600 B. C., when the Saṁhitā text[2], *i. e.* the text settled in accordance with the rules of *saṁdhi,* which control Classical Sanskrit, was formed. Since that date the text of the Ṛigveda has been preserved with almost faultless accuracy.

The Ṛigveda deserves to be called 'the most important'[3] of the Vedas, because it is the oldest and largest collection of Vedic hymns and the source of much of the material found in the *Saman, Yajus* and *Atharvan.* Of the 20,000 metrical stanzas in Vedic literature (omitting variants) about 10,000, or fully one-half occur in the Ṛik[4]. Of the 1549 stanzas of the Sāmaveda 1474 are derived from the Ṛik, and also one-fourth of the matter of the Yajurveda. Besides a considerable portion in prose, the Atharvaveda contains about 6000 poetic stanzas, one-fifth of which, namely 1200 stanzas, occur also in the Ṛv.[5]. The Ṛigveda,

[1] Bloomfield refers to his own "rapidly growing conviction that the Ṛv., as we have it, in common with the other Vedas, is a liturgic collection". *Relative Chronology*, JAOS., 1901, p. 45.

[2] Macdonell, SL. 46-50; Hopkins ION. 27.

[3] Macdonell, SL. in IGI. II. 209.

[4] Bloomfield, *op. cit.* 42-43.

[5] Macdonell *op. cit.* 227-229.

then, is a great documentary source for the other three Vedas, very much as the Gospel of Mark is an important source for the Gospels of Matthew and Luke.

Vedic literature covers three classes of literary productions in the Vedic age, *viz.* (1) *Mantras* or Vedic stanzas produced largely in the creative period and afterwards collected in the form of the four Vedas; (2) *Brāhmaṇas,* exposition and further elaboration of the ritualistic element in the Vedas, and also of the philosophical element[1]; and (3) *Sūtras,* mnemonic compendia dealing with Vedic ritual and customary law. Thus by Veda we mean, in a narrow sense, the Ṛigveda; in a wider sense, any or all of the Four Vedas; and, in the widest sense of all, the whole cycle of Vedic literature according to the threefold division of *Mantra, Brāhmaṇa,* and *Sūtra.* The extent of the existing Vedic literature may be estimated from the fact that about one hundred and twenty texts have contributed to the *Vedic Concordance* of Prof. Bloomfield[2]. The Ṛigveda is about equal in bulk to the Iliad and Odyssey combined. Being 'the most ancient literary monument of India', it is the foundation not only of Vedic literature, but of Indian literature in general. Thus for Indian history, religion, philosophy and civilization the Ṛigveda is a book of origins. As prophetic of the lines of future development it may also be called a collection of 'first fruits.

2. THE TEXT OF THE ṚIGVEDA.—The Ṛigveda contains 1017 hymns, or 1028, if we add the supplementary *Vālakhilya* hymns. But the number can be easily increased by breaking up some of the larger wholes into separate hymns, as we seem forced to do on critical grounds[3]. Thus out of the total collection of 1028 hymns E. V. Arnold finds about 220 which are composite and consist of 780 parts,

---

[1] The elaboration of the philosophical element in the Vedas is, of course, the work of the *Upaniṣads,* philosophical appendices to the Brāhmaṇas.

[2] Bloomfield, ṚV. 18.

[3] Hillebrandt, *Alt-Indien,* 53.

usually short hymns of three verses each[1]. The hymns are arranged in ten books or *maṇḍalas* (lit. 'cycles').

Books II-VII are the so-called 'family books', because each is assigned by tradition to the eponym ancestor of a particular priestly family[2]. That these groups of hymns were produced within the families to which they are ascribed is sufficiently proved by internal evidence. The hymns of the family books are arranged on a uniform plan, which seems to reveal the editorial work of a single school. Each major group or *maṇḍala* is a collection of smaller groups of hymns arranged according to the deities addressed, the first sub-group consisting of hymns to Agni, the second to Indra, and so forth. Within these smaller groups the position of any hymn is determined by the number of stanzas it contains, the hymn containing the largest number of stanzas being placed first, and so on. Hymns which break this rule are to be regarded either as complexes of smaller hymns, or as containing later additions. Again books II-VII seem to have been arranged according to the number of hymns they severally contain (not counting later additions); for the second book contains the smallest number of hymns (43) found in any of the family books, and the seventh book the largest number (104). Thus the 'family books' clearly form one great group.

The first, eighth and tenth books agree together in the fact that the groups of which they consist are based on identity of authorship, actual or assumed. The eighth book and Part A (hymns 1-50) of the first book have a certain affinity with each other due to the strophical arrangement which exists more or less in both and also to the fact that the family of the *Kāṇvas* figures in the authorship of each. The ninth book is unique, in that all of its hymns are addressed to Soma. Its groups depend upon identity of

---

[1] *The Ṛigveda and Atharvaveda*, JAOS. 1901, p. 312.

[2] The names of these *Ṛishis* are: Gṛitsamada, Viśvāmitra, Vāmadeva, Atri, Bharadvāja, Vasiṣṭha.

metre[1]. We see, then, that there are three principles which lie at the basis of the groups within the several books, *viz.* identity of the deity addressed, as in the family books, identity of authorship, as in the first, eighth and tenth books, and identity of metre, as in the ninth book. The first and tenth books have each the same number of hymns (191), and together they contain the great mass of all the Atharvanic or 'popular' stanzas in the Ṛigveda.

On the basis of these uniformities of arrangement by which various sections of the Ṛv. are linked together, it is plausible to assume more or less independent redaction for several of the larger wholes of which the Ṛv. consists. Professor Hopkins[2] thinks that a threefold process of grouping lies at the basis of the present arrangement; books II-VII, the 'family books', furnishing the nucleus, books I and VIII adding a framework, and books IX and X completing the collection. This, or something like it, must have taken place. If Hopkins' view is correct, then we have a kind of threefold canon in the Ṛv.

The canonical form of the Ṛv., as we have seen, is known as the *Saṁhita* text, that is, the text in which the words are united according to the rules of combination current in Sanskrit, and is not earlier than 600 B. C. Several schools existed, each with its own text, distinguished by unimportant differences; but the text has come down to us only in the recension of the Śākala school[3].

As soon as the Ṛv. 'collection' was made, an extraordinary set of devices was invented, in order to guard the purity of the text. Soon after the formation of the *Saṁhita* or synthetic text, the *Pada* or analytic text was constructed. In the *pada* or 'word'-text each word of the *Saṁhitā* was reproduced in its separate, unmodified and (generally) older

---

[1] See for this whole section Macdonell, *Sanskrit Literature*, Chap. III.

[2] ION. 26-27.

[3] This single recension of the Ṛv. reminds us of the similar textual history of the Qurān, the single recension of Othmān being responsible for all later copies of the Bible of Islām.

form. It is easier to read metrically from the *pada* than from the *saṁhita* text. Further devices for safeguarding the text were the *Krama-paṭha* 'step-text', the *jaṭa-pātha* 'woven text', and the *ghana-paṭha,* a still more complicated text. Representing the words of a Vedic stanza by the letters of the alphabet, we may illustrate the three safeguarding texts by the three following formulas: (1) ab-bc-cd-de, etc., (2) ab-ba-ab; bc-cb-bc, etc. (3) ab-ba-abc-cba-abc; bc-cb-bcd, etc. By these complicated processes of dislocation and repetition forwards and backwards, the aim was to make impossible the slightest change in the sacred text. Besides the five forms of the text mentioned above, there were two more safeguards in the shape of the *Prātiśakhyas,* which explain all the changes necessary for converting the *pada* into the *saṁhita* text, and the *Anukramaṇis* or 'Indices', which define the contents of each hymn from various points of view, and also furnish a statistical account of the Ṛv. as a whole[1]. The result was that from the time that these safeguarding devices began to be applied, the Śākala recension of the Ṛv., like that of Othman's recension of the Qurān, was preserved in a unique state of purity. Before that time, however, some textual corruption had taken place[2].

It should be mentioned also that for a long time the Vedic texts were in all probability orally transmitted. If writing was introduced into India in the 8th century B. C., as Bühler[3] thinks, its use for long centuries was confined largely or entirely to commercial transactions and the like. Doubtless the Brāhmanical community had an interest in keeping the sacred texts as a kind of priestly monopoly. Such a monopoly could be maintained only if the texts were taught orally and not reduced to writing.

---

[1] 1028 hymns, 10,402 verses, 153,826 words and 432,000 syllables. Max Müller, *Physical Religion,* 66.

[2] For evidences of this see Oldenberg, *Hymns to Agni,* SBE. XLVI.

[3] Indian Paleography in IA. vol. XXXIII. Appendix 15-16.

The extraordinary machinery for safeguarding the text of the Ṛv., the like of which is not found elsewhere in the world, indicates the existence of a well-grounded fear that the textual history of the Vedic hymns in the past would repeat itself in the future; in other words, that "the text would continue to be corrupted, modified, modernized, as without such precautions it had been changed in the past"[1]. The textual history of the hymns of the Ṛv. before the 'collection' was stereotyped in the form of the canonical text, was undoubtedly a history of *linguistic levelling*. On this point the testimony of experts may be cited. Macdonell[2] admits that "there are undeniable corruptions in detail belonging to the older period." Hopkins[3] holds that the hymns of the Ṛv. collection—hymns of very different periods originally—had been already reduced pretty much to one linguistic level, at the time the canonical text was formed. Grierson and Barnett[4] also remark that the songs of Lallā, or Lāl Ded, the Kāshmirī female ascetic, furnish a valuable example of the manner in which the language of the Vedic hymns must have changed from generation to generation, before their text was finally established. The effect of such linguistic levelling was to obscure more or less the data for the existence of different dialects in the Ṛv. and the evidence for different periods of composition. The *saṁhitā* text stereotyped the form of the Ṛv. very much as the grammar of Pāṇini fixed the form of Sanskrit.

What has the extant text of the Ṛv. to say regarding the material out of which it is composed? As an answer to this question Bloomfield[5], the editor of the great Vedic Concordance, remarks: "Of the 40,000 lines of the Ṛigveda

---

[1] Hopkins, ION. 26.

[2] Sanskrit Literature 47.

[3] *op. cit.* 26.

[4] *Lallā-Vākyāni*, 1920, p. 128, note 1.

[5] *On Certain Work in Continuance of the Vedic Concordance*. JAOS. 29 (1908) pp. 287-288.

about 5000 are repeated[1] lines........ Not far from 2000 verse-lines occur two, three, or more times........ This collection as a whole is the last precipitate, with a long and tangled past behind it, of a literary activity of great and indefinite length........ Every part seems to be conscious of and assimilated to every other part." And in another place the same scholar[2] writes that "the earliest books of the Ṛv. are not exempt from the same processes of secondary grouping and adaptation of their mantras, though they are less frequent and less obvious than is the case in the Atharvaveda". In harmony with this Hopkins[3] declares that "the Ṛigveda Collection itself is a composite consisting largely of the same material disposed in various ways". And he draws the conclusion that "the hymns are founded on older material, the wreck of which has been utilized in constructing new poetic buildings, just as many of the temples of India are to a great extent built of the material of older demolished temples". This is certainly true to some extent. But may not many of the phenomena of repetition in the Ṛv., even as in the O. T. Psalms and in the Qurān, be due to a stereotyped religious vocabulary, in which the same phrases would naturally tend to recur?

3. THE LANGUAGE OF THE ṚIGVEDA. — The centre of gravity of the Indo-Aryan world at the time that the Ṛv. collection was made (circa 600 B. C.) was most probably in *Brahmarṣideśa*[4] (the country of the Holy Sages) in the region between the upper Jumna and Ganges. It is clear that the earlier hymns were produced in the western Punjab, while the later hymns were composed further East and probably largely in the vicinity of the sacred river Sarasvatī[5]. Now an outstanding fact in the linguistic

---

[1] *Cf.* Bloomfield, *Rigveda Repetitions* in HOS., Vol. 20.

[2] SBE. XLII, p. LXXII.

[3] ION. 24.

[4] Rapson, CHI. I. 46.

[5] *Manusmṛti* II. 17; Hopkins, ION. 31, 34, and JAOS. 19, p. 20; Grierson, JRAS. 1904, p. 476.

history of Aryan India is the distinction emphasized in Sanskrit literature between the 'Midland' *(Madhyadeśa)* and the 'Outland'[1]. The Midland extending approximately from the Himālayas to the Vindhya Hills and from Sirhind to Allahabad was regarded as the true home of the Aryan people, language, religion and culture. The Outland, namely, Punjab, Sind, Gujarāt, Rājputāna, Oudh and Bihār, was also peopled by Aryan tribes, each with its own dialect. Now in the opinion of Grierson, the Superintendent of the Linguistic Survey of India, "a comparison of the modern vernaculars[2] shows that these outer dialects were more closely related to each other than any of them was to the language of the Midland". To account for this linguistic condition of things, he assumes that the latest invaders "entered the Punjab like a wedge into the heart of the country already occupied by the first immigrants, forcing the latter outwards in three directions, to the East, to the South and to the West"[3]. The result of course would be the creation of a kind of linguistic cleavage between the language of the Midland, on the one hand, and the various dialects of the Outland, on the other, such a cleavage as is suggested by the linguistic facts imbedded in the modern Indo-Aryan vernaculars. If this is a correct interpretation of the facts, then the Aryans of the Midland as distinguished

---

[1] See chapter on *Languages* by Grierson in IGI. I. 349 ff.

[2] Grierson's classification of the Indo-Aryan Vernaculars of India is as follows: —

A. Language of the Midland, *Western Hindī*.

B. Intermediate Languages.

a) More nearly related to the Midland: *Rājasthānī, Pahāṛī, Gujarātī, Punjābī*.

b) More nearly related to the outer band, *Eastern Hindī*.

C. Outer Languages.

a) North Western Group: *Kaśmīrī, Kohisthānī, Lahṇḍā, Sindhī*.

b) Southern Group: *Marāṭhī*.

c) Eastern Group: *Bihārī, Oriya, Bengālī, Assamese*.

[3] Grierson IGI. I. 358 (following Hœrnle)

from the Aryans of the Outland, were the last to arrive, but the first to achieve great things.

This interpretation of the linguistic facts lies at the foundation of the assumption of two widely separated gates by which the Aryans entered India, the Khyber Pass and the route through Chitrāl and Gilgit. This view is not supported by the general consensus of opinion. If certain scholars, such as Hœrnle, Grierson and Risley[1] favour it, other equally great scholars like Macdonell[2], Keith[3] and Rapson[4], who occupy the Sanskrit chairs at Oxford, Edinburgh, and Cambridge, oppose it. Rapson suggests an alternative theory to account for the linguistic facts.

The language of the Ṛigveda was naturally the dialect of the region where the hymns were composed, namely, the northern and eastern part of the Punjab, with its centre probably at the sacred river Sarasvatī. It was, without doubt, the literary form[5] of a living vernacular, and Grierson[6] sees in it "the earliest Prākṛit, of which we have any cognizance". The language of the Ṛv. doubtless represents a more archaic dialect than was commonly spoken. The later hymns, we have reason to believe, were largely imitative and presuppose a fixed tradition of the kind of speech proper for a sacred song. If, as Hopkins holds, the earlier Ṛigveda hymns have suffered from 'linguistic levelling', it is probably equally true that the later hymns have suffered from the opposite process of linguistic heightening, so to speak, through the conscious archaizing of their authors[7].

The speech of the Ṛv. may be called Vedic to distinguish

---

[1] IGI. I. 303 ff.

[2] Vedic Index.

[3] CHI. I. 119, 123.

[4] CHI. I. 50.

[5] Keith, CHI., I, 109-110.

[6] *op. cit.* 360.

[7] This may be illustrated from the religious hymns or *bhajans* of North India. Even to-day Hindī hymns are usually written in the archaic dialect of the *Rāmāyaṇa* of Tulsī Dās.

it from the elaborate and artificial form given to the language by the grammatical canons of Pāṇini (circa 350 B.C.). The main difference, then, between Vedic and Sanskrit is the difference between an earlier and relatively unpruned popular speech and a later pruned and polished speech. In fact, Vedic as the vernacular of a limited region in and near the upper Gangetic Doāb is referred to by Grierson as the only known specimen of "the Primary Prākṛits of India"[1]. The language of the Ṛv., then, was in its time as truly a vernacular speech as the Hebrew of the Old Testament or the so-called 'Biblical' Greek of the New Testament; at the same time, as the hieratic speech, it was "the first literary dialect of India"[2]. There are of course other differences between Vedic and Sanskrit. Vedic is much richer in conjugational forms, having numerous subjunctive, infinitive, and aorist forms, which do not occur in Sanskrit. Phonetically, there is little difference between the two. Of course, many Vedic words were obsolete by the time of Pāṇini and the beginnings of classical Sanskrit. On the whole, Vedic and Sanskrit differ from each other very much as Homeric differs from Classical Greek or as the language of Chaucer differs from that of Milton.

The processes of levelling down and levelling up, to which reference has already been made[3] — the old being assimilated to the new and the new to the old — have naturally more or less obscured any traces of dialectical differences which might otherwise have existed in the Vedic text. The distinction between 'hieratic' and 'popular'

---

[1] Grierson distinguishes between primary, secondary and tertiary Prākṛits. The language of the Ṛv. illustrates the first; the Pāli of the Buddhistic writings, the second; and the modern Indo-Aryan vernaculars, such as Hindī and Punjābī, the third. It is noticeable that these various vernaculars, Vedic, Pāli, Hindī and Punjābī, have furnished the literary vehicles for such religious books as the *Ṛigveda*, the *Tripiṭaka* of Buddhism, the *Rāmāyaṇa* of Tulsī Dās, and the *Granth Sāhib* of the Sikhs.

[2] Farquhar, ORLI. 8.

[3] pp. 61, 64.

language in the Ṛv. is a real distinction, if priestly and popular hymns belong to the same age; if not, it may mark simply chronological sequence. Such a distinction, however, between two varieties of Vedic speech, one more learned and technical, and the other more popular, would be very natural according to all analogy. We would expect that the priests as the learned class of the Vedic age would have a 'class' speech, technical and professional. There are also some linguistic phenomena in the Ṛv., which suggest as their causes the existence of different Indo-Aryan dialects, notably the multitudinous present, aorist and infinitive forms[1].

The language of the Ṛv. is closely akin to that of the Avesta, the Bible of the Zoroastrian religion. In fact, as already shown[2], Vedic and Avestan are simply dialects of the same Indo-Iranian speech. Entire passages of Avestan can be rendered into Vedic and *vice versa* merely by making the necessary phonetic changes[3]. And a knowledge of Vedic is the best preparation for the study of Avestan.

But Vedic, as we have seen[4], is related not only to Avestan, but also to Greek, Latin, Celtic, Teutonic and Slavonic. It is, in other words, a member of the great Indo-European family of languages, the only rival of which in historic importance is the Semitic family. If Assyro-Babylonian, Hebrew and Arabic were important vehicles of ancient culture, none the less were Vedic, Avestan, Greek and Latin. But in modern times the languages of the Indo-European family have far outstripped in importance the languages of the Semitic family (except perhaps Arabic). As modern representatives of the Indo-European family there may be mentioned nearly all the languages of Europe, including such tongues as English, French, German, Russian

---

[1] "The wealth of inflectional forms in the Vedic age may be partly explained as the result of a mixture of dialects". Rapson, JRAS. 1904, p. 440.

[2] p. 21.

[3] Jackson, *Avesta Grammar*, Part I (1892), p. XXXI.

[4] pp. 2-6.

and Italian, and in Asia Persian[1], Hindī, Bengālī, Punjābī, Marāṭhī, etc. Thus Vedic belongs to that potent and widely conquering family of languages which more than any other (except possibly the Semitic) has furnished literary vehicles for the best thought of the ages past, and is apparently bound up, to a large extent, with the future linguistic destiny of mankind. Vedic, as the Indian branch of the Indo-European family, has shared with the other branches in the common tendency to spread and conquer. What was first simply the dialect of a district became the language of a caste and a religion, and afterwards (in the form of Sanskrit) the language of religion, politics and culture throughout India[2].

4. THE CHRONOLOGY OF THE ṚIGVEDA.—Brief references have already been made to the migrations and settlements[3] of the Western Indo-Europeans, as bearing upon the problem of the date of the Ṛigveda. It seems desirable to consider this question from the point of view also of Indian history and archæology. There is as yet no unanimity among scholars concerning the age of the Ṛigveda. Brāhmanical orthodoxy holds that the Vedas are eternal[4]. Modern critical scholars have hitherto been divided into three

---

[1] If the superstructure of Persian is Semitic (Arabic), its foundation is Indo-European

[2] Rapson, *op. cit.* 456.

[3] p. 19.

[4] *Manu* I. 21-23, XII. 94-100. The view embodied in *Manusmṛiti* (circa 100 A. D.) is that in the beginning Brahmā fashioned from the words of the Veda the several names, functions and conditions of all creatures, and that in order to the performance of sacrifice he drew forth from *Agni*, *Vāyu* and *Sūrya* the triple eternal Veda. According to scholastic Brâhmanism, then, the Veda is at once a *creative* and a *sacrificial* program. Kullūka-Bhaṭṭa (15th Cent. A. D.) who builds on Govindarāja (12th Cent. A D.) interprets Manu to mean that at the beginning of the present mundane era *(Kalpa)* Brahmā drew forth the Vedas from Agni, Vāyu and Sūrya. The Ārya Samāj, which has broken with Brāhmanical tradition at so many points, holds fast nevertheless to the Brāhmanical theory of the antiquity of the Vedas and teaches that the Four Vedas were revealed to four sages, Agni, Vāyu, Sūrya and Angiras at the beginning of the present mundane age over one hundred billion (!) years ago.

camps, according as they have favoured an early, a late, or an intermediate date. Professor Hopkins[1] of Yale, a great authority on the Epic literature of India, and Professor Jackson of Columbia, well known as a Zoroastrian scholar, both agree in urging a late date, 1000-600 B.C. Briefly stated their grounds are as follows: (1) The date of Zoroaster is now generally fixed at B.C. 660-583[2] by *e.g.* Geldner[3], West[4] and Jackson[5]; and since there is only a dialectic difference between the language of the Ṛv. and that of the Avesta, there can be no great interval in time between the two works, the date of Zoroaster, of course, determining the date of the oldest part of the Avesta. (2) The change in language between the Ṛigveda and the Upaniṣads is not greater than that between Chaucer and Milton, and hence it is fair to suppose that about 200 years would suffice in the one case as well as in the other. The two hundred years within which Hopkins and Jackson place the bulk of the Ṛigveda hymns are B.C. 800-600. (3) The Ṛishis who composed the hymns may very well have been in large measure contemporary with one another, and certain differences in vocabulary and style may be accounted for simply by variety of authorship. According to this view, then, the Ṛigveda is roughly contemporaneous with the bulk of early Hebrew literature.

At the opposite pole from Hopkins and Jackson stand Tilak[6] and Jacobi[7], who on the basis of astronomical calculations would carry the period of the composition of the Ṛigveda back beyond 2500 B.C., as far at least as 3500, and according to Tilak farther still. Jacobi places the

---

[1] ION. 30.

[2] Oldenberg demurs. See *Orientalische Religionen*, 78, in *Die Kultur der Gegenwart* (1906), I. 3, 1.

[3] Art. on *Zoroastrianism* in *Encyclopædia Biblica*, IV. 5431.

[4] SBE. XLVII, p XLII.

[5] *Zoroaster the Prophet of Iran*, 16.

[6] *Orion or Researches into the Antiquity of the Vedas*, Poona, 1916.

[7] ZDMG. XLIX. 218-230; JRAS. (1909) 721 ff., and (1910) 456 ff.

Vedic age within the period 4500-2500 B. C. but refers the composition of the Ṛigveda to the second half of this period. Tilak dates the oldest period of Aryan civilization between 6000 and 4000 B. C., when he thinks certain 'sacrificial formulæ' were 'probably in use'. He places the composition of the Ṛigveda hymns, as we have them, within the period 4000-2500 B. C.[1] The Tilak-Jacobi thesis has met with severe criticism from Weber, Whitney, Oldenberg[2], Thibaut[3], Hopkins, Macdonell, and Keith[4]. Apart from the assumed astronomical data, however, Jacobi urges that the norm of European progress cannot be applied to India on account of its isolated position and the consequently independent character of its development. And he emphasises the fact that the dates assumed by himself for the Vedic period are not greater than are accepted by scholars for the civilization of the Euphrates and the Nile[5]. The late Professor Bühler[6] was of the opinion that the conquest and brahmanization of India requires a much earlier date than 1200-1000 B. C. Following him, Winternitz[7] declares that from the standpoint of Indian history there is nothing against the view that Vedic literature goes back to the third millennium and the beginnings of Indian culture to the fourth millennium B. C. Prof. Bloomfield[8], too, declares himself "now much more inclined to listen to an early date, say 2000 B. C., for the beginnings of Vedic literary production, and to a much earlier date for the beginnings of the institutions and religious concepts" thereof.

---

[1] Tilak, *Orion*, 206.

[2] ZDMG. XLIX. 470 ff.

[3] *Antiquity of Indian Literature and Civilization* (Hindustân Review, January 1904).

[4] JRAS. (1909), 1095 ff., and (1910) 464 ff.

[5] The Tilak-Jacobi hypothesis is, to some extent, recommended by the fact that each sponsor discovered and formulated it independently of the other.

[6] IA, XXIII. 245 ff.

[7] GIL. 254.

[8] RV. 20. and JAOS (1908) p. 287 ff.

The third group of scholars stands between these extremes. Their convictions are based largely upon considerations of the time necessary for the linguistic, literary and historical development in India. It was Max Müller who suggested the chronological system we refer to, in his brilliant pioneer volume, *A History of Ancient Sanskrit Literature,* published in 1859. Here are the essential features: —

1200-1000 B.C. the *Chhandas* period, when the earlier hymns of the *Ṛigveda* were composed.

1000-800 „ the *Mantra* period, when the later hymns were composed and the *Sāmaveda* and the *Yajurveda* were compiled.

Most British scholars and many belonging to other lands have followed him; and it now seems as if his ideas were likely to have a far wider range. The first volume of *The Cambridge History of India*, published in April 1922, is a magnificent piece of collaborative scholarship. The book consists of chapters written by fourteen great scholars — eleven British, two American, one Swedish, — Sir Halford Mackinder, Prof. Rapson, Peter Giles, Master of Emmanuel College Cambridge, Prof. A. Berriedale Keith, Prof. Jarl Charpentier of Upsala, Prof. T. W. Rhys Davids, Mrs. Rhys Davids, Prof. Hopkins of Yale, Prof. Jackson of Columbia, Dr. George Macdonald, Mr. E. R. Bevan, Dr. F. W. Thomas, Dr. Barnett and Sir John Marshall — ; and the whole group accept for the early Vedic period the chronological scheme proposed sixty-three years ago by Max Müller. It is noticeable that the two brilliant men, who are mentioned above as favouring later dates, are included in this group. Their views have doubtless been modified during the intervening years.

But, although this scheme seems to be steadily gathering the suffrages of a larger number of scholars, the grave differences which separate them from those thinkers who favour far earlier dates make it quite clear that positive dates are as yet lacking for determining the chronology of the Vedic period. Scholars who bring forward considerations based upon the length of time assumed to be necessary for a particular development, linguistic, literary or historical, as the case may be, sometimes forget that in literature and history as well as in religion one day may be as a thousand years and a thousand years as one day[1]; that is to say, the literary and political development may at one time drag very slowly and at another time proceed with leaps and bounds. If the development of the invading Aryan tribes was rapid — and the development of an invading population is more likely to be rapid than that of a stationary population — then a period of four hundred years might well suffice for the composition of the Ṛigveda hymns, as is shewn by the development of the new world after its discovery in 1492. If, on the contrary, the development was slow, then the period suggested by Jacobi and Winternitz may be none too large.

What is needed in order to set all this uncertainty at rest is the discovery of positive data. Such data must clearly be *archæological.* The appearance of Iranian proper names[2] in one of the Tel-el-Amarna letters (1400 B. C.), the occurrence of the name *Assara-Mazās* (Ahura Mazda) in an Assyrian list of gods[3], and Winckler's discovery at Boghaz-Köi[4] are suggestive of the kind of evidence needed. And there is good reason to hope that the needed evidence will be forthcoming in the future. If it is true, as Bloomfield[5] says that "from the entire Vedic period we have not one single piece of antiquarian or archæological material, not one bit of real property; not a building, not a monument, not a coin, jewel or utensil", it is equally true that "the archæology of India is, at present, almost

[1] 2 Peter III.

[2] Bloomfield calls this "the earliest direct record of Indo-European chronology". AJP. XXV. 10.

[3] Hommel, PSBA. 21 (1899) p. 137.

[4] Meyer, GA. I[2] (1909), p. 802.

[5] RV. 20.

an unworked field[1]", at least so far as pre-Buddhistic sites are concerned. One needs but to visit the Punjab and see the numerous ancient mounds scattered over its surface, in order to be convinced that material bearing upon the Vedic period will almost certainly be forthcoming, when these mounds have been adequately explored.

A glance at the map of Asia is also instructive. Leaving out China, there are three river basins which are among the earliest culture-centres of mankind, *viz.* the Nile, the Euphrates-Tigris, and the Indus-Ganges. The Euphrates-Tigris basin lies between the Indus on the east and the Nile on the west. It is well known that there were close relations, political, diplomatic and commercial, between Babylonia and Egypt at a remote period. While there were probably no political relations equally ancient between the Euphrates and the Indus, it is certain that there was an early trade[2]. Bühler's[3] conclusions concerning the origin of the earliest Indian script presuppose such trade relations at least as early as the 8th century B. C. Kennedy also on the basis of all the evidence available concludes that "in the ninth century B. C. some trade existed between the Punjab and Assyria", and that "maritime commerce between India and Babylonia flourished in the seventh and sixth century B. C."[4]. The sea-route between Babylonia and the mouth of the Indus was relatively not a long one, the distance from the base of the Persian Gulf to the Indus being less than from the same point on the Persian Gulf to Babylon. Hitherto archæological research in the Punjab,

---

[1] Quoted from Prof. Rhys Davids by Vincent Smith, JRAS. 1902, p. 288. During the last twenty years (1900-1920) there have been great developments in Indian archæology, but the sites selected for excavation have been largely Buddhistic. For example, at Taxila, the first and oldest city represented by the *Bhir* mound, the occupation of which probably reaches back to the Vedic age, is as yet hardly touched by the spade.

[2] Kennedy, *The Early Commerce of Babylon with India*, JRAS, 1898, p. 241 *ff.*

[3] *Indian Paleography* in IA., Vol. XXXIII, Appendix, 15-16.

[4] *op. cit.* 264, 270.

as already stated, has done practically nothing toward the discovery and excavation of the earliest sites of Vedic culture. We may well cherish the hope that there may yet be found some dateable objects, such as inscribed seals or tablets or other articles from Babylonia or Egypt, which by establishing a lucky synchronism, may solve the chronology of the Vedic age. But as yet Winternitz's formula, x to 500 B.C., expresses the facts of our knowledge or lack of knowledge concerning the chronology of the Vedic period. Theoretically x may mean any date between 1000 and 6000 B.C. as determined by future investigation. This is but giving to the Indus valley a chance to prove for its culture a like antiquity with that of the Euphrates and Nile. In the light of the extraordinary discoveries of recent years (*e.g.* the discovery of the relics of Buddha at Peshawar) Max Müller[1] seems to be too pessimistic when he says that "the date assigned to the poetry of the Veda is and will always remain hypothetical". As yet it is hypothetical. That it will always be so, remains to be seen.

While, then, the lack of evidence precludes the fixing of the Vedic age with anything like certainty, yet a tentative and provisional chronology may be adopted, subject to modification or even rejection in the light of future discovery. The present writer would accordingly present the following system of chronology found in the Cambridge History of India as the best available to-day: —

B. C.	
2500	Probable date of the beginning of the Indo-European migrations.
1800 onward.	Period during which, in Northern Asia Minor and eastward through Northern Mesopotamia to Media, Indo-European peoples can be traced.
1500	Probable date of the first Aryan invasion of India.
1400	The Boghaz-köi tablets, containing Indo-Aryan deities in Vedic form. These clearly come from

[1] Physical Religion (1891) p. 22.

Aryans who have not made "the Iranian shift". Possibly we should think of them as Aryan tribes, who had stopped on the way, while their brethren had already passed on and settled in Iran and in India. At a later date we find Aryan gods at Babylon, whose names are still of the old forms.

B. C.	
1200-1000	Early hymns of the *Ṛigveda* composed probably for the most part in the western Punjab, notably the hymns to Uṣas and to Varuṇa.
1000-800	Later hymns of the *Ṛigveda* composed in Brahmāvarta. The *Sāmaveda* and the *Yajurveda*. Beginnings of the Brāhmaṇa literature.
800-600	The existing Brāhmaṇas.
600	Formation of the *Saṁhitā* text of the Ṛik[1].

This scheme has the merit of not being extremist either upwards or downwards. It fits into the latest and most trustworthy ethnological opinion as to the chronology of the dispersion of the Indo-European peoples, and harmonizes well with the conclusions of students of prehistoric IE. archæology, such as Schrader, Hirt, Feist and Giles[2], and students of ancient history such as Eduard Meyer. It makes possible a reasonable interpretation of all the evidence recently found in Asia Minor, Mesopotamia and elsewhere. The Indian dates were originally based on the literary and cultural evidence of Indian literature; and the majority of our greatest scholars still agree that, from this point of view, these dates are the most natural. Finally it makes possible a common chronology for India and Persia. If we place Zoroaster circa 1000 B. C., as Oldenberg, Moulton and others suggest, then the linguistic phenomena of the early Avesta and of the early Vedic hymns become clearly

[1] CHI. Vol. I. 1922, pp. 76, 112-113, 697.

[2] Schrader, RIA. and Indogermanen; Hirt, Indogermanen I and II; Feist, KAHI.; Giles, CHI. I. 65 ff.

comprehensible; while we are able to understand at once the Zoroastrian reformation in Persia, and in India the rise of Varuṇa and the composition of the great Varuṇa hymns. This becomes all the more natural and credible, if we accept the suggestion that there was intercourse in those days between the early Zoroastrians in Bactria and a special group of their brethren in the Punjab. It is altogether within the limits of possibility that the personal influence of Zoroaster reached the Punjab, whether by the actual sending of preachers or in the ordinary intercourse of trade. It is certainly not too much to believe that some reverberation from that mighty voice—for as a personality he is surely comparable with the Buddha himself — would be heard in the Punjab.

5. THE INTERPRETATION OF THE ṚIGVEDA[1].—The Ṛigveda is not only 'the most ancient literary monument of India', but also 'the most ancient literary document of the Indo-European peoples'[2]. Covering, as it does, several centuries at least, it may be characterized as nothing less than 'a library and a literature'[3]. As already pointed out, it forms a connecting link between India and the West. For while, on the one hand, it fulfils itself in the later history and literature of India, on the other, its roots run deep into the Indo-Iranian and even Indo-European period. Its discovery laid the foundation of the sciences of Comparative Philology and Comparative Mythology. In view of its intrinsic importance in so many fields of thought, linguistic[4], mythological, religious, literary, and historical, it is not at all strange that an unusually large proportion of Sanskrit scholars have been attracted to its study.

The Ṛigveda is not an easy book. Its dialect is archaic, and there are a very large number of words which occur

---

[1] Oldenberg, *Vedaforschung*; Gray, *Interpretation (Vedic)*, ERE. VII; Macdonell, VRS. XXIX-XXXI, and *Principles* (Bhandarkar, CV. 3 ff.).

[2] Bloomfield, RV. 17.

[3] Arnold, *Vedic Metre*. p. 1.

[4] Sanskrit lies at the foundation of Indo-European Comparative Grammar.

only once. The vocabulary is priestly, full of mystic allusions to the technique of the sacrifice. Hence, while a considerable part of the Ṛv. is fairly clear, there are many single stanzas and even whole hymns which still remain obscure. Moreover, there is hardly a single hymn in the Ṛv., in which there is not some obscure word or difficult phrase. A comparison together of the various translations is the best proof of the difficulty of the Ṛigveda text.

The traditional text of the Ṛigveda and its traditional interpretation constitute, as it were, the *given element,* the data to be critically examined. The traditional text was fixed (circa 600 B. C.) in the form of the *Saṁhitā* text. This is open to a limited amount of conjectural emendation[1], in correction of errors which preceded the final editing of the Ṛv. When Yāska wrote his *Nirukta* (Etymology) about 500 B. C., the meaning of many Vedic words had already become unintelligible; for he quotes one of his predecessors as saying that the Vedic hymns are 'obscure, unmeaning and mutually contradictory'. This was only one of seventeen predecessors of Yāska, whose opinions often disagreed. Accordingly Yāska has a way of assuming alternative roots and meanings for the same word, from which we conclude that there was no unbroken tradition. Yāska's weakness is his too great dependence on etymology.

About eighteen centuries after Yāska, Sāyaṇa (14th Cent. A. D.) wrote his great commentary on the Ṛv. It is extremely valuable[2] as setting forth the Indian tradition,

---

[1] The late Prof. Oldenberg, while at Lahore in 1913, expressed in the hearing of the author his regret at having carried the conjectural emendation of the Ṛv. text too far, an example of the humility of the true scholar. Compare Macdonell, *Principles* (Bhandarkar, CV. 18): "Advancing study has proved many emendations made by earlier scholars owing to imperfect knowledge, to be unnecessary. Conjectural corrections of the text should, therefore, be resorted to only in extreme cases".

[2] At the basis of all modern study of the Ṛv. is Prof. Max Müller's *magnum opus,* his critical edition of the *Ṛigveda-Saṁhitā* together with the Commentary of Sāyaṇācārya, vols. I-VI, 1849-1874, a library in itself.

in Sāyaṇa's time, of the meaning of the Ṛigveda. Sāyaṇa leaned heavily upon Yāska, and like him put too much dependence upon etymology. He fails to deduce the meanings of words by a comparison of parallel passages. We may note in passing that the Vedic interpretation of Swāmī Dayānanda Sarasvatī (1824-1883), the founder of the Ārya Samāj, outstrips Yāska and Sāyaṇa in its over-emphasis on etymology, neglect of the consideration of parallel passages, and appeal to later and non-Vedic usage[1].

The history of the modern interpretation of the Ṛigveda is the story of various attempts to penetrate its secret, different schools of investigators emphasizing different points of view. The traditional interpretation as represented by Sāyaṇa was regarded by H. H. Wilson[2] as adequate and trustworthy; and so he reproduced it in his English translation of the Ṛv. Roth, the founder of the 'critical' school, was impressed with the primitive and natural poetry in the Ṛv. For him it was 'the oldest religious lyric'. His principle was that we must gather the meaning from the texts themselves with the help of comparative philology. He overlooked, however, the importance of the Indian commentators and of a knowledge of the ritual literature. His merits and defects are both reflected in his lexicographical work[3]. Bergaigne[4] employed an allegorical method and emphasized the single meanings of words, but interpreted the Ṛv. from too narrow a standpoint. Dayānand Sarasvatī[5] built upon the theistic element in the Ṛv., especially on such passages as I. 164, 46 and X. 114, 5, which seemed to him to indicate that the multitudinous divine names in the Ṛv. refer to a single exalted divine being; and on the basis of this interpretation helped out by his

---

[1] Griswold, *The Dayānandī Interpretation of the word 'Deva' in the Ṛigveda*, Ludhiana, 1897 (out of print).

[2] *Ṛigveda Saṃhitā*, Eng. trans., vols. I-VI, 1850 and following years.

[3] PW. I-VII.

[4] *La Religion Védique*, I-III, Paris, 1878-1883.

[5] *Ṛigvedādibhāṣyabhūmikā*, Ajmer (Sanskrit with explanation in Hindī).

gift for etymologizing, he laid the foundation of an indigenous theistic society in North India. Pischel and Geldner[1] represent a reaction against the school of Roth in favour of a more indigenous method of interpretation. Their principle is that the Ṛigveda is a purely Indian book, and that accordingly the later Indian literature is the key to its interpretation. It was a vigorous attempt, in the words of Oldenberg[2], to rehabilitate the indigenous Vedic exegesis which had fallen into disrepute. In the opinion of Pischel and Geldner the Ṛv. hymns do not reflect a primitive state of society, but rather an advanced culture with all its evils, such as greed for gold and a highly developed *demimonde.* The weakness of Yāska and Sāyaṇa are reproduced along with their method, namely endless etymologizing and the assumption of multitudinous meanings for words. The one solid contribution of Pischel and Geldner is their emphasis upon the necessity of making the fullest use of the resources of indigenous scholarship in the elucidation of the Vedic text. Brunnhofer[3], the Ishmael among Sanskritists, lays hold of the fact that the roots of the Ṛv. run deep into the Indo-Iranian period. It is for him almost as much an Indo-Iranian as an Indian book. Hillebrandt and Oldenberg stress the importance of the later Vedic ritual for the understanding of the Ṛv. Macdonell and Keith cherish well-balanced views on Vedic topics and avoid eccentric opinions.

Such are some of the different points of view from which the Ṛigveda has been studied,—the adequacy of the traditional interpretation, the allegorical method, the Indian or the pre-Indian character of the Ṛv., and the presence in it of a primitive lyrical, a theistic, and a ritualistic element. Devotion to a particular point of view has inevitably meant exaggeration, but has at the same time accomplished the end of bringing out whatever truth

[1] *Vedische Studien*, I-III.

[2] *Vedaforschung*, 21.

[3] *Urgeschichte der Arier*, I-III, 1889-1893, and *Arische Urzeit*, 1910.

is contained therein. The exaggerations of opposing schools of Vedic research tend to correct one another, very much as in the case of Old Testament research. The truth lies in the middle[1].

The tendency of the best Vedic scholarship at the present time is to emphasize the largeness of the context in which the Ṛigveda is to be set and studied. In the first place, the Ṛv., as Roth held, is its own best commentary. Moving out from this in ever enlarging circles we should use as aids to Vedic interpretation the indigenous exegesis as found in Yāska and Sāyaṇa, the Avesta, the younger Vedic texts containing the 'ritual' literature, the later literature of India, present day religious custom and folklore as found, *e. g.* in the writings of Crooke[2] and Mrs. Stevenson[3], the great Western IE. literary works, Iliad, Odyssey, Æneid, Eddas and Niebelungenlied, and the mythology and anthropology of all the nations. To illustrate the new emphasis on the importance of studies in the modern religion and folklore of India in their bearing on the elucidation of the Ṛigveda, attention may be drawn to the bibliography at the end of Hopkins' chapter on *The Vedic Religion of India*[4] in which Crooke's *Popular Religion and Folklore of Northern India* occupies the first place, standing even ahead of Macdonell's *Vedic Mythology*. In like manner as illustrating the contribution, which general mythology and folklore may make to Vedic study, Caland[5] points out the striking similarity which exists between the sacred formulas of the Cherokees[6] and those of the *Kauśika Sūtra*.

---

1 Winternitz, GIL. 65.
2 PR.
3 RT. and HJ.
4 Chapter XI of *The History of Religions*, N. Y. 1918.
5 *Altindisches Zauberritual*, 1900, pp. IX-XI.
6 Published by James Morney, 1891.

PART B.

RELIGIOUS CONTENTS OF THE ṚIGVEDA

CHAPTER IV.

THE VEDIC WORLD OF GODS AND DEMONS

1. INTRODUCTORY.—It is a commonplace of psychology that thinking is conducted under the pressure of practical needs[1]. Primitive man found himself in an environment partly helpful and partly untoward and perilous. There were all about him friendly objects and forces such as sunshine, rain, fire, dawn, rivers, etc. The very epithet 'friendly' applied above to 'objects' and 'forces' indicates incipient personification and shows the naturalness of the process. Then there were other forces which were hostile and perilous, such as drought, darkness and the mysterious causes of the blighting of crops, of disease, and of death. The friendly forces became gods and the hostile forces demons. All nature thus divided into friendly and hostile forces was regarded as an aggregate of animated entities[2]. This attitude of mind toward its environment began undoubtedly with the very first manifestation of the religious consciousness in the dim pre-historic past, and extended down far beyond the Vedic age. It is the well-known doctrine of animism[3], which has had such a wide sway in the early stages of mankind, and forms in a sense the background of all our religious thinking. To ascribe life, will and agency to inanimate nature was just as natural for man in his childhood stage as it is for children to personify their play-things. Animism presented itself at the beginning as probably only a haunting sense of the

---

[1] *Cf.* James, *Psychology*, 1900, p. 358: "Reasoning is always for a subjective interest".

[2] Macdonell, VM. 1.

[3] Oldenberg, RV. 39.

mystery and potency of the world and its forces. This primitive attitude based on the experience of both harmful and helpful powers was made gradually more articulate through the interpretation of the powers of nature as animals *(theriomorphism)* or as men *(anthropomorphism)*.

2. Process of Personification. -- The book which deals most fundamentally with this topic has already been mentioned[1]. Usener's main thesis is that the stage of 'personal gods' was preceded by that of 'special gods'. In the case of a 'special god'[2] the name of the thing is the name of the god, *e.g. dyaus* 'sky', *agni* 'fire', *sūrya* 'sun', *uṣas* 'dawn', *vata* 'wind', etc. Furthermore, the province of a special god is limited to the sphere of activity indicated by his name, that is to say, Agni had to do originally only with fire, Vāta with wind, etc. The special god enjoyed only an incipient degree of personification. But "all the special gods had the capacity of annexing the sphere of activity of others"[3]. The more a special god annexed the territory of his neighbours, and the more fully emancipated he became from his own 'primitive nature significance', the more completely personalized he was. Accordingly in the case, *e.g.* of Dyāus 'Heaven' and Pṛithivī 'Earth' the personification is very rudimentary, whereas *Varuṇa* and *Indra* are the most completely personalized gods of the Vedic pantheon. One reason was that the names Dyāus and Pṛithivī remained 'transparent', meaning quite simply 'heaven' and 'earth'. Hence the personifying imagination was checked by their constant presence and obvious physical nature. It was not so with Varuṇa, Indra and the Aśvins, whose original physical basis had been almost or quite forgotten. In general, we may say, then, that the survival of the 'transparent' name of a god such as Agni 'god fire', Sūrya 'god sun', Uṣas 'goddess dawn', Vāta 'god wind', etc. prevents to a greater or less degree the full personification

[1] Usener, *Götternamen*. See above, p. 13.

[2] Called by Usener 'Sondergott', *op. cit.* 75.

[3] Schrader, *Aryan Religion*, ERE. 11.

of the god. Even here, however, other influences work, so that the personification of Agni 'the priestly god' *par excellence* is in some respects much more complete than that of Sūrya 'god sun'.

Usener's first stage is that of the 'special god'. The name of anything in nature or in culture which impressed primitive man as mysterious, haunting, potent for good or for ill, might be the starting point of a process of personification[1]. This tendency to ascribe specialization of function to the gods, a tendency which Usener finds amply illustrated in the Litu-Prussian and ancient Roman religions is regarded by Schrader[2] as a primitive Indo-European characteristic. It is a fruitful cause of the tendency to create what Hillebrandt aptly calls 'mythological synonyms'[3], a tendency which is well represented in the Ṛigveda. Just as verbal synonyms are words which have much the same significance, while each possesses its own special shade of meaning; so 'mythological synonyms' are gods which in general are in charge of the same department of nature or life, while each one has his own special physical basis, distinguishing characteristic and theophanic moment. Thus, according to the Ṛigveda, we have as gods of the sky, Dyāus and Varuṇa (?); as gods of the sun, Sūrya, Mitra (?), Savitar, Pūṣan, Viṣṇu, etc.; as gods of the lightning and the storm, Indra, Trita Āptya, Apāṃ Napāt, Mātariśvan, Ahi Budhnya, Aja Ekapād, Rudra and the Maruts; as priestly, and sacrificial gods, Agni and Bṛihaspati. Usener[4] points out the minute 'division of labour' which existed in the same department (*e. g.* agriculture) among

[1] *Cf.* Hillebrandt. VM. III. p. VII: Alles was die Einbildung erregt, Furcht, Freude erweckt, was den Geist im Traum oder Wachen bewegt, wird oder kann zum Ausgangspunkte einer Gottheit oder "Dämons werden"; also Rhys Davids *Buddhism* (American Lectures), p. 12: "The gods were ideas, a rough kind of scientific hypothesis. The arrival of a new god meant the birth of a new idea"

[2] ERE. art. *Aryan Religion* II. 32.

[3] VM. II. 12-13; III. p. XV.

[4] *Götternamen*, 75-122.

the Roman and the Lithuanian gods, and by the same analogy was later extended to the Lithuanian Church saints. According to Varro's account[1] every separate fact and process of agriculture, *e.g.* first, second and third ploughing, dragging, sowing, growth, blossoming, etc. was under the care of a special deity. So also with the Lithuanians, *e.g.* in the matter of cattle raising. Even after the Lithuanians were christianized the same primitive tendency asserted itself in the form of a minute specialization of the functions of their numerous patron saints; *e.g.* in the department of healing Apollonia curing toothache, Augustinus warts, Ita headache, Deicolus cramps and Eutropius dropsy. A similar tendency may be invoked to help explain the 'mythological synonyms' of the Ṛigveda[2]. The sky is the home of light by day (*Dyaus*) and by day and night is all-encompassing (*Varuṇa*). The sun has many distinguishable aspects and functions. It is a bright orb (*Sūrya*), a light-giving friendly power of nature (*Mitra*), a great stimulator of life and activity (*Savitar*), a nourisher and protector of cattle, shepherding them and finding them when lost (*Pūṣan*), wide-striding from earth through mid-air to zenith, 'he of the three steps' (*Viṣṇu*), and the one who at dawn shines in every direction (*Vivasvant*). The functions of the gods of the lightning and the storm are similarly differentiated. Thus the lightning fighting to release the cows of the sky manifests itself as an impetuous warrior (*Indra*); it is the third or aerial form of fire dwelling in the clouds (*Trita Āptya*); it is born of the heavenly waters (*Apāṁ Napāt*); it grows in the mother cloud and brings fire down from heaven to earth (*Mātariśvan*); it looks like a serpent in the lower atmosphere (*Ahi Budhnya*); it leaps down from the cloud-mountains in a single streak of fire like a 'one-footed goat' (*Aja Ekapad*); it strikes the

---

[1] Based largely on the Roman *Indigatamenta*. See Art. by Wissowa in ERE. VII. 217-218.

[2] Hillebrandt, VM. II. 14.

earth, shatters trees and kills animals and men (*Rudra*); accompanied by thunder, wind and rain, it manifests itself in numerous lightning flashes (*Maruts*)[1].

The formation of such 'special gods', each originally with delimited province and function, was not confined to the Indo-European or even the Indo-Iranian period. There were plenty of such creations in the Ṛigveda, as, *e. g.* (1) the abstract agent gods, *Savitar* 'stimulator', *Dhātar* 'creator', *Vidhātar* 'disposer', *Dhartar* 'supporter', *Tratar* 'protector', *Netar* 'leader', *Tvaṣṭar* 'artificer', and *Viśva-karman* 'all-creating'; (2) compounds in *pati*[2] 'lord', as *Prajāpati* 'lord of creatures', *Bṛihaspati* 'lord of prayer', *Vāstospati* (VII. 54) 'lord of the house', *Kṣetrasya pati* 'lord of the field' (IV. 57, 1), and perhaps some others of the same formation[3]; (3) the abstract goddesses *Śraddha* 'faith', *Anumati* 'favour', *Aramati* 'devotion', *Sūnṛita* 'bounty', *Asunīti* 'spirit-life' and *Nirṛiti* 'decease' or the goddess of death; probably also *Aditi* and *Diti;* (4) the wives of the great gods as *Indrāṇī*, *Agnayī*, *Varunanī* and *Aśvinī;* (5) deified objects connected with the ritual, as *Gravan* 'press-stone for crushing the soma-plant', *Āpas* 'sacrificial waters mixed with Soma, *Ghṛita* 'sacrificial oil' (IV. 58), *Barhis* 'the sacrificial litter' upon which the

---

[1] Macdonell. VM.; Keith, *Indian Mythology*.

[2] *Cf.* Hillebrandt, VM. II. 19.

[3] These names in *pati* might, so far as the form is concerned, belong to the Indo-European period. Compare the Greek δεσπότης 'lord of the house' and the Lithuanian *wiesz-pats* (=*Viśpati*) 'lord of the clan'; also the Lithuanian divine names *Dimstipatis* 'lord of the house and home' (*cf.* Vedic *Dampati* 'house-lord' and *Stipā* 'household protector'), *Raugupatis* 'lord of the leaven', *Laukpatis* 'lord of the field'. *Zemepatis* 'lord of the land' (*cf.* Persian *zamin*), and the Litu-Prussian *Wejo-patis* 'lord of the wind'. Usener, *Götternamen*, 89, 100, 105. There are many other names in *pati* in the Ṛv. such as *sadasaspati*, *gaṇapati*, *satpati*, *somapati*, *vanaspati*, *rathaspati*, *gāthapati*, etc., but these are probably all used as epithets of the great gods. It is conceivable, however, that prior to their use as epithets some of them may have been true 'Sondergötter'. Schrader (ERE. II. 35 note) regards the Lithuanian divine names ending in *patis* as very old.

gods sit (I. 13, 5), *Yūpa* (*Vanaspati*) 'the sacrificial post', to which the victim was bound (I. 13, 11), and *Dakṣiṇā* 'largess', the deified fee of the priest (I. 18, 5), etc., etc.; (6) the deified implements and objects of agriculture[1] such as *Lāṅgala* 'plough' *Śunāsīra* 'plough-share', *Urvarā* 'plough-land', *Sītā* 'furrow', etc.; and (7) the deified weapons of war, Bow, Arrows, Quiver, Car, etc. (VI. 75).

It is obvious that such gods whose designations are merely appellative, the name of the god being the name of the thing or concept, would in general be inconspicuous and shortlived, never attaining to the dignity of the 'great gods', unless they represented some dominant aspect of nature, as *Agni* 'fire', or were fundamentally important in the ritual of worship, as *Agni* and *Soma,* or were caught on the tide of a new and growing conception, as *Prajāpati.* We have already quoted Schrader's statement that 'all the special gods had the capacity of annexing the sphere of activity of others' (ERE. II. 35). When thus annexed, many 'special gods' undoubtedly became merely epithets of one or other of the great gods, their entire being having been absorbed[2]. Such annexation was doubtless furthered by the principle of congruity. In general, harmonious elements would attach themselves, *e. g.* to Varuṇa the 'holy' god, that is, attributes corresponding to his nature; and in like manner Rudra in his development would attract to himself such semi-demonic qualities as were akin to his original character as probably the destructive aspect of lightning[3], such qualities for example as are celebrated in the *Śatarudrīya* litany[4], and such as have made him in the Yajurveda period the god of diseases[5], as well as of healing.

---

[1] IV. 57, 4-5, 7-8.

[2] One is impressed with the wealth of epithets which adorn such Vedic gods of the first magnitude as Indra, Varuṇa, Agni and Soma.

[3] Macdonell, VM. 77.

[4] *Taittirīya Saṁhitā* IV. 5, 1-11. Translation, Keith (in HOS.), II. 353-362.

[5] According to Oldenberg (RV. 216-224) Rudra is probably to be taken as a god who sends chills and fevers from his dwelling place in the forests and

Doubtless other factors also co-operated in the making of the gods. The Aryan tribes brought with them from their earlier home beyond the Hindu Kush a fairly elaborate mythology and cult, as may be seen at a glance by referring to the table of Vedic-Avestan equivalents[1]. Probably, too, the Aryan tribes came in at different times covering a period possibly of centuries. At any rate, we know there were different tribes and different priestly families, each tribe and priestly family probably having its own special beliefs and rites in addition to the things held in common. These conditions would naturally produce a multiplicity of gods and rites of worship, which would tend to become common property. As Hillebrandt[2] well puts it, Vedic mythology is not a system, but a conglomerate, a kind of mythological 'confusion of tongues', which arose through the coming together and fusion of the traditions of different clans.

With the changes geographical, climatic and ethnological there would naturally be changes in the gods themselves, reflecting as they did the changing environment and experiences of the Aryan tribes. Accordingly, like earthly rulers, one god would increase his domain at the expense of another, or himself be despoiled of some or all of his attributes. Thus Varuṇa, the majestic god of the Ṛigveda, became later a night-god and finally only a god of lakes and pools, so completely did he lose his sublime attributes of holiness and sovereignty. After having been one of the most completely personalized gods of the Ṛv., he is gradually depersonalized and de-ethicised, until his final estate is like his first, that of a 'special god' in charge of a limited

mountains of the North. Hillebrandt (VM. II. 179-208) thinks that Rudra was a god of the terrors of the tropical climate, connected very specially with the feverish time immediately following the monsoon. Such opinions doubtless hold good for the later Vedic period, but not so certainly for the Ṛigveda.

[1] p. 21.

[2] VM. III. p. XII.

province of nature. This illustration brings out the fact that, like the sun, the Vedic gods have their times of rising and setting. They appear above the horizon, go on waxing until they reach the zenith of their influence, then begin to wane in importance, and finally reaching 'the twilight of the gods' pass away for ever. The gods of the Ṛigveda are all to be found somewhere within these various stages. Indra, Agni and Soma are at the zenith. Varuṇa has just passed the zenith. Vivasvant and Trita are distinctly waning gods. Prajāpati, the chief god of the Brāhmaṇas, is just appearing above the horizon. Viṣṇu and Rudra (Śiva), destined to such a distinguished career extending even to modern times, have not yet reached the zenith of their influence.

The Vedic gods, then, have varying degrees of personification, extending all the way from that, for example of *Śraddha*[1] 'faith', which at least in the Ṛv. is little more than a poetic symbol or at most a candidate for the honours of full apotheosis, on to that of Varuṇa and Indra, the most completely personalized of all the gods of the Ṛigveda. If, as already stated, the more a god enlarged the sphere of his activity and emancipated himself from the limitations of his original nature as a 'special god', the more completely personalised he became, then it follows logically that complete personification would be attained only in a condition of monotheism, when one God had taken to himself the attributes and functions of all gods[2].

The various stages of personification existed side by side. If some gods were waxing, others were waning. If some were passing below the horizon, others were rising above the horizon. The 'special god' was capable of

---

[1] X. 151.

[2] This is regarded by Usener (Götternamen 347-349) as the logical goal of all polytheisms, but he admits that in the case of Greece and Rome the vested interests of the priesthood were too strong and that the monotheistic movement had to come from Palestine through the Christian Church.

creation at any time[1]. It was through the birth of new special gods that the loss through the passing of the old gods was made good.

3. Gods and Demons. -- The Vedic gods, as we have seen, are in general personifications of natural phenomena. This is equally true of the Vedic demons. The contrast between god and demon is not so much one of power, for the demons also are strong, as of benevolence. The gods are kindly and benevolent; the demons, as a rule, malevolent and injurious. The psychology of this distinction is not difficult to discern. The activities of nature are partly helpful and partly noxious. A beneficial force or activity like fire or water or wind, when personified, becomes a god. Injurious activities or experiences such as drought, blasting of crops, darkness, illness, etc. are personified as demons. It was seen that the thunderstorm by producing a vast downpour of rain destroys the drought. What more natural than to think of a struggle between Indra the storm-god and Vṛitra the withholder of the rain. In the fight Indra pierces with his bolt *Vala,* the 'cave' where the cows of the sky are confined, and slays Vṛitra the 'obstructor', thus releasing the waters. The whole imagery is reminiscent of cattle-lifting. As thieves carried off cattle and hid them in the caverns of the mountains, so Vṛitra 'obstruction', then more concretely conceived as 'obstructor' carried off the cloud-cows and hid them in a cave. The 'cave' itself, *Vala,* becomes in time personified as a cave-demon. In a time of drought, when the heavens were as brass and no clouds were visible, the conclusion was that the cloud-cows had been stolen. This is but one example of how cosmic phenomena were interpreted after the analogy of, and in terms of, human experience.

---

[1] Keith (*Indian Mythology,* 97), referring to the new creations of the Brāhmaṇa period, remarks that "they serve to show how full of semi-divine figures was the ordinary life of the people, who saw a deity in each possible form of action". This is quite after the manner of the Roman *Indigatamenta* as interpreted by Varro.

Such is the most probable origin of gods and demons, at least in the Indo-European world. The concept 'gods' was distilled, as it were, from the contemplation of the gracious and kindly powers of nature[1]; and in the same way the concept 'demons', from the experience of nature's grim and hostile forces. The psychology of the whole process is found in the working of the principle of analogy. Man naturally gave an anthropomorphic interpretation to the physical powers and phenomena in the midst of which he was placed, by finding in his own nature as man the key to their interpretation. As there was a human race *(mānuṣajana)* so over against and above it there was a heavenly or divine race (*daivyajana*), which was suggested by the human race. And as the human race for the Vedic Indians was divided into Aryans and Dasyus mutually hostile to each other, so the superhuman powers incarnate in sun, lightning, storm, darkness, drought, disease, death, etc., were divided by analogy into gods and demons. The correspondence between Dasyu and Demon was so close that the same term 'Dasyu' covered both human enemies and superhuman enemies, producing frequently considerable uncertainty in interpretation.

It has already been pointed out that there was a considerable development of demonology[2] in the Indo-Iranian period, together with corresponding magic practices. Words for 'ghost', 'demon' and 'evil spirit'[3] were in use before the breaking up of the Indo-Iranian unity. Hence the Aryans brought with them into India a belief in demons as well as in gods. The Ṛigveda as devoted to the worship of the higher gods gives relatively little attention to the demons, that is, the Ṛv. as contrasted with the Atharvaveda and the Brāhmaṇas. The great atmospheric demon is

[1] Compare Rom. 1. 20: "The invisible things of Him since the creation of the world are clearly seen, being perceived through the things that are made, even His everlasting power and divinity".

[2] P. 26.

[3] *būiti, yatu, druj* = Vedic *bhūta, yātu, druh*. See p. 21.

Vṛitra[1], from whom comes Indra's cult name *Vṛitrahan* 'slayer of Vṛitra'. There are other atmospheric demons such as *Śuṣṇa*[2] 'scorcher' or 'hisser', *Śambara, Pipru, Varcin,* etc., although some of these may have been aboriginal chiefs or aboriginal gods. In the Ṛigveda Indra as the powerful atmospheric god purges his own domain of the demons of the air. What is often described is the single combat between Indra and Vṛitra after the fashion of a Homeric struggle between two champions. The *Rakṣasas,* as earth demons, are driven off by Agni the fire-god of earth, whose cult name accordingly is *Rakṣohan* 'slayer of Rakṣas'. Thus Indra and Agni, gods respectively of lightning and fire, are the great antagonists of the demons of darkness. Of the three domains, heaven, mid-air and earth, the demons are confined to the last two. They do not intrude upon the heavenly abode of the gods and the glorified 'fathers'. The demons are referred to by a variety of group names, as *Dasyus*, *Paṇis* 'niggards', *Rakṣasas* 'injurious' or 'to be guarded against', *Druhas* 'deceivers', *Arātis* 'illiberalities', *Yatus* 'demons', *Yātudhānas* 'sorcerers', and *Asuras,* the standing designation for the demons in the later Vedic literature. According to the Ṛv. the numerous demons are smitten either singly or collectively by some one or other of the great gods, who is always victorious. This way of stating the case seems to be a reflection of the successful and optimistic character of the Ṛigveda period. Later on it is no longer a conflict between single god and demon or demons, but between the collective Devas on one side and the collective Asuras on the other, the Devas being often worsted in the fight. Does this reflect the more difficult climatic conditions and consequently more pessimistic outlook of life further east in the Ganges valley?

---

[1] Of whom *Vala* is a mere doublet.

[2] Also called *Kuyava* 'who causes bad harvests'. The Mussoorie hills at this time (May 1921) look as if they were under the power of Śuṣṇa, the demon of drought. The spring crops have largely failed for lack of rain.

4. **Specimen of Vedic Demonology.**—While, as already stated, the Ṛigveda is chiefly concerned with the mythology and worship of the great gods, it nevertheless incidentally through many a vivid phrase as well as through two entire hymns throws light, all the stronger because undesigned, upon the demonology of the Vedic age. In order to bring forward the matter concretely, the hymn VII. 104 is presented in a metrical version with now and then a phrase adopted from Griffith[1].

To Indra-Soma VII. 104 (= AV. VIII. 4).

1. O Indra-Soma, burn, destroy the *Rakṣasas,*
Thrust down, ye strong ones, those that flourish in the dark;
Annihilate the fools, consume them utterly,
Smite, thrust and overthrow the greedy *Atriṇas.*

2. O Indra-Soma, 'gainst the sinner and his sin
Let heat boil up like kettle glowing with the flame;
Against prayer-hating, raw flesh-eating, dreadful-eyed
Kimīdin, keep hostility, unceasingly.

3. O Indra-Soma, plunge the evil-doers down
Into the pit, the gloom profound and bottomless,
So that not one of them may ever thence emerge;
Such wrathful strength and might be yours to conquer them.

4. O Indra-Soma, hurl your weapon from the sky
And earth, your weapon crushing the malignant one;
From the cloud-mountains forge a whizzing thunderbolt,
Wherewith ye may consume the waxing Raksas foe.

5. O Indra-Soma, shoot ye forth from out the sky,
With your fire-heated sling-stones, heavenly thunderbolts;
With glowing darts unfailing hurl the *Atrinas*
Down the abyss, and let them into silence sink.

6. On all sides, Indra-Soma, may this song of ours
Beset you both, as girth surrounds two mighty steeds,—
Which song as offering I with wisdom send to you,
These prayers, O lords of men, do ye inspire and speed.

7. Remind yourselves in your effective manner,
Smite the *Druhas* and *Rakṣasas,* the tricky ones;

[1] Indebtedness is also acknowledged to Hillebrandt's translation, LR. 112-114.

No bliss be to the wicked, Indra-Soma,
Whoso at any time against us plots with guile.

8. Whoso accuses me of walking falsely,
With lying words, although my heart is guileless,
May such a liar come to naught, O Indra,
Like water which in shut hand seized escapeth.

9. Those who the good man's speech delight to slander,
And those whose habit is to harm the righteous,
May Soma hand them over to the serpent,
Or to the lap of Nirṛiti consign them.

10. Whatever one, O Agni, tries to injure
The substance of our food, steeds, kine or persons,
May such thief, robber, trickster go to ruin,
Sink to destruction both himself and children.

11. May he be taken off himself and children,
Under all three earths let him lie imprisoned;
May his fair glory, gods, dry up and wither,
He who by day or night desires to harm us.

12. Good wit is his who has discrimination,
Truth and untruth, both words oppose each other;
Of these twain what is true and what is upright
That indeed Soma helps, untruth he smiteth.

13. Never aids Soma him whose ways are crooked,
Nor him who falsely claims the Kṣatriya title;
He smites the Rakṣas, smites the falsehood—speaker,
Both lie entangled in the snare of Indra.

14. Is it that I to false gods was devoted,
Or held the gods as a delusion, Agni?
Why art thou angry with us, Jātavedas?
Deceivers shall experience thy destruction.

15. Let me at once die, if I practice witchcraft,
Or have oppressed the life of any mortal;
Likewise may he be severed from ten kinsmen,
The one who falsely calls me witchcraft-monger.

16. Who calls me witch, me innocent of witchcraft,
Who claims he's pure, although himself a Rakṣas;
May Indra smite him with his mighty weapon,
May he fall down the lowest of all beings.

17. What owl-like creature cometh forth at night-time,
With trickery and guile herself concealing,

May she plunge into bottomless abysses;
May press-stones with their clatter smite the demons.

18. Spread out and search among the clans, O Marut host,
Seize ye the Rakṣasas and crush them utterly,
Who fly about at night-time in the form of birds,
Or at the worship of the gods display their tricks.

19. Indra, hurl forth from heaven thy stony weapon,
Maghavan, sharpen it, made sharp by Soma;
In front, behind, and from above and under,
Smite thou the Rakṣasas with rocky missile.

20. These fly about in form of demon-dogs and seek,
Harm-lovers they, Indra to harm, whom none can hurt.
Śakra makes sharp his weapon for the slanderers;
Now at the witchcraft-mongers may he hurl his stone.

21. Indra is the destroyer of the Yātu-fiends,
Disturbers of the sacrifice with aim malign;
Now verily 'gainst the Rakṣasas doth Śakra go
As axe against a wood, like vessels splitting them.

22. Smite the owl-fiend and owlet-fiend, O Indra,
Dog-fiend, or him who comes in guise of cuckoo,
The fiend in form of eagle or of vulture,—
As with a mill-stone crush thou every Rakṣas.

23. Let not the demon of the sorcerers near us come,
With light may (Agni) drive *Kimīdins* off in pairs;
Let earth protect us well from every earthly woe,
Mid-air deliver us from such as comes from heaven.

24. O Indra, buffet the male *Yātudhāna*,
The female also boasting of her magic;
Neck-broken may the *Mūradevas* perish,
And see no more the sun as he arises.

25. Look straight ahead, look on each side,
Indra and Soma, watch ye both;
Your weapon hurl against the fiends,
Against the sorcerers your stone.

This hymn is addressed principally to Indra and Soma, to Indra as the great demon-slaying god of the atmosphere, and to Soma as the deified sacrificial drink by which Indra was strengthened and exhilarated for his tasks. It is probably a late hymn, standing as it does at the end of book VII;

quite likely, too, it is composed of several fragments originally distinct, which differ in metre and (a more important consideration) in thought. Very similar to it in spirit is X. 87[1].

The following comments are made:—

a) We may recall Hillebrandt's observation[2] that whatever excites the imagination and awakens fear or joy, and whatever moves the spirit in dream or waking hours, will or at least can become the starting point for a god or demon. Accordingly almost every Vedic demon can be traced back to the experience of something either hurtful or uncanny, that is, to the actual experience of cold, darkness, drought, disease, etc. or to the tendency to people the dark with ghostly and uncanny creatures, and in general to find for every unhappy experience a demonic origin. As human troubles and calamities are multitudinous, so are the demons that cause them. As stated above, some demons are the reflection of physical ills, while others are creatures of the imagination postulated as causes to account for mental ills. A Vedic demon was the embodiment, then, of every fear and dread, of every illness and calamity as well as of every physical evil such as cold, drought, etc. that besets mankind. A demon in the hymn under consideration is called in general *rakṣas*[3] or *yātu*[4].

b) From *rā́kṣas* 'demon' there was formed *rakṣás* 'sorcerer' by shifting the accent to the last syllable. And from *yātu* were formed a number of words also meaning 'sorcerer'[5]. Thus there was a close connection between demons and sorcerers. They were hand in glove with each other. The demon was apparently thought of as entering

[1] X. 87 and VII. 104 reappear in AV. VIII, 3, 4 with some changes in the order of stanzas and some textual variations. They are both distinctly Atharvanic in quality.

[2] p. 82, n. 1.

[3] VII. 104, 1, 4, 13, 22, 23.

[4] VII. 104, 21. Hindi derivative *jādu*, 'sorcery'.

[5] *Yātudhāna, yātumant, yātumāvant*. VII. 104, 15, 16, 20, 23.

the sorcerer as a familiar spirit, and the sorcerer used the demon for his purposes[1]. Hence in some passages there is little or no distinction between the demon who dwells in the sorcerer and the sorcerer who is indwelt by the demon. The sorcerers were the 'sensitives' or 'mediums' of the Vedic age.

c) The demons are described as 'devourers'[2], eating raw flesh[3], the flesh of men[4] as well as of cattle and horses. They flourish in the dark (v. 1). They delight to injure the sacrifice[5]. Demons and sorcerers are alike in ethical quality. They are fools[6], haters of prayer (v. 2), evil-doers (vv. 3, 7), tricky (v. 7; X. 87, 22), false accusers and slanderers[7] (vv. 8, 9, 20), thieves and robbers (v. 10), liars (vv. 8, 13, 14-16), and malicious[8]. Ethically this is a notable statement of the close relationship existing between evil spirits and evil men. The sin of lying is specially emphasized.

---

[1] Oldenberg RV. 263, n. 1 and 268. Compare the expressions *rakṣoyuj* 'yoker of the rakṣas', *rakṣas . . . . Yātumāvatām* 'rakṣas of the sorcerers', etc. See Oldenberg RV. 272, as translated: 'Every moment of life, every activity and every dwelling is threatened by troops of invisible fiends, *the allies of human evil-doers.*'

[2] *Atriṇah* VII. 104, 1, 5.

[3] *Kravyād* VII. 104, 2; X. 87, 2, 19. Kravyād is applied to the corpse-devouring Agni in X. 16, 9-10. Agni is called in later Sanskrit the *all-eater* and at the same time the *all-purifier*.

[4] X. 87, 16. This looks like a cannibal trait borrowed from the barbarous habits of the aborigines.

[5] VII. 104, 18, 20, 21.

[6] *Acitaḥ*, v. 1.

[7] Thus the Vedic like the Hebrew demon was conceived as a 'calumniator' (διάβολος) and an 'adversary' (שטן I. Sam. XXIX. 4.)

[8] With *anṛita* 'falsehood' the *Yātudhāna* smites *ṛita* 'truth' (X. 87, 11). Compare: "He (the devil) is a liar and the father thereof" (John VIII. 44), and "without are the dogs and the *sorcerers* . . . . and every one that loveth and maketh a *lie*" (Rev. XXII. 15). The worst charge the enemies of Christ could make against Him was to say He had a demon, that is, was in league with evil spirits (Matt. XII. 24, John VIII. 48). Note that the same kind of accusation is mentioned in Rv. VII. 104, 15-16.

d) The demons are lovers of darkness and accordingly often appear in the form of night-birds such as owls, or in the form of dog, cuckoo, vulture, eagle, etc. creatures with strange uncanny cries; or even in the form of the *roots* of plants used for purposes of sorcery[1]: They are both male and female, female demons being much more prominent in the demon world than are the goddesses in the aristocratic world of the great gods[2]. They are dreadful-eyed (v. 2) and cloven-hoofed[3]. The Kimīdins go about in pairs[4], but in the two great hymns under consideration[5] the names for 'demon' and 'sorcerer' are usually in the plural.'

e) Agni, the sacrificial fire of earth and Indra the lightning fire of the mid-air, are the natural enemies of the demons of darkness. Hence with an ample use of synonyms they are besought to smite, crush, pierce, burn, destroy, annihilate, etc. their demon foes. Doubtless there is a reference to the cosmic conflict between light and darkness, but already in the two great 'demon' hymns of the Ṛv. there is mingled with the literal meaning of darkness the metaphorical meaning of evil and sin. The demons who roam about at night and seek to spoil the sacrifice and injure good people are lovers of darkness both literally and figuratively. As is their nature, so is their doom. Their place is the bottomless pit of darkness[6], an abyss[7],

---

[1] *Mūradeva* 'whose god is a root', *mūra=mūla*. VII, 104, 24; X. 87, 2, 14. So Oldenberg, RV. 266 n. 3, and Geldner *Glossar*. This epithet, like *śiśnadeva* 'whose god is the phallus', doubtless reflects the religious beliefs and practices of the aborigines. We may compare *sahamūla* III. 30, 17 and *sahamūra* X. 87. 19; also X. 87, 10 'the Yātudhāna's *root*' *(mūla).*

[2] Oldenberg, RV. 265.

[3] Śaphāruja either 'cloven-hoofed' (Hillebrandt, LR. 115), 'hoof-breaking' (Whitney-Lanman, AV. VIII, 3, 21), or 'hoof-armed' (Griffith). If 'cloven-hoofed' is correct, then there is a point of contact with the mediæval representation of Satan.

[4] VII. 104, 23; X. 87, 24. [5] VII. 104 and X. 87.

[6] *Tamasi anārambhaṇe* 'in the darkness which offers nothing to take hold on', therefore bottomless (VII. 104, 3). [7] *Parśāna.*

a covert or hole having no end[1]. Into this they are hurled by the fiery bolts of Indra[2]. The imagery is Miltonic and reminds one of Paradise Lost. The demons go to their own place. By implication all who are akin to the demons in character go to the same place. There is here an implicit doctrine of *hell*.

f) In both VII. 104 and X. 87 there is a distinctly ethical element. Good men take the side of Agni and Indra, the gods in whom is 'no darkness at all', against the demons of darkness and the evil men who are their confederates. The ethical antithesis between light and darkness, truth and untruth[3] is firmly drawn. And yet both hymns were used as spells or charms, certainly as incorporated in the Atharvaveda and possibly as originally very late hymns of the Ṛv. It shows the close connection that existed in Vedic India between the prayer that persuaded the gods and the magic that compelled them. The difference in the point of view of prayer and magic is somewhat uncertain and subjective. What for one was *brahman* 'prayer' might be for another *brahman* 'spell'. This ambiguity in the meaning of *brahman* 'sacred formula'[4], illustrates the subtle intermingling of both points of view in the hymns and ritual of the Vedic age. What is certain is that the magical conception of *brahman* was on the increase, culminating finally in the magical theory of sacrifice as held in the Brāhmaṇa period, when the sacrifice in its potency was everything and the gods were little or nothing.

---

[1] *Vavra* (*vṛi* 'to cover') 'hole', 'hell', with the epithet *ananta* 'endless' (VII. 104, 17, cf. v. 3).

[2] VII. 104, 4, 5.

[3] *Sat* and *asat* VII. 104, 12.

[4] The fixed religious formula tends to have a magical character. Not to mention the formula in the Roman Mass which causes 'transubstantiation', reference may be made to the repeated use of the Lord's prayer in some forms of worship and to the closing formula of prayer 'for Jesus Christ's sake'. Whether a magical character is attributed to these formulas depends upon the attitude of the worshipper.

5. **Father Dyāus and his Children the Devas.** — The conception of a heavenly clan with *Dyēus*[1] as head began, as we have seen[2], in the Indo-European period, extended through the Indo-Iranian period[3], and appears in a faded and vanishing form in the Vedic age. Dyāus 'Heaven' is celebrated in six hymns in conjunction with *Pṛithivī* 'Earth', the two appearing in the dual compound *Dyāvāpṛithivī* 'Heaven and Earth'. Dyāus apart from Pṛithivī has not a single hymn in his honour, in this respect falling behind the lady Earth, who is celebrated alone in one hymn. As specimens of Vedic thought concerning these oldest of the gods there are here presented metrical translations of Ṛv. VII. 53 and I. 160.

To Dyāus-Pṛithivī, VII. 53.

1. With sacrifice devotedly I worship
The Heaven and Earth, adorable and mighty;
For ancient sages praising them have given
Pre-eminence to them, whose sons are *Devas*.

2. Bring these two parents ancient-born for worship,
With newest praise-songs, to the seat of *Rita*.
Come, Heaven and Earth, with all the heavenly people
Hither to us, for great is your protection.

3. Full many are your treasures to be granted,
O Heaven and Earth, to every liberal giver[4].
To us may what you grant be not deficient;
Ye gods, with welfare evermore preserve us.

To Dyāus-Pṛithivī, I. 160.

1. These two, indeed, the order-observing Heaven and Earth,
To all beneficent, support the mid-air's sage;
Between the fair-creating hemispheres divine
Goes the resplendent sun according to fixed law.

---

[1] Primitive IE. form postulated by scholars.

[2] P. 14.

[3] It was, of course, interrupted and modified during the Iranian period by the Zoroastrian reformation.

[4] Or 'to King Sudās'.

2. The twain, far-reaching, mighty, inexhaustible,
Father and mother-like, all creatures guard and keep.
Like two most proud fair women are the Heaven and Earth,
Because the Father has in beauty them arrayed.

3. Conductor, purifier, son of two parents, he,
The sage, by occult power all creatures purifies;
From out the speckled earth-cow and the heavenly bull,
The rich in seed, he always milks the shining fluid.

4. Of all the active gods most active is that one
Who made the heaven and earth, the all-beneficent;
He who with insight measured out the spaces twain,
With props unaging, — he receives the general praise.

5. Thus lauded, O Great ones, great fame may ye bestow,
On us, O Heaven and Earth, and lofty governance;
Such strength as worthy is of all praise bring to us,
Whereby o'er all the peoples we may ever spread.

Heaven and Earth bear exclusively the characteristic epithet *devâputre,* 'they whose sons are gods'[1], and they are besought to come to 'the seat of *ṛita*' or sacrifice along with their children, who constitute the heavenly clan[2]. They are parents[3] of Agni in his sun or lightning form[4]. In their majesty and beauty they are like two proud fair women. As parents they protect all creatures and bestow treasures, fame and dominion.

The conception of the parenthood of Heaven and Earth is very ancient and widespread, being found in the mythology of many peoples[5]. In the Ṛv. the picture which the hymns conjure up before us is that of Father Dyāus bending down in love over Mother Earth and bestowing his seed in the form of rain, by which the earth is fertilized and made fruitful. In VI. 70, 1-5 rain is probably referred to under the figures of ghee, honey and milk.

---

[1] VII. 53, 1; I. 185, 4; IV. 56, 2.

[2] *Daivya jana* VII. 53, 2.

[3] *Pitarā,* lit. 'two fathers' (VII. 53, 2; I. 160, 3) or *mātarā* 'two mothers' (I. 159, 3) explained in I. 160, 2 as 'father and mother'.

[4] I. 160, 1, 3.

[5] Tylor, *Primitive Culture,* London, 1871, I. 290 ff.

Reference has already been made to the equation *Dyāuṣpitar*[1] = Ζεῦ πάτερ = *Jupiter,* as proving the existence of the conception of Father Heaven in the IE. period[2]. Zeus and Jupiter were the heads respectively of the Greek and Roman pantheon. They were no mere 'departmental' deities, but were enriched and thoroughly personalized through the annexation of departments of activity which did not originally belong to them, especially that of the thunderstorm. They were no longer gods merely of the bright shining sky. Dyāus, as he is pictured to us in the Ṛv. is very inadequately personalized. For one thing his name Dyāus 'sky' and 'day' was very transparent, perhaps somewhat more transparent than Zeus and Jupiter, and as regards gender Dyāus was both masculine and feminine. Then, too, the most exalted moral attributes, as we shall see, had been appropriated by Varuṇa, while Indra and certain other gods almost monopolized the thunderstorm. Hence Dyāus and Pṛithivī are in the Ṛv. little more than conventional figures, mythological fossils, as it were, which possibly bear witness to a time when the conception of Father sky was taken more seriously than it was in the Vedic age. The fact that the Vedic Dyāus is a waning god does not necessarily prove that he had never been in the *ascendant*[3].

---

[1] Ṛv. VI. 51, 5. Note that *Dyāuṣpitar* is in the vocative, as are its equivalents in Greek and Latin.

[2] P. 14.

[3] Schrader (ERE. II, *Aryan Religion*) thinks that the IE. *Dyāus* had a position of honour as compared with the other heavenly ones. V. Bradke (*Dyāus Asura* 110) in like manner holds that IE. polytheism had a decidedly monarchical character with Father Heaven as the patriarchal head. Oldenberg (RV. 34 n. 1), while admitting that presumably Father Heaven occupied a position of honour among the gods, holds that his fatherhood was not taken very seriously, and that the IE. gods were too fluid and shifting to permit us to think of them as an ordered pantheon (like the Greek) ruled over by a supreme god. With this Macdonell (VM. 22) agrees, criticising v. Bradke's view that *Dyāus* was the supreme god of the Indo-European age, while at the same time admitting that he must have been 'the greatest among the deities of a chaotic polytheism'. Meyer

We have already noticed that the chief anthropomorphic trait of Dyāus is fatherhood. But even this characteristic of Dyāus is not taken very seriously in the Ṛv. In I. 160, 4, Heaven and Earth, the universal parents, are spoken of as themselves begotten or created, and the suggestion is thrown out that the one who begot them must have been the most active and skilful of all the active gods; and in v. 2 mention is made of the Father of heaven and earth who arrayed them in beauty. Hence, in the Ṛv. at least, fatherhood was little more than a 'fluid and shifting' conception which (within certain limits, of course) could be ascribed rather miscellaneously according to the fancy of the individual poet. Anything within the sphere of heaven and earth might be called their child. There were other relationships also which suggested fatherhood, such as antecedent in relation to consequent, head of a group in relation to the members of a group, etc.[1]

The IE. conception of Father Sky and his children the 'shining ones', after all necessary abatements have been made, remains still a very significant one. It means, as we have seen[2], that the heavenly powers and phenomena, such as sun, moon, dawn, lightning, rain, etc., were already conceived anthropomorphically after the analogy of an earthly family. Heaven and earth, which are always with us, and within whose sphere the various phenomena come and go, were very naturally conceived as father and mother. They are the primeval parents, the 'ancient-born[3]', since their existence, as we would say, is the presupposition of everything else. The phenomena which come and go within

---

(GA. I[2], 775 ff.) refers to the dominating position of the Heaven god in IE. religion, and holds that Dyāus in India was thrust into the background through the growth of a multiform pantheism, thereby losing much of his original greatness. The present writer accepts Meyer's view as probable. Varuṇa in post-Vedic times was denuded and depersonalised. The pre-Vedic Dyāus may have been treated in the same way.

[1] Macdonell, VM. 12.

[2] Pp. 14-16.

[3] *Purvaje*, VII. 53. 2.

the sphere of heaven and earth are, with equal naturalness for the primitive mind, called children of heaven and earth. The significant thing in all this is the analogy which holds between earthly clan and heavenly clan. Bergaigne's[1] constructive principle in his study of Vedic religion is the analogy which he thinks holds between heavenly phenomena and the Vedic sacrifice, the latter being interpreted by him as an imitation of the former. Whether this principle be true or not, it is certain that the conception of Father Sky and his children the Devas is the reflection of human society. The devas are often referred to in the Ṛv. as a heavenly clan, generation, tribe, nation, race[2], standing over against the human race[3]. The parallel is very complete. In most cases the singular or dual is used, but sometimes the plural is used of the gods as well as of men[4], thereby indicating perhaps that the gods as well as men are split up into groups.

The gods may be grouped according to several principles of division. As in Hebrew thought heaven and earth embrace the universe, so in Vedic thought they are the two world-halves[5] that comprehend everything. Within this scheme there are three levels, heaven, mid-air, and earth[6], for which there are thirty-three[7] gods, eleven apparently for each different level. This is the oldest classification, being found in the Ṛv. itself. The human race is bisected into males and females. By analogy the

---

[1] RV. I. Pp. VII-VIII.

[2] *Daivya jána, janúṡ, jánas, jániman, jantú, jánman* and *viś*.

[3] *Mānusa jána, janúṡ, jánas, jániman, jantú, jánman* and *viś*.

[4] *e. g. daivyāni mānuṣā janūnṣi* 'heavenly and human tribes' VII. 4, 1.
,, *pārthivāni janma* 'celestial and terrestrial generations' V. 41, 14.

[5] *dhiṣaṇe, rodasī*.

[6] Compare the tripartite Hebrew division into 'heaven above', 'earth beneath' and 'water under the earth' (Ex. XX. 4). The Vedic Indians had knowledge of rivers and of river-confluences *(Samudra)*, but only slightly of the ocean. The Hebrew lived on the borders of the great sea (Mediterranean). Hence the difference.

[7] *Cf. Yasna* I, 10 'thirty and three lords'.

divine race will have the same division, and so there are goddesses as well as gods. The goddesses may be subdivided into three groups: (a) those having a natural basis, as *Uṣas* 'Dawn', *Sarasvatī* the deified 'Sarasvatī' river, *Pṛithivī* 'Earth', *Rātri* 'Night', *Pṛiṣṇi* the 'mottled' storm-cloud and *Vāc* 'Speech'[1]; (b) abstract feminine nouns personified as goddesses, *e. g. Puraṁdhi* 'Plenty', *Iḷā* 'Nourishment', *Dhiṣaṇā* 'abundance', *etc.*; (c) goddesses as wives of the great gods, as *Indrāṇī, Varuṇānī* and *Agnāyī*. The great gods are furnished with wives in order to make the parallel between the human race and the divine race complete. No public functions are ascribed to them. They are 'house-wife' deities, Mistress Indra, Mistress Varuṇa, Mistress Agni. This detail may be taken as reflecting the attitude of the Ṛigvedic age as regards the proper sphere and functions of married women.

Again, the human race is broken up into small groups. By analogy the divine race will have similar groups, *e. g. Ādityas, Vasus, Rudras,* the semi-divine *Aṅgirasas,* and among the lower deities the *Ṛibhus, Apsarasas* and *Gandharvas,* and finally *Viśvedevāḥ* 'all-gods', a term designed to cover them all. As a tribal chieftain is represented as the head of his tribe, so Agni is the head of the *agnis* 'fires', Soma of the *somas* 'soma drops', Rudra of the rudras 'lightning flashes' (?) and Uṣas of the *uṣasas* 'dawn gleams'.

The gods may be divided according to function. As in Vedic society there were priests, warriors and commons, so among the gods Agni and Bṛihaspati were priests, Indra and the Maruts warriors, Tvaṣṭar and the *Ṛibhus* artizans. The agricultural community, whether Vaiśyas or Śūdras, had special agricultural deities such as *Kṣetrapati*[2] 'lord of the field', *Urvarā* 'she of the ploughland', *Sītā* 'she of the furrow', and perhaps *Pūṣan,* the 'thrift'-god, guardian of flocks and herds.

---

[1] Probably originally the voice of thunder. *Cf.* קול יהוה in Ps. XXIX.

[2] Reminds one of the Hindī *Bhūmiyā* 'land-lord'.

We may also classify the gods according to certain great functions in which, as groups, they share. There is the work of rain giving, in which, to a greater or less degree, Parjanya, Varuṇa, Indra, Dyāus, Rudra and the Maruts all participate. As gods of the lightning there are Indra, Trita Āptya, and so forth; as physician gods Rudra and the Maruts, Varuṇa, Soma, Aśvins, Vāta and the Waters; as demon-slayers Agni and Indra and in general the gods of light; and as gods of song Bṛihaspati, the Maruts and the Aṅgirasas.

The so-called 'dual divinities' constitute the smallest groups of Vedic gods. The union of man and wife is the human analogy followed in the primeval conception of the marriage of Heaven and Earth. So compelling was this analogy that in harmony therewith the great Vedic gods had to be joined in wedlock, *e. g.* Indra with Indrāṇī, Agni with Agnāyī, Varuṇa with Varuṇānī. There must also have been 'David and Jonathan' friendships among men in the Vedic age. At any rate, after the analogy of *Dyāvāpṛithivī* 'heaven and earth', a considerable number of male deities were joined together so as to form dual gods, *e. g. Mitrā-Varuṇā* 'sunlight and sky', or possibly as Oldenberg and Hillebrandt think 'sun and moon', *Indrā-Agnī* 'lightning-flash and altar-fire', *Indrā-Varuṇa* 'lightning flash and sky', *Indrā-Vāyū* 'lightning-flash and storm-wind', *Indrā-Somā* 'the drinking god and the drunken liquor', *Sūryā-Māsā* 'sun and moon', *Indrā-Viṣṇū* 'lightning and sun', etc.; also one group of two female gods *Naktā-Uṣasā* 'night and dawn'. In the case of each dual divinity there is distinct contrast in the constitutive elements as well as close association of the same in sphere and function. The *Aśvinā* 'two horsemen' may also be mentioned here, since they are essentially dual gods, meaning probably either 'morning star and evening star' or 'the twin-lights before dawn, half dark and half light'[1]. In either case they are almost 'mythological synonyms' of 'night and dawn'.

[1] Macdonell, VM. 53.

Thus the whole 'clan of the devas' is conceived anthropomorphically after the analogy of human society. They wear ornaments of gold, ride in cars drawn by horses, and have houses. They fight against the demons, as Aryans fight against the Dasyus. They are glorified Kṣatriyas. Some gods are male, others are female. Indra, god of the lightning-flash and thunder-roll, is suitably represented as a man; Uṣas, the many-coloured dawn, as a fair and richly-dressed woman. The gods are related together anthropomorphically. Examples of wedded gods have already been given. Some gods are represented as parents, *e. g. Dyāvā-Pṛithivī,* and others as children. Some are related as brothers and sisters. Uṣas[1] is the daughter of Dyāus, the sister of Bhaga, the kinswoman of Varuṇa, and the wife (or mistress) of Sūrya. Night and Dawn are sisters. Agni[2] is the son of Dyāus and the brother of Indra. The principle of 'division of labour' exists among the gods. Each deity is in charge of some special aspect of nature or of life. While there is considerable overlapping of function, as explained in another place[3], yet on the whole the Vedic gods are 'departmental deities', although in some cases new and extensive functions have been added in the course of time to their original tasks. As the members of a human clan act together and mutually support one another, so is it with the clan of the Devas. There is much mutual helpfulness and interchange of services among the gods, as is natural in a clan consisting of members related as husbands and wives, parents and children, brothers and sisters, etc., in general kinsmen, children of Heaven and Earth. Thus Varuṇa prepares a path for Sūrya (I. 24, 8), and in turn Sūrya reports to Mitra and Varuṇa concerning the sinfulness of men (VII. 62, 2). Agni serves Indra, since Indra drinks Soma with the tongue of Agni (III. 35, 9-10) and

---

[1] I. 124, 3; 123, 5, 10.

[2] III. 3, 11; VI. 59, 2.

[3] P. 82.

Indra serves all the gods (including Agni) by gaining the victory over Vṛitra and so giving freedom to the gods (III. 34, 7). Agni, too, serves all the gods by acting as their messenger. The Maruts, who constitute the host of Indra, serve him as his soldiers (III. 35, 9). Tvaṣṭar fashioned the bolt of Indra and sharpened the metal axe of Bṛihaspati (V. 31, 4; X. 53, 9). Soma stimulates Indra to perform great cosmic deeds. Viṣṇu helps Indra in the fight with Vṛitra, etc., etc. The gods in general are thus conceived as living together in a state of harmony and mutual helpfulness. The only exception of importance is in the case of Indra, the violent and changeable weather god, the shifty nature of whose tasks helps perhaps to excuse the note of discord which he sometimes introduces among the gods.

6. COMMON CHARACTERISTICS OF THE VEDIC GODS.—As we have seen, the Vedic gods are a celestial folk, the clan of the shining ones. The members of the heavenly clan, as is natural, have a family resemblance one with another. Certain common features characterize them as a group. In the first place, they are all *Devas* 'bright heavenly ones', whose proper habitat is the sky[1] and proper nature light[2]. While the term *Asura* 'mysterious lord' is not explicitly applied to all the gods, yet in general it is one of their epithets, emphasizing their 'mysterious' nature, which expresses itself through *māyā* 'occult power'. In sharp contrast to mortal men the gods are described as '*immortal*'. As might be expected, *brilliance* is a common characteristic of the race of gods whose very nature is light. Since the Vedic gods in general preside over cosmical functions, *power* is an attribute of them all. So with

[1] In the case of such terrestrial deities as Agni and Soma, their heavenly origin and subsequent 'descent' to earth is expressly stated. The deified 'Waters' and 'Rivers' manifestly descend from the sky in the form of rain. Deified terrestrial 'Mountains' may be regarded as having their prototype in the cloud-mountains of the sky.

[2] *Cf.* 'Who coverest thyself with light as with a garment', Ps. CIV. 2.

knowledge. Each god being in charge of a special department must have knowledge and power adequate to his task. *Beauty* is commonly ascribed to the gods. As distinguished from the malevolent demons, the gods as a class are benevolent, and, on the whole, are upholders of moral order. The attributes of power, wisdom, beauty, benevolence and righteousness though possessed by all, are not possessed by all in the same degree. Thus Uṣas, the lady 'Dawn', has more beauty than knowledge and strength; Indra, the warrior god, more strength than knowledge and righteousness. Of all the Vedic gods Varuṇa possesses the best combination of physical and moral attibutes. Agni, as a priestly god, is well endowed with knowledge, *Jātavedas* 'knowing all generations' being his exclusive epithet.

The mutual relationships and mutual interchange of services that held among the Vedic gods have already been traced out with some detail. Every department of nature and of life is brought under the control of some deity. All the deities together function as a unity. The unity of the divine activity is not the unity of an individual will as in monotheism, but the unity formed by the collective will[1] of a clan, the clan of the devas. The multiplicity[2] of the Vedic gods reflects the multitudinous aspects of nature and of life; and the unity which, on the whole, pervades the diverse activities of the gods reflects, in like manner, the unity of nature, the fact that the universe is a cosmos, an ordered whole. One of the great conceptions of the Ṛigveda is that of *Ṛita* 'order', a conception which goes back to the Indo-Iranian period and the roots thereof to the IE. period. As the Greek and Roman gods are linked up with Fate (*Moira, Fatum*), so the Vedic gods are connected with *Ṛita,* 'Eternal Order'. The relation which the gods sustain to *ṛita* is variously

[1] *Cf.* X. 33, 9, 'Beyond the will *(vrata)* of the gods lives not even the hundred-lived.'

[2] Like the multiplicity of Greek, Roman and Lithuanian gods.

stated. Heaven and Earth are called the ancient parents (*mātarā*) of *ṛita* (VI. 17, 7), and in the same passage they bear the epithet *devȧputre* 'whose sons are gods'. Heaven and Earth, then, are parents of the gods and parents of *ṛita*. In other words, the devas, each in his own proper sphere, are *ṛita*, express *ṛita*, are the guardians and cherishers of *ṛita*. For example, Uṣas is not independent of Eternal Order. She was born in *ṛita* (*ṛitejā* I. 113, 12), and so her task is to cherish and protect it. She does not infringe the heavenly ordinances[1], the law of *ṛita*[2], but rather follows its rein (I. 123, 13), for day by day she returns to the place appointed. In the thought of *ṛita* being expressed by the daily recurrence of dawn we have the idea of the *uniformity of nature*. Of all the gods the two chief Ādityas, Varuṇa and Mitra, are most intimately connected with *ṛita*, so that what seems in some passages to be the work of *ṛita*, in others is referred to as the work of Varuṇa.

All the gods, then, are alike in either determining[3], or expressing or guarding some aspect or other of *ṛita*, which may be translated as 'the course of things', 'nature', or 'cosmic order'. Through the great conception of *Ṛita* the multiplicity of nature is reduced to a unity and the multiplicity of the gods (corresponding to the multiplicity of nature) is seen to reflect a single will, because all are 'labourers together' in maintaining a single all-comprehensive cosmic order. Thus the tendency of Ṛigvedic religion was toward some form of unity, whether monotheistic or pantheistic.

7. We may finally note the bearing of all this upon two recent theories of the Ṛigveda:—

a) Max Müller's theory of '*Henotheism*'[4], namely 'the belief in individual gods alternately regarded as the

---

[1] *Daivyāni vratāni* I. 92, 12.

[2] *Ṛitasya dhāma* I. 123, 9.

[3] As in the case of Varuṇa.

[4] Oldenberg, RV. 101, note; and Macdonell, VM. 16.

highest'. We have seen that the gods form a heavenly 'caste'. All participate in deity. All possess in superabundant measure the qualities of power, sovereignty, wisdom, beneficence and beauty. Where there are so many gods, there must necessarily be considerable indefiniteness of outline; and, as we have seen, there is a tendency to the recognition of an underlying unity, and so to fusion. Hence the loftiest attributes might properly be ascribed to any and every *deva*, simply because he was a member of the 'clan of the devas', and because all alike participated in divinity. This did not imply in the least that a god thus addressed was regarded as the 'highest' in contradistinction to all the rest, but simply that he had his full share of divinity. Of course, exaggerations and inconsistencies are found in the Vedic hymns, but so are they in other religious literature [1]. Where there is more than one deity or divine person, it is difficult always to keep the right balance, especially when the one worshipped is an *iṣṭa devatā*.

Swāmi Dayānand Sarasvati's theory of '*Monotheism*' in the Ṛigveda. Taking his cue from the late passages Ṛv. I. 164. 46 [2] and X. 114, 5 [3], the founder of the Ārya Samāj held that all the gods mentioned in the Ṛv. are simply variant names for one god. This process of reduction from multiplicity to unity would have been easier, if there had been no dual gods or group gods mentioned in the Ṛv. It has already been remarked that the tendency of Ṛigvedic polytheism was toward unity of some sort, either monotheistic or pantheistic. Swāmi

[1] Farnell (*Greece* and *Babylon*, 1911, p. 84) refers to the "tendency very marked in the Babylonian liturgies, to exalt the particular divinity to whom worship is at that moment being paid above all others", with the result that "the ecstatic poet is always contradicting himself".

[2] 'The one Being priests speak of in many ways: they call it Agni, Yama, Mātariśvan.'

[3] 'Priests and poets with words make into many the bird (= the Sun) that is but one.'

Dayānand was not a pantheist. In reading into the Ṛigveda a monotheistic doctrine as opposed to pantheism, he virtually declares that instead of issuing in pantheism or at most in an unstable monotheism, Vedism ought to have issued in a clear-cut and definite monotheism. The monotheistic interpretation of the Ṛigveda involved on the part of Swāmī Dayānand much wild and unscientific exegesis. For this, however, we may be thankful that as between theism and pantheism Swāmī Dayānand took the side of theism.

CHAPTER V.

VARUṆA THE ETHICAL GOD

1. **Introductory.**—Varuṇa is the most impressive deity among all the Vedic gods. As a prehistoric god he is more or less opaque, his nature substratum (if he ever had one) being a matter of dispute. He certainly dates from the Indo-Iranian period, being the Indian analogue of Ahura Mazda; and by some he is carried back to the Indo-European period and connected with the Greek Ouranos. The two greatest German authorities on Vedic mythology[1] both agree in finding in the moon Varuṇa's original physical basis. Varuṇa stands in the midst of the group of Ādityas as one of them, possibly seven in number, which the late Professor Oldenberg thought represented originally sun, moon and five planets, in his opinion loan gods from the Semitic world. The Vedic Ādityas as a group remind one distinctly of the Avestan *Amesha Spentas.* Varuṇa is as closely connected with Mitra in the Ṛv. as Ahura Mazda is with Mithra in the Avesta; and both names Mitra and Varuṇa occur in the Boghaz-kői tablets (1400 B.C.). The name 'Varuṇa' has vanished entirely from Iranian unless it be represented by the word *Varena;* but the nature of Varuṇa is clearly manifest in the impressive character of Ahura Mazda[2]. For as the 'wise' Ahura gathered up in himself the attributes and functions of the *daevas* whom he supplanted, so it is equally true, in the words of Barth, that "if we combine into one all the

---

[1] Oldenberg and Hillebrandt.

[2] It is certain that Varuṇa and Ahura Mazda originally were either identical, as Oldenberg thinks (RV. 95, "Varuṇa, der Ahura des Avesta"), or were parallel forms of the same conception. See Keith CHI. I. 103: "Varuṇa bears the epithet Asura, which serves to show his parallelism with Ahura Mazda, the highest of Iranian gods". *Cf.* also v. Schrœder, AR. I. 325 ff.

attributes of sovereign power and majesty which we find in the other gods, we will have the god Varuṇa[1]. As Ahura Mazda represented the actuality of ethical monotheism in ancient Irān, so Varuṇa represented its possibility in ancient India. If the one may be rightly called 'the Iranian Yahweh', the other with almost equal justice may be called 'the Indian Yahweh'.

2. **Distribution of the Ṛigvedic Material.**—Since the group of the Ādityas must be considered in connection with Varuṇa, we have the following statistics. There are addressed to Varuṇa hymns II. 28, V. 85, VII. 86-89, VIII. 41-42 and I. 24-25, ten in all; to Mitra-Varuṇa 23, of which eleven are in Book V and six in Book VII; to Indra-Varuṇa 9, of which 4 are in Book VII; to Mitra only one, III. 59; and to the Ādityas 6, of which 3 are in Book VII. Although none of these hymns is found in Bk. X, yet there are isolated references to Varuṇa in no less than 35 hymns belonging to that book. From the prominence of Bk. VII in connection with Varuṇa, one might infer that the priestly family of the Vasiṣṭhas was very specially the guardian of this worship during the pre-Vedic or the Vedic age.

3. **The Prehistoric Varuṇa.**—If connected etymologically with Οὐρανός, Varuṇa goes back to the period of IE. unity. There is, indeed, a slight phonetic difficulty, but nothing so serious as to prevent its acceptance by competent scholars[2]. In Greek mythology Ouranos is represented as an ancestor of Zeus, a consciousness of his great antiquity being perhaps thereby revealed. In IE. times Zeus (Dyāus) and Ouranos (Varuṇas) may both have

---

[1] RI. 16.

[2] "There has been some phonetic scepticism about the equation Varuṇas = οὐρανός which time has not justified. Greek οὐρανός is Indo-European *u̯oru̯-n̥nos* or *u̯oru̯-enos*; Sanskrit Varuṇas is Indo-European *u̯oru̯-nos*. The two forms differ no more than, for instance, Vedic *nūtanas* and *nūtnas* 'recent', or Greek στεγανός and στεγνός 'covered'"—Bloomfield RV. 136.

been descriptive appellations of the one physical fact of the sky, Zeus 'the bright' and Ouranos 'the encircling', two names for the same thing, or one perhaps an epithet of the other. Before the IE. clans had separated, these words had already parted company. In Greek and Vedic both words survive; in Avestan both are lost[1], a fact probably due to the Zoroastrian reformation. In Greek mythology Zeus is the great personality, not Ouranos; the opposite is true in the Ṛv.[2] There is very much, then, to be said in favour of regarding Varuṇa as originally the same as Ouranos, both words being derived from *vṛi* 'to encompass', therefore 'encompassing' as an epithet of Zeus (Dyāus). This seems to the present writer to be, on the whole, the most satisfactory conclusion[3]. In the nature of the case there is no absolute proof. But whether Varuṇa is connected with Ouranos or not[4], nearly all scholars regard the word as derived from *vṛi* 'to encompass', meaning the same as if it were connected with Ouranos, namely 'encompassing sky[5]. It is possible too that folk etymology has been at work, the word Varuṇa naturally suggesting to the popular mind some connection with *vāri*

---

[1] This statement must be qualified to this extent that in the textually uncertain Yasht III. 13 *dyaoš*, abl. of *dyav* 'sky', occurs (only here in Avesta). 'Headlong down from heaven fell he'.—Moulton's trans. As regards Varuṇa there is the possibility of a connection with *varena* and *varenya*.

[2] "In so far as Zeus has a parallel, it is in Varuṇa not in Dyāus". Keith, IM. 21.

[3] The latest and best statement of this position is found in Schrœder, AR. I. 322 ff. Other scholars who connect Varuṇa with Ouranos are Muir, OST. V. 76; Barth, RI. 16; Grassmann, *Wörterbuch*; Roth, PW.; Bohnenberger, AGV. 22; Darmesteter, OA. 53, 78; Bloomfield, RV. 136-137. Such authorities on Comparative Philology as Brugmann, *Grundriss* 2. 154, and Prellwitz EWGS, have not rejected this connection.

[4] "Joh. Schmidt writes to the effect that till the relation of the Æolic ὄρανός and ὤρανος to οὐρανός has been determined, it is impossible to say whether Varuṇa is connected with οὐρανός or not."—Macdonell, VM. 1897, Addenda and Corrigenda.

[5] So Macdonell, VM. 27-28, and Keith IM. 25; as well as the scholars mentioned under note 3 above.

'water', and *var-ṣa* 'rain'[1], just as ὀυρανός might suggest a connection with οὐρεῖν 'to make water'[2].

4. MITRA AND VARUṆA.—The divine names Mitra and Varuṇa[3], discovered by Winckler on the Boghaz-köi tablets (1400 B.C.) indicate the existence of the two gods at that early date. The question whether these divine names are Indo-Iranian, Iranian or Indian has already been raised[4]. They clearly belong to a people and language in which *s* had not been changed to *h*[5], and in which Indra and Nāsatyā (u) were gods and not demons. Hence the period before the Zoroastrian reformation and before the Iranian consonantal shift. The inscriptions represent, then, either the undivided Indo-Iranian, the pre-Zoroastrian Iranian, or the Vedic Indian; or possibly they are the work of Indo-European speaking tribes, who had stopped in Upper Mesopotamia on their way eastward, or of Aryan people, who had migrated westward from Bactria. At any rate, whatever the facts are, the Divine names are mentioned along with Mitānian kings, whose names seem to be genuinely Aryan[6].

The appearance of Varuṇa in the midst of an environment of Iranian royal names at such an early date is a reason for reviving the older view that the late Avestan

---

[1] "Varuṇa is the covering sky united with the sun, or *he whose covering is rain and dew*". Hopkins RI. 71.

[2] Pischel (VS. I, 88) regards it as not impossible to bring Varuṇa into connection with οὐρεῖν. Æschylus in a fragment calls the rain the seed of ἁγνὸς Οὐρανός, and in the Rv. rain is virtually called *divo retaḥ*.

[3] *Mi-it-ra-aš-ši-il u-ru-w-na-aš-ši-el* variant *a-ru-na-aš-ši-el*. Aššil is clearly a combining suffix; hence the divine pair Mitra and Varuṇa. Meyer, GA. I[2] 802.

[4] See p. 23.

[5] Indra and Nāsatya occur on the same tablets as gods along with Mitra and Varuṇa; and Nāsatya is the form which appears, and not the later Avestan *Nāonhaithya*, in which the Iranian consonantal shift from *s* to *h* has taken place.

[6] The letter of Dushratta, the King of Mitāni, in the Tel-el-Amarna correspondence contains the Iranian names *Artashumara* and *Artatāma*. Keith, *Indo-Iranians* in Bhandarkar, CV. 84 *ff*; Giles, CHI. I, 76; Bloomfield, RV. 12.

varena[1], name of an earthly district, is connected with Varuṇa. Zoroaster clearly made a clean sweep of the old gods, even the noblest of them such as Varuṇa and Mitra. They were doubtless too closely connected with the physical aspects of nature to suit his reform. So he cast them out of heaven[2]; and Varuṇa who undoubtedly was the highest fell the lowest, for he was apparently transformed into a demon of lust[3]. With the counter-reformation of the later Avesta Mitra returned, but not Varuṇa. The reason clearly was that the noble aspects of the Iranian Varuṇa had been conserved and retained under the name of Ahura Mazda, while the ignoble side of Varuṇa to which his name still apparently clung had nothing that even the later Avesta wished to revive. The earlier fellowship of Mitra and Varuṇa as seen in the Boghaz-Köi inscription and revealed in so many passages of the Ṛv. was restored in the later

---

[1] So Darmesteter, OA. 69-70; Hillebrandt in his early book *Varuṇa und Mitra*, 1877; and recently Prellwitz, EWGS., and L. v. Schrœder, *Arische Religion* I. 332. A conversation at Ithaca with Prof. Jackson left the impression that he was prepared to leave the question open. From *varena* is formed *varenya daēvas* (Vend. X 14), by hypothesis οὐράνιοι θεοί, and also the phrase *varenya drvantō* (Yasht X. 68, 97). The degradation of meaning may have been from *devas* in heaven to demons in heaven and finally to demons in the Varena land, demons of lust and doubt. In the Pahlavi texts there is a *Varenō*, a demon of lust. See Jackson in Iranian *Grundriss* I. 655,660. It must be mentioned, however, that Spiegel who earlier (AP. 181) accepted the equation Varuṇa = Varena, in a later article (ZDMG. 32, [1878], 716-723) considers the identification questionable, while not rejecting it out and out. In favour of the identification is the fact that in nouns formed from roots in *r*, a succeeding *a* is changed to *u*; e. g. *dhṛi, vṛi* and *tṛi* give *dharuṇa, Varuṇa* and *taruṇa* instead of *dharana, varana* and *tarana*. Against the identification is the fact that the Iranian forms *karena, parena* and *varena* seem to have as their equivalents in Sanskrit *karṇa* 'ear', parṇa 'feather' and *varṇa* 'covering'. Then, too, Skt. *varuṇa* would seem to require as its Iranian ẹquivalent *vauruna*, since Skt. *taruṇa* = Iran. *tauruna* and Skt. *aruṇa* = Iran. *auruna*. But at any rate *varena* is clearly derived from *vṛi* in some one of its numerous meanings, and that is the main point.

[2] Neither Mithra nor Varuṇa is mentioned in the Gāthās.

[3] Dinkard VIII. 9, 3; IX. 32, 3; Dādistān ı Dīnīk XXXVII. 44, XCIV. 2.

Avesta in the comradeship of Mithra and Ahura[1]. In this way we are able with a considerable degree of confidence to reconstruct portions of Iranian religious history which do not lie on the surface; for, as Prof. Oldenberg says[2]: "We must try to read the Avesta like a palimpsest; under the writing of the Zarathustrians we discover the clear traces of a more ancient text which very closely resembles the Veda".

The existence of the copulative compounds, *Mithra-Ahura* and *Mitra-Varuṇa,* in both the later Avesta and the Ṛigveda presupposes a similar conjunction of these names before the breaking up of the Indo-Iranian unity. This is also supported by the Boghaz-köi inscription, in which Mitra and Varuṇa are linked together by the combining suffix *aššil.* See p. 114 n. 5. Mithra in the Avesta means 'compact[3]', and in the Ṛv. friendship (neut.) and friend (masc.). It looks as if Mitra were originally a 'Sondergott', 'he of the compact', just like Janus 'he of the door'. Mitra, then, would be the god who watches over truth-speaking and sincerity between man and man in the matter of contracts, promises, treaties. Now there has ever been recognized an inner affinity between truth and light[4]. Truth is an inner light; and light is a kind of external truth. We do not know which idea emerged first in connection with Mitra, but probably Meillet is right in giving the priority

---

[1] "Ahura Mazda spake unto Spitama Zarathushtra, saying: 'Verily when I created Mithra . . . . . . I created him as worthy of sacrifice, as worthy of prayer as myself, Ahura Mazda'".—Yasht X. 1, *Cf.* also: "We sacrifice unto Mithra and Ahura, the two great imperishable holy gods".—Yasht X. 145. Darmesteter's translations, SBE. XXIII, pp. 119-120, 158.

[2] JRAS. 1909, pp. 1097-98.

[3] 'Vertrag, Abmachung, Kontrakt'—Bartholomæ AW. 1183. Brugmann (*Grundriss,* 2nd ed. 1906 II. 1, p. 346) explains the word as originally meaning 'austauschen, verkehren', indicating especially *friendly intercourse* (das freundliche Verkehren); *mei* 'to exchange', *mayate* 'he exchanges', Lat. *communis.* *Cf.* Oldenberg RV. 186, n. 1.

[4] "He that doeth the *truth* cometh to the *light*"—John III. 21. God is "*true*" (I. John V. 20) and God is "*light*" (I. John I. 5).

to the ethical idea[1]. It really makes little difference. The original Mitra stands for truth and compact-keeping[2]. His business was to help men 'to walk in the light' of covenant-keeping faithfulness as between man and man and tribe and tribe, and to punish them, if they did otherwise. It may not be without significance that among all the IE. tribes the first to form a confederacy were the Aryans. We may perhaps see in this the influence of Mitra, the god presiding over the great social principle of faithfulness to compacts. Such was Mitra's ethical sphere, and his physical sphere sooner or later was the light. Some scholars, as Moulton puts it, have been too prone to antedate the ultimate identification of Mithra with the sun[3]. The passage from sunlight to sun was, of course, natural and inevitable, and the transition was effected in Persia by the time of the later Avesta[4]. The physical meaning, then, of the two divine names, Mitra and Varuṇa, was most probably 'sunlight and encircling sky'. These two separate entities, light and sky, naturally fuse together into one conception.

Why did the Zoroastrian reform find no place for Mithra? For one thing he is represented in the *Mihr Yasht* as a fighter, a god of battles[5]. This was another side of his character—the militant side—which probably appealed with special force to the robber hordes who had little use for a god of good faith. For this or other reasons Zoroaster transferred to *Asha* 'Truth', 'Ethical Order', the care of covenant faithfulness and loyalty—a charge which Mitra had apparently forfeited. But, as we have seen, Mithra came back in the later Avesta as a *yazata* or 'angel'. Later on as the *Sol Invictus* of Mithraism the

---

[1] Journal Asiatique, 1897, II. 143 ff.

[2] Moulton, EZ. 151; Schrœder, AR. 367-383.

[3] Moulton, EZ. 151; Schrœder, AR. 381.

[4] Schrœder, AR. 382, denies that the Indian Mitra ever was a sun-god.

[5] A natural development from the conception of Mitra as a god of light, since the early mythologies are full of the conflict between light and darkness.

worship of Mithra penetrated the Roman Empire[1]. As a warrior god and the patron of the blunt honesty and straightforwardness which soldiers love, he was very specially the god of soldiers. The golden period of Mithraism in the West was between 100 and 300 A. D. For a time it was uncertain whether Christianity or Mithraism would win the day.

Only one hymn of the Rv. is addressed to Mitra, III. 59.

A

1. Mitra mankind uniteth, to them speaking;
Mitra the earth upholdeth, and the heaven;
Mitra with eye unwinking sees the tillers;
To Mitra offer the oblation oily.

2. Pre-eminent be that man who brings oblation,
Who serves thee duly, Mitra the Āditya;
Never is slain or vanquished whom thou helpest,
From neither far nor near doth trouble reach him.

3. Free from disease, in sacred food delighting,
Standing firm-kneed upon broad earth's expanses,
Abiding by the will of the Āditya.
May we continue in the grace of Mitra.

4. Adorable and gracious is this Mitra
A king with fair dominion, born disposer;
May we abide in his auspicious favour,
The loving-kindness of the holy Mitra.

5 We must approach with awe the great Āditya,
Mankind-uniter, to the singer gracious;
To him most highly to be praised, to Mitra
Into the fire pour this oblation pleasant.

---

[1] As India exported Buddhism eastward, so Persia exported Mithraism westward. Something of Mithraism entered India also, for in the first century A. D. and later (see Farquhar, ORLI. 152) there was continuous Iranian influence in North India (*cf*. the Iranian symbols on the Kanishka coins), and Hindu Sun-worship was carried on almost entirely in accordance with Iranian rules. Magian Priests entered India in large numbers and not only became Priests in temples of the sun, that were also recognized as Brāhmans. Farquhar *op. cit.* 152, 205.

B

6. Mitra the god upholds the folk,
His favour bringeth ample gain,
His wealth conspicuous renown.

7. The fair-famed Mitra is the one
Who by his might excels the sky,
And by his lofty fame the earth.

8. To Mitra, mighty one to help,
The peoples five submit themselves,
'Tis he supporteth all the gods.

9. 'Mongst gods and mortals, for the man
Who spreads the straw, hath Mitra made
Provision by his will and law.

This hymn (really two hymns) contains, as we shall see further on, almost nothing which could not have been said with equal truth and appropriateness of Varuṇa. Mitra is described as upholding heaven and earth (1), the folk (6) and even the gods (8); as greater than heaven and earth (7); as beholding man with unwinking eye (1); as a king whose 'ordinance' (*vrata*) is to be observed (3, 9); and as a god of grace (3, 4) who helps and delivers, and grants health, wealth and prosperity (2, 3, 6, 8). The only attribute mentioned in this hymn which seems specially to belong to Mitra is *yātayajjana*[1], 'uniting men' (vv. 1, 5). Unfortunately the particular meaning of the verbal root *yat* is not very definite[2]. Nevertheless the various interpretations given in the foot-note are not so very far apart. There is a social reference. Mitra stirs up men and sets them at their respective tasks in friendly

[1] Occurs in only three other passages in the Rik: V. 72, 2 of Mitra-Varuṇa; I. 136, 3 of Mitra, Varuṇa and Aryaman; and VIII. 91, 12 of Agni who 'Mitra-like unites men'.

[2] For example *yātayati* (v. 1) has received the following interpretations: sets men at their respective tasks (Sāyaṇa); indicates to men their place (Hillebrandt, LR. 73); incites to emulation, that is to say, sets a good example (Geldner, VS. III. 15); sets in motion (Ludwig on passage); stirs men (Macdonell, VRS. 79); inspects (Bergaigne RV. III. 165); unites (Roth PW., Oldenberg RV. 287 note 1) Grassmann, *Uebersetzung* I. 102, V. Schrœder, AR. 369); and makes men keep their engagements (Meillet, JA. X (1907), 2. 148).

emulation and co-operation. As Geldner finely interprets it, 'he who calls himself Mitra (friend) incites to emulation of himself'. He the divine 'friend' as he is called in the Ṛv., and the guardian of compacts according to the Avesta, incites men by his own example to friendly and co-operative, that is, to social activities, in the performance of which there must necessarily be mutual faithfulness and loyalty to engagements. Other evidence in the Ṛv. for an interpretation of Mitra similar to that of the Avesta is found in X. 89, 9, 'Men of evil ways who injure Mitra, injure Aryaman, injure *agreements (saṅgiraḥ)*, injure Varuṇa'. The word 'agreements' set in the midst of the three Ādityas suggests that to do violence to 'agreements' is the same thing as to do violence to the three gods. Ṛv. IV, 55, 5, "May the Lord (Varuṇa) protect us from distress caused by strangers; Mitra, from distress *'caused by friends'*" may also be cited, if this translation is correct[1].

As the Avestan Mitra had a luminous character, so had the Vedic Mitra. Both ultimately were identified with the sun, Mithra in the later Avesta and Mitra in the younger Veda. The first texts clearly indicating the identification of the Vedic Mitra with the sun are AV. XIII. 3, 13 and IX. 3, 18, according to which Mitra at sunrise is contrasted with Varuṇa in the evening, and Mitra is asked to uncover in the morning what has been covered up by Varuṇa. Certain Ṛigvedic passages also may be cited which point more or less clearly in the direction of this ultimate identification, *e. g.* X. 8, 4, Agni at the head of the dawns generates Mitra for himself; III. 5, 4 and V. 3, 1, Agni when kindled becomes Mitra; V. 81, 4, Savitar becomes Mitra because of his laws; Vāl. 4, 3, Viṣṇu took his three steps by the laws of Mitra[2].

On the whole, then, while an indefinite luminous character cannot be denied to the Ṛigvedic Mitra, such as

---

[1] It is supported by Grassmann, and by Whitney-Lanman on AV. II. 28, 1.

[2] Macdonell, VM. 29-30.

belonged to the Ādityas as a class and indeed to the Devas in general, yet on the basis of the earliest evidence, Vedic and Avestan, the original Indo-Iranian Mitra must be assumed to have been the apotheosis of the friendly compact, the 'gentleman's agreement'[1].

5. Varuṇa and Ethical Order.—Ṛv. VII. 86 is almost entirely penitential in character, and as such vividly reminds one of the Hebrew and Babylonian penitential psalms:

1. Wise are the generations through the greatness
Of him who propped the two wide worlds asunder;
Pushed forth the great and lofty vault of heaven,
The day-star, too; and spread the earth out broadly.

2. With mine own self I meditate this question:
"When shall I have with Varuṇa communion?
What gift of mine will he enjoy unangered?
When shall I happy-hearted see his mercy?

3. Wishing to know my sin I make inquiry,
I go about to all the wise and ask them;
One and the self-same thing even sages tell me;
'Varuṇa hath with thee hot indignation."

4. O Varuṇa, what was my chief transgression,
That thou wouldst slay a friend who sings thy praises?
Tell me, god undeceived and sovereign, guiltless
Would I appease thee then with adoration.

5. Set us free from the misdeeds of our fathers,
From those that we ourselves have perpetrated;
Like cattle-thief, O king, like calf rope-fastened,
So set thou free Vasiṣtha from the fetter.

6. 'Twas not mine own will, Varuṇa, 'twas delusion,
Drink, anger, dice, or lack of thought, that caused it;
An older man has led astray a younger,
Not even sleep protects a man from evil.

7. O let me like a slave, when once made sinless,
Serve him the merciful, erewhile the angry.
The noble god has made the thoughtless thoughtful;
Hẹ speeds the wise to riches, he a wiser.

---

[1] So Oldenberg, RV. 186 note 1, "die Verkörperung des Vertrags"; Schrœder, AR. 372; and Meillet, JA. X (1907), 2, p. 145: "Mitra est la personnification du contrat".

8. May this my praise-song, Varuṇa, sovereign ruler,
Reach unto thee and make thy heart complaisant;
May it be well with us in rest and labour,
Do ye protect us evermore with blessings.

Ṛita, as has been pointed out, means 'order' cosmic, ethical and ritualistic. The kind of *ṛita* celebrated in this hymn is predominantly ethical, the first and last verses alone having to do with cosmic and ritual order respectively. The following comments may be made: —

a) Varuna inflicts disease as a reminder and punishment of sin. — Some member of the priestly family of the Vasiṣṭhas was fettered[1] with disease (v. 5) and so was in peril of death (v. 4). Like Job he did not know the exact nature of his transgression (vv. 3-4). The wise assured him that he must be a sinner, because his illness was proof that Varuṇa who hates sin was angry with him (v. 3)[2]. He

---

[1] There are many references to 'the fetters of Varuṇa' (I. 24, 15; 25, 21; VII. 88, 7, etc.), the term *pâśa* being characteristic of him. This clearly refers to the suffering entailed by sin. Here, too, we have the working of analogy. As an earthly king binds criminals with fetters, so does the heavenly king Varuṇa deal with those who violate his ordinances, binding them with the fetters of disease and death.

Cf. "The *cords* of Sheol were round about me,
The *snares* of death came upon me". Ps. XVIII, 5.

Also: "His own iniquities shall take the wicked,
And he shall be holden with *the cords of his sin*". Prov. V, 22.

This punitive aspect of Varuṇa's character has perhaps been brought into harmony with the meaning of the name Varuṇa through the working of popular etymology. The root *vṛt* means 'to obstruct', 'to beset', as well as 'to encompass', as seen in the name Vṛitra 'the obstructor'. Varuṇa 'besets' with illness those who violate his ordinances, becoming the antagonist, the enemy (meaning in Iranian) of all evil-doers. Thus Varuṇa is a kind of ethical Vṛitra for all who disobey his laws. The Vedic Indians recognized many demons of disease. Varuṇa, too, caused disease, but he was not a demon. His chastisements were those of a holy god, which are blessings in disguise, leading as they often do to repentance and amendment.

[2] The same point of view is found in the Babylonian penitential hymns concerning which Prof. Morris Jastrow (RBA. Chap. XVIII) writes: "The two parts which presented themselves with overpowering force to the penitent were the anger of the deity and the necessity of appeasing that anger... .... The man afflicted

accepts this opinion as correct, asserts that he did not mean to err, mentions as possible causes of his sin, strong drink, anger, dice, thoughtlessness, bad example, and evil dreams (v. 6), and prays that he may be released from all misdeeds, whether committed by himself or by his ancestors[1] (v. 5). Through the infliction of suffering Varuṇa rendered thoughtful the thoughtless one who had sinned through thoughtlessness[2]. Like the prodigal son in the parable[3] 'he came to himself' through the insight which comes from suffering. The same general situation is brought before us in VII. 89, in which there is an apparent reference to dropsy as the peculiar infliction of Varuṇa:

1. I do not wish, King Varuṇa
   To go down to the home of clay,
   Be gracious, mighty lord, and spare.
2. Since like one tottering I move,
   O slinger, like inflated skin,
   Be gracious, mighty lord, and spare.
3. Somehow through weakness of my will
   I went astray, O shining one;
   Be gracious, mighty lord, and spare.
4. Thirst found thy singer even when
   He in the midst of waters stood;
   By gracious, mighty lord, and spare.
5. Whatever wrong we men commit against the race
   Of heavenly ones, O Varuṇa, whatever law
   Of thine we here have broken through thoughtlessness,
   For that transgression do not punish us, O god.

Here too disease is regarded both as a penalty for sin causing suffering and death and as a reminder of sin.

---

was a sinner, and the corollary to this position was that misfortunes come in consequence of sin. .... Within this circle of ideas the penitential psalms of Babylonia move. ...... An ethical spirit was developed .... that surprises us by its loftiness and comparative purity."

[1] Note the conception of the *solidarity* in sin as between the fathers and their children, an idea belonging to a primitive tribal state of society, where the unit of responsibility is the family or tribe rather than the individual.

[2] *acitti* 'thoughtlessness' *acit* 'thoughtless', *acetayat* 'made thoughtful'.

[3] Luke XV. 17.

b) Fellowship with Varuṇa is broken by sin.—This is brought out in VII. 86, 2 and more fully in VII. 88, 4-5:

4. Varuṇa took on board with him Vasiṣṭha,
Made him a Ṛishi by his mighty working;
The Sage on gladsome days made him a singer,
As long as days, as long as dawns continue.
5. But now what has become of this our friendship,
When lovingly we walked together erstwhile:
When, sovereign Varuṇa, to thy lofty palace,
Thy thousand-gated house I had admittance?

We have here two pictures of the intimacy which Vasiṣṭha enjoyed with Varuṇa; first, when he was in a boat at sea alone with Varuṇa, and again when as the guest of Varuṇa he had free access to his thousand-gated house. But alas! this intimacy was broken through sin. The violation of Varuṇa's ordinances involves loss of communion with him as well as penalty in the form of disease and death. Varuṇa as a holy god has righteous indignation[1] against the sinner.

c) Varuṇa is besought to loose the sinner from sin and its penalty.—As specimens of Vedic prayer for release from sins, we have the following:—

Set us free from the misdeeds of our fathers,
From those that we ourselves have perpetrated;
Like cattle-thief, O king, like calf rope-fastened,
So set thou free Vasiṣṭha from thy fetter. VII. 86, 5.

As from a bond release me from transgression.
. . . .
Remove far hence the debts by me contracted,
Let me not suffer, king, for guilt of others. II. 28, 5^{a}, 9^{a-b}.

Against a friend, companion, or a brother,
A fellow-tribesman, or against a stranger,
Whatever trespass we have perpetrated,
Do thou, O Varuṇa, from that release us.
If we, like those that play at dice, have cheated,
Have really sinned, or done amiss unwitting,
Cast all these sins away, as from us loosened;
So may we, Varuṇa, be thine own belovéd. V. 85, 7-8.

[1] VII. 86, 2, 3, 7; I. 24, 11, 14; I. 25, 2, etc.

A hundred are thy remedies, a thousand,
Wide be thy grace and deep, O sovereign ruler;
Far, far away from us drive off Destruction,
And make us free from every sin committed.
O Varuṇa, we deprecate thine anger
By bowings down, oblations, sacrifices;
Sage Asura, thou sovereign widely ruling,
Release from us the sins we have committed. I. 24, 9, 14.

A god who is thus appealed to is conceived as a merciful and gracious god. There are many references to the *grace*[1] of Varuṇa, which is clearly the basis of the hope of the worshipper who is conscious that he has violated Varuṇa's laws and so is the object of his wrath. Varuṇa is the lord of life and death. If he has 'weapons' with which to consume the evil-doer (II. 28, 7), he has also a hundred, a thousand 'remedies' (I. 24, 9) with which, as the divine physician, to heal and restore the penitent. The forgiveness of sin is conceived as a removing of sin, that is, of its penalty, and as a release, separation and losing therefrom[2]. The conception of sin as a defilement and of forgiveness as a cleansing from such defilement is not found explicitly stated in the Ṛv.[3] Sin itself is viewed as transgression and indebtedness[4]. There are, as

---

[1] *sumati, mṛiḷika* VII. 86, 2, 7; 87, 7; 88, 1; 89, 1; I. 24, 9; 25, 3, 5, 19, etc.

[2] Such verbs are used a *ava-sṛij, śrath, vi-śrathaya, parā-sū, vi-as, pra-muc.* We may cite the following parallels from the Bible:

"As far as the east is from the west,
So far hath he *removed* our transgressions from us" (Ps. CIII. 12).

"Behold the Lamb of God, that *taketh away* the sin of the world" (John. I. 29); "Unto him that loveth us, and *loosed* us from our sins by his blood" (Rev. I. 5); "Jehovah also hath *put away* thy sin," (2 Sam. XII. 13).

[3] With this compare the following: "The inward defilement of sin, *i. e.* its power to defile the conscience of the sinner, is well represented in the Old Testament penitential psalms, but is hardly referred to, at least not explicitly, in the Vedic penitential hymns." Griswold, *Repentance as illustrated from the Old Testament Psalms and from the Varuṇa hymns of the Ṛigveda*, Madras, 1919, p. 10.

[4] Transgression, *enas, drugdha* and *āgas;* debt *ṛina. Cf.* "Forgive us our *debts*" Matt. VI. 12. Also *anṛita*, 'falsehood' and *vṛijina* 'crookedness'.

we have seen, two consequences of sin, the loss of the fellowship of the holy Varuṇa, and the physical penalty of disease or death. Prayer to Varuṇa for the remission of sin seems to cover both needs alike. There is certainly prayer for deliverance from disease and death [1]. There is also (by implication) prayer for the restoration of Varuṇa's friendship [2]; and the feeling is expressed that Varuṇa's grace deserves 'slave-like' devotion (VII. 86, 7); for through the grace bestowed those who have been the objects of Varuṇa's wrath become his *beloved* (V. 85, 8), and stand before him and his law *guiltless* [3] and so *happy-hearted* (VII. 86, 2).

d) Sin is 'the transgression of the law' of Varuṇa [4].—This is the burden of VII. 86, and it is implied wherever there is an appeal to Varuṇa for the remission of sin. For example:—

Whatever ordinance *(vrata)* of thine,
God Varuṇa, we violate,
As human beings day by day;
Yet to the stroke subject us not,
Death-dealing of the angry one,
The wrath of the incenséd one. I. 25, 1-2.
Whatever wrong against the heavenly race we do,
Being but men, O Varuṇa, whatever law
Of thine we may have broken through thoughtlessness,
For that transgression do not injure us, O god. VII. 89, 5.

According to one passage the moral ordinances and laws [5] are an expression of Varuṇa's character and will, being built, as it were, upon him:

---

[1] See VII. 86, 4; I. 24, 9, 12-15; II. 28, 7.

[2] VII. 88, 4-5; 86, 2.

[3] *Anāgas* VII. 86, 7, I. 24, 15.

[4] Other gods have to do in a lesser degree with the punishment or remission of sin, as will be pointed out in the proper place.

[5] The terms employed are *vrata* 'ordinance' I. 25, 1; II. 28, 8, etc.; *dharman* 'statute' VII. 89, 5; *dhāman* 'decree' IV. 5, 4; VI. 67, 9, etc.; *kratu* 'will' IV. 42, 1-2; *dakṣa* 'will' in *pūtadakṣa* 'whose will is pure' VII. 65, 1, etc. *Cf.* also VII. 86, 6. The terms used of the will of Varuṇa are the same whether applied in the sphere of nature or of morals. *Cf.* Bohnenberger, AGV. 50.

For on thee, undeceivable one, are founded,
As on a mountain, ordinances unshaken. II. 28, 8.

No wonder, then, that the gods follow the will and ordinances of Varuṇa[1]. The laws of Varuṇa, like the laws of the Medes and Persians, change not. His is the characteristic epithet *dhṛitavrata* 'whose ordinances are fixed'[2].

As regards special sins, we meet with such implicit prohibitions on the part of Varuṇa as not to kill (I. 41, 8), not to curse (I. 41, 8), not to deceive (II. 27, 16, VII. 65, 3, VIII. 49, 3), not to gamble (II. 29, 5), or at least not to cheat at gaming (V. 85, 8) and not to indulge immoderately in wine, anger and dice (VII. 86, 6)[3]. Vedic ethics was, on the whole, tribal, as might be expected at that early age, moral obligation being largely limited to the clan. But there is in V. 85, 7 a reference to the possibility of sinning against a stranger, and in the next verse the distinction is drawn between deliberate sinning and such sin as is committed unintentionally.

As regards the causes of sin the Vedic Indians clearly believed that "to err is human" (I. 25, 1, VII. 89, 5). They plead as excuses for sin thoughtlessness, weakness of will, wine, anger, dice, bad example and evil dreams[4]. Besides being responsible for one's own sins, there is also the suggestion in VII. 86, 5 and II. 28, 9 that one may be responsible for the sins of others, especially for the sins of one's ancestors, who are bound up with one in the same bundle of life[5].

e) As omnipresent and omniscient, Varuna is a witness of the deeds of men.—For this aspect of Varuṇa's character I. 25 is important:

---

[1] IV 42, 1-2; V. 69, 4; VIII. 41, 7.

[2] I. 25, 8, 10, etc. There is the suggestion that moral law is as fixed as physical law. *Ṛita* covers both ideas.

[3] *Cf.* Bohnenberger, AGV. 52.

[4] VII. 86, 6; 89, 3, 5.

[5] *Cf.* Ex. XX. 5, Ps. LI. 5, Rom. VII. 20.

7. He knows the path of birds that through
The atmosphere do wing their flight,
And ocean-dwelling knows the ships.

8. He knows, as one whose law is firm,
The twelve months with their progeny,
Knows too the month of later birth.

9. He knows the pathway of the wind,
The wide, the high, the mighty wind,
And those that sit enthroned above.

10. Enthroned within his palace sits
God Varuṇa whose law is firm.
All-wise for universal sway.

11. From there the observant god beholds
All strange and secret happenings,
Things that are done or to be done.

12. Let him the all-wise Āditya
Make all our days fair-pathed for us;
May he prolong our earthly lives.

13. Wearing a golden mantle, clothed
In shining garb, is Varuṇa;
His spies are seated round about.

14. He whom deceivers do not dare
Try to deceive, nor injurers
To harm, nor th' hostile to defy.

Quite in the same spirit is I. 24, 6:

Thy realm, O Varuṇa, thy might, and anger,
Even these winged birds have not attained to,
Nor yet the waters that go on for ever,
Nor (mountains) that obstruct the wind's wild fury.

Here Varuṇa's separateness and ethical transcendence are emphasized. His realm is 'beyond the flight of birds', beyond the utmost surge of the waters and beyond the farthest reach of the wind-breaking mountains. Within the highest heaven he sits enthroned in his thousand-gated palace, wielding universal sway, surrounded by his spies[1],

---

[1] The spies (*spaśaḥ*) of Varuṇa might be interpreted as the rays of the sun, moon and stars, which, as it were, search out and reveal the doings of men. It is possible, however, to see here the working of analogy, the heavenly king Varuṇa being equipped like an earthly king with a 'secret service' of spies to discover evil-doers. In them is embodied the all-seeing might of Varuṇa (Oldenberg RV. 286). The Iranian Mithra also has spies.

the all-wise observer of the deeds of men. The "heaven and the heaven of heavens cannot contain" him; but on the contrary, the three heavens and the three earths are deposited in him (VII. 87, 5), and he is all-embracing (VIII. 41, 3, 7). His omnipresence is such that a man cannot escape from Varuṇa by fleeing far beyond the sky[1] (AV. IV. 16, 4). He knows the flight of birds in the sky, the path of ships in the sea and the course of the wind; and he beholds all the secret things that have been or shall be done. Thus past, present and future, far and near, are all alike to him. As such he cannot be deceived[2]. Whatever thing two sitting down together talk about, Varuṇa as a third knows (AV. IV. 16, 2). He surveys the truth and falsehood of men (VII. 49, 3). No creature can even wink without him (II. 28, 6), and the winkings of men's eyes are all numbered by Varuṇa (AV. IV. 16, 2). Varuṇa's omniscience is distinctive and typical, Agni being compared to him in this respect (X. 11, 1)[3].

f) Means of gaining the mercy of Varuṇa.—Among the means expressed or implied may be mentioned moral seriousness in trying to discover one's 'hidden faults' (VII. 86, 3-4), confession of sin (VII. 86, 6; 88, 6; 89, 3), longing to be justified in the sight of Varuṇa (VII. 87, 7; I. 24, 15), prayer for the remission of penalty (often)[4], purpose after new obedience (VII. 86, 7), oblations and sacrifices (I. 24, 14), and hymns of praise. As examples of praise are the following:—

May this my praise song, Varuṇa, sovereign ruler,
Reach unto thee and make thy heart complaisant. VII. 86, 8a-b

May we thy heart by means of song
For grace, O Varuṇa, release,
As charioteer a tethered steed.

[1] *Cf.* Ps. CXXXIX.

[2] *dūḷabha*, VII. 86, 4; I. 25, 14; II. 28, 8.

[3] Macdonell, VM. 26.

[4] VII. 86, 5; 88, 6; 89, 1, 5; I. 24, 9, 11-15; 25, 1-2; V. 85, 7-8, II. 28, 5-7, 9.

Away indeed in search of good
My (hymns) propitiatory fly,
Ev'n as the birds unto their nests. I. 25, 3-4.

In the prayers for the pardon of sin there is undoubtedly too great an emphasis on the removal of the temporal consequences of sin; and some of the Varuṇa hymns are rather conventional and possibly late[1]. Such literary monuments, however, as we have of the worship of Varuṇa represent the fullest consciousness of sin that is found anywhere in the hymns of the Ṛik; and most of them were probably produced within some special Aryan tribe or priestly family, such as the Vasiṣṭhas[2].

The Vasiṣṭha hymns to Varuṇa, Mitra-Varuṇa, Indra-Varuṇa and the Ādityas in Bk. VII (17 in all out of 104 hymns, *i. e.* one-sixth of Book VII) are the most notable in the Ṛigveda.

The hymns addressed to Varuṇa, e. g. VII. 86, are most probably to be regarded themselves as in some sense sacrifices[3], and, as such, means for propitiating Varuṇa. As soon as Vasiṣṭha learns the nature of his sin against Varuṇa, he purposes to appease him[4] by means of adoration. In the later Vedic literature are described many ritualistic devices for accomplishing the same end[5]. But in the Varuṇa hymns of the Ṛv. the sacrifices which receive the emphasis are the outpourings in confession and prayer of what seems

---

[1] Hopkins, RI. 64-65.

[2] We must remember that Bactria is only three or four hundred miles from the Punjab. It is possible that the family of the Vasiṣṭhas remained in touch with Bactria, and advanced in spiritual worship *pari passu* with the worship of Varuṇa or his equivalent in Irān. Keith (*Indo-Iranians* in Bhandarkar CV. 89) holds that "the spread of the people over Irān and India did not at first and in itself cause complete severance". This is probable. If then the suggestion of continued intercourse between the Punjab and Bactria is accepted, we can take the Varuṇa hymns and the Zoroastrian reformation as parallel chronologically, and place both about 1000 B. C., or a little earlier.

[3] Oldenberg, RV. 318.

[4] *ava-i* VII. 86, 4, *cf.* I. 24, 14.

[5] Oldenberg, RV. 319-326.

almost 'a broken and a contrite heart'. It is because of a change of attitude on the part of the sinner toward his sin that Varuṇa can show himself just while justifying the sinful[1]. Because Varuṇa is gracious and merciful, he delights to respond to the cry of the penitent. By way of the ritually appointed oblations and sacrifices (I. 24, 14; VII. 86, 2) the sincere penitent doubtless offered the Vedic equivalent of 'a broken spirit'.

It is just because Varuṇa is ethically so exalted and because there is hardly a hymn of his which does not contain some reference to sin and its remission, that there is such danger of committing the 'psychologist's fallacy', that is, the fallacy of importing modern and especially Christian feelings and conceptions into the hymns.

g) Varuṇa grants protection and happiness to his worshippers.—Happy are they who experience the mercy of Varuṇa (VII. 86, 2) and continue in his ordinance (II. 28, 2); for Varuṇa represented by the sun has a thousand boons to give (VII. 88, 1). He guards the thoughts of men (VIII. 41, 1), grants protection[2] (II. 28, 3, VII. 88, 6, VIII. 42, 2), removes fear (II. 28, 6, 10), delivers from thief, wolf and inauspicious dreams (II. 28, 10) and furnishes the singer with a wealthy patron[3] (II. 28, 11).

h) Varuṇa as Lord of the Ethical Order is a holy God.—

---

[1] *Cf*. Rom. III. 26.

[2] The word *varūtha* 'protection' is derived from *vṛi* in the meaning to 'encircle', 'protect'. Popular thought may have found a connection between the name Varuṇa and the protective aspect of Varuṇa's activity. We are reminded of the Biblical phrase:"

"As the mountains are round about Jerusalem,
So Jehovah is round about his people". Ps. CXXV. 2.

[3] The *dānastuti* character of the mention of a 'wealthy patron' need not disturb us even in a Varuṇa hymn, when we recall that Zarathushtra in one of the genuine Gāthās reminded Ahura Mazda that he had been promised as a reward "ten mares with a stallion and a camel", besides "the future gift of welfare and immortality" (Yasna XLIV. 18). It was felt by these ancient seers that godliness is profitable not only for "the life that is to come", but also for "the life that now is". Then, too, stanza 11 in II. 28 may be an editorial addition.

This is his distinctive province. Other gods share with him in his cosmic activities, such as the creation and direction of the world, sending of rain, etc., but outside of his own circle of the Ādityas none have to do so fully as Varuṇa with the moral life and destiny of mankind. In passages, the context of which is ethical, Varuṇa is referred to as 'the support[1] of *ṛita*', as possessing 'the fountain of *ṛita*' (II. 28, 5) and as the one on whom as on a mountain everlasting ordinances are based (II. 28, 8). The conception of ethical order was covered and explicated by the statutes (*dharman*), decrees (*dhāman*), and ordinances (*vrata*) of Varuṇa. The term *vrata*, which is so often used in connection with Varuṇa is to be derived from *vṛi* to 'choose', 'will', therefore 'ordinance', 'will'. The word suggests that the laws of morality are to be referred immediately to the holy will[2] of Varuṇa. The best Vedic equivalent of the New Testament expression 'the will of God[3] would accordingly be *Varunasya vratam*, 'the will of Varuṇa.' 'The great conception of *Ṛita* 'Order' stands in the closest connection with Varuṇa, whether in its cosmic or its ethical application. Thus:

> The Āditya distributed the waters,
> *The rivers follow Varuṇa's holy order;* (cosmic)
> Unwearied do they flow and never tarry,
> Like birds that speed them quickly on their courses.

---

[1] *dharṇasi* I. 105, 6.

[2] Meillet (JA. X. (1907) 2, p. 157) proposes to connect Varuṇa with *vrata* 'ordinance', Avestan *urvata, urvaiti* 'contract', *urvāta* 'order', 'law'. Accordingly Varuṇa would be originally a personification of the idea of *order*, a Sondergott 'he of order', like Mitra 'he of the compact'. But is it not also possible that this derivative *vrata*, from the fertile root *vṛi*, may have been through popular etymologizing brought into connection with Varuṇa so as to form a kind of etymological support for the thought of the will, ordinances, statutes, decrees of Varuṇa? The Aryans of India love to etymologize, and Sanskrit lends itself peculiarly well to such treatment.

[3] Θέλημα τοῦ Θεοῦ I Thess. IV. 3, etc.

As from a bond release me from transgression,
May we swell, Varuṇa, thy spring of order,[1] (ethical)
May no thread break as I weave my devotion,
Nor mass of work before the time be shattered. II. 28, 4-5.

The prayer 'May we swell, Varuṇa, thy spring of order' seems to imply co-operation with Varuṇa through the practice of righteousness and reverent devotion. Varuṇa's 'ordinances' are fixed and changeless, nevertheless man is free either to obey them or to disobey them. To obey them is life and health; to disobey them is death'.[2]

Ṛita, then, in its ethical connection meant the moral law. It was an impersonal conception. With the passing of Varuṇa in the post-Vedic period, the content of *ṛita* was taken up into that of *dharman* 'law' and *karman* 'retribution'. The conception of *ṛita* in the Indo-Iranian and Vedic periods is a striking witness to the belief that the world-order is essentially righteous, and that morality belongs to the inmost nature of things. Being embodied in the will of Varuṇa *Ṛita* was made concrete and personal. As the guardian and cherisher of moral order Varuṇa was called *ṛitāvan* 'holy' and *pūtadakṣa* 'whose will is pure'. Thus on that 'far-off bank and shoal' of time the Vedic Indians were not without the conception of a law of righteousness viewed as the will of a holy God.

6. Varuṇa and Cosmic Order.

a) Creator and Sovereign.—Varuṇa's creative activity is expressed in such passages as the following:

Wise are the generations through the greatness
Of him who propped the two wide worlds asunder;
Pushed back the great and lofty vault of heaven,
The day-star, too; and spread the earth out broadly. VII. 86, 1.

Varuṇa cutteth for the sun his pathways,
Causeth the river floods to hasten seaward;

[1] The expression Khā ṛitasya 'spring of *ṛita*' (II. 28, 5), as Bloomfield points out (RV. 126), is 'sound for sound the same' as the Avestan *asahe khāo,* Yasna X. 4.

[2] I. 24, 9, 11, 15; 25, 1-2, 21; II. 28, 5, 7, 9. *cf.* "The wages of sin is death". Rom. VI. 23.

Digs for the shining days their mighty channels,
Guiding them as a racer guides his horses.

Thy breath, the wind, resoundeth through the mid-air,
Like a wild beast that smites its prey in pasture;
Between these two world-halves, the great, the lofty,
Are, Varuṇa, all thy lovéd habitations. VII. 87, 1-2.

In baseless space king Varuṇa, the holy,
Sustains erect the summit of a great tree;
Its rays, whose root is high above, stream downward;
Among us be deposited these gleamings.

King Varuṇa hath made a spacious pathway,
Wherein the sun may travel on his journey;
Feet for the footless made wherewith to stay him,
And by his ban removes heart-piercing trouble.

The stars that show themselves by night in heaven
Placed high above,—where are they gone by daylight?
Inviolable are Varuṇa's regulations,
And through the night the moon wide-gleaming wanders.
I. 24, 7-8, 10.

Ṛita, as already pointed out, embraces both cosmic and ethical order. Varuṇa's creative power is manifested especially in the great vault of heaven, through which he has made a path for the sun to travel by day, and for the moon and stars by night. As compared with the moon and stars, the sun in the Ṛv. receives the emphasis, being called the 'day-star' (*nakṣatra*, VII, 86, 1), the 'tree of the sky' (I. 24, 7), the 'mighty beast' (VII. 87. 6), 'the heavenly measuring line' (V. 85, 5), 'the lofty bull' (VII. 88, 1), 'the golden swing' (VII. 87, 5), 'the eye of Mitra and Varuṇa' (VI. 51, 1), and 'the bright beautiful face of *ṛita*' (VI. 51, 1). The wind is Varuṇa's breath[1] and his habitat or domain is the great space between heaven and earth (VII. 87, 2).

---

[1] Does the description of Varuṇa as having the wind for his breath, the sun for his eye, and the space between heaven and earth for his home, bear upon his original physical substrate? All that can be said is that it fits in well enough with the assumed derivation from vṛi 'to encompass', namely 'encompassing sky'. As a matter of fact Varuṇa has become so entirely spiritualized in the Ṛv. that nothing can be proved with certainty as regards his original nature.

Varuṇa is a divine pathmaker, having dug out channels for the rivers and the days as well as for the sun. The appearance and disappearance of sun, moon and stars and their courses are all subject to the regulations (*vratāni,* I. 24, 10) of Varuṇa. There seems to be the suggestion in all this that the order which rules in the physical world should also rule in the moral world. Through his creative might he makes men wise[1].

Like Ahura Mazda, Varuṇa is represented as the creator of the best things:

> The Air hath Varuṇa placed among the tree-tops,
> Milk in the cows and strength in the swift horses,
> Wisdom in hearts and fire within the waters,
> In heaven the sun and soma on the mountain. V. 85, 2.

As creator Varuṇa is naturally ruler. The attribute of sovereignty *(kṣatra)* is very specially his. He is 'the king of all that is' (VII. 87, 6), 'the king of the whole world' (V. 85, 3). The title *samrāj*[2] 'universal monarch' is so often applied to him that it may be regarded as peculiarly his. *Svarāj* 'self-dependent,' *i. e.* independent ruler (II. 28, 1), is also given to him as a title. Varuṇa's sovereignty embraces both the physical and the moral spheres. Varuṇa sits enthroned within his heavenly palace, fully equipped for universal sway (*sāmrājya* I. 25, 10).

The sun as the eye *(cakṣus)* of Varuṇa and the face *(anīka)* of *ṛita* (VI. 51, 1) may be regarded as a visible symbol[3] of Varuṇa. We may compare the following:—

---

[1] *Cf.* Ps. XIX. and Job XXXVIII-XLI.

[2] V. 85, 1.

[3] Only a symbol, be it noted. The metaphors of the sun and light are used in connection with Varuṇa, just as the same metaphors are used of God in the Bible. For example, God is 'a sun and a shield', and 'the sun of righteousness', Ps. 84, 11; Mal. IV. 2. If we had to choose between the sun and the moon as the original physical basis of Varuṇa, we should, on the basis of Ṛigvedic evidence, have to choose the sun.

Now that at last I have come near and seen him,
The face of Varuṇa looks like that of Agni;
To see his beauty may the master lead me
Unto the sun in heaven or to the darkness. VII. 88, 2.

Here, too, the sun as the heavenly form of Agni resembles the face of Varuṇa. But the beauty of Varuṇa may be seen either by looking at the sun in heaven by day or by night looking at moon or star. The theophany of Varuṇa is given at both times to the spiritually illumined.

Again:

Like Dyāus, god Varuṇa sank into the Sindhu,
Like a white drop, or mighty beast, descended;
Ruling in depths and measurer of the mid-air,
King of this world, whose empire is fair-bounded. VII.87,6.

This verse presupposes some place on the Indus where sky and water meet, and where the light-bearers (sun, moon and stars) as revelations of Varuṇa seem to sink into the sea-like bosom of the great river. Varuṇa as represented by the sun is compared, when he sinks into the sea, with a white drop or ball or with a mighty beast.

b) Varuṇa and the Waters. — We may cite the following stanzas from V. 85, 3-6: —

3. Varuṇa caused the cloud-cask opening downwards
To stream forth over heaven and earth and mid-air:
Therewith the king of all the world doth moisten
The ground, just as the rain the fields of barley.

4. What time Varuṇa longeth for the cloud-milk,
He moisteneth the ground, yea earth and heaven,
The mountains clothe themselves then in the rain-cloud,
Their firm foundations the strong heroes loosen.

5. Let me declare this mighty deed of magic
Of Varuṇa the glorious and the godlike,
Who standing in the air's mid region meted
The earth out with the sun as with a measure.

6. This, too, is the all-wise god's deed of magic,
A mighty deed, which none hath ever challenged,
That all the streams that pour themselves out quickly
Do never fill the one sea with their waters. V. 85, 3-6.

He knows the path of birds that wing
Through air their flight, knows too the path
A boat takes, ocean-dweller he. I. 25, 8.

The Āditya distributed the waters;
The rivers follow Varuṇa's holy order;
Unwearied do they flow and never tarry,
Like birds that speed them quickly on their courses. II. 28, 4.

Varuṇa, as lord of cosmic order, has control of the waters. The connection of Varuṇa with this department of nature is so emphasized as to require special explanation. The great encircling vault of the sky is sometimes 'clothed with light as with a garment', majestic in its repose and calm, the very picture of sovereignty and order. Again it is covered with dark rain clouds. By day it is traversed by the sun; at night, by moon and stars, and Uṣas displays her beauty in the morning. It is the same mighty vault—by hypothesis the same Varuṇa as originally conceived—that undergoes these magic transformations. It is suggestive that the word *māyā* 'occult power' is specially used, in connection with such changes. In the ten hymns addressed to Varuṇa *māyā* occurs only four times (V. 85, 5, 6 and VIII. 41, 3, 8) and then in hymns, which especially emphasize Varuṇa's connection with water. Through his 'occult power' he measures the earth by the sun as with a measuring line (V. 85, 5), brings it about that the constantly flowing streams never fill the one sea (V. 85, 6), and establishes the dawns (VIII. 41, 3). With his shining foot he scatters magic wiles (*māyāḥ* VIII. 41, 8), doubtless the evil magic of the demons of darkness.

Varuṇa bears the title *samudriya* 'oceanic' (I. 25, 8) and is called a 'hidden ocean' (*samudraḥ apīcyaḥ* VII. 41, 5), both references being primarily to his atmospheric character. The fact that the rain falls from the sky proves that there is in the sky an invisible ocean, as the source of supply, 'the waters above the firmament'. Varuṇa 'he of the all-covering sky' is thus naturally conceived as 'he of the all-covering rain', the two appearing at times as one and the same. A similar development of meaning is seen in Dyāus, Zeus and Jupiter, each originally meaning 'the bright, shining sky', and each coming to have in addition a 'rainy' character[1], just as in the case of Varuṇa. Furthermore Varuṇa by a natural development[2], very much as in the parallel case of Indra, comes to be the lord of the earthly as well as of the heavenly waters[3].

7. VARUṆA AND THE ĀDITYAS.

The Ādityas are a group of gods with Varuṇa the Āditya *par excellence* at their head. They may be characterized in general as 'the gods of celestial light'[4]. The group, however, is somewhat indefinite both as to the number of gods it includes and as to their names. In II. 27, 1 six are mentioned, namely Mitra, Aryaman, Bhaga, Varuṇa, Dakṣa and Aṁśa. In IX. 114, 3 the number is given as seven[5], in X. 72, 8 as eight. In the later Vedic literature twelve is the usual number of the Ādityas, to correspond apparently with the number of the months.

In addition to the names given above there are sometimes mentioned Dhātar, Indra, Vivasant, Mārtāṇḍa, Sūrya and Viṣṇu. There seem to be certain points of contact between the seven *Amesha Spentas* of Zoroastrianism and the Vedic Ādityas (likewise assumed to be seven). In order, however, to make up the list of seven Ādityas, it is necessary to add one to the number given in II. 27, 1, Sūrya as Macdonell thinks[6], or possibly Parjanya[7].

---

[1] *Cf. Jupiter Pluvius* and Ζεὺς ὕει (Zeus rains).

[2] "Der Gott, der über den Regen gebietet, wird sich leicht zu einem Gott alles Wassers und so denn auch des Meeres entwickeln"—Oldenberg, ZDMG. L. 59.

[3] The conception of Varuṇa as regent of the waters would find a support in popular etymology, if Varuṇa were connected with *vṛi* 'to cover' in the sense of 'he whose covering is rain and dew', or with such words as vāri 'water' and *varī* 'river'. See Hopkins RI. 60 n. 1, 71. Pischel (VS. II. 124-125) holds that the watery character of Varuṇa is original and fundamental.

[4] Macdonell, VM. 44.

[5] So Yasna 47. 1 as interpreted by Oldenberg, ZDMG. L. 53.

[6] VM. 44.

[7] Schrœder, AR. I, 408-423.

a) Varuṇa and Mitra, the Āditya Chiefs.—Of the approximately seven Ādityas the most distinct and individualised are Varuṇa and Mitra. Mitra has not a single quality which is not found in Varuṇa[1]. What is said of Varuṇa alone is said equally of Mitra-Varuṇa. Thus Mitra and Varuṇa are related to *ṛita* (V. 62, 1) and are even identified with *ṛita* (V. 68, 1), have the sun for their eye (VII. 63, 1), are kings and imperial rulers (V. 62, 3; 63, 2), wield dominion (*kṣatra* V. 66, 2, 6), are *Asuras* and possess *asura*-hood (VII. 65, 1, 2), are the guardians of *ṛita* (VII. 64, 2) and of the word (V. 62, 9), manifest creative activity by establishing heaven and earth (V. 62, 3) and setting the sun in heaven (V. 63, 7), possess steadfast and inviolable ordinances (V. 69, 1, 4), have spies and watch with unwinking eye the deeds of men (VII. 61, 3), take account of sin[2] (VII. 60, 1, 5, 9; 65, 3), manifest anger (VII. 62, 4), are the chastisers of *anṛita* (VII. 60, 5; 61, 5), strengthen and cherish *ṛita* (V. 65, 2; 67, 4), are observers of *ṛita, i.e.* 'order-loving' (*ṛitāvānā* VII. 62, 3), are pure-minded (*pūtadakṣasā* V. 66, 4), are gracious and merciful (V. 70, 1; VII. 60, 10), are wise (V, 63, 7) and givers of wisdom (VII. 60, 6, 7), are uniters of people (V. 65, 6; 72, 2) and upholders of mankind (V. 67, 2), wield occult power (māyā V. 63, 3, 4) and through it effect magic transformations of the sky (V. 63, 4, 6), send forth the rain (V. 63, 1-3, VII. 65, 4), are lords of rivers (*sindhupati* VII, 64, 2), and together mount their car in the highest heaven (V. 62, 5, 7-8; 63, 1).

Hymn V. 63 emphasizes the rainy aspect of Mitra-Varuṇa and its connection with *māyā* 'occult power',

---

[1] With the exception possibly of *yātayajjana* 'uniting men', which however is really implicit in Varuṇa, if not actually predicated of him in I. 136, 3.

[2] Mitra-Varuṇa are *bhūripāśāv anṛitasya setū, i.e.* 'barriers, furnished with many fetters, against falsehood'. See Macdonell, VM. 26. It is worthy of note that the group of Vasiṣṭha hymns to Mitra-Varuṇa (VII. 60-66) contains references to sin, whereas the corresponding Atri group (V. 62-72) is devoid of such reference, at least explicitly.

containing also allusions to the Maruts or 'storm-winds' and Parjanya the deified 'rain-cloud'. It reminds one of V. 85, a hymn to Varuṇa already considered[1], and also of V. 83 a hymn addressed to Parjanya.

To Mitra-Varuṇa V. 63.

1. In highest heaven ye twain united mount your car,
Joint guardians of order, ye whose law is true;
What man here, Mitra-Varuṇa, is blessed of you,
To him from out the sky the rain with sweetness streams.

2. As joint imperial rulers govern ye the world,
O Mitra-Varuṇa, sunlike at the sacrifice;
The rain, your boon, we crave, and immortality,
The thunderers traverse the heaven and the earth.

3. Joint kings, strong bulls, and lords of heaven and earth are ye
O Mitra-Varuṇa, present and active everywhere;
With gleaming storm-clouds girt ye twain attend the roar,
And through the Asura's[2] magic power cause heaven to rain.

4. Your magic power, O Mitra-Varuṇa, in heaven resides;
The sun, a gleaming weapon, as a light, doth roam;
Him in the sky with cloud and rain ye do obscure;
The honied drops, Parjanya, then bestir themselves.

5. Their easy-running car the Maruts yoke for pomp,
Even as a hero, Mitra-Varuṇa, in battle strife;
The thunderers traverse the gleaming atmosphere;
Ye twain all ruling, sprinkle us with milk of heaven.

6. A voice, in truth, refreshing, gleaming, shattering,
Parjanya utters now, O Mitra-Varuṇa; [power;
The Maruts clothe themselves with clouds through magic
Cause ye the sky to rain, the red, the spotless one.

7. Through law and through the Asura's magic power ye guard
The ordinances, Mitra-Varuṇa, wise gods:
Through *ṛita,* holy order, rule ye all the world;
The sun in heaven ye stationed as a gleaming car.

Professor Leopold von Schrœder in a recently published work[3] seeks to find the seventh Āditya in Parjanya, which

[1] p. 136.

[2] The Asura mentioned here (vv. 3, 7) is either Dyāus or Parjanya. See Macdonell, VM. 24; Griffith on the passage; v. Bradke, *Dyāus Asura* 55, 60.

[3] *Arische Religion* 1914, pp. 408-423.

he regards as originally an epithet of Dyāus, and a parallel form of Dyāus and Varuṇa in their capacity as heavenly rain-givers. Whether this view be correct or not, the great hymn to Parjanya (V. 83) is worthy of insertion, because of its correspondence with similar utterances addressed to Varuṇa and Mitra-Varuṇa[1].

V. 83. *To Parjanya*[2]

1. Salute the mighty one with these thy praise-songs,
Parjanya laud, with reverence seek to win him.
The bull, the bellowing one, whose gifts enliven,
Places his seed in vegetation, germ-like.

2. The trees he shatters and he smites the Rakṣasas,
The whole world is afraid of the great-weaponed one.
Even the guiltless man before the strong one flees,
What time Parjanya thundering smites the evil-doers.

3. Like charioteer with whip his horses urging hard,
He maketh manifest his rainy messengers;
From far away arise the lion's thunderings,
What time Parjanya constitutes the rainy sky.

4. The mighty winds break forth, the lightnings flash and fly,
The growing plants shoot up, the heavens stream with rain;
For the whole world of being refreshment is produced,
What time Parjanya quickeneth the earth with seed.

5. Under whose law the broad earth bendeth lowly,
Under whose law hoofed creatures leap and gambol;
Under whose law the plant-forms grow diversely,
As such, Parjanya, grant us mighty shelter.

6. Bestow on us, ye Maruts, rain from heaven;
Pour forth the genial streams of the strong stallion.
Come hither with this thunder, O Parjanya,
Shedding the floods as Asura our father.

---

[1] See Ṛv. V. 85 and V. 63, pp. 136 and 140.

[2] If the word *Parjánya*, in spite of phonetic difficulties, proves finally to be identical with the name of the Lithuanian thunder-god *Perkúnas*, then it goes back to the IE. period. Possibly the phonetic difficulties may be removed by assuming with Grassmann and v. Schrœder a derivation from the root *parc* 'to fill, satisfy' *i. e. Parcanya*, this through the working of popular etymology having been turned into *Parjanya*, the rain-cloud which generates (*jan*) the plants. See v. Schrœder, AR. 422, n. 2.

7. Bellow and thunder thou, the germ deposit:
With wagon water-laden fly around us.
Draw well thy water-skin unloosened downward,
Let heights and valleys all alike be level.

8. Draw up the mighty vessel, pour it downward;
May the streams thus released flow forward rushing,
Moisten and drench with ghee the earth and heaven;
May there be found good drinking for the cattle.

9. When thou, Parjanya, bellowing,
And thund'ring smitest evil-doers,
This whole world, thereupon exults,
Yea everything upon the earth.

10. Rain thou hast shed, pray grant us its cessation;
Thou hast made passable the wildernesses.
Plant-life thou hast begotten for man's sustenance,
And from thy creatures hast received a praise-song.

This hymn reminds us vividly of Psalms 29 and 65, the thunder and rain Psalms of the Old Testament. As there, so here, as well as in V. 85 and 63, we have the revelation of deity in storm and rain. The imagery is theriomorphic. Parjanya is the bellowing bull of the sky[1]. Through the rain represented as his seed he quickens the earth and generates the plants providing food and drink for man and beast. The 'will' *(vrata)* of Parjanya governs all things within the sphere of his activity (v. 5). There is a distinct ethical element. With his weapon the lightning, Parjanya smites the demons and the evil-doers (vv. 2, 9), and causes the whole world to rejoice at the vindication of righteousness. So terrible is he that even the guiltless man flees before him. In v. 6 Parjanya receives the remarkable epithets 'asura' and 'father' — the Asura who is at the same time 'our father' — epithets which elsewhere are almost entirely confined to Dyāus and Varuṇa[2]. As regards ethical quality there is nothing in this hymn which might not have been addressed to Varuṇa[3].

---

[1] So Dyāus V. 58, 6.

[2] Father Asura in X. 124, 3 is probably Varuṇa. *Cf.* v. Schrœder AR. 319, n. 1 and 416; but see also Oldenberg, *Ṛigveda Noten,* 342-343.

[3] Hopkins RI. 102-104.

b) Common Characteristics of the Āditya-group.—Varuṇa stands out clear and distinct with sharply defined characteristics. Mitra his companion and double is in most matters simply the replica of Varuṇa. What is true of Mitra is true of all the other Ādityas in their relation to Varuṇa their head. They have little or no individuality or real personality. They indeed form a system with Varuṇa, revolving about him, as it were, like planets about a central sun. But in relation to Varuṇa they are little more than expressions of his divine nature, personified aspects of the same,—in short, little more than names of the great god. Thus Mitra and Aryaman explicate the social nature and laws of Varuṇa. Mitra, 'he of the compact', signifies that Varuṇa is a covenant-keeping god and demands that men should be like him in this respect. Aryaman 'the loyal', 'the true' with special reference to the marriage contract means that Varuṇa desires truth and loyalty in the marriage relation. Bhaga, 'he of bounty', and Aṁśa 'he of the due share' emphasize the bountiful and gracious character of Varuṇa who 'gives to all men liberally', and to every man his due. Dakṣa 'he of strength, cleverness, insight, will' emphasizes the creative purpose, power and skill of Varuṇa. In a word, if the Ādityas are 'in the aggregate sense gods of celestial light'[1], they are also, 'in the aggregate sense', gods of truth and righteousness, the creators and directors of an eternal and inviolable world-order, both physical and moral. Being observers of order' *ṛitāvānaḥ, i. e.* 'holy' themselves, they are able to say with one voice: "Be ye holy, for I am holy"[2]. With some slight abatement[3] the saying of Macdonell is true that "there is no hymn to Varuṇa (and the Ādityas) in which the prayer for forgiveness of guilt does not occur, as in the hymns to other deities the prayer

---

[1] Macdonell, VM. 44. *cf.* I John I. 5.

[2] I Peter, I. 16.

[3] See p. 139. n. 2. The Varuṇa hymn Ṛv. VIII. 41 has also no explicit ethical reference.

for worldly goods"[1]. Ethically then the Ādityas are the highest gods of the Vedic world. No myths are told of Varuṇa and the Ādityas.

c) Place of Aditi among the Ādityas.

Aditi[2] is clearly an abstract goddess, 'she of bondless freedom'[3], hence a personified idea. The Ādityas are represented as the sons of Aditi, sons of her who is the expression and embodiment of freedom from the bonds of sin and suffering. Roth conjectured that Aditi herself is the seventh or last Āditya[4]. Better is it to consider her the mother — the common nature[5] — that binds all of the Ādityas into a unity. In addition to motherhood, Aditi's most basic function is to free from sin. In I. 24, 15 the prayer is to be guiltless *(anāgas)* before Aditi. She is besought to release her worshipper like a thief that is tied (*baddha* VIII. 67, 14). The emphasis in the case of Aditi, as well as in that of her sons, is on the ethical. Aditi is represented as the holy mother of holy sons. But, as we have seen, Aditi herself is an abstraction, a purely Indian goddess, the product of reflection, historically younger than most of her sons. What does this mean except that under the figure of a mother a common nature or essence is postulated for the Āditya-group. The Ādityas as brothers or parallel forms express each the common nature of the whole group, and that is the quality of guiltlessness and the capacity to make even sinful men guiltless.

---

[1] VM. 27, *cf.* Roth, *Ueber die höchsten Götter der arischen Völker,* ZDMG. VI. 72.

[2] From *dā* to bind, *diti* 'binding', *a-diti* 'unbinding'. Āditya is a metronymic formation from aditi, meaning 'son of aditi'. The expression *aditeḥ putrāḥ* may have meant in the pre-Vedic period simply 'sons of freedom', just as *sahasaḥ putrāḥ* means 'sons of strength'. We may compare the Hebraic expressions 'sons of Belial', and 'sons of thunder'. Aditi being feminine and described as having a son would easily become personified as a mother.

[3] So Oldenberg, RV. 203-207; Macdonell, VM. 122; v. Schrœder, AR. 295-407.

[4] ZDMG. VI. 76.

[5] In VII. 51, 1 the nature of Aditi *(aditiva)* is defined as guiltlessness *(anāgāstva)*.

As an abstraction from the Ādityas, Aditi is not only ethical, but also luminous. She is asked for light (IV. 25, 3), her imperishable light is celebrated (VII. 82, 10), and Dawn is called 'the face of Aditi' (I. 113, 19). This is the aspect of Aditi which Hillebrandt makes central — Aditi as the light of day in its boundlessness and imperishability[1]. In X. 63, 2 occurs the expression *dyāur aditi* 'Aditi the sky' or 'boundless sky'. On the basis of this and similar expressions Max Müller[2] thought of Aditi as the unlimited expanse of space visible to the eye, and Roth[3] as the boundlessness of the sky as opposed to the finite earth. In I. 72, 9 Aditi seems to be identified with the earth[4]. This is the view of Pischel[5] following the *Naighaṇṭuka.* The earth for Pischel is 'the inexhaustibly creative and generous one'. In a late passage (I. 89, 10) Aditi stands for universal nature in a Pantheistic sense. These various cosmological and mystical extensions of the meaning of Aditi are made possible by applying the idea of 'boundlessness', 'lack of limitation' to different aspects of nature[6], such as heaven, earth and the totality of existence. Such speculations based upon the etymology of Aditi are quite after the manner of Indian thought, and are a Ṛigvedic anticipation of the methods of the Brāhmaṇas.

d) Ādityas and Amesha Spentas. — Reference has already been made[7] to the similarity which holds between these two groups of gods. The points of resemblance have been impressively drawn by Oldenberg[8]. Ahura Mazda

---

[1] VM. III. 106-108.

[2] SBE. 32, 241.

[3] PW.

[4] *Pṛithivī ....mātā.... aditiḥ,* i. e. 'boundless mother Earth' or 'spacious Mother Aditi'.

[5] VS. II. 86.

[6] Max Müller defines Aditi as "what is free from bonds of any kind, whether of space or time, free from physical weakness, free from moral guilt". SBE. 32, 241.

[7] p. 25.

[8] RV. 29-30, and ZDMG. 50 (1896), 43-68.

stands at the head of the (seven)[1] Amesha Spentas, as Varuṇa at the head of the (seven) Ādityas. As Mazda is an Ahura, so Varuṇa is an Asura. Ahura Mazda is the lord of right (*asha*) and Varuṇa of order (*ṛita*), both bearing the same epithet, *ashavan ṛitāvan* 'righteous', 'holy'. In the Avesta Ahura and Mithra appear clearly conjoined[2], just as Mitra and Varuṇa in the Ṛv. In the Avesta the sun is 'the eye of Ahura Mazda' (Yasna I. 11); in the Veda, 'the eye of Mitra and Varuṇa' (VI. 51, 1, etc.). As Ahura is related to Spenta Mainyu 'Holy Spirit', so Varuṇa is related to Aditi, the holy mother whose nature is freedom and guiltlessness. The Amesha Spentas "are parts of the divine hypostasis, sharing with Mazda the name Ahura 'Lord'...... The Ahuras are not really separate from Mazda or subordinate to him; they seem to be essentially part of his own being, attributes of the Divine endowed with a vague measure of separate existence for the purpose of bringing out the truth for which they severally stand."[3] The same view is to be taken of the Ādityas in their relation to Varuṇa. "Alongside of Varuṇa the uniquely great Āditya, the other Ādityas appear as little more than expressions of his divine nature, personified aspects of the same—yes, hardly more than names of the one great God"[4]. Thus the Ādityas represent the 'holy of holies' of Vedic religion, even as the Amesha Spentas, 'Immortal Holy Ones', hold the same place in Avestan religion.

How are the similarities which hold between Ādityas and Amesha Spentas to be explained? Two such similar

---

[1] Neither the Ādityas nor the Amesha Spentas appear as a definitely closed group. The number seven is in each case comparatively late. What determined the selection of candidates for the place of honour next to Ahura Mazda and Varuṇa respectively was not the demands of a fixed number, but rather ethical and spiritual congruity.

[2] Yasna I. 11, *Ahuraeibya Mithraeibya* (Dvandva-compound).

[3] Moulton, EZ. IX. 97, 293-295.

[4] v. Schroeder, AR. 355.

lines of development almost certainly presuppose, as already stated[1], a common starting point in the undivided Indo-Iranian period. The Zoroastrian reform obscured many resemblances which must have existed by leaving not one name in common in the two lists. The seventh book of the Ṛv. is specially connected with the worship of Varuṇa, and it is possible that the priestly family of the Vasiṣṭhas, the authors of the seventh book, maintained some connection with the mother country Bactria[2] before and during the progress of the Zoroastrian reform. As the pure doctrine of Yahweh was mediated through a small group of Hebrew prophets, so may it have been with the high doctrine of Varuṇa and the Ādityas. The real ethical and spiritual earnestness connected with the worship of Varuṇa, the 'holy' god, was probably displayed only in a limited quarter and among a select few. It may be that these 'select few' continued in contact with their 'separated brethren' across the mountains, both giving and receiving spiritual inspiration. It is even possible that some of the stimulus toward the Zoroastrian reform came from India, or *vice versa.*

e) Semitic Influence possibly to be recognized in the Ādityas and Amesha Spentas. This hypothesis was brought forward by Oldenberg[3] to account for three things: (1) the sevenfold number of the Ādityas and Amesha Spentas, (2) the implications involved in the close association of Mitra (assumed to be a sun-god) with Varuṇa (hence taken to be a moon-god) and with five other Ādityas (hence taken to be the five planets), and (3) especially the appearance of such exalted ethical deities as Ahura Mazda and Varuṇa in the Aryan world. To account for these things Oldenberg assumed that there was a borrowing of seven planetary gods from the Semitic (or Accado-Sumerian) world, and that of these the moon-god

[1] p. 25.

[2] From Peshāwar to Bālkh it is less than 400 miles as the crow flies.

[3] RV. 185-195; ZDMG. 50 (1896), 43-68.

(Varuṇa) was the bearer of the noble ethical qualities of the later Ahura Mazda and Varuṇa, since there was an earlier ethical development in the Semitic than in the Indo-European world. It may be admitted at once that the discovery of the names of Mitra and Varuṇa on the Boghaz-kōi tablets counts to some extent in favour of Oldenberg's view. So also does the highly probable Semitic origin of the later Avestan goddess *Ardvī Sūra Anahita*[1]. Babylon too was probably responsible for fixing the Amshaspands as seven—a secondary trait—in the time of the later Avesta; and Babylon, the teacher of astronomy to the nations, knew of the seven heavenly bodies, sun, moon, and five planets, possibly the origin of the sacred number seven.

It is true also that the Babylonian moon-god *Nannar-Sin* is described in language which reminds us strongly of the Varuṇa hymns[2]. He is a 'merciful one' ......whose 'strong command produces right and proclaims justice to mankind' ...... a 'king of kings', whose 'sovereignty is in heaven and on earth'[3]. It must be admitted, too, that in the development of any god it is not the original physical substratum (whether moon or what not) that is of importance, but rather the degree in which the god represents the highest ethical ideals and brings under his authority all departments of nature and of life. But all due admissions having been made, what is the result? The sevenfold number of the Ādityas and Amesha Spentas is apparently not primary, as is required by Oldenberg's hypothesis, but secondary and late. So is the sun-nature of Mitra, which therefore cannot serve to prove that Varuṇa was originally the moon. The only question that remains is this: May there not have been an influence, if

---

[1] *Cf.* Strabo 15, 3, 15; Carnoy, *Iranian Views of Origins*, JAOS. 36 (1917), pp. 301-303; Moulton EZ. 238 ff.

[2] Jastrow, RBA. 303 ff; Oldenberg, ZDMG. 50, p. 67; Carnoy IVO. in JAOS. 36 pp. 307 ff.; Griswold, GVR. 28.

[3] Jastrow, RBA. 303 ff.

not direct, at least indirect, subtle, and almost telepathic [1], over the religious thinking of the undivided Indo-Iranian people in Bactria on the part of the culturally and religiously more developed Babylonians? The Indo-Iranians themselves had something on which to build, the lofty conception of Dyāus as Father and Lord, which had come down to them from the time of the undivided IE. period, and the great ethical conception of *Asha-ṛita* 'order, righteousness, truth'. It may be that these ideas were fructified [2] and helped to come more speedily and fully to fruition through the influence of Babylonia [3]. The hypothesis of Professor Oldenberg has rendered a service in emphasizing the unique significance of Varuṇa and the Ādityas in the religion of the Ṛigveda.

---

[1] Compare Renan *Vie de Jesus*, Eng. trans. by C. E. Wilbour, N. Y. 1868, p. 65: "The delicate and *clairvoyant* Virgil seems to respond, as by a secret echo, to the second Isaiah".

[2] "The admirable conception of the *ṛita* is probably superior to all that is found in Babylonian religion and philosophy, and gives proof of an exalted mentality among the Indo-Iranians. *This does not, however, preclude the fecundation of Aryan thought on this point by the contact with their neighbours at a very early period*". Carnoy, IVO. in JAOS. 36, p. 308.

[3] The influence postulated is of the subtle, telepathic sort that made the period 600-400 B. C. so notable in the religious and ethical history of the world. For example, it was the period of Jeremiah, Ezekiel and Second Isaiah 600-500, Confucius 551-478, Buddha 560-477, Socrates 469-399, possibly too of Zoroaster 660-583 B. C.

Even direct intercourse between Babylonia and Bactria during the period of the Indo-Iranian unity (B. C. 2500-1500 circa) must be admitted as possible. During all that period Babylonia was in close touch with Egypt. If as the crow flies, it is about 800 miles from the Euphrates to the Nile, it is only about 1200 Miles from the Euphrates to the Oxus. This bears upon the possibility of a Babylonian origin for the sacred number seven in both Veda and Avesta. Keith (*Numbers, Aryan,* ERE. IX) on the basis of all the evidence declares that 'three and nine are Aryan numbers', the implication being that seven is possibly Semitic, since it is prominent in Babylonian and Hebrew. Among all the IE. branches, seven as a sacred number is apparently found, apart from Christian influence, only in Iranian and Indian, *i. e.* in the Avesta and Veda. Bactria was near enough to Babylonia and the Indo-Irānian period was early enough for such a loan of the number seven to be made in connection doubtless with trade. This view becomes even more plausible, if we hold that the route by which the Aryan clans travelled eastward to Bactria and India lay across the upper Euphrates and Tigris.

CHAPTER VI.

AGNI THE PRIESTLY GOD.

1. INTRODUCTORY.—The Ṛigveda recognises a threefold division of the universe into heaven, mid-air and earth, in connection with each of which a form of fire is found. The altar-fire on earth, the lightning in mid-air, and the sun in heaven, are the same in nature, but differ in location, function and attendant circumstances. This is the earliest Indian triad, the centre of much mystical speculation. Thus Agni is threefold (I. 95, 3; IV. 1, 7)[1] for thus the devas made him to be (X. 88, 10), has three heads (I. 146, 1), three stations, tongues, bodies (III. 20, 2), three dwellings (VIII. 39, 8) and three kindlings (III. 2, 9)[2]. On the basis of the threefold classification in I. 139, 11 of the 33 gods into eleven each for sky, earth and aerial waters, together with the three forms of Agni as mentioned above, there existed a very early view quoted by Yāska, according to which the three groups of eleven deities reduce respectively to *Agni* on earth, *Vāyu* or *Indra* in air and *Sūrya* in heaven. A possible proof-text for the identification of the intermediate form of Agni with lightning is found in I. 164, 1, according to which the heavenly Agni (=the sun) has two brothers, of whom 'the middlemost is lightning' *(aśna)* and

---

[1] Threefold are those, the highest, true, and lovely,
The births of this god Agni. Close enveloped
Within the infinite has he come hither,
The shining, gleaming and resplendent Aryan. IV. 1, 7.

[2] As the three stations and dwellings of Agni are probably earth, mid-āir and sky, so his three heads, kindlings and tongues probably represent his three forms, altar-fire, lightning and sun. This triad of Vedic Agnis doubtless lies at the basis of the three later ritualistic fires, *gārhapatya, āhavanīya* and *dakṣiṇāgni*. But in view of such texts as II. 36, 4 'Sit down in the three yonis', and V. 11, 2 'Men have kindled Agni in his threefold seat', it is possible that the three ritualistic fires may be Ṛigvedic.

the other is 'butter-backed' (the altar-fire)[1]. But in VIII. 18, 9 the three are represented as Agni, Sūrya and Vāta 'wind', the same being also implied in I. 164, 44. The ambiguity in the Ṛigvedic texts between the meanings 'lightning' and 'wind, explains the view referred to by Yāska that the regent of the air is 'Vāyu or Indra'.

Agni is celebrated in about 200 hymns, being next to Indra the most prominent of the Vedic gods. The Agni-hymns stand at the beginning of each of the 'family-books' (II-VII) and every one of the ten books of the Ṛv. except two, begins with a hymn to Agni. The cult of fire has been maintained in India down to the present time — 3000 years at least. Since the name of the god is also the name of the thing, Agni 'fire' is a thoroughly transparent Sondergott — 'he of the fire'. Hence in contrast with Varuṇa and Indra Agni's personification is very rudimentary, the process being constantly arrested by the fact that his nature as fire is so obvious. Thus Agni is called butter-backed, butter-faced, butter-haired, etc., with reference to the oblations of ghee which he receives, and flame-haired, burning-jawed, thousand-eyed, thousand-horned, etc., with reference to his flames[2]. For further illustrations of this compare the following:

2. Seizing his own food for himself, th' unaging one,
Agni stands greedy mid the brushwood, full of thirst;
When ghee-besprinkled shines his back like racer swift,
Like heaven's exalted ridge he thundering doth roar.

4. Wind-driven, with the sickle, Agni ladle-fed
Spreads lightly through the brushwood with his mighty roar;
When, bull-like, thirstily thou rushest on the sticks,
Black is thy course; unaging god with fiery waves.

---

[1] So Ludwig and Macdonell. Hillebrandt (VM. 2. 128) and Geldner (Glossar) take *aśna* in the sense of 'eater' or 'hungry'. Since it is clear that Vāyu 'wind' is one of the three in I. 164, 44, it is reasonable to look for Vāyu or Vāta in I. 164, 1. *cf*. X. 158, 1.

[2] I. 58, 5; 79, 12; III. 1, 18; V. 4, 3; VIII. 49, 2. See Macdonell VM. 88-89.

5. Fire-jawed, wind-driven, there blazes down upon the wood
Agni, like a strong bull that rushes on the herd,
Mounting the everlasting air with streaming light, —
Then both things fixed and moving fear the winged one.

I. 58, 2, 4, 5.

In these stanzas Agni is little more than 'an assortment of fire-qualities' linked together by a slight measure of personification. At any rate, the poet is very conscious of the fiery nature of Agni.

2. THE PREHISTORIC AGNI.—Agni 'fire' is the Latin *ignis* and the Lithuanian *ugni*. Hence the word comes down from the undivided IE. period. During the long cold winters of their northern home the hearth-fire must have been the centre of the domestic life of the IE. clans, and as such must have been a place connected with religious rites. It is highly probable that the hearth-fire itself received offerings in connection with the custom of making gifts to the gods in fire[1]. But the *Sondergott* 'fire' in that early period was probably little more than the name of an element at once friendly and terrible, and as such surrounded with a halo of mystery[2]. The special sanctity of the house-fire was inherited by the Iranians from Indo-European antiquity[3].

There are many points of contact between Agni and Ātar[4], *e.g.* Agni (Ṛv. I. 26, 10) and Ātar (Yasna 2, 12, etc.) are both adored together *with all fires*. Ātar is the son of Ahura Mazda, and Agni of Dyāus. Corresponding to the three Vedic fires there are in the Avesta probably a house-fire, a village-fire and a community-fire[5]. As Agni is called 'house-lord' in the Ṛv. so Ātar is called 'the

---

[1] Oldenberg, RV. 103.

[2] The wide diversity of the IE. names for fire, such as Skt. *Agni*, Lat. *ignis*, Lith. *ugni*; Gr. pūr, Eng. fire; Gr. *Hestia*, Lat. *Vesta*; Iran. *Ātar*, *cf.* Lat. atrium, the room containing the hearth; Lat. *tepor*, Sk. *tapas*, etc., shows that there was no catholic name for fire-god in the IE. period.

[3] Moulton, Art. *Iranians* in ERE.

[4] Avestan word for fire.

[5] See Yasna 62, 5, and Spiegel, AP. 152.

house-lord of all houses' in the Avesta (Yasna 17, 11). It is clear that there was a developed fire-ritual in the period of Indo-Iranian unity, out of which sprang the worship of both Agni and Ātar in later times[1]. The fact that Ātar was retained by the Zoroastrian reform shows that in the pre-Zoroastrian period it had no unworthy associations. It was simply the house-fire or hearth, and is to be compared with Hestia and Vesta[2]. In the later Avesta Ātar is sometimes reckoned as a *Yāzata* or angel (Yasna 17. 1-11) and sometimes as an Amesha Spenta or archangel (Yasna 1. 2). According to Yasna 62. 4 Ātar as Ahura Mazda's son is besought to give 'glory ......nourishment ....booty....understanding...virile power .... offspring'. We are reminded of similar statements in many of the hymns to Agni. For example:

Agni bestows the swift prize-winning racer,
Agni gives heroes famed, in duty steadfast;
Agni pervades the two great worlds, anointing,
Agni the fruitful wife makes teem with heroes. X. 80, 1.

As in the sun the rays are firmly centred
So in Vaiśvānara are placed all treasures;
Whether in mountains found, or plants, or waters,
Or in mankind, — thou art the king of all that. I. 59, 3.

Come to us, Agni, with thy gracious friendship,
With thy great blessings, great one, swiftly speeding;
Vouchsafe to us wealth plentiful victorious,
Our share make laudable and full of glory. III. 1, 19.

Here Agni is represented as a cosmic, generative force intimately connected with the origin and growth of plant and animal life. But the generative Agni is at the same time the economic Agni. If fire is the condition of the existence and growth of life, both vegetable and animal,

---

[1] "The history of religion practically includes only two genuine fire-gods—Agni of Hinduism and Ātar of Zoroastrianism". Crawley, Art. *Fire, Fire-gods* in ERE. VI. 28.

[2] Ātar is referred to seven times in the Gāthās, three times together with the spirit or thought of Zoroaster, quite as in Matt. III. 11 the Holy Ghost is associated with fire.

then fire may also be regarded as the cause of food, wealth and prosperity, as it actually is regarded in the stanzas quoted above.

The two most primitive aspects of Agni are undoubtedly his 'domestic' *(damūnas)* character as 'house-lord' *(gṛiha-pati)*, and his function as a dispeller of darkness, evil spirits and hostile magic. The Ṛv. offers abundant illustrations of both points:

a) Agni's domestic character as his first primitive trait:

Who o'er the Five Tribes bearing sway
Hast set him down in every home,
Sage, youthful, *master of the house.* VII. 15, 2.

Doing his work he dwells in earthly houses,
Though god he wins the fellowship of mortals. IV. 1, 9.
As god *domestic* thou hast settled mortals. III. 1, 7.

Thus, as Macdonell says, Agni's "association with the dwellings of men is peculiarly intimate"[1]. It is from this point of view that Agni is called by such names as kinsman, friend, father, brother, son and mother. For example:

As is a *father* to a son,
Agni be easy of access;
Stay with us for prosperity. I. 1, 9.
Thee, Agni, men do make their *father* through the rites,
A *brother* through sacrifice, O thou of shining form;
Thou dost become a *son* to him who worships thee,
As a kind *friend* thou dost protect from all attack. II. 1, 9.

These stanzas were written from the point of view of the developed sacrificial system, but they doubtless presuppose a more primitive condition. As Macdonell says, "such terms seem to point to an older order of things, when Agni was less sacrificial and, as the centre of domestic life, produced an intimate relation such as is not easily found in the worship of other gods"[2]. This characteristic of Agni naturally connects him more closely than any other god with the past. In him is perpetuated,

[1] VM. 95.

[2] VM. 96; *cf.* Oldenberg, RV. 132.

as it were, the usage of the fathers[1]. Thus there is mentioned an Agni of Bharata, Devavata, Trasadasyu, Divodāsa and Vadhryaśva[2]. Agni is called an Aṅgiras (I. 1, 6), and he is besought to respond to his worshippers as he did to Manus, Yayāti and Aṅgiras in the days of old (I. 31, 17).

b) The second primitive trait of Agni is his character as a dispeller of darkness, night-foes, hostile magic, demons and illness.

First, then, Agni's function in dispelling darkness:

Over against the Dawns resplendent Agni
Has been awakened, priest and guide of sages;
Of ample splendour, by the pious kindled,
The carrier-god throws back *the gates of darkness.* III. 5, 1.

Shepherd of clans is he; *by his night-shining rays*
All the two-footed and four-footed creatures walk;
The great bright splendour of the dawn art thou.
In thine own friendship, Agni, may we live unharmed. I. 94, 5.

O Agni god, whose wealth is light,
Beaming with radiance like the sun
Boldly *thou dost the darkness slay.* VIII. 43, 32.

Swallowed by darkness was the world and hidden;
At Agni's birth the light became apparent. X. 88, 2.

Secondly, Agni repels enemies. The dispelling of darkness is closely connected with the discomfiture of enemies, for undoubtedly the Vedic Aryans experienced night-attacks from their foes. The opportune rising of the sun would often mean the flight of the enemy.

Through fear of thee the clans of dusky colour
Have fled at random leaving their possessions;
When thou, fierce-glowing Agni, stronghold-piercing,
Hast shone, Vaiśvānara, on behalf of Pūru. VII. 5, 3.

Thirdly, Agni wards off hostile magic. Anthropological researches have abundantly shown the large place that magic holds in the life of primitive man.

---

[1] Macdonell, VM. 96; Hillebrandt, VM. II. 57.

[2] Ṛv. II. 7, 1; III. 23, 3; VIII. 19, 32; 92, 2; X. 69, 1.

Should any one bring on us sin, transgression[1],
On him of evil spells inflict the evil;
Destroy, O knowing one, such imprecation,
O Agni, of the man that harms by falsehood. V. 3, 7.

Ghee-offered and resplendent one,
Burn thou against the mischievous,
Yea, Agni, 'gainst the sorcerers. I. 12, 5.

May our curse overcome the evil-minded ones.
. . . .
With thy dread weapons beat away all those who curse,
Devourers, evil-minded, be they far or near. I. 94, 8[b], 9[a-b].

These passages indicate a strong belief in the potency of the magic spell. A conflict between two hostile tribes was often a conflict between sorcerers using magic[1]. From the point of view of the Vedic hymns the magic of their enemies was the magic of 'evil-minded sorcerers', and so belonged to the works of darkness.

Fourthly, Agni destroys the demons or puts them to flight. The belief in demons and goblins of the night is an article of the primitive faith of mankind—a belief vastly antedating the composition of the Vedic hymns. The distinction between sorcerer and demon is not always clear.

Agni expels the Rakṣasas,
God of clear radiance, deathless one,
Bright, cleansing, worthy to be praised.
Agni protect us from distress,
With hottest flames, unaging god,
Burn thou against our enemies. VII. 15, 10, 13.

The raksas-slaying racer I besprinkle,
Mitra approach for most capacious shelter;
Kindled and sharpened by the potent off'rings
May Agni guard us day and night from mischief.

Kindled, with flame attack the *Yatudhanas*.
O Jātavedas, armed with metal grinders;

[1] Just as in the O. T. Balak hired Balaam to curse the children of Israel, Numbers XXII-XXIV.

With fiery tongue assault the *Mūradevas*,
Rend, place within thy mouth the raw-flesh eaters.

Annihilate with heat the *Yātudhanas*,
With fiery force annihilate the *Raksas:*
Annihilate with flame the *Mūradevas*,
Burning against the life-destroying monsters[1]. X. 87, 1, 2, 14.

The modern man has no difficulty in understanding the primitive man's tendency to associate demons and ghosts with darkness. With the breaking of the day how quickly the mind-created goblins of the night take themselves off.

Fifthly, Agni banishes illness, or perhaps more strictly illness-demons, for this is the primitive point of view. As Macdonell[2] says, "evils closely connected with human life, such as disease proceed from lesser demons". The hygienic value of fire, warmth and light must have impressed primitive man.

To the sage Agni render praise,
Him of true rules in sacrifice,
God, banisher of illnesses. I. 12, 7.

The last line might just as well be translated: 'God, banisher of illness-fiends'.

Thus far we have considered the aspects of fire which would naturally impress primitive man — the function of the fire on the hearth as the centre of domestic life, its function as a dispeller of darkness, demons and hostile magic, and its function as a cosmic force vitally connected with the growth of animal and vegetable life, and so the cause of food, wealth and prosperity. These aspects of fire are all most primitive, although they are often found side by side with more modern conceptions.

3. The Sacrificial Agni. — The discovery of fire as a means of preparing food was one of the most epoch-

[1] According to Oldenberg (RV. 336-340) a distinction must be drawn between the sacrificial fire and the magic fire. The fire which is besought to expel or destroy demons belongs to the latter category.

[2] VM. 18.

making experiences of mankind. It probably came about accidentally through forest-fires caused by lightning. We may assume that wild animals would be killed by the fire and roasted[1]. Primitive man always hungry would thus get his first taste of roasted flesh, and at the same time it would be easy for him to snatch a fagot from the burning forest, and keep it alive. In some such way as this the great discovery was made. Cooked food was seen to be more palatable than uncooked food. And so food prepared by fire would be set before a guest, in order to do him honour. After the same analogy the gods being conceived anthropomorphically as the divine guests of men would be entertained and fed with fire-prepared food. Such is undoubtedly the psychological origin of the chief sacrificial use of fire[2], stated very roughly.

A distinction must be drawn between fire-offerings and fireless offerings. Fire offerings are those which, whether prepared by fire or not, are consumed in fire and go up in flame and smoke to the gods. Fireless offerings, on the other hand, are those that, whether consisting of cooked or uncooked food, are not consumed in fire, but are laid out for the gods to eat. Of the two types of offerings the fireless variety would seem to be the more primitive. The well-known passage in Herodotus (I. 132) describes a Persian sacrifice of the fireless sort, according to which the dismembered parts of the animal victim, after being seethed, are laid out on a carpet of the tenderest herbage[3]. This carpet of grass corresponds to the Vedic barhis[4], the

---

[1] See Charles Lamb's *Dissertation upon Roast Pig* in the "Essays of Elia.".

[2] Oldenberg (RV. 347) refers to two early uses of fire, which may stand in close connection with the sacrificial fire, namely the fire that scares away demons, and the fire in which the remnants of the sacrifice as possibly dangerous to men (*cf*. Lev. VII. 15), are consumed.

[3] Moulton, EZ. 394; Oldenberg, RV. 341-347; Schrader, ERE. II. 41-42.

[4] The tender grass mentioned by Herodotus reminds us of the description of *barhis* as 'soft as wool', ūrṇamradāḥ, Ṛv. V. 5, 4. *cf*. Avestan *barezish*, 'mat', 'bolster'. Note that the *barhis* is so closely connected with the gods at their

sacred 'strew' or 'litter' on which the gods are invited to sit and partake of the sacrificial food. Herodotus tells us that the old Persians had no fire-altar in connection with 'the carpet of herbage'. In the Ṛv., however, the juxtaposition of *barhis* 'litter' and *vedi* 'altar', would seem to be an indication at once of the primitive method of fireless sacrifice and of the later innovation of the fire-altar[1]. Both the old and the new, as so often seen in Indian practice, are thus brought together, the *barhis* which requires the gods to come to earth for their feast, and the *vedi* which carries in flame and smoke the sacrifice to heaven. As illustrating the two points of view there may be quoted the two following stanzas of I. 1: —

Agni is worthy to be praised
By former Ṛishis and by new;
May he the devas hither bring. I. 1, 2.

That is, to sit on the *barhis* and partake of the food (originally laid out on it). And for the second point of view:

Agni, the rite and sacrificc
Which thou encirclest on all sides,
That to the devas truly goes. I. 1, 4.

That is, the sacrifice, when encircled by fire and so consumed, goes to the gods in heaven.

Under the head of Fire as a sacrificial element we may roughly classify the Vedic material as follows: —

a) Agni dwells in the *vedi* or fire-pit, where he (or it) is kindled at dawn (the morning sacrifice).

To th' altar-seated fair-established, brilliant (god),
To Agni proffer drink-like the encircling ghee. I. 140, 1.

---

earthly feasts and with Agni in connection with the altar-fire that it receives apotheosis and in the Āprī hymns is adored as a form of Agni. According to Taitt. Saṁh. VI. 3, 8, 3, so holy is the barhis that the offering is not lost, *i. e.* defiled by falling upon it.

[1] Oldenberg, RV. 343.

Over against the Dawns resplendent Agni
Has been awakened, priest and guide of sages,
Of ample splendour, by the pious kindled. III. 5, 1.

Agni arrayed in many-coloured garments
Is seated *in the navel* of the broad earth,
Born ruddy in the place of sacrifices. X. 1, 6.

As such, O Agni, be to us the nearest,
For help the closest, *while this dawn is breaking*. IV. 1, 5.

Agni's abode being in the form of a round fire-pit is called 'the navel of the earth'. The round altar of earth corresponds to the round sun in the sky[1].

Navel of earth and head of heaven is Agni. I. 59, 2.

b) Agni is strengthened with fuel, ghee and soma for his various tasks.

The lofty one has by receiving fuel
Propped up the sky, the highest light becoming. III. 5, 10.
Men with oblations magnify thee ever,
Agni the agile[2] one, *to act as envoy*. VII. 11, 2.

O Agni, magnified with ghee,
On lightest car *bring near the gods;*
Thou art a hotar Manus-made. I. 13, 4.

This is thy goodness that when kindled in thy house,
And soma-fed, thou dost awake, most merciful.
Treasure and wealth thou givest to thy worshipper;
In thine own friendship, Agni, may we live unharmed. I. 94, 14.

Thus by means of fuel, ghee, etc. Agni is made to blaze up fiercely, and so is enabled to do his work.

c) Agni as the sacrificial fire is the mediator and messenger between gods men.

Through thee who art their mouth the guileless deathless gods
All eat the off'ring which is sacrificed to them. II. 1, 14.
However constantly to all
The gods we offer, yet in thee
Alone the sacrifice is made. I. 26, 6.

---

[1] *Cf.* Hillebrandt, VM. II. 135: The arrangement of the place of sacrifice is a copy of the heavenly world.

[2] *ajira* 'agile' from *aj* to drive (Lat. ago, Gr. ἄγω) a possible etymology of *agni* as the 'agile' or 'nimble' element.

To kindle thee may we be able; speed our prayers;
In thee the gods do eat the offered sacrifice. I. 94, 3.
Agni, the other fires are thine own branches,
In thee the immortals find exhilaration. I. 59, 1.
Splendour of sacrifice, great art thou; never
Without thee are the gods exhilarated.
With all the deathless ones come on thy chariot,
Sit down here, Agni, as the first of hotars. VII. 11, 1.

The strength-begotten deathless hotar downward smites[1],
What time Vivasvant's messenger he has become;
By straightest paths the atmosphere he has traversed,
Invites the gods in heaven by sacrificial food. I. 58, 1.

To eat th' oblation, bring the devas, Agni;
With Indra leading let them here be joyful.
In heaven among the gods place this our off'ring:
Ye gods, protect us evermore with blessings. VII. 11, 5.

O Agni, mayest thou announce
Among the gods this newest song
Of ours, a potent *gāyatra*. I. 27, 4.

As god domestic thou hast settled mortals;
As charioteer, the gods directly seekest. III. 1, 17.
Delight the yearning gods and bring them, youngest,
Knowing right times, O lord of times and seasons. X. 2, 1.

Awaken thou the yearning ones,
What time as envoy thou dost go;
Sit with the devas on the straw. I. 12, 4.

By Agni Agni kindled is,
The sage, house-master, youthful god,
Oblation-bearing, spoon-mouthed one. I. 12, 6.

Agni doth send the sacrifice to heaven. X. 80, 4.
Ḥotar is he; he knows the work
Of messenger; goes to and fro
'Twixt heaven and earth, knows heaven's ascent. IV. 8, 4.

Bring forth a praise-song for the mighty Agni,
For him, the manager of earth and heaven. VII. 5, 1.

Navel of earth and head of heaven is Agni,
He has become the steward of the two worlds. I. 59. 2.

Thee, Agni god, the gods have ever set to work
Unanimously as their representative. IV. 1, 1.

---

[1] Or perhaps better *'never tires'*, after Oldenberg's conjectural emendation. See SBE. XLVI. 46.

Under this head an unusually large number of texts are cited, since the doctrine of Agni as sacrificial mediator is the central doctrine of the sacrificial fire. In and through Agni men offer sacrifice to the gods (I. 26, 6) and in and through Agni (II. 1, 14; I. 94, 3) the gods eat the sacrifice and are exhilarated (VII. 11, 1, 5). Thus Agni is the mouth of the gods (II. 1, 14). Ghee as a drink of the gods is poured into the fire with a spoon and so Agni is called spoon-mouthed[1]. Then he mounts up toward heaven, bearing in flame and smoke the oblation to the gods (I. 12, 6; VII, 11, 5; VIII. 80, 4); and the flames of Agni crackle and roar, calling out to the gods, as it were, to come to the sacrifice (I. 58, 1; VII. 11, 1, 5). Agni as the roaring fire awakens the gods (I. 12, 4), and perhaps from this point of view he is called a *hotar* (VII. 11, 1, etc.) or *invoking*[2] priest. Agni announces among the gods not only sacrifices, but also hymns (I. 27, 4). Agni has a golden chariot[3] with which he traverses the mid-air by straightest paths (I. 58, 1), seeks the gods directly (III. 1, 17), and brings them on lightest car to the sacrifice (I. 13, 4). The twofold direction of Agni's car, heavenward and earthward, may have been suggested by the upward movement of the altar-flame and the downward movement of the lightning, when it falls to the earth. Agni rising in flame from the altar heavenward and falling in the form of lightning from heaven earthward is the mediator between the two worlds. On earth Agni is the sacrificial fire on the altar, the 'navel' or centre of earth; in heaven he is the sun as well as lightning. Thus Agni as the sacrificial representative[4] of the gods belongs to both worlds, and as messenger

---

[1] *Juhvāsya*, I. 12, 6, 'whose mouth is a spoon', or more probably 'having a spoon in his mouth'.

[2] *Hū* 'to call', as well as *hu* 'to sacrifice'.

[3] IV. 1, 8. doubtless referring to the ruddy flame as it mounts heavenward.

[4] *Arati* IV. 1, 1; VII. 5, 1.

moves freely to and fro between them. His connection with the two worlds is thus emphasized[1].

4. AGNI'S HEAVENLY ORIGIN.—According to the Ṛv. both Agni and Soma, the sacrificial fire and the sacrificial drink, came down from heaven. Mātariśvan brought Agni from afar (III. 9, 5; VI. 8, 4). We have here in general the Vedic equivalent of the Greek myth of Prometheus. There is some difference of opinion as to whether Mātariśvan in the Ṛv. means lightning[2] or wind[3]. Wind is the usual meaning from the Atharvaveda onward. If, however, we recall that lightning and wind usually go together in a thunder-storm, there will be no difficulty in making Mātariśvan[4] to mean in the Ṛv. lightning accompanied by wind. The isolated texts[5] in which Mātariśvan is mentioned indicate sufficiently his fiery quality, but do not overlook altogether his windy nature[6]. We may regard Mātariśvan, then, as the lightning form of Agni with a windy character. We know that lightning is attended by wind, is to some extent guided by draughts of wind, and at any rate the swiftness of lightning is like that of the wind. The lightning element, which was primary at the beginning, finally dropped out leaving in the later Mātariśvan only a windy character, just as in the parallel case of Varuṇa nothing was left finally but the headship of pools. For the Vedic Aryan the lightning and wind of the thunder-storm were an indissoluble unity. The lightning was windy and the wind was bright and gleaming[7]. The original meaning of

---

[1] Ṛv. II. 6, 7; III. 1, 3; 3, 2; IV. 2, 3, etc.

[2] Macdonell, VM. 72.

[3] Hillebrandt, VM. II. 149-154.

[4] Lit.—'growing in his mother' the rain-cloud (Macdonell. VM., 72), hence probably a mythological synonym of *Apām Napāt* 'Son of the (heavenly) waters'.

[5] Only 27 in all.

[6] Thus when fashioned in his mother, he became 'the swift flight of wind', III. 29, 11; and Agni as a raging serpent in the air (lightning) is compared with the rushing wind I. 79, 1.

[7] In V. 87, 6 the Maruts are compared with fires.

the myth clearly is that fire was brought to earth by means of lightning (and wind)[1]. Agni, then, though as the deified altar-fire a god of earth, yet in origin is a *deva* 'a bright heavenly one', brought 'from afar'. The bringing down of Agni and Soma from heaven are the earliest instances of 'descents' in the history of Indian religion[2]. Agni's title as 'guest' may refer to the same circle of ideas.

5. AGNI AS THE GREAT HIGH PRIEST. — Since the sacrificial fire was the centre of the Vedic ritual, it was natural to ascribe to Agni priestly functions.

a) Agni is the divine counterpart of the earthly priesthood.

Thine, Agni, is the Hotar's, thine the Potar's task,
Thine, too, the Neṣṭar's; thou art Agnidh for the good;
Thine the Praśāṣṭar's office, thine Adhvaryu's too,
The Brahmán-priest art thou, House-master in our house.
II. 1, 2.

Agni I praise, domestic priest,
God, minister of sacrifice,
The Hotar, giver best of gifts. I. 1, 1.

Th' Adhvaryu art thou and the ancient Hotar priest,
Praśāṣṭar, Potar and by birth Purohita;
Knowing all priestly duties, thou dost give success.
In thine own friendship, Agni, may we live unharmed. I. 94, 6.

There was division of labour among the Vedic priests, their tasks being distributed among seven or eight different persons, not to mention the *Purohita* or 'domestic priest'. Agni knows and performs the functions of each priest. Thus Agni's priesthood is essential and architypal. Over against the many priesthoods of men there is the one divine priesthood of Fire, for through Agni alone men worship the gods. Thus Agni as the sacrificial element of fire was the great high priest of the Vedic period. This fact may

---

[1] This interpretation fits in well with the early view quoted by Yāska that the god of the middle region is Vāyu or Indra, *i. e.* wind or lightning.

[2] They introduce the idea of 'descents', such as are found in the *avatāras* of Viṣṇu in the form of animals and men.

help to account for the position of the Agni hymns in the Ṛv. collection. They stand first in the 'family books' and in general occupy the most prominent position in the whole collection. At the time when the Ṛik text was finally fixed (circa 600 B.C.), the priestly caste had gained the supremacy over the warrior caste. This condition of things may be symbolized by the fact that the hymns dedicated to the *priest* Agni are given a more prominent position than those ascribed to the *warrior* Indra. At any rate as Macdonell says, Agni's priesthood is the most salient feature of his character, he being the great priest as Indra is the great warrior[1].

b) Agni is the king of sacrificial rites:

In the abode of mortals has th' immortal,
The *king* sat down, performing acts of worship. III. 1, 18.
Lord of the mighty sacrifice is Agni,
Yea, lord of all oblations that are offered. VII. 11, 4.

He who at eve and dawn receives
Praise for his beauty, house by house,
Whose ordinance is inviolate. II. 8, 3.

King of the clans, the wonderful
Director of the rites,—I praise
This Agni; may he hear our call. VIII. 43, 24.

Thou who art *king* of holy rites,
Guardian of *ṛita*, shining one,
Increasing in thine own abode. I. 1, 8.

Delight the yearning gods and bring them, youngest,
Knowing right times, O lord of times and seasons. X. 2, 1.

O Agni, long-tailed[2] like a horse,
Thee let me greet adoringly,
The sovereign lord of sacred rites. I. 27, 1.

According to these specimen passages selected at random Agni is the king, superintendent and sovereign[3] of rites and sacrifices and of sacrificial times and seasons. He is the guardian of *ṛita* and his ordinance *(vrata)* is inviolate.

[1] VM. 97.

[2] The shifting flame is compared with a horse's tail.

[3] *Rājan, adhakṣa, samrājan.*

Agni as the sacrificial element *par excellence* and the archi-type of every human priesthood is the very embodiment of ritualistic order[1]. He possesses the priestly function and wields the priestly authority.

c) Agni, as the wise priest, is able to correct mis-takes in worship[2].

If ever we violate your regulations,
O ye sage gods, we who are poor in knowledge;
Wise Agni, then, corrects the matter wholly,
So as to give each god his proper season.

When, simple as they are, weak-minded mortals
Fail to bethink themselves of sacrificing,
Then may the hotar Agni, wise, discerning,
Worship the gods, best worshipper, in season. X. 2, 4-5.

Agni is the very embodiment of priestly wisdom. He knows all priestly duties (I. 94, 6) and is as wise as a sage[3]. Especially as the ritualistic god is Agni interested in the production of prayers and hymns. He is the deviser of brilliant speech (II. 9, 4), the first deviser of prayer (VI. 1, 1). As the master of every thought he promotes the worship-per's meditation (IV. 6, 1).

6. AGNI AS INTERCESSOR AND JUDGE.

In relation to sin Agni plays a part only second to that of Varuṇa and the Ādityas[4].

a) Agni is an all-seeing god. He has eyes (II. 2, 4, X. 21, 7), 100 eyes (I. 128, 3), 1000 eyes (X. 79, 5), with which to behold the deeds of men. Like Varuṇa, he has spies which he sends forth (IV. 4, 3). He knows accordingly the 'hidden part' (*apīcya* VIII. 39, 6) of men. He can

---

[1] Of the three strands of meaning in *ṛita* 'order, namely cosmic, ethical and ritualistic, the meaning ritualistic order is naturally prominent in connection with Agni.

[2] With Agni as the perfector of human worship compare Rom. VIII. 26-27, where the Holy Spirit is represented as helping our infirmity, himself making intercession for us, and so enabling us to offer acceptable worship.

[3] *Kavikratu* I. 1, 5.

[4] Oldenberg, RV. 201.

distinguish the wisdom and folly of mortals like straight and crooked backs of horses (IV. 2, 11). Thus Agni is the eye and guardian of mighty *ṛita*[1], and is to be identified with Varuṇa when the latter strives after *ṛita* (X. 8, 5)[2].

b) Agni takes account of sin and punishes it. He publishes the guilt of sinful men before Varuṇa and the Ādityas, nay, before all the gods (IV. 3, 5-8). He brings evil upon the man who utters evil spells, imprecations and falsehood (V. 3, 7) and consumes with his hottest flame those who violate the fundamental principles *(dhāma)* of Varuṇa and Mitra:

May Agni rich in wealth with flame most scorching,
Agni the sharp-toothed one, consume those people
Who break the laws by Varuṇa established,
The dear abiding rules of watchful Mitra.
Roaming about like girls that have no brothers,
Of evil ways like wives that trick their husbands,
Being unrighteous, lost to truth and goodness,
They for themselves have this deep place created[3]. IV. 5, 4-5.

c) Agni intercedes with Varuṇa for sinners and deprecates his wrath.

Therefore, O Agni, turn to brother Varuṇa,
The god who graciously accepts the sacrifice.
O Friend, to (Varuṇa) thy friend turn promptly thou,
Like a swift wheel, like two car-steeds in rapid course.
O Agni, *mercy* find for us with Varuṇa.
Knower of Varuṇa mayest thou, O Agni,
For us appease the god's fierce indignation.
Best agent of the gods, best sacrificer,
Flaming remove far from us every hatred.
As such, O Agni, be to us the nearest,
For help the closest, while this dawn is breaking;
Make Varuṇa go away by sacrificing;
As liberal one, have *mercy*, heed our prayer.
IV. 2, 1a-b, 3a-b, d, 4, 5.

---

[1] Certainly ethical order here as well as ritualistic.

[2] Is the common relation to *ṛita* on the part of both Varuṇa and Agni the basis of their identification in such passages as II. 1, 4; III. 5, 4; V. 3,1; VII. 12, 3?

[3] The grammatical uncertainties are not such as to affect the general sense. See Oldenberg, RVN. I. 270-271.

A very notable passage. Varuṇa is angry. He must be appeased. The one who can find mercy with Varuṇa and remove his anger is Agni. This he can do, because Varuṇa is his friend and brother. Agni the sacrificial god, shows his mercy[1] toward the sinful by appealing to the mercy of Varuṇa on their behalf. Thus Agni the priestly god fulfils the role of an intercessor.

d) Agni is besought to forgive whatever sin has been committed (VII. 93, 7), to pardon the sin which has been perpetrated through thoughtlessness by those who are only human (IV. 12, 4), to release from 'great guilt' and its penalty 'the prison of gods and mortals' (IV. 12, 5), to make men guiltless before Aditi (IV. 12, 4), to grant Diti and keep off Aditi (IV. 2, 11), to protect from Varuṇa's *dhūrti* (harmful purpose I. 128, 7), and to put away the wrath of the gods (IV. 48, 10).

In relation then to sin and its punishment or remission Agni who dwells in the homes of men is the counterpart of the heaven-dwelling Varuṇa[2].

7. Agni and Bṛihaspati.—Bṛihaspati[3] 'the lord of prayer' shares in the activities of both Agni and Indra, as the following hymn together with other passages indicates:

To Bṛihaspati IV. 50

1. The one who propped with might earth's ends asunder,
The charming tongued, three-seated, loudly roaring,
Him god Bṛihaspati the ancient Ṛishis
And sages pondering made their priestly leader[4];

2. They who with noisy rush, exhilarated,
For us, Bṛihaspati, stormed the extensive
Dappled, conspicuous, uninjured cattle;
Bṛihaspati, guard thou the kine recovered[5].

---

[1] The word 'mercy' *(mṛiḷika)* is the same in verses 3 and 5.

[2] Bergaigne, RV. III. 169-174; Oldenberg, RV. 201, 298-299.

[3] Alternative form *Brahmaṇaspati*, lit. 'lord of Brahman'.

[4] *i. e.* made their *purohita* (purodhā).

[5] For this very difficult stanza see Macdonell, VRS. 85-86; Oldenberg, *Noten* I. 305-306; Hillebrandt, LR. 59.

3. Bṛihaspati from farthest distance coming
The *Rita*-lovers have for thee been seated;
For thee the springs dug out or milked with press-stones
Of mead drip superabundance in all quarters.

4. Bṛihaspati, when first receiving being
From the great light that is in highest heaven,
With seven mouths, strong-born, with sevenfold radiance,
Dispersed with his vast roar the glooms of darkness.

5. He with his troop exultant, jubilating
Burst open with his roar th' enclosing *Vala;*
Bṛihaspati bellowing drove out the cattle,
That, red and lowing, sweeten the oblation.

6. Thus the strong sire of all gods would we worship
With sacrifices, homage and oblations;
Bṛihaspati, we would be lords of riches,
Begirt with children fair and warrior offspring.

7. That king, indeed, with power and might heroic
Doth meet and overcome all hostile forces,
Who tends and keeps Bṛihaspati well-nourished,
Honours and lauds him who receives first portion.

8. Truly he dwells well-set in his own mansion;
To him the sacred food yields ever plenty;
To him spontaneously bow down his subjects;
The king with whom the Brahman has precedence.

9. He irresistible obtains the riches
Of both his enemies and his own people;
The king who for the succour-needing Brahman
Secures relief and help, the gods assist him.

10. Drink ye the soma, Indra and Bṛihaspati,
Glad in this sacrifice, O ye of mighty wealth;
The invigorating drops shall enter both of you,
Bestow upon us riches linked with hero sons.

11. Bṛihaspati and Indra, make us prosper,
Let that benevolence of yours be with us;
Assist our prayers, stir plenteous bestowals,
Weaken hostilities of foe and rivals.

The points of contact between Bṛihaspati and Agni are numerous. Both are three-seated[1] and were born in the

[1] *triṣadhastha*, IV. 50, 1; V. 4, 8, referring either to heaven, mid-air and earth, or to the three sacrificial fires.

highest heaven (IV. 50, 4; VI. 8, 2); both are identified with Mātariśvan (III. 26, 2; III. 29, 11), Narāśaṁsa (I. 18, 9; III. 29, 11) and Aṅgiras (II. 23, 18; I. 1, 6); both are associated with the Aṅgirasas (X. 67, 2-3; IV. 3, 11), and are friends and allies of Indra (I. 18, 6; II. 23, 18; VI, 59, 2,); both are purohitas or 'family priests' (II. 49, 9: I. 1, 1), and *brahmāṇas* or 'praying priests' (X. 141, 3; II. 1, 2); both offer sacrifice (I. 139, 11; I. 45, 10) and inspire hymns (I. 18, 7; VI, 1, 1); both dispel darkness (IV. 50, 4; VIII. 43, 32), drive away disease (I. 18, 2; I. 12, 7), protect from evil charms (I. 18, 3; I. 12, 5), and destroy rakṣasas (II. 23, 14; X. 87, 2); both bear the title', 'son of strength' (I. 40, 2; III. 1, 8) and both are sages (II. 23, 1; I. 12, 6); each is like a father (VII. 97, 2; I. 1, 9), etc.

Not less closely related are Bṛihaspati and Indra. Like Indra, Bṛihaspati is associated with a band of singers[1] does exploits as soon as born, cleaving Vala, winning the kine, dispersing the darkness; is a warrior, drinks Soma, gives kine and horses; was generated by Tvaṣṭar[2]; wields the thunderbolt (*vajra*)[3], roars like a lion, bellows like a bull and thunders; shakes things unshaken, rent the forts of Śambara; has a bow and arrow; is a pathmaker, is called *maghavan*, and should be worshipped with faith[4].

It is not strange, then, that the opinion of scholars is divided between the two types of affinity pointed out above, Max Müller[5], Macdonell[6] and Keith (*Indian Mythology*

---

[1] Aṅgirasas belong to Bṛihaspati, Maruts to Indra. Hence both B. and I. bear the title *gaṇapati* 'lord of a host' (II. 23, 1: X. 112, 9). Note, however, that the companions of Bṛihaspati are once called 'boars' (*varāha* X. 67, 7), a name given elsewhere to Rudra (once I. 114, 5), and to the Maruts (once I. 88, 5), but not to the Aṅgirasas, unless in X. 67, 7. Bṛihaspati is, however, sometimes mentioned along with the Maruts (I. 40, 1-2) as Indra with the Aṅgirasas.

[2] As Indra's *vajra* was generated, I. 32, 2.

[3] Only once of Bṛihaspati (I. 40, 8) and once of the Maruts, VIII. 7, 32.

[4] Śraddhāmanas II. 26, 4. *cf*. II. 12, 5 for Indra as an object of faith.

[5] SBE. 32, 94.

[6] VM. 101-104.

45) regarding Bṛihaspati as a variety or 'parallel form' of Agni, while Weber and Hopkins[1] consider him to be a priestly abstraction of Indra. But Bṛihaspati may be approached from another angle. Recall the Indo-Iranian and Vedic constituents of worship, namely soma-drink, fire-offering and sacred utterance[2]. Corresponding to them are Soma, Agni and Bṛihaspati, the deified sacrificial 'drink', 'fire' and 'formula'. Soma and Agni (or Ātar) are Indo-Iranian, while Bṛihaspati looks like a purely Indian deity[3]. If Soma and fire are concrete, bráhman as the sacred formula (only heard) is intangible and abstract. Each received apotheosis, Soma and Agni as concrete deities and Bṛihaspati as an abstract god, 'the personification of the mighty power which lies at the heart of the *bráhman* or 'holy word', and manifests itself in the wonderful effects of the sacred formulas'[4]. This seems to be in general the view of Roth[5], Oldenberg[6] and Strauss[7].

The name of *Brahmaṇaspati* expresses his nature. He is the supreme king and generator of prayers (*bráhma*), assists holy thoughts (*dhiyaḥ*) and promotes their preparation, pronounces the formula (*mantra*) in which the gods take pleasure, places in the mouth of the earthly priest an effective word (*vāc*), and punishes those who hate prayer[8]. Most of the Vedic gods share in the function of helping the priests in the production of effective prayers, but Bṛihaspati as Strauss truly says, is a 'specialist'[9] in the department of inspiration.

---

[1] RI. 136.

[2] Farquhar, ORLI. 6; Yasna IX. 1.

[3] The name *Bṛihaspati* is relatively archaic, being interpreted by the form *Brahmaṇaspati*. It belongs at least to 'the beginning of the Ṛigvedic period' (Macdonell). Some compounds in *-pati*, however, go back to the IE. period. See p. 84 n. 3.

[4] Griswold, *Brahman*, 8.

[5] ZDMG. I. 73.

[6] RV. 65-68.

[7] *Bṛihaspati im Veda, 1905.*

[8] I. 18, 7; 40, 5; II. 23, 1-2, 4; IV. 50, 11; X. 98, 2.

[9] BV. 23.

Bṛihaspati is the divine embodiment not only of the sacred utterance (*bráhman*)[1], but also of the sacred order of the priesthood (*bráhman*)[2]. In IV. 50, 7-9 the king's cherishing of Bṛihaspati is identified with his giving precedence to the Brahmán and helping him in his need, and in X. 141, 3 Bṛihaspati is actually called a Brahmán. Furthermore he is closely linked up with a band of singers, undoubtedly to be identified with the Aṅgirasas, the semi-mythical ancestors of the Brāhmans. Thus Bṛihaspati is a priest, the prototype of the earthly priesthood, and the embodiment of the mysterious potency which dwells both in bráhman, the holy word, and bráhman, the holy order of the wielders and custodians thereof. As Agni is the apotheosis of agni 'fire', so Brahmaṇaspati is the apotheosis of bráhman 'word'.

It is uncertain in what way the abstract 'lord of prayer' gained concrete content, such as is revealed in the hymns addressed to him. Since the curse or spell had a very definite military value and priests like Viśvāmitra (III. 33) accompanied expeditions of war, it is possible that Bṛihaspati after the same analogy was conceived as the Brāhman *purohita* of the warrior Indra[3]. This would probably account for the numerous points of contact between Bṛihaspati and Agni, on the one hand, and between Bṛihaspati and Indra on the other. There is another possibility. Both the Maruts and the Aṅgirasas are represented as singers. The song of the Maruts is

---

[1] The meaning of *bráhman* as already pointed out (p. 97) halts between 'prayer' and 'spell', according as its aim is either to persuade the gods or to compel them. In the following passages *bráhman* is clearly used in the sense of 'spell': I. 82, 6; II. 2, 7; 17, 3; 24, 3; V. 40, 6; VI. 65, 5, etc. *Cf.* Strauss BV. 57-58, and Hillebrandt Art. *Brahman* in ERE. Oldenberg and Strauss have much to say about a '*Zauberfluidum*' or magic element, which operates in both the sacred priesthood and the sacred utterance, like *māna* among primitive peoples. It is regarded as constituting the very nature of bráhman. *Cf.* Strauss BV. 20, n. 4.

[2] *Cf.* the terms '*Brahma ca Kṣatram ca*' in the later Vedic literature.

[3] Strauss, BV. 43.

clearly the song of the thunder and wind, as heard in a thunderstorm. The Aṅgirasas like the Bhṛigus and Atharvans were ancient priestly families, probably historical, most likely reaching back to the Indo-Iranian period[1]. They are, however, heavily clothed upon with mythical elements, as was natural, being associated with the gods Bṛihaspati and Indra in their exploits. Quite likely we may detect the working of popular etymology in the mythical drapery[2] that has overspread the original Aṅgirasas. The fiery nature of the Aṅgirasas, as indicated by the probable connection of the word with *aṅgāra* 'live coal', may have suggested to the myth-making imagination a 'fiery' career akin to, or even identical with, that of the Maruts. Bṛihaspati, the lord of *bṛih*[3] or *brahman*, 'formula' 'incantation', was in origin a purely ritualistic deity, but unlike Soma and Agni had no physical nature except sound. It is antecedently probable, however, that Bṛihaspati as lord of the effective spell would be linked on to something analogous in nature. What would that be except the thunder[4], which might easily be regarded as the song or mantra of a heavenly priest, a most effective 'charm' to release the heavenly waters.

---

[1] The probable connection of these names with *aṅgāra* 'live coal' and ἄγγελος 'messenger', bhrāj and Φλέγω 'to shine', *atharyú* 'flaming' VII. 1, 1 and *ātar* 'fire', helps to support the view that they were ancient fire-priests. So Hillebrandt, VM. II. 155-178; *cf.* Macdonell, JRAS. (1900), 383.

[2] Oldenberg has made it probable (RV. 151-162) that the Dasyu chieftains Śuṣṇa, Pipru, Śambara, et al., were aborigines dressed up in the livery of the demon world. According to the same analogy we may regard the Aṅgirasas as an ancient Aryan priestly family arrayed in the habiliments of the world of the devas. In this sense they came to be 'a race of higher beings intermediate between gods and men' (Macdonell, VM. 143).

[3] Oldenberg connects the word *bṛih* or *brahman* with the Irish *bricht* 'magic', 'Magic formula' (LU. 46 n. 1). *Bricht* is related to the Icelandic *bragr* 'poetry' and so *brahman* is the 'ceremonially conceived' word as used in magic. Hillebrandt, Art. *Brahman* in ERE.

[4] *Cf.* the thunder in Hebrew as the קוֹל יְהוָה, 'voice of Yahweh', in Psalm XXIX; also John XII. 28-29.

The Aṅgirasas as singing priests would naturally accompany Bṛihaspati, the great high priest of the sky, just as the Maruts as young warriors accompany Indra. There is more or less mutual assimilation between the Aṅgirasas and the Maruts, the Aṅgirasas becoming military and the Maruts priestly[1]. Perhaps the Aṅgirasas and the Maruts are largely 'mythological synonyms', parallel forms of each other. Possibly by this very weak bridge might be secured an interpretation of the Maruts as 'personifications of the souls of the dead', the dead thus embodied in the storm-winds being the ancient Aṅgirasas. The love of music and song which has ever characterised India lends some weight to an interpretation which would emphasize the play of the Vedic imagination along musical lines. If the great musical composers have drawn part of their inspiration from the music of the elements, the songs of the thunder[2] and wind, probably the Vedic singers had imagination enough to find in the same music the heavenly analogue of the 'song' or 'incantation' of the earthly priest.

As regards his relation to *ṛita*, Bṛihaspati is *ṛitaprajāta* '*ṛita*-born'; that is to say, he represents an aspect of eternal order, mounts the shining car of *ṛita*, has a bow the string of which is *ṛita*, punishes and avenges guilt[3], is the upholder of great *ṛita*, consumes *(tap)* enemies, the bráhman-hater and rakṣasas, manifests wrath and remits debt (or guilt) according to his own will *(vaśa)*[4]. Here *bráhman*, the mysterious power of 'prayer' or 'spell' is represented as an expression or instrument of eternal order, serving it by both the punishment and the remission of guilt.

To sum up, Agni and Bṛihaspati, as ritualistic gods, have many functions in common. Only in this general

---

[1] *Cf.* V. 29, 3, *Brahmaṇo Marutaḥ*.

[2] Bṛihaspati is represented as roaring, bellowing and thundering (X. 67, 3, 6, 9; VII 97, 5), and as 'born of the great light in the highest heaven', IV. 50, 4 (*i. e.* the lightning which is followed by thunder as its child).

[3] *Ṛiṇacit, ṛiṇayā* II. 23, 17.

[4] II. 23, 3, 15, 17; II. 24, 8, 13-14.

sense however can Bṛihaspati be called a 'variety' or 'aspect' of Agni, for each is the apotheosis of a different cult object.

The great interest connected with Bṛihaspati is that 'the lord of bráhman' is one of the links in the chain that led from the primitive conception of bráhman as a kind of *'mana'* or *'Zauberfluidum'*, on to the supreme conception of it as the central reality of the universe. Three notions of fundamental importance in the Ṛv. remain impersonal, *viz. ṛita* 'order', *bráhman*[1] 'word' and *māyā* 'power'. Of these bráhman alone became personalized in Brahmaṇaspati, who as the divine brahmán priest was the prototype of *Brahma*, the first person of the later Hindu triad[2].

8. VEDIC NATURE STUDIES ON THE SUBJECT OF FIRE.—There remains a great mass of material pertaining to Agni, which while most interesting, can receive only the briefest reference. It may be studied in detail in Macdonell's Vedic Mythology. Agni dwelt in the homes of the Vedic Indians as the hearth-fire and the altar-fire. He was mysterious, potent for both good and evil, at once friendly and terrible. With his apotheosis as one of the great gods he became the object of most careful study and the centre of the earliest Vedic speculation. The result was that we have in the Ṛv. a most elaborate series of nature studies on the subject of fire[3]. We have already referred to the three

---

[1] Oldenberg remarks that not one of the powers that aspired to the place of Universal Being belonged to the sphere of physical nature. (*Die älteren Upanishaden*, 45.).

[2] No reference has been made to Prof. Hillebrandt's view of Bṛihaspati as a lord of plants and a personification of the moon. The present writer finds himself incapable of appreciating the arguments which have led the learned author to the conclusions he adopts.

[3] Once while at Gureis, Kashmīr, I sought to test the accuracy of the Ṛigvedic descriptions of the behaviour of fire when ghee is poured on it. The three altars were dug under the direction of a Srinagar pandit, the round *Gārhapatya* westward, the square *Āhavanīya* eastward, and southward the *Dakṣiṇāgni* in the form of a half-moon. Each fire-pit was dug about six inches deep. Fuel was heaped in the *Gārhapatya* fire-pit, and when the darkness came on the pile was lighted and ghee

forms of Agni, the earliest Indian triad. Very often also Agni is called *dvijanman* 'having two births', one in heaven and the other on earth. Then there was the fact of the indefinite multiplicity of fires. What was the relation between fires and Fire? It was the first emergence in Indian thought of the problem of the one and the many, a problem destined to receive such a radical solution in the Vedānta philosophy. Sometimes Agni is invoked with the agnis[1] as Indra with the Maruts. At other times it was observed that Agni is 'of like appearance in many places' (VIII. 11, 8), and so the conclusion was drawn that there is 'only one Agni though many times kindled' (VIII. 58, 2)[2]. Already multiplicity had begun to give way before unity. Then there is the distinction between the latent and the manifested, so important in the later philosophy of India. For example, Agni is latent in the heavenly waters[3] until he is born in the form of lightning, and also in the plants until through the twirling of the fire-sticks he is brought to birth. Because of the strong friction necessary to produce fire, Agni is called 'son of strength'. The mystery of fire is the ground of many Vedic paradoxes. Agni is at once young and old, heavenly and earthly, latent and manifested. As soon as born he devours his parents.

---

was poured on, accompanied with the recitation of Vedic fire-mantras. I was exceedingly impressed with the vividness and accuracy of the language used in describing the rushing flames. A Hindu servant some years after referred to it as our *pūjā!*

[1] VII. 3, 1; VIII. 18, 9, etc.

[2] Oldenberg, RV. 43-45.

[3] Hence called *apām napāt*, 'son of the waters'.

CHAPTER VII.

INDRA THE WARRIOR GOD.

INTRODUCTORY.—Indra is celebrated in not less than 250 hymns of the Ṛv. and in approximately 50 more he is praised conjointly with other deities. Judging then from the fact that he is celebrated in nearly one-fourth of the total number of hymns, we must conclude that he was a favourite deity in the Vedic age. The name 'Indra' is of uncertain derivation[1] and meaning, being more 'opaque' than that of any other divine name in the Ṛv. The result is that there is some uncertainty as to his original physical basis. For most scholars Indra is a storm-god, who sends thunder and lightning, but for Hillebrandt he is an ancient sun-god. In the Boghaz-köi list Indra is mentioned in the form 'In-dar' along with Mitra, Varuṇa and Nāsatya (1400 B. C.). Hence he must have been recognised at that time as a great god. In the Avesta he is mentioned twice[2] in the variant form Indra or Añdra. The name occurs in the list of demons; hence it is clear that Indra like the other pre-Zoroastrian daēvas was reduced at the great reform to the status of an evil spirit[3]. Indra is perhaps the most completely anthropomorphised of all the Vedic deities. While the anthropomorphism of Varuṇa's personality is more fully developed on the moral than the physical side (Macdonell, VM. 23), the opposite holds true of Indra. As might be expected, then, Indra represents

---

[1] Derivations which have been suggested are the following: *indu* 'drop'; *idh* 'kindle'; *in* 'stir' 'urge'; *ina* 'strong', hence perhaps In(d)ra; *aner*, an(d)ros 'man', hence An(d)ra, In(d)ra 'manly', *ent* 'giant' in Anglo Saxon, etc.

[2] Vend. X. 9, XIX. 43, the second passage not being found in all manuscripts.

[3] While the Vedic *Vṛtrahan* is a regular epithet of Indra, its Avestan equivalent *Verethraghna* is quite separate from the Avestan demon Indra or Añdra, and is regarded as a *yazata*, the 'genius of victory', created by Ahura and clothed with the light of sovereignty. Vend. XIX. 37. *cf.* Spiegel, AP. 194-198.

12

the apotheosis of naked might, the embodiment of the martial and imperialistic tendencies of the Vedic Indians. No phenomenon of nature is so suggestive of ruthless might as the lightning stroke. Indra is Agni's twin brother (VI. 59, 2), a way of expressing the close relation between the lightning-fire and the altar-fire.

2. **Indra the Slayer of Vṛitra.**—Indra's most notable exploit is set forth with great vividness and energy in the following hymn:

To Indra, I. 32[1].

1. Let me tell out the manly deeds of Indra,
Which he accomplished first of all, bolt-weaponed:
He slew the serpent, opened up the waters,
And cleft in twain the belly of the mountains.

2. He slew the serpent lying on the mountain;
Tvaṣṭar for him the heavenly[2] bolt had fashioned;
Like lowing cattle downward sped the waters
In rapid flow descending to the ocean.

3. With bull-like eagerness he sought the soma;
Out of three vats he drank the pressed out liquor;
Maghavan took in hand his bolt, the missile,
And smote therewith the first-born of the serpents.

4. When, Indra, thou didst smite the serpent's first-born,
When thou didst spoil the wiles of the enchanters,
Anon the sun and sky and dawn disclosing;
Thou didst not then a single foe discover.

5. The Vṛitra Vyaṁsa worst of Vṛitras, Indra
Smote with his bolt, smote with his mighty weapon;
Then just like trunks of trees laid low by axes,
The serpent lies stretched out along earth's surface.

6. For, like a drunken weakling, Vṛitra challenged
The mighty hero, the impetuous warrior;

---

[1] Indebtedness is acknowledged to Oldenberg's translation of this hymn (RV. 136-138) and to his Ṛv. Noten 31-33.

[2] *Svarna* 'gleaming', Ludwig; 'roaring' Geldner and Oldenberg; 'whizzing' Macdonell.

He did not meet the clash of Indra's weapons,
Broken[1] and crushed he lay, whose foe was Indra.

7. Footless and handless battled he with Indra,
Who on the back of Vṛitra hurled his missile;
With scattered limbs lay the dismembered Vṛitra,
Emasculate, who tried the Bull to equal.

8. On this wise, as he lay like ox[2] dismembered,
Over him ruthlessly did sweep the waters,
Which Vṛitra by his greatness had surrounded;
Down at their feet low lieth now the serpent.

9. The strength of her whose son was Vṛitra withered;
Indra his weapon brought to bear against her,
The mother lay above, the son was under,
Dānu lay like a cow her calf alongside.

10. There lay her body midst the watercourses,
That never cease, that never rest from flowing;
Through Vṛitra's secret place the waters speed them;
In lasting gloom sank he whose foe was Indra.

11. Dāsa-controlled and guarded by the serpent,
The waters stood like cows confined by Paṇis;
The orifice of the waters which was fastened,
That opened Indra, having slaughtered Vṛitra.

12. A horse-tail[3] didst thou then become, O Indra,
What time the foe, as if sole god, assailed thee;
Didst win the cows, didst win the Soma, hero,
And didst set free to flow the seven rivers.

13. Lightning and thunder profited him nothing,
Nor mist nor hailstorm which he spread around him;
When Indra and the serpent fought their battle,
Maghavan won the victory for ever.

---

[1] *Rujānāḥ*, either correct to *rujānāḥ* 'broken' (Oldenberg, RV. 136) or divide into *rujā + anāḥ* (Oldenberg, Noten 32) "Durch Zerschmetterung ist der Mundlose (Nasenlose?) zermalmet worden". Note that 'noseless' goes well with 'footless' and 'handless'. Accordingly it may be translated: Crushed was the noseless Indra-foe when smitten.

[2] Or: 'like broken reed'—Macdonell, HR. 48.

[3] Agni's flame (I. 27, 1) is compared to a horse with a tail. Indra became a 'horse-tail' apparently, when he appeared as the lightning flash. The translation of stanza twelve is only tentative.

14. Whom didst thou see to avenge the serpent, Indra,
When terror filled thy heart that thou hadst slain him,
When like a frightened eagle through the mid-air
Thou didst cross over nine and ninety rivers?

15. Indra is king of that which moves and moves not,
Of tame and hornéd creatures, too, bolt-weaponed;
Over the tribes of men he rules as monarch;
As felly spokes, so holds he them together.

A description of the great battle between Indra and Vṛitra, which resulted in the slaying of Vṛitra and the release of the imprisoned waters. The following points may be noted:—

a) Since *Vṛitrahan* 'slayer of Vṛitra' is Indra's most characteristic epithet, the exploit referred to constitutes Indra's mythological essence. Three questions arise. What is Vṛitra, a demon of drought or a demon of cold? What is Indra, lightning or sun? And what are the waters, atmospheric or earthly? An answer to these questions is complicated by the fact that Indra is confessedly a prehistoric god belonging to the Indo-Iranian and possibly even to the Indo-European period[1]. Hence with the change of environment and climatic conditions his own nature and attributes may have suffered a change, since he was the reflection largely of natural phenomena. The great majority of Vedic scholars regard the slaying of Vṛitra and the release of the waters as referring to the atmospheric drama of the thunderstorm in which the demon of drought is pierced by the lightning and made to surrender the pent-up waters, which fall to the earth in the form of rain. The two chief German authorities on Vedic Mythology, Oldenberg and Hillebrandt, would, however, introduce important modifications into the traditional explanation. Oldenberg follows the traditional view in holding that the original pre-Vedic conception was the freeing of the waters from the prison of the cloud-mountain, but thinks that this conception in the Ṛigvedic environment was trans-

[1] Oldenberg, RV. 34, (n. 1), 134.

formed into the freeing of the earthly waters from the earthly mountains. This transition was favoured by the identity of the heavenly and the earthly waters, which made it natural to think that the freeing of the earthly waters must be the work of the same god who freed the heavenly waters[1]. The changes which Hillebrandt would introduce into the traditional view are much more radical. For him Vṛitra 'the encompasser' was originally a personification of cold and ice, a 'winter-giant'. Only the sun could be the antagonist of such a demon. Hence Indra must have been originally a sun-god. Indra and Vṛitra then represent the antithesis between summer sun and winter cold, as was natural in a northern environment. With the change from such a climate to that of the Punjab where drought, not cold, was the great enemy, Indra was transformed from a sun-god into a storm-god or simple rain-god. Indra's original task was to free the waters from the clutch of the ice-demon. His later development as a rain-god was doubtless helped by his early connection with water[2]. Thus according to Hillebrandt both Indra and Vṛitra owe their pre-Vedic character as god of summer warmth and demon of winter cold to pre-Vedic climatic conditions. The theory is brilliantly stated, but in its totality is not convincing. It will be profitable to compare Indra with Varuṇa in their capacity as water-gods. Varuṇa as a sky-god[3], sends rain from heaven and wets the earth (V. 85, 3-4). But not only is he a rain-god, but also a river-god (id. v. 6). By analogy Varuṇa's function was extended from rain-giving to river-digging[4]. Assuming with Oldenberg that Indra's original function was that of a storm-god wielding the thunderbolt and slaying the

---

[1] Oldenberg, RV. 51, n. 1.

[2] Hillebrandt, VM. III. 195-197.

[3] Whether he was originally the 'encompassing sky' or the 'moon' makes no difference in this connection.

[4] *Cf*. X. 75, 2, Varuṇa *dug (rad)* the bed for thy course, O Sindhu. So Indra dug out *(rad)* the Vipāś and Śutudrī (III. 33, 6).

rain-withholding demon, one can easily see how by analogy his domain in the Punjab would be enlarged so as to cover rivers, quite as in the parallel case of Varuṇa. Especially would this be natural and inevitable, if the standing metaphors of the Indra-Vṛitra myth[1] had a pre-Vedic origin. The cloud-mountains and the cloud-waters of the myth would fit in well with the literal mountains and mountain streams of the northern Punjab[2]. At any rate, it seems clear that Indra like Varuṇa was a regent of both heavenly and earthly waters. Vṛitra may be interpreted, then, as anything which obstructs the waters, whether drought-demon in the case of the heavenly waters, or mountain barriers or snow in the case of the earthly

---

[1] Mountains (= clouds) and waters (= rain or rivers).

[2] The deep cut through the mountains by which the Jhelum river flows from Kashmīr down to the Punjab must have impressed the Vedic Indians. There are traditions of a large body of water anciently held back in the mountains — a tradition amply attested by geology. The Himâlayas are the scene of violent thunderstorms. In view of the language of the original myth, what more natural than to think of the deep cleft of the Jhelum 'in the belly of the mountains' as hollowed out by Indra? To this day the people of Kashmīr refer many changes to the action of lightning. A Śrīnagar Paṇḍit asserted that the mountains were once full of the caves of ascetics. On being asked where the caves were, he replied that the lightning had destroyed them. About the 20th June 1911, while our boats were tied up in the *Tsuṇṭh Kul*, Śrīnagar, a terrific storm of thunder and lightning came on at night. Not very much rain fell at Śrīnagar, but a good deal must have fallen on the mountains. The next morning the water had risen so much that we were compelled to move our boats to another place. It was a warm rain which melted much snow. The evening of the thunder-storm was marked by a marvellous display of lightning. On the far-off horizon the lightning would dart down apparently from heaven to earth. The phenomenon might very well have been interpreted by primitive man as a sky-deity smiting with his weapon some atmospheric or earth demon reclining on the mountains. It may be that the Indra-Vṛitra myth was extended by analogy to cover such cases as this, and to this extent Hillebrandt's theory may be true. As seen from a long distance a white cloud and a snow-capped mountain are practically indistinguishable. A cloud looks like a mountain. As a matter of fact, the cloud-mountains and the snowy mountains of eastern Bactria must have made possible from the beginning a double application of the Indra-Vṛitra myth, namely to the cloud-waters obstructed by the drought-demon and the mountain-waters obstructed by the snow-demon.

waters. Indra must be regarded throughout as the wielder of the lightning.

b) Vṛitra, the chief enemy of Indra, seems to be the name of those cloud or atmospheric appearances which promise much in the matter of rain, but perform little or nothing, an abortive rain-storm, as it were.

Vṛitra manipulates lightning, thunder, mist[1], darkness[2] and hail (v. 13; I. 80, 12). He is clothed in the habiliments of Indra, 'Satan transformed', as it were, 'into an angel of light'. His 'snorting' is several times referred to (V. 29, 4; VIII. 85, 7), and he is called a muttering or bellowing snake (*navantam ahim* VI. 17, 10). His mother is *Dānu* 'drip', a name of the rain-cloud which sprinkles only a few drops. 'She of the drip' is the mother of a demon-brood[3], of which Vṛitra is the first-born. As thus interpreted Vṛitra means a false thunderstorm with little or no rain, while Indra means a thunderstorm followed by abundance of rain. Vṛitra is also called *Ahi* 'serpent', the same epithet being applied to the chief atmospheric demon in the Ṛv., as is applied to Satan in the Bible. Agni is once called 'a raging

---

[1] Śuṣṇa 'hisser' or 'scorcher', one of the demon-brood is called *mihonapāt*, 'son of mist', V. 32, 4.

[2] Vṛitra as 'son of mist' moves in darkness and waxes in sunless gloom (V. 32, 4, 6). Is there any reference here to the phenomena of dust-storms, so characteristic of the Punjab before the rains?

[3] Ṛv. X. 120, 6 mentions seven Dānus (Dānavas), sons of the Cow Dānu. As drought-demons they probably cover different aspects of the sky in the dry season, *e.g.* Vṛitra 'the obstructor' of the heavenly waters being the entire dry weather sky (*cf.* Varuṇa from the same root), and associated with him probably *Śuṣṇa* 'the scorcher' who spoils the harvests, personification of the intense pre-monsoon heat, *Aurṇavābha* 'son of the wool-weaver, possibly referring to the woolly look of the dry-weather sky or to the whitish dust-haze which hangs over the Punjab in the very dry season. As soon as Vṛitra is smitten and the rains fall, all the other drought-demons take themselves off. Hence Vṛitra as the most important drought-demon is called 'the first-born of the dragons' (I. 32, 3). In May and June 1921 both on the plains and on the hills at Mussoorie the drought and heat were intense. Vṛitra had withheld the waters, Śuṣṇa had spoiled the winter crops in the hills, and over all the mountains a thick, whitish dust and smoke-haze was spread, possibly *Aurṇavābha's* work.

serpent like a rushing wind' (I. 79, 1), and the Maruts, or 'storm-winds and lightning flashes', bear the epithet *ahi-bhānavaḥ* 'shining like ahi' (I. 172, 1). The name 'serpent' may refer to the subtle deceptive nature of Vṛitra, to his appearance as lightning, or to the wide-spread tradition that serpents guard treasures, especially water-springs. So the word *nāg* 'serpent' is applied generally as a name for 'spring' in Kashmir. We may draw an instructive comparison between Ahi Vṛitra and *Ahi Budhnya.* Both have their habitat in the atmospheric ocean. It looks as if both were very much the same, the only difference being that Ahi Budhnya 'the serpent of the deep' is a parallel form of Indra and hence a deva, while Ahi Vṛitra 'the serpent obstructor' is a demon[1]. As is fitting for a snake, Ahi Vṛitra is represented as footless, handless and perhaps noseless (I. 32, 6-7; III. 30, 8). Being armed with thunder, lightning and magic devices *(māyā),* Vṛitra is no mean antagonist.

c) Indra's equipment for the fight with Vṛitra. The gods constituted him for this purpose (III. 49, 1) and made him their champion (VI. 17, 8). To this end he was strengthened with food, drink and song[2]. Indra is represented as a mighty eater and drinker[3]. He eats the flesh of bulls[4] and buffaloes, and drinks enormous quantities of Soma.

---

[1] Macdonell, VM. 72-73.

[2] Since agni 'fire' could be literally increased *(vṛidh)* by pouring in ghee, the same general idea of strengthening was carried over by analogy to Indra (*cf.* II. 11, 1-2) and the other gods. It may be that the growth of the storm from 'a little cloud like a man's hand' was viewed as the growth of Indra.

[3] The anthropomorphic representation of the gods in India is frequently symbolical. Large activity and heroic deeds are often represented by multiplying the number of hands and feet, or as in the case of Indra by multiplying the amount of food and drink consumed. *Big eating* among the Vedic Aryans was doubtless the preparation for *big doing.* So by analogy among the gods. It is safe to say that the Greek with his artistic restraint and sense of form would not have used such a metaphor as 'he like an ocean-has made room in his belly (for Soma)' I. 30, 3.

[4] 'They dress for thee bulls', *pacanti te vrisabhān,* X. 28, 3. Thus Indra the 'bull' eats bull-meat.

As friend for friend Agni made ready quickly
Three hundred buffaloes, to meet his longing;
Indra at once three lakes of pressed-out Soma,
As Manus ordered, drank for Vṛitra's slaughter.

"When thou three hundred buffaloes' flesh hadst eaten,
And drunk, as Maghavan, three lakes of Soma,
All the gods raised as 'twere a shout of triumph,
To Indra praise because he slew the Dragon."

V. 29, 7-8 (Griffith's translation of v. 8).

Indra's weapon *par excellence* is the *vajra* or 'bolt', clearly a mythological name for the lightning stroke. It is described as golden, heavenly, hundred-edged, thousand-pointed, roaring, shattering, etc.[1] Synonyms[2] are 'heavenly stone', 'burning dart' and 'moving weapon'. It is the weapon exclusively appropriate to Indra[3], though assigned a few times to Rudra, the Maruts and Manyu. Through it Indra shakes all things:

Even the heavens and earth bow down before him,
And at his vehemence the mountains tremble[4]. II. 12, 13.

Indra then settles the things shaken and fixes the unsteady:

He who the quivering earth hath firm established,
And set at rest the agitated mountains. II. 12, 2.

What Indra shakes and agitates by his thunderbolt, he also calms and settles. What are the facts of the thunder-storm? First, the heavy peals of thunder *shake* the world. Then after the storm has passed a great *calm* succeeds[5]. As the Vedic Aryan interpreted it, Indra first shakes[6] all things and then makes fast the quivering and the agitated.

Indra and Vṛitra are both furnished with *mayā*. This

---

[1] I. 57, 2; 61, 6; II. 11, 9-10; VI. 17. 10.

[2] I. 176, 3; III. 30, 17; 32, 6.

[3] Macdonell, VM. 55.

[4] *Cf.* Judges V. 4-5; Ps. XVIII. 7; XXIX. 4, 8.

[5] *Cf.* Psalm XXIX for both aspects of a thunder-storm.

[6] Earthquake tremors are very common in the Punjab. It is possible that these are included in the agitation mentioned. The great Kangra earthquake of 1905 synchronized with dust storms and other meteoric phenomena.

very pregnant word occurs in about thirty Indra hymns[1]. In these there are about twenty references to the *māyā* of Vṛitra, Śuṣṇa, etc. and about ten to the *māyā* of Indra. The word *māyā* signifies occult, incomprehensible, superhuman power[2], and so easily passes into the meanings, trick, magic, illusion[3], etc. We have already noticed that the atmosphere is the scene of the *māyaḥ* or magic transformations of Varuṇa[4]. So it is with Indra. He frustrates the tricks of the tricky (I. 32, 4). With his *māyā* he blew away the tricky ones, that is to say, he dispersed Vṛitra and his company[5]. Indra through his *māyā* can assume all forms:

> "Maghavan weareth every shape at pleasure,
> Effecting magic changes in his body"; and
> "Indra moves multiform by his illusions".
> II. 53, 8 and VI. 47, 18 (Griffith's translation).

It is craft played off against craft. Indra is equipped with thunder, lightning, mist[6], wind, etc., which constitute the armoury of his *māyā,* while Vṛitra and his company, like the magicians of Egypt, do "in like manner with their enchantments" (Exodus VII. 11). But all in vain. Vṛitra cannot meet the clash of Indra's weapons. So strong is Indra that fighting on his part is 'appearance', not reality.

> That is thy magic power which men call battles,
> Never foe hast thou found, to-day or erstwhile. X. 54, 2.

d) Closely connected with the slaying of Vṛitra and the liberation of the waters is the winning of light. The lightning flash 'makes light where no light was', *cf.* VI. 24, 5. Indra generated the lightnings of the sky (II. 13, 7), and

---

[1] Prabhu Dutt Śāstrī, *The Doctrine of Māyā*, London, 1911, pp. 7-8.

[2] Oldenberg, RV. 163-166, 293-295.

[3] We may compare the later meaning of *māyā* as the cosmic illusion.

[4] V. 63 and 85, pp. 140, 136.

[5] I. 51, 5. *cf.* Indra blew the great snake out of the mid-air, VIII. 3, 20, and Indra blew the Dasyus from the sky with his weapon, X. 55. 8.

[6] Veiled in *mist (mih)* Indra rushed upon his foe (II. 30, 3), and cast forth mists *(mihaḥ)* and darkness (X. 73, 5).

also the sun, the sky and the dawn (I. 32, 4; VI. 30, 5). What is the Vedic point of view? Indra's supreme manifestation is the lightning flash with the accompanying 'bolt' *(vajra)*. The wonder of the lightning is that light *all-illuminating* (*cf.* Matthew XXIV. 27) suddenly appears, where all was darkness before. But the light of morning also appears, where all was darkness before. The Vedic conception seems to be that the same power that produces the lightning flash produces also the light of the dawn and sun which reveals the whole 'heaven'. Indra in both exploits appears in his characteristic guise as a *warrior*, slaying the drought-demon Vṛitra and also the darkness-demon of the night; and thereby releasing the cloud-cows and the dawn-cows. It is to be noted that the point of departure is the lightning flash. With this as his characteristic theophanic appearance Indra embraces all phenomena of light and fire.

3. INDRA AND THE EARTHLY WATERS.—Indra, like Varuṇa, had to do with both the heavenly and the earthly waters. His relation to the latter is well brought out in Viśvāmitra's conversation with the rivers:—

To Indra, III. 33.

1. (Viśvāmitra)
Forth from the bosom of the mountains, eager,
Like two mares racing side by side, loose-coupled,
Like two bright mother cows that lick each other[1],
Vipāś and Śutudrī pour down their waters.

2. Sent forth by Indra, begging him to speed you,
Ye twain move seaward, as it were on chariots;
Running together, swelling with your billows,
Ye lucid streams, to each draws nigh the other.

3. Now have I reached the most maternal river,
We have approached Vipāś, the broad, the blessed;
They are like mother cows that lick their offspring,
Flowing on toward their common home together.

---

[1] Or: 'As cows a calf lick, lapping earth, the fair streams'. Hopkins, ION. 48.

4. (Rivers)
Swelling with floods of water we move forward
Unto our place of meeting, god-appointed;
Not to be halted is our stream, full-flooded,
What would the seer have, calling to the rivers?

5. (Viśvāmitra)
Halt for a moment at my potent saying,
Ye streams law-loving, on your ocean journey;
To you ward is addressed my purpose lofty.
I, Kuśika's son, call on you, succour needing.

6. (Rivers)
Indra the bolt-armed hollowed out our channels,
Drove Vṛitra off, obstructor of the rivers;
God Savitar has led us, the fair-handed;
In his propulsion we go forth wide-ranging.

7. (Viśvāmitra)
For ever memorable is that deed of Indra,
The valiant deed, that he dismembered Ahi;
Broke open with his bolt the strong enclosures,
Forth flowed the waters, for their course desirous.

8. (Rivers)
Never forget this utterance, O singer,
Which later generations shall re-echo;
O bard, in these thy hymns be toward us friendly;
Humble us not 'mongst men; to thee obeisance.

9. (Viśvāmitra)
Give ear, O sisters, to the bard; he cometh
To you from far away with cart and chariot.
Bow down yourselves, please give an easy passage;
Floods, with your waves remain beneath our axles.

10. (Rivers)
We will give heed unto thy words, O singer,
Thou comest from afar with cart and chariot;:
Low like a nursing mother will I bend me,
Will yield myself like maiden to her husband.

11. (Viśvāmitra)
Now when the Bharatas have crossed thee safely,
Indra-impelled, a horde in search of booty,
Then may your stream full-flooded flow as ever;
Of you the worshipful I beseech the favour.

12. The booty-seeking Bharatas crossed over;
The sage enjoyed the favour of the rivers.

Rush forward, swelling, speeding, pouring riches,
Fill full your channels, hasten swiftly onward.

13. Your wave the yoke-pegs merely touch,
Ye waters, spare the chariot-thongs;
And never may the bullocks twain,
Faithful and steady, come to grief[1].

This notable hymn celebrates the crossing of the Beās and the Sutlej by a cattle-raiding band of the Bharatas accompanied by the sage Viśvāmitra, the reputed author of the third Maṇḍala. The rivers were in flood, but Viśvāmitra by his prayer caused the waters to subside[2], so that the Bharatas passed over safely. Already reference has been made to the military significance of the rivers of the Punjāb[3]. The god who could so control their waters as to cause them to rise or subside at will[4] was in very truth a war-god. While the Beās and Sutlej are represented as deified streams, the personification is only of the slightest. The hymn is addressed to Indra. It is he who dug the channels of these two rivers and sent forth their waters from the mountains to the sea (vv. 1-2, 6). Since the Beās and Sutlej as well as the war-band of the Bharatas were all alike under the control of Indra (vv. 2, 11), it was a simple thing for Indra at the request of his devotee Viśvāmitra to send the Bharatas across the streams 'on dry ground' as it were. We may compare the crossing of the Red Sea and of the Jordan in Hebrew story[5]. Yahweh, like Indra, is 'a man of war' (Ex. XV. 3), and the crossing of the Red Sea, as well as the crossing of the

---

[1] Indebtedness is acknowledged to Hillebrandt, LR. 137-138 and Hopkins, ION. 48-50.

[2] *Cf.* Vedic Index, II. 310-311.

[3] pp. 31-32.

[4] There are other references to a similar control of the rivers. Thus 'even the wide-spreading floods Indra made for Sudās into passable fords' (VII. 18, 5). 'The great Ṛiṣi (Viśvāmitra) stayed the billowy river' (III. 53, 9, a reference to the crossing of the Beās and Sutlej); and Indra arrested the streams for Turvīti and Vayya to cross (II. 13, 12; *cf.* also II. 15, 5 and I. 61, 11).

[5] Exodus XIV-XV; Joshua III-IV.

Beās and Sutlej is celebrated by a hymn. It is probable that no great chronological difference separated the Vedic and Hebrew events. The Vedic hymn is in the form of a dramatic dialogue between Viśvāmitra and the rivers, an interesting anticipation of the later Indian drama. The whole hymn may have been used in later times as a charm against accidents in crossing swollen streams[1]. Especially was the last stanza, which is looks like a later addition, thus used as a magic spell[2].

It is to be observed that the mountains, channels and rivers of this hymn all belong to the earth. The Beās and Sutlej flow from the mountains, and Indra hollowed out their channels[3]. In connection with this there is mentioned Indra's supreme exploit, the slaying of Ahi-Vṛitra (vv. 6-7). Indra dismembered Ahi and broke open with his bolt the obstructing enclosures, so that the waters flowed freely. Whether this refers to the obstruction of heavenly or of earthly waters is uncertain. Probably to both, for the release of the heavenly waters is the fundamental condition of the flooding of the earthly rivers, even more fundamental than the melting of snow. Since Indra is certainly connected with the lightning and the thunder, why not think of the whole process of the release of the waters as beginning with the sky and including the melting of snow on the mountains, the piercing of the springs[4] of the rivers, the hollowing out of channels[5], the swelling of

[1] The writer has had experiences in crossing the Kṛiṣṇa at Sangli and an arm of the Ganges near Kasgañj, when an effective spell (!) would have been most welcome.

[2] Hillebrandt, LR. 138, n. 3; Oldenberg, Ṛv. Noten 245.

[3] These are clearly literal rivers, but they are assimilated to the sky-scheme, for Indra hurled away Vṛitra, obstructor of the waters (v. 6). Such a process of assimilation by analogy is common in the Ṛv.

[4] *Cf.* 'He pierced with his bolt the fountains of the rivers', II. 15, 3. Springs in Kashmir are called *nāgas*, lit. 'snakes', a memorial of the time when every fountain was thought of as guarded by a snake. It reminds one of the heavenly fountain guarded and confined by the heavenly snake, Vṛitra.

[5] Thunder and lightning go with the kind of rainfall that *digs channels* (*cf.* Habakkuk III. 9) and produces *floods* (Hab. III. 10; Nahum I. 8; Judges V. 21).

the waters, and their advance in flood to the Samudra? Wherever the streams are flooded, there is seen the work of Indra, the releaser of the waters, whatever the immediate occasion of their release may be[1].

4. INDRA THE WAR-GOD OF THE VEDIC ARYANS. As Indra first released the heavenly waters, and then was brought down to earth, as it were, to release and guide the earthly waters, so he began his martial career in the atmospheric fight with Vṛitra, extending it so to speak to become the war-god of the Vedic Indians in their struggle with the aborigines. The parallel development of Yahweh is so striking and significant that some reference must be made to it. In the earliest poetry of the Old Testament Yahweh is represented as a kind of Hebrew Indra, a storm-god wielding the weapons of thunder, lightning[2] and wind, hailstones and flood, earthquake and (possibly) volcanic fire. Yahweh is also, like Indra, a national war-god, 'the lord of hosts and god of battles'. Quite as in the case of Indra, Yahweh employs the artillery of the sky against the enemies of his people, thundering from heaven against them (I Sam. VII. 10) and smiting them with hailstones (Joshua X. 11). On earth Yahweh so manipulated the waters of sea, river and flood as to save his people and drown their enemies[3]. It is the military, rather than the economic aspects of water that are emphasized in the great Hebrew war-songs,—the Song of Moses (or Miriam) in Ex. XV, and the Song of Deborah (Judges V). So is it also in such Vedic war-songs as III. 33, the crossing of the

---

[1] Thus Hillebrandt's theory, while contributing an important element, is too narrow and exclusive. Moreover it is based upon just as indirect evidence as is the traditional theory. If clouds and rain are not as a rule mentioned in connection with the release of the waters, no more are snow and ice.

[2] The tetragrammaton *yhwh*, is possibly to be connected with Arabic *hawa*, 'to fall', that is, 'He who causes lightning or rain to fall'. So Wellhausen and Robertson Smith. See *Hebrew Lexicon*, Brown, Driver and Briggs, 1906, under *Yahweh*.

[3] Ex. XIV-XV; Joshua III-IV; Judges V.

Beās and Sutlej, and VII. 18 the battle of the Ten Kings. Thus both Yahweh of Palestine and Indra of the Punjab were storm-gods and war-gods. In each case the god who presided over 'the war of the elements' naturally became the leader of his people in the wars against their earthly foes.

The hymn now to be translated contains interesting reference to the military side of Indra's activity.

To Indra, II. 12[1].

1. He who as soon as born keen-thoughted, foremost,
Surpassed the gods, himself a god, in power;
Before whose vehemence the two worlds trembled
Through his great valour; he, O men, is Indra.
2. He who the quivering earth hath firm established,
And set at rest the agitated mountains;
Who measured out the mid-air far-extending,
And sky supported: he, O men, is Indra.
3. Who slew the snake and freed the seven rivers,
Drove out the cattle by unclosing *Vala;*
Who fire between two rocks hath generated,
In battles victor: he, O men, is Indra.
4. Who hath made all things in this world unstable,
The Dāsa colour humbled or destroyed it;
Who takes the foe's possessions, as a gambler
Stakes of his rival; he, O men, is Indra.
5. The terrible one, of whom they ask, 'where is he?'
Concerning whom they also say, 'he is not';
Like player's stake the foe's wealth he reduces,
Have faith in him; for he, O men, is Indra.
6. He who of rich and poor alike is helper,
And of the supplicating Brāhman singer;
Who fair-lipped[2] aids the one who presses Soma,
Making the stones work; he, O men, is Indra.

---

[1] *Cf.* the translations of Hillebrandt, LR. 40-41, and Macdonell, VRS. 45-56 and HV. 49-50.

[2] *Suśipra* is probably to be rendered 'fair-lipped' in the sense of 'well-lipped'. One may recall the *protuberant* lips of the *Trimūrti* figures in the Elephanta Caves (Farquhar, PH. 99) or in the late Mr. Justice Ranade's statue at Bombay. *Cf.* Macdonell, VRS. 50. Note also the phrase *apruthyū śipre* III. 32, 1 'having puffed out his lips'.

7. He under whose control are steeds and cattle,
Clan-villages and every kind of chariot;
Who hath begotten sun and dawn of morning,
Guide of the waters; he, O men, is Indra.

8. Whom rival hosts appeal to, joined in battle,
On both sides foes, the farther and the nearer;
On self-same chariot mounted two invoke him,
Each for his own self; he, O men, is Indra.

9. Apart from whom men never are victorious,
Whom they when fighting call on for assistance;
Who is for every one a match, who moveth
The things immovable; he, O men, is Indra.

10. Who with his arrow slays the perpetrators
Of grievous sin, when such fate not expecting;
Who pardons not the arrogant man his arrogance[1],
Who slays the Dasyu; he, O men, is Indra.

11. He, who discovered in the fortieth autumn
Śaṁbara dwelling on the lofty mountains;
Who slew the serpent as he lay defiant,
The son of Dānu; he, O men, is Indra.

12. Who as the mighty seven-rayed bull releases
The seven streams so that they flow in torrents;
Who, bolt in arm, spurned *Rauhiṇa* the demon
As he scaled heaven; he, O men, is Indra.

13. Even the heavens and earth bow down before him,
And at his vehemence the mountains tremble;
Who, bolt in arm, is known as Soma-drinker,
With hands bolt-wielding; he, O men, is Indra.

14. Who with his aid helps him that presses Soma,
Him that bakes food, sings praise, does sacrifices;
For whom prayer is a means of strength, and Soma,
And this our offering; he, O men, is Indra.

15. Faithful and true art thou, the fierce, exacting
Largess for Soma-presser and food-baker;
We being evermore of thee belovéd,
Would, Indra, with strong sons thy worship utter[2].

It will be necessary to add only a few comments, since Vedic warfare has been sufficiently treated in the sections

[1] Or: 'Who yields not to the boasting foe in boldness'. Macdonell, HR. 50.

[2] Or: 'address the synod', Macdonell, HR. 50: Hillebrandt LR. 41.

of Chapter III on 'Aryans', 'Dasyus' and 'Conquest of the Land'. As the gods chose Indra to be their champion against Vṛitra and the other atmospheric Dasyus (vv. 11-12), so the Aryans chose him to be their champion against the earthly Dasyus (vv. 4, 10)[1]. Indra is a match for every one, whether demon or man (v. 9). The resources of language are exhausted in describing his irresistible might: He is a bull, mightier than the mighty, the lord of strength, the might-lord of might, having a hundred powers[2], etc. If forty or more epithets celebrate his matchless strength, about the same number glorify him as a victorious warrior. Indra made a broad place for the afflicted sky (or for Dyāus, VI. 18, 14) by slaying Vṛitra, that is to say, by sending a thunderstorm and clearing the atmosphere of dust and mist. He filled the spacious mid-air, and by battle gave enlargement and freedom to the gods (VII. 98, 3; III. 34, 7). Such enlargement and victory he gives also to his friends and worshippers among men (IV. 24, 2, 6; X. 43, 11), that is, to those who press soma for him (II. 12, 6, 14-15). For the 'Strong Soma' makes Indra strong (v. 14) and everything connected with Indra is also strong.

> The vessel of the *strong* flows forth, the flood of meath,
> Unto the *strong* who feeds upon the *strong*, for drink;
> *Strong* are the two Adhvaryus, *strong* are both the stones,
> They press the Soma that is *strong* for him the *strong*.
>
> *Strong* is thy thunderbolt, yea, and thy car is *strong*;
> *Strong* are thy bay steeds and thy weapons too are *strong*.
> *Strong* Indra, thou art lord of the *strong* gladdening drink,
> With the *strong* Soma, Indra, satisfy thyself.
>
> (II. 16, 5-6, Griffith's translation with slight changes.)

---

[1] The word Dasyu or Dāsa is ambiguous, referring as it does to both human foes and demon foes. Both are Dasyus, fiends, devils. *Cf.* Roosevelt, WW. I. 110. "Appalling by their craft, their ferocity, their fiendish cruelty, they (the Algonquins) seemed to the white settlers *devils* and not men". Or perhaps it was this way. As the Devas were conceived after the image of the Kṣatriyas, so the demons were conceived according to the image of earthly Dasyus, the enemies of the Aryans.

[2] V. 40, 1, 4; VI. 20, 3; X. 22, 3; II. 16, 8.

Thus it is 'in the exhilaration' of Soma that Indra performs his martial as well as his cosmic exploits. No one can overcome him in battle when he has drunk of it (VI. 47, 1). The epithet *Somapā*, 'Soma-drinker' (v. 13) is characteristic of him. It is well known that men offer to the gods in sacrifice the food and drink which are regarded by them as the best. The offering of Soma to Indra presupposes, then, the use of strong drink as a beverage by the Vedic Aryans. Indra after the analogy of a Vedic warrior is *heartened* for the fray by Soma. We may reason from the effects ascribed to Indra's drinking of Soma back to the results in the way of victory, winning of plunder, etc. which the Kṣatriya warrior doubtless ascribed to the use of strong drink as a producer of valour in battle. It is from this point of view that Soma is called a 'victor, unconquered in fight' (I. 91, 21)[1]. Indra as the war-god of the Vedic Indians humbled the Dāsa foes and gave their possessions to his worshippers (vv. 4-5). He dispersed 50,000 of the black race and rent their forts (IV. 16, 13). Rival Indra-worshipping foes[2] appeal to him for assistance, without which men never are victorious (II. 12, 8-9). Through Indra's help the Aryan wins cattle (VI. 26, 2) and corn-land (*urvarā*, VI. 20, 1; 25, 4). The following are samples of Vedic prayers to Indra for help in battle:

Indra, bestow on us the power heroic,
Skilled and exceeding strong, that wins the booty;
Wherewith, by thy assistance, we may conquer
Our foes in battle, *be they kin or stranger.*
VI. 19, 8 (Griffith's translation).

The cup whence Indra drinks the draught is present;
The Amṛit dear to Indra hath been drunken,
That it may cheer the god to gracious favour,
And keep far from us hatred and affliction.

[1] When 'Pussyfoot' Johnson was 'ragged' in the streets of London by the Medical students, they carried banners inscribed with the words. *What won the war? Rum!*" New York Times, November 14, 1919.

[2] We are reminded of the Great War, in which Protestants and Catholics, Muhammadans and Jews fought on both sides.

Therewith enraptured, hero, slay our foemen,
Th' unfriendly, Maghavan, *be they kin or strangers;*
Those who still aim their hostile darts to smite us,
Turn them to flight, O Indra, crush and kill them.

VI. 44, 16-17 (Griffith's translation).

These passages reveal at least so much of history as to make it clear that the Vedic Indians were often at war among themselves. The references to historical events are confined largely to the military exploits of tribes and individuals, just what we would expect in hymns composed almost entirely for sacrifices instituted and financed by Kṣatriyas. Indra, the war-god of the Vedic peoples was naturally also the patron and guide of the Aryans in their migrations eastward[1].

5. HEROIC DEEDS WROUGHT BY INDRA.—

In the O. T. the 136th Psalm is a hymn of praise to Yahweh for his wonderful works in creation and redemption, each stanza ending with the refrain 'his loving kindness endureth for ever'. In the cosmic sphere Yahweh made the heavens, spread out the earth, and made great lights, the sun to rule by day and the moon to rule by night. In the sphere of deliverance and redemption Yahweh smote Egypt in their first-born, brought out Israel from among them, divided the Red Sea and made Israel pass through the midst of it, overthrew Pharoah and his host in the Red Sea, led his people through the wilderness, smote great kings, Sihon King of the Amorites and Og King of Bashan, and gave their land to his people for a heritage. Similar exploits and works of deliverance are ascribed to Indra[2]. In the cosmic sphere as we have seen Indra generated the matchless lightnings of the sky, slew Vṛitra and released the waters, pierced the cattle stall, found heaven and earth which were hidden, made the earth visible to heaven and the sun visible to earth, separated

[1] Oldenberg, RV. 167-168.

[2] See especially I. 32; II. 12; III. 33. translated entire, pp. 178 ff., 192 ff., 187 ff.; also II. 15 and X. 49.

and supported heaven and earth, spreading out the earth and fixing the sky, when he was born for the Vṛitra fight[1]. In this way Indra generated the sun, the sky and the dawn (I. 32, 4). In the human sphere Indra, the warrior-god, wrought deliverance for many Aryan chieftains. He arrested the floods so that Turvīti and Vayya could cross over (II. 13, 12); on behalf of Dabhīti he overcame Ćumuri and Dhuni with sleep, and bound the Dasyus without cords (II. 15, 9; II. 13, 9); for the sake of Divodāsa he demolished Śambara's nine and ninety forts (II. 19, 6); he broke down the forts of Pipru and helped Ṛijiśvan at the slaughter of the Dasyus (I. 51, 5); he through the prayer of the Vasiṣṭhas helped Sudās in the battle of the ten kings (VII. 33, 3) and drowned his foes in the Paruṣṇi (VII, 18, 9), etc., etc. Such deliverances of ancient Aryan heroes on the part of Indra remind us of the similar exploits of Yahweh on behalf of Moses and Joshua, Samson, Deborah and Barak, Gideon, etc.

It is on the basis of his exploits that Indra is declared to be unique and incomparable. The word *eka* 'one' 'alone' is often applied to Indra to express his uniqueness[2]. He is unique in shaking what is unshaken and in slaying Vṛitra (III. 30, 4-5), in filling earth and heaven with food and treasure (III. 30, 11), in becoming master of the kine (III. 31, 4) and in being the king of all the world (III. 46, 2); also in being the one strong champion of the gods in the Vṛitra-fight (VI. 17, 8), in conquering men (VI. 18, 2), in subduing people to the Aryan (VI. 18, 3), in bestowing treasure (VI. 30, 1), in being lord of wealth (VI. 31, 1), etc.[3] Indra is incomparable. He has no match among

---

[1] II. 13, 5, 7; I. 32, 1, 5; VI. 17, 1, 3; VIII. 85, 16; V. 29, 4, VIII. 78, 5.

[2] Every Vedic deity as a 'special god' is unique in his own department, but the uniqueness of Indra is emphasized.

[3] The passages in which the uniqueness of Indra is emphasized are chiefly found in books III. and VI., the hymn-books of the Kuśika and Bharadvāja clans. In the passages quoted from Maṇḍala III. food and treasure are linked up with the slaughter of Vṛitra and the winning of the (heavenly) kine; in those quoted from Maṇḍala VI. wealth is connected especially with Indra's exploits as a war-god.

those born or to be born (IV. 18, 4). Even the two boundless worlds are but a handful to him, when he seizes them (III. 30, 5)[1]. With his greatness he has filled earth and heaven, and even beyond this his greatness extends (IV. 16, 5). Heaven trembles at the birth of his blinding splendour (IV. 17, 2). Indra makes the non-existent existent (VI. 24, 5). The unique and incomparable character of Indra is without doubt grounded ultimately upon the uniqueness of the thunderstorm with its accompaniments of lightning, wind and downpour of rain.

6. CHARACTER OF INDRA.—

a) Indra's relation to Varuṇa. In nine hymns Indra and Varuṇa are addressed conjointly as a dual divinity. While they seem to have originated in different circles, Varuṇa perhaps among the Vasiṣṭhas and Indra among the Kuśikas and Bharadvājas, yet on the basis of common attributes and functions they are, as it were, amalgamated. The uniting bonds are their similar cosmic qualities[2]. If Varuṇa as the 'encompassing sky' includes day-sky, night-sky and rainy sky, Indra through the lightning flash, whether by day or night, lights up the whole heaven; and by finding the light at sunrise does the same thing, while with the release of the heavenly waters there is little difference between the two gods as regards 'rainy' character. In most matters referred to in the nine hymns Varuṇa is assimilated to Indra, that is to say, Indra-Varuṇa functioning as a unity drink Soma, overcome Vṛitra, hollow out the channels of the waters, set the sun in motion in the sky, aid in battle, grant victory, bestow wealth and prosperity, cast their mighty bolt against the wicked, and bind with bonds not made of rope[3]. But there is revealed at the same time a consciousness that

---

[1] *Cf.* Isa. XL. 15.

[2] Other things may have contributed to this union, as *e. g.* political alliances between tribes or the development of the ritual.

[3] Ṛv. VI. 68, 2, 10-11; VII. 82, 3; IV. 41, 4, 7, 11; I. 17. 7-8; VII. 84, 2.

however closely allied Indra and Varuṇa may be in cosmic matters, yet in the most fundamental things they will not fuse. Varuṇa as a sky-god can easily be made to wield the thunderbolt and slay Vṛitra, but Indra is ethically too far removed from Varuṇa to be easily assimilated to him[1]. Hence in the Indra-Varuṇa hymns there are drawn no less than six contrasts between Varuṇa and Indra. Varuṇa is king, possessor of the most-exalted *Asurahood,* whose will[2] the gods follow; whereas Indra loves battle and stirs the dust of conflict (IV. 42, 2, 5). Indra with his bolt slays Vṛitra, while Varuṇa as a sage (*vipra*) keeps to the settlements (VI. 68, 3). Varuṇa is a god of peace and quiet (*kṣema*), whereas Indra associated with the Maruts is a warrior seeking glory (VII. 82, 5-6). Indra in the conflicts slays the Vṛitras, whereas Varuṇa evermore guards his ordinances (*vrata* VII. 83, 9). Prayer is made that the wrath of Varuṇa may pass us by, while Indra is besought to make wide room (VII. 84, 2). Varuṇa upholds the terrified[3] people, while Indra smites resistless foemen (VII. 85, 3). In these significant antitheses Varuṇa is represented as watching over his ordinances, as one whose will the gods follow, as a sage who in peace and quiet abides in the settlements, and as one whose anger punishes the evil-doer. On the other hand, Indra loves battle, smites Vṛitra and makes wide room for gods and men. The difference is manifest. In connection with the Zoroastrian reformation, as we have seen, Indra was reduced to the status of a demon, while Varuṇa—the Ahura of the Avesta—was exalted to the supreme position. In India, however, the fortunes of these two chief gods of the Vedic pantheon-rivals, as it were, for supreme honour—were the reverse of what they were in Irān. The influence of the soma-

[1] Some indications of an attempt at assimilation are found in the seventh and tenth books.

[2] *kratu*.

[3] Pravikta from *vij* 'to slink away frightened' (Oldenberg Ṛv. Noten). Geldner (RV. *Glossar*) derives it from *vic* 'to separate' hence 'chosen' people.

cult and of both Brāhman and Kṣatriya sentiment told in favour of Indra. Varuṇa was too remote and inflexible, too august and holy, to be popular. Hence the popularity of Indra gradually increased at the expense of Varuṇa. For in the Brāhmaṇa period Indra became chief of the Indian heaven, while Varuṇa was reduced to the lordship of lakes and pools[1].

b) Indra's relation to Ṛita. In general it may be said that each Vedic deity, while respecting the 'order' of the other departmental gods, especially represents and protects the order within his own department. Neither gods nor mortals infringe the ordinances (*vrata*) and statutes (dhāma) of Indra, (III. 32, 8; VI. 21, 3); and on the other hand, Indra as a deva does not infringe the statutes of the devas, be they Ādityas, Vasus or Rudriyas (X. 48, 11). Within his own sphere Indra is strong and active through law (*dharman* X. 44, 1). He distributes through law the plants and the streams (II. 13, 7): and the rivers follow his ordinance (I. 101, 3). Through *ṛita* he lighted up the many dawns (VI. 39, 4). The *Śiśnadevāḥ* are not to approach Indra's *ṛita* (VII. 21, 5). Thus the emphasis is on the cosmic and ritualistic. There is little reference to *ṛita* in the ethical sense. It is to be remarked, however, that three stanzas in praise of *ṛita* (vv. 8-10 of IV. 23) occur in the middle of an Indra hymn, containing the notable lines:

> The thought of *Ṛita* slayeth crookednesses (v. 8); and
> Of *Ṛita* sure and firm-set are the bases (v. 9).

The first line contains, or at least we would like to read into it, the thought of the supremacy in conscience of the moral law, and the function of the moral law in making sin known and so checking it[2]. Neither line, however, is closely linked up with Indra. As consciousness has the three aspects of knowing, feeling, and willing, so *ṛita* has

---

[1] Oldenberg, RV. 94-97; Macdonell, VM. 65-66.

[2] *Cf.* "By the law is the knowledge of sin". Rom. III. 20.

three strands of meaning, cosmic, ritualistic and ethical. Varuṇa is the Lord of ethical law, Agni of ritualistic law and Indra of cosmic law as displayed in the flash of the lightning, the roar of the thunder, and the downpour of the waters. Varuṇa is depicted as a king seated on his heavenly throne, while Indra is sketched as a warrior hurling the bolt at Vṛitra or leading the Aryans in their struggle with the aborigines. The one is characterised by 'passive sway'; the other, by 'energetic action'[1]. Being primarily a storm-god, Indra manifests a shifty and arbitrary temper as compared with Varuṇa. Thus Indra is represented as having shattered the wain of Uṣas with his bolt (II. 15, 6)[2], quarrelled with the Maruts (I. 170, 2) and fallen out with Sūrya over the heavenly chariot race. Doubtless cosmic myths underlie these episodes. If one thinks of Indra's stormy nature, his love of the intoxicating Soma, his military braggadocio and his uxoriousness—qualities doubtless all found in the Vedic 'Yunkers'—one is not surprised that he does not cut a better ethical figure than he does. But even so Indra is the apotheosis of heroic action rather than of meditative calm. The 'strenuous life' in the person of Indra receives the praise in the largest number of hymns addressed to any god in the Ṛv. It is striking that the national god of the Vedic peoples exemplifies this quality—a quality which the Indian Aryans lost more or less through the influence of the climate and of fusion with the aborigines. That the majestic and reposeful Varuṇa shows up better than the active, Soma-drinking, fighting Indra simply illustrates the fact that a negative character who does nothing bad appears often to much better advantage than a man of action who does great deeds, but commits many faults in the doing of them.

---

[1] Macdonell, VM. 64.

[2] Not a very gallant procedure on the part of Indra to strike the lady Dawn! Mythologically, either the obscuration of the dawn by a thunderstorm, or the extinction of her light after the rising of the sun. Oldenberg, RV. 169; Macdonell, VM. 63; Griffith, Eng. Trans. 2nd Edition, Vol. I. 1896, p. 432, footnote 8.

c) Indra's relation to the wicked. Indra smites the earthly foes of the Aryans as well as the atmospheric Vṛitras and Asuras. With his arrow he slays the perpetrators of great sin, and pardons not the arrogant (II. 12, 10). He is often called 'guiltless' (III. 32, 9, etc.). In the earlier books of the Ṛv. there is little more than this. In the seventh book, however, Indra is once represented as a 'saviour even from great sin' (VII. 20. 1); there is a reference to the sinless Varuṇa as the beholder of sin (VII. 28, 4); and we read that both the crooked *(vṛijina)* and the deceiver lie in the net[1] of Indra (VII. 104, 13). It would seem that in the Vasiṣṭha book, which so exalts Varuṇa, Indra also gets, at least by assimilation to Varuṇa, a considerable degree of ethical character. For he (like Varuṇa) observes sin, punishes the sinner, and saves from even great sin. The most notable passage, however, is found in X. 89, 8-9, probably a late hymn:

8. Indra thou art a clever debt-exactor;
As sword a joint, so cleavest thou the wicked[2],
Who break the law of Varuṇa and Mitra,
Even as people wrong a friend and ally.

9. Those men of evil ways who break agreements,
And injure Varuṇa, Aryaman and Mitra,—
Against such enemies, puissant Indra,
Sharpen thy heavy, strong and ruddy weapon.

On the whole, then, Indra in his ethical function is represented as little more than an executioner who punishes those who break the laws of the Ādityas. With him the ethical is not primary as with Varuṇa, but secondary. It is something, however, that he serves Varuṇa, and the Ādityas at least in the capacity of executioner.

7. INDRA AND THE MARUTS. — Thirty-three hymns[3] are devoted to the Maruts, besides several in which they are addressed conjointly with other gods, especially with Indra.

---

[1] *prasiti*. *cf.* the pāśa, 'noose' of Varuṇa.

[2] *vṛijina*, lit. 'crooked'.

[3] Eleven in V., eleven in I. and eleven in all the other books.

They constitute a band or troop[1], the sons of Rudra and of the cow Pṛiśni[2]. Their close connection with Indra as his helpers in the fight with Vṛitra throws light upon the nature of Indra, on the principle that 'a man is known by the company he keeps'. The following hymn sets forth their activity:

To the Maruts, I. 85.

1. As wondrous sons of Rudra, racers of the sky
Who on their course, like women, beautify themselves,
The Maruts have indeed made heaven and earth increase;
Th' impetuous men rejoice in rites of sacrifice.

2. Having waxed strong, they unto greatness have attained,
In heaven the Rudras have established their abode;
Singing their song and generating Indra-might,
Glory have they put on, the Pṛiśni-mothered ones.

3. When they, cow-mothered, deck themselves with ornaments'
With brilliant weapons arm themselves, the shining ones;
Then every adversary and foe they drive away,
And fatness flows abundantly along their paths.

4. Who as great warriors shine resplendent with their spears'
Shaking with might even the things unshakable,
When ye, O Maruts, swift as thought have to your cars
The spotted mares yoked, ye whose hosts are powerful;

5. When ye have yoked the spotted mares to chariots,
Speeding the stone, ye Maruts, in the conflict,
Streams of the ruddy steed of heaven discharge they[3],
And as with water-skin earth's surface moisten.

6. Let your swift-gliding racers bring you hitherward,
Advance swift-flying with your mighty arms outstretched;
Be seated on the straw, the wide seat made for you;
Delight yourselves, ye Maruts, in the honied juice.

7. Strong in themselves, they have increased through mightiness,
Have climbed the sky, and made themselves an ample seat.
When Viṣṇu helped the Soma-drunken bull of heaven,
Like birds on the dear sacrificial grass they sat.

---

[1] *gaṇa* and *śardhas*.

[2] That is of lightning in its destructive aspect and of the mottled storm-cloud. See Macdonell, VM. 77, 78.

[3] Change of second to third person.

8. Like heroes bold, like warriors speeding in the fray,
Like glory-seekers, they in fights array themselves;
All creatures are afraid of the fierce Marut-band,
Like kings of aspect fierce and terrible are the men.

9. When Tvaṣṭar, skilful workman, turned the thunder-bolt,
Well-wrought, with thousand edges, and of gold compact,
Then Indra took it to perform his manly deeds,
Slew demon Vṛitra and forced out the water-flood.

10. Up have they pushed the bottom of the well with might,
Even the firm cloud-mountain have they cleft in twain;
Blowing their pipes the Marut heroes bountiful
In Soma's rapture have accomplished glorious deeds.

11. Prone have they laid the heavenly well so as to flow,
For thirsty Gotama poured they out the water-spring.
Of brilliant splendour they approach the sage with help,
By mighty deeds may they his wishes gratify.

12. The shelters which you have to give the zealous
Extend them threefold, Maruts, to the pious;
Extend them to us also, O ye Maruts,
Grant wealth to us with hero sons, ye mighty.

From this and other Ṛigvedic material the Maruts may be described as follows: They are born of the laughter of lightning (I. 23, 12): are 'sons' 'heroes' and 'males' of the sky (X. 77, 2; I. 122, 1; III. 54, 13); are brothers who have grown together, all equal in age and of one mind (V. 60, 5; V. 56, 5; I. 165, 1; VIII. 20, 1); are closely associated with the lady *Rodasī*[1]; shine like tongues of fire and have the brilliancy of serpents (X. 78, 3; I. 172, 1); hold lightnings in their fists and are 'lightning-speared' (V. 54, 11; 52, 13); wear golden ornaments such as armlets or anklets (*Khadi*), with which they shine like the sky with stars (II. 34, 2); have chariots of lightning drawn by spotted steeds, and yoke the winds as horses to their pole (III. 54, 13; II. 34, 4; V. 58, 7); are playful like calves, and also terrible like wild beasts (VII. 56, 16; II. 34, 1); with thunder and blasts of wind cause the mountains to quake (I. 23, 11; VIII. 7, 4); sow the mist, milk the

[1] Perhaps a personification of the lightning, since she is described as 'self-luminous' and 'like light', VI. 66, 6.

udders of the sky, cover the eye of the sun with showers, make darkness with the cloud when they wet the earth, and milk the thundering well (VIII. 7, 4; I. 64, 5, 6; V. 59, 5; I. 38, 9); are singers of the sky, who generate Indra-might while singing their song, and cleave the mountain while blowing their pipe (V. 57, 5; I. 85, 2, 10); co-operate with Indra in slaying Ahi and Śaṁbara and in performing all his celestial exploits (III. 47, 3-4; I. 100, etc.)[1]. To sum up the picture of these confederates of Indra and warriors of the sky, they have spears on their shoulders, anklets on their feet, golden ornaments on their breasts, splendours on their chariot, lightnings in their fists, golden helmets on their heads (V. 54, 11).

It is clear from all this that the Maruts are conceived as storm-gods, their nature being defined in terms of lightning, thunder, wind and rain. In a thunderstorm there are numerous lightning flashes and peals of thunder, the 'winds' blow, and 'showers' of rain fall. For such a description it is natural to use the plural. As conceived by the Vedic poets a thunderstorm is a theophany of Indra, who goes forth at the head of his army the Maruts to smite Vṛitra and release the waters[2]. We are surprised that Indra had to go outside of his own circle, as it were, and find his helpers in the circle of Rudra. For the Maruts[3] as the sons of Rudra are called Rudras or Rudriyas. It may be that the distinction between Agni and Agnis, Rudra and Rudras, Uṣas and Uṣasas, Soma and Somas, Vāyu and Vāyus, etc.[4] belongs in its very nature to

---

[1] See Macdonell VM. 77-81.

[2] Indra at the head of the heavenly host of the Maruts fighting against Vṛitra and the other atmospheric demons is the Rigvedic analogue and anticipation of the later struggle between the Devas and Asuras.

[3] From *mar* 'to die', 'to crush', or 'to shine', probably the last. See Macdonell, VM. 81 and VRS. 22.

[4] That is, collective Fire and individual fires, collective Lightning (in its destructive aspect) and individual lightning-flashes, collective Soma and individual soma-drops, collective Wind and individual blasts of wind. There are no Indras

transparent names and not to an archaic and opaque name like Indra. At any rate Indra had no family of sturdy sons to help him in toil and fight, and so had perforce to adopt as it were, the numerous[1] sons of Rudra as his children[2] and co-workers. The Maruts are frankly storm-gods 'racers of the sky', whatever else they may be[3], whereas Indra is described predominantly as cleaving the mountains and digging the channels of rivers. On the other hand, Indra's characteristic weapon is the bolt (*vajra*) which is only once placed in the hands of the Maruts (VII. 7, 32). The different terminology[4] employed in describing the exploits of Indra and the Maruts respectively probably indicates that they originated at different times and in different circles. The fact that Indra uses as his soldiers the Marut band of 'storm-gods' is sufficient proof that he too is essentially a storm-god[5]. We may reasonably expect

---

or Indriyas as there are Rudras and Rudriyas. There is a Varuṇa but no Varuṇas. Possibly it is the uniqueness and exaltation of Varuṇa and Indra that has precluded any lesser Indras or Varuṇas. To this extent like Allāh they are *lā-sharīk*.

[1] Thrice seven or thrice sixty, I. 133, 6; VIII. 85, 8.

[2] Strong with the Rudras *as with sons*, I. 100, 5.

[3] Hillebrandt thinks that the name 'Rudras' combines two meanings, 'storm-winds' and 'the spirits which cause harm and illness' (VM. III. 301).

[4] If the forces and phenomena of the sky are, under the influence of human analogies, poetically conceived sometimes as animals (*Pṛśni* 'Cloud-cow' *Dānu*, water-cow, *Ahi* 'serpent', etc.) and sometimes as men (Varuṇa, Mitra, Indra, Maruts, etc.), it is not at all strange that under the same working of analogy the clouds should be poetically depicted as mountains and their showers of rain as rivers. *Cf.* Psalm LXV. 9 "The river of god (clearly from the context the atmospheric river) is full of water". It requires no very vivid imagination to see mountains and forts in the sky, the cloud-shapes are so suggestive of such interpretation.

[5] On the general subject of Indra and the Maruts as storm-gods the following vivid description of a thunderstorm may be quoted: "An awful storm overtook us. The night settled in. The black clouds eclipsed the light of every star..... The silence became as still as the famous half-hour of silence in heaven...... Then came the rushing of mighty winds. It seemed as if all the spirits demoniac as well as celestial (*cf.* Hillebrandt's theory) were sweeping past me and meeting in mighty conflict. Then the whole heavens became sheets of fire. North, east, south and west, everywhere the heavens were ablaze..... After the thunders had

congruity between Indra and the Maruts as well as between Varuṇa and the Ādityas.

8. INDRA THE BOUNTIFUL.—Indra's most characteristic epithet apart from *Vṛitrahan* 'Vṛitra-slayer' is *Maghavan* 'bountiful'. Indra is the leader in battle of both human tribes and heavenly clans (III. 34, 2). As troop-leader (*śardhanīti*) Indra led the Maruts in the fight against Vṛitra, and as the great war-god of the Vedic people he led them in their struggle with the Dasyus. Accordingly two types of exploit seem to provide the basis for Indra's epithet 'bountiful', *viz.* his release of the waters (heavenly and earthly) through the slaughter of Vritra, and his victories over the Dasyus on behalf of his people. Through the release of the waters Indra becomes a 'god of fertility'[1] giving good crops, food, cows, horses and store of hero sons. Indra's gifts, however, are frequently the result of his victories over the earthly foes of his worshippers or favourites. Through battle he wins from the aborigines ploughland, horses, cows, gold, etc. (II. 21, 1; IV. 17, 11), which he as 'spoil-winner' (III. 42, 6) gives as booty. Indra bestows also wives upon his worshippers (IV. 17, 16; V. 31, 2)[2]. In all of these ways Indra is generous and bountiful toward those who offer him libations. He is a 'treasure-lord of treasures'[3]. As a sample of the highest type of prayer addressed to Indra is the following:

rolled and swelled and died away,....then, suddenly, every tree, rock, every hillside, would come out as clear in outline as during the day. Then midnoon in an instant would be changed into midnight. Power, power, omnipotent, infinite power!"

Rev. Frank De Witt Talmage, D. D. in the Christian Herald, July 19, 1905.

[1] See *Indra as God of Fertility*, Hopkins, JAOS. 36, 1917, pp. 242-268. The numerous references to sexual relations in the Indra hymns are probably to be interpreted from the point of view of Indra as a fertility god. *Cf.* Hopkins, *op. cit*, pp. 262-265.

[2] It is frequently uncertain in what manner Indra gives food, cows, etc., whether through victory over Vritra and consequently 'rain from heaven and fruitful seasons', or through the winning of booty from earthly foes. Wives may have been captured in battle, or good harvests and plenty of food may have made marriages easy and numerous.

[3] *Vasupati vasūnām* III. 36, 9.

Indra bestow on us the best of riches,
Discernment of the practical, good fortune;
Increase of substance, welfare of our bodies,
Sweetness of speech, and pleasantness of weather. (II. 21, 6.)

And to illustrate the enthusiasm and confidence with which men called upon Indra:

Hurrah, let us invoke large-hearted Indra,
Most manly in the fight for gain of booty;
Mighty, a very present help in battle,
Slayer of Vṛitṛas, winner he of riches. (III. 34, 11.)

CHAPTER VIII.

SOMA THE DEIFIED SACRIFICIAL DRINK

1. Introductory. — Of the three ritualistic gods Agni, Bṛihaspati and Soma, the last is, in one respect at least, the most important, since the Soma sacrifice furnished the centre and framework[1] for the whole Ṛigvedic ritual. As the importance of Agni is suggested by the fact that his hymns occupy the first place in the family books, so that of Soma is indicated by the equally significant fact that one whole book, the ninth, is devoted entirely to his praise. About 120 hymns are addressed to Soma, so that he ranks third in importance in the Ṛv., if judged by statistical standards. Like Agni, Soma is a thoroughly transparent deity. His physical nature as the Soma plant and juice was so obvious as to prevent that completeness of the anthropomorphic process which is seen in the more opaque gods, Indra and Varuṇa. The fact that Soma-Haoma was prominent in both the Indian and the Iranian ritual proves sufficiently that the divine drink was known to the undivided Indo-Iranian tribes. There are only two references to Haoma in the Gāthās of Zoroaster, one mentioning *Dūraoša*[2] 'the averter of death', the standing epithet of Haoma in the later Avesta, and the other alluding to 'the filthiness of this intoxicant'[3]. These allusions are sufficient to prove that the intoxicating *Haoma* was under the ban of the great reformer[4]. But in the later Avesta Haoma, like so many others of the old daēvas, came back

[1] The Soma sacrifice is the *soul (ātmā yajñasya* IX. 2, 10; 6, 8) of the Vedic ritual.

[2] Yasna, XXXII. 14.

[3] Yasna, XLVIII. 10.

[4] Moulton, EZ. 71-72. Even if the force of these allusions be challenged, the result remains the same. Haoma was certainly pre-Zoroastrian, and the name constantly appears in the Younger Avesta. This means simply that Haoma was banned by Zoroaster. See Jackson, *Grundriss* (Iranian) II. 644.

again, and according to Yasna IX-X was in almost every respect the same as the Vedic Soma. The details of the following hymn will be compared with the corresponding Avestan account:

To Soma, VIII. 48.

1. Of the sweet food I have partaken wisely,
That stirs good thoughts, best banisher of trouble,
On which to feast, all gods as well as mortals,
Naming the sweet food 'honey', come together.

2. Hast thou within gained entrance[1], thou becomest
Aditi, appeaser of the gods' hot anger.
May'st thou, O Indu, Indra's friendship choosing,
To riches speed us as a mare the car-pole.

3. We have drunk Soma, have become immortal,
Gone to the light have we, the gods discovered.
What can hostility now do against us?
What, O Immortal, mortal man's fell purpose[2]?

4. Joy to our heart be thou, when drunk, O Indu,
Like father to a son, most kind, O Soma;
Thoughtful like friend to friend, O thou of wide fame,
Prolong our years that we may live, O Soma.

5. These glorious freedom-giving drops by me imbibed
Have knit my joints together as straps a chariot;
From broken legs may Soma drops protect me,
May they from every illness keep me far removed.

6. Like friction-kindled fire inflame me, Soma,
Make us more opulent and us illumine;
For in thy rapture, Soma, I regard me
As wealthy. For prosperity, then, enter.

7. Of thee pressed out with mind devoted, Soma,
We would partake as of paternal riches.
Years of our life do thou prolong, King Soma,
Even as the sun prolongs the days of springtime.

8. Be gracious unto us for good, King Soma;
We are thy devotees; of that be certain.
When might and wrath display themselves, O Indu,
Do not abandon us, as wished by foemen.

---

[1] *I. e.* When thou hast been imbibed.

[2] "And what, immortal god, the spite of mortals?". Macdonell, HR. 80.

9. Protector of our body art thou, Soma,
In every limb hast settled man-beholding:
If we infringe thine ordinances, be gracious
As our good friend, O god, for higher welfare.

10. May I with that kind friend be close united
Who, Lord of bays, when quaffed shall harm me never.
As for the juice deposited within us,
Indra, prolong our years for its enjoyment.

11. Ailments have fled away, diseases vanished,
The powers of darkness have become affrighted.
With might hath Soma mounted up within us;
The dawn we've reached, where men renew existence[1].

12. The drop imbibed within our hearts, O Fathers,
The immortal drop in mortals hath found entrance;
That Soma we would worship with oblation,
Rest in his loving kindness and fair favour.

13. Uniting with the Fathers hast thou, Soma,
Thyself extended over earth and heaven.
Thee, Indu, would we worship with oblation,
And we ourselves become the lords of riches.

14. Ye gods, protectors, speak for us defending;
Let neither sleep nor prattle overpower us.
May we belovéd evermore of Soma
With hero sons attended utter worship.

15. Soma, thou art our strengthener on all sides;
Light-finder art thou; enter us, man-beholder.
Do thou, O Indu, with thine aids accordant,
Grant us protection both in front and rearward[2].

This hymn written by a member of the priestly family of the Kaṇvas describes the effects of Soma when quaffed by mortals. It protects the body, preserves from accident, removes illness, banishes trouble, gives joy and comfort, prolongs life, speeds to riches, scares away the powers of darkness, averts hostility, preserves from the wrath and malice of enemies, gives exhilaration, inflames and illumines, gives good thoughts, makes one think one is rich[3], appeases

[1] 'We have arrived where men prolong existence'. Macdonell, HR. 81.

[2] Acknowledgment is made of indebtedness to translations of this hymn by Macdonell, VRS. 152-164; HR. 79-81; Hillebrandt, LR. 35-36.

[3] So through the drinking of Soma the singer thinks himself to be a Rishi, III. 43, 5.

the anger of the gods, and makes immortal. In the Avesta likewise Haoma is best for drinking and most nutricious for the soul, heals illness, gives health of body and long life, furnishes prosperity, overcomes enemies, warns off thief, murderer and wolf, is a cause of good exhilaration, and drives away death[1]. It should be observed that, according to the Vedic hymn just translated, the wonderful effects of Soma in the individual are bound up with and conditioned by, the actual drinking of Soma[2]. Soma mounts up with might, and settles in every limb (vv. 9, 11). With it one is 'filled'. Peoples and mortals in general, and wealthy Kṣatriya patrons, besides priests, are referred to as drinkers of Soma[3], but the evidence is insufficient to show that it was a popular drink[4]. The Soma-juice *as freshly prepared* three times a day could hardly have been intoxicating, except when allowed to stand for a sufficient time in which to ferment, as when pressed two days before using.

Hymn X. 119 is clearly a monologue, in which some one, when exhilarated with Soma, boasts of his prowess. It is usual to think of Indra as the one[5], but Oldenberg[6]

---

[1] Yasna IX. 16-21; X. 8-19. *Cf.* L. H. Gray's fine translation of Yasna IX. 17 according to the original metre (the same as that of Longfellow's Hiawatha):

Thee I pray for might and conquest,
Thee for health and Thee for healing,
Thee for progress and for increase,
Thee for strength of all my body.

Carnoy, *Iranian Mythology* in volume VI. of *The Mythology of All Nations*, p. 282.

[2] vv. 1, 2, 3, 4, 5, 6, 7, 9, 10, 12, 15.

[3] *Sūrayaḥ* IX. 99, 3; *Kṛṣṭayá* III. 49, 1; *martyāsaḥ* VIII. 48, 1.

[4] See *Vedic Index* under *Soma* and *Surā.* It may be that the difference between *surā*, the evil effects of which were frankly recognised (VII. 86, 6) and *Soma* was this, that Soma was used chiefly for religious purposes and was freshly and liturgically prepared, whereas surā was a 'commercialised' article of trade. Possibly it was the mode of preparation, sacramental in the one case, secular in the other, that helped to make the difference. At any rate *surā* was a popular and *Soma* a hieratic drink.

[5] So Muir, OST. V. 90-91; Geldner and Kaegi, SL. 81-83; Macdonell, VM. 65.

[6] Ṛv. Noten, II. 339.

following Bergaigne prefers to think of the poet himself as describing his feelings after drinking Soma. Both interpretations are possible and it makes little difference whether the hymn is placed in the mouth of Indra or in the mouth of a priestly devotee who through participation in Indra's drink [1] became mystically identified with Indra[2]. Each stanza has the same refrain; 'Have I not drunk of Soma juice?' Leaving out the refrain, the hymn reads as follows:—

> Thus even thus my purpose is to win a cow, to win a horse.
> Like violent winds, the draughts I drink have lifted and transported me.
> As the swift horses move the car, so have the draughts excited me.
> To me has come the hymn of praise, like lowing cow to darling calf.
> As carpenter a chariot-seat, so with my heart I frame the hymn.
> Not ev'n as mote within the eye do the 'five tribes' appear to me.
> The heavens and earth themselves are not the equal of even half of me.
> In greatness I surpass the sky, surpass also this spacious earth.
> Hurrah! let me deposit earth, and set it either here or there.
> In one brief moment will I smite this broad earth either here or there.
> One half of me is in the sky; the other half I cause to trail.
> I am superlatively great, have been exalted to the skies.

Such a monologue, as the above, shows clearly that Soma, when imbibed, did produce a certain exhilaration or intoxication, call it what you will. A distinctive characteristic of the experience was a feeling of strength and greatness. The poor man thought himself rich (VIII. 48, 6). Psychologically, Soma would never have been thought of as stimulating the strength of Indra, if it had not been known in

[1] Soma is called in IX. 85, 3 the 'soul (*ātmā*) of Indra', and even 'the generator of Indra', IX. 96, 5.

[2] In fact, the ascription of the hymn to *Lava Aindra*, 'Indra as Lava' or 'Lava the Indra-like' would seem to suggest this. We have found (p. 95) such mystical identification of demon and sorcerer as largely to obliterate the difference between them. This suggests the possibility of a similar identification of god and devotee.

experience to stimulate[1] the strength of men. In Vedic battle doubtless each side was fearful of the other, and afraid to make a desperate onset. Whatever, then, like Soma (or *surā*), would help to banish 'collateral trains of thought'[2] connected with caution, personal safety, etc. and furnish *a feeling of strength* until the rush of battle was accomplished, would ordinarily bring about victory. Soma in IX. 77, 1 is called 'the bolt *(vajra)* of Indra'. The rush of warriors in battle was due to Soma, just as the rush of the lightning.

The mysterious qualities of the Soma juice as seen in its exhilarating the warrior and helping him to perform valiant deeds were also seen in the inspiration which it gave to the priestly singer and in the healing it furnished to the sick. Soma himself was a singer[3], and as such was a source of inspiration to singers[4]. He is called 'generator of hymns...... leader of poets, Ṛishi of sages' (IX. 96, 5-6). He is 'Ṛishi-minded' and a 'Ṛishi-maker'. Soma, like Bṛihaspati, was a 'specialist' in the work of inspiring hymns. Thus in X. 119, 2 the poet sings:

> 'Like violent winds the draughts I drink have lifted me and borne me on[5]'.

Soma was also the sick man's medicine (VIII. 61, 17). Thus, as shown above, god Soma was the guardian of men's bodies, occupying their every limb, knitting together their

---

[1] I. 82, 5 suggests that Soma stimulates the sexual instinct. For the similar effect of wine compare Gen. XIX. 30-36, 2 Sam. XI. 13. Once while in camp in India, a low-caste (Chamār) servant got intoxicated. When expostulated with he replied: "If one does not use strong drink, how can one beget children?"

[2] See article on *Alcohol and the Individual* by H. S. Williams, M.D. in McClure's Magazine, October 1908, p. 705.

[3] *Rebha* IX. 7, 6, etc.

[4] Similar spirituous sources of the divine afflatus are not unknown in modern times.

[5] This reminds one of 2 Peter I. 21: "Men spake from god, being moved (φερόμενοι, lit. 'borne along') by the Holy Spirit"; and also of Eph. V. 18-19, "Be filled with the spirit; *speaking* one to another in psalms and hymns and spiritual songs".

joints, protecting from broken legs, causing ailments and diseases to vanish, and so bestowing long life[1] (VIII. 48, 5, 7, 9, 10, 11). Not only did Soma bestow health of body, but also health of mind, giving good thoughts, a sense of peace with the gods, joy, rapture, illumination, forgiveness[2]. Soma is a very wise sage (IX. 12, 4). As such he bestows 'a happy mind, practical skill and mental ability' (X. 25, 1). Here the nature and effects of Soma are idealized, very much as wine is idealised in the lines of a certain Christian hymn[3]. Victory over enemies, composition of hymns, and recovery from disease, as manifestations of the grace of Soma, are well illustrated in X. 25, 9-11.

2. The Origin and Habitat of Soma.—

a) Soma's heavenly origin.—Like Agni Soma came from heaven[4]. The celestial origin of the two is mentioned once together:

> Mātariśvan fetched one of you from heaven;
> The eagle twirled the other from the cloud-rock. I. 93, 6.

There is reason for holding that Mātariśvan and the eagle, although belonging to different myths, are yet 'mythological synonyms', both referring to the lightning form of Agni. There is no doubt in the case of Mātariśvan. Bloomfield makes it highly probable for the eagle also[5]. There is no difficulty in understanding the eagle as the lightning, since Agni is often called a bird, and is once termed 'the eagle of the sky'[6]. The Maruts, whose lightning-nature is so manifest, are also called 'eagles of the sky' (X. 92, 6). Soma is represented as a 'child of the sky', whom, though heavenly in origin, earth received.

---

[1] The writer recalls meeting with an Indian civilian in 1890 who declared that if it had not been for whiskey he would have died long ago.

[2] VIII. 48, 1, 2, 4, 6, 9.

[3] "He brings a poor vile sinner
Into his 'house of *wine*'".

[4] See Kuhn, HFG.

[5] *The Legend of Soma and the Eagle*, JAOS, 16, (1896), pp. 1-24. Bloomfield's interpretation is favoured by Macdonell, VM. 111-112, and Keith, IM. 47.

[6] *Divaḥ śyenaḥ* VII. 15, 4.

High is the birth of thee, the plant;
Thee being in heaven the earth received. IX. 61, 10.

The eagle brought Soma from afar, from heaven, flying swift as thought[1]. That is to say, the lightning as the eagle of the sky darts down from the cloud, bringing with it the nectar of the skies, in other words 'the water of the cloud'. In one hymn especially the myth of the rape of Soma is summarized:

IV. 27. To the Eagle.

(Agni the lightning)

1. While yet within the womb[2] I was acquainted
With all the generations of the *devas;*
A hundred metal forts kept me well guarded,
Then with all speed I flew forth as an eagle.

(Soma)

2. Not easily did he effect my capture,
Yet in heroic strength was he triumphant;
As bountiful he far outstripped the niggards,
O'ertook the winds and passed them, he the mighty.

(Poet)

3. And so when from the sky down rushed the eagle,
Or when from there (the gods) brought him, the bounteous;
Then furious in his mind Kṛiśānu[3], th' archer,
An arrow aimed at him and loosed the bow-string.

4. From heaven's zenith swift the eagle bore him,
As from afar the Aśvin pair bore Bhujyu[4];
Then downward fell meantime the flying feather
Of that bird hasting forward on his journey.

The myth of the heavenly origin of a divine beverage

---

[1] IX. 68, 5; 77, 2; VIII. 89, 8.

[2] *i. e.* the cloud-womb, in which the lightning form of Agni was shut up by a hundred metal forts, as it were.

[3] Probably a Gandharva, a guardian of the celestial Soma. Kṛiśānu is possibly to be identified with the demon *Karesāni* mentioned once in the Avesta (Yasna IX. 24). Kṛiśānu may be compared with Vṛitra.

[4] The translation of this line gives only the general sense as gathered from other passages. For the various attempts to interpret or amend *indrāvataḥ* see Ludwig, *Uebersetzung* II. 593, V. 468; Pischel, VS. I. 206-216; Bloomfield, JAOS. 16 (1896), 13-24; Hillebrandt, LR. 29; and Oldenberg, *Ṛv. Noten*, I. 292-293.

conceived as a kind of honey-mead[1] may be Indo-European. At any rate there is the myth of the nectar-bringing eagle of Zeus and the metamorphosis of Odin as an eagle to carry off the mead, both myths agreeing in general with that of the Soma-bringing eagle of Indra[2]. These three myths clearly refer alike to the downward swoop of the lightning-bird bringing therewith the rain as the *madhu*[3] or *amṛita* of the sky.

b) Soma's earthly habitat.—In several passages Soma is called 'mountain-dwelling'[4], and once 'mountain-grown'[5]. His origin is closely connected with 'rock'[6]. While the same ambiguity may beset some of these texts as adheres to the special vocabulary of Indra ('mountains' and 'rivers' as either heavenly or earthly), yet it is clear from both the Ṛv. and the Avesta[7] that Soma-Haoma was a mountain-grown plant. It is connected with the mountain Haraiti in the Avesta, and with Mūjavant in the Ṛv.

As draught of Maujavata[8] Soma, so doth,
Th' enlivening Vibhīdaka delight me. X. 34, 1.

---

[1] Skt. *madhu*, Gr. μέθυ, Anglo-Saxon. Medu, Eng. Mead.

[2] Oldenberg, RV. 176; Macdonell, VM. 114; Kuhn, HFG. 153, 177.

[3] *Madhu*, because of its wonderful intoxicating effects, was conceived as the drink of the gods. It must naturally then have been a heavenly drink, which was brought down to earth, this being the function of the nectar-bringing eagle in the three mythologies. The connection between rain-water and madhu was sufficiently explained by the fact that water is a constituent of the honey-mead. And the close connection between waters and plants provided a sufficient nexus between the rain and the soma-plant.

[4] *giriṣṭha* III. 48, 2; V. 43, 4; IX. 18. 1, 62, 4.

[5] *parvatāvṛidh*, IX. 46 1.

[6] *adri* V. 85, 2; I. 93, 6.

[7] According to Yasna X. 4, 10-12, 17, Haoma is represented as placed on the high mountain *Haraiti* by a skilful god, whence holy birds carried it everywhere to the heights, where it grew both on the lofty tablelands and in the mountain valleys.

[8] The mountain Mūjavant (if it was a mountain and not simply the name of a people; *cf.* Hillebrandt, VM. I. 65), being closely connected with the Gandhāris (AV. V. 22, 5, 7, 8, 14) must have been situated somewhere between Bactria and the Punjab. In the *Tait, Saṃh.* I. 8, 6, 2 and the AV. passages referred to above the Mūjavants are taken as a type of distant folk, to which Rudra with his fever-bearing bow is entreated to depart. In fact Mūjavant is as far off and mysterious as the river *Rasā*. Possibly both embody dim reminiscences of the undivided Indo-Iranian days.

3. The identification of the Soma plant.

Not much need be said under this head. When the Indo-Iranian tribes left the original IE. home, they experienced along with the change in their habitat a change also in their drink. The IE. *madhu* 'honey-mead' was replaced by the Indo-Iranian Soma. Soma-Haoma means literally 'extract' or 'juice', from *su* = *hu* 'to press'[1]. In the Ṛv. Soma and madhu are often used interchangeably and each in the form of an adjective may qualify the other[2]. Soma 'juice' and madhu 'sweet' are too general in meaning to be confined necessarily to any one drink. It is true the Avestan account in Yasna X would seem to indicate that the Haoma juice was produced from a particular plant which grew in a particular place. The preparation of Soma-Haoma, as we have seen, belonged to the undivided Indo-Iranian period. With their 'trek' into India the Vedic Aryans probably had to give up largely the use of the Iranian Soma plant and find substitutes nearer their new home[3]. This was not difficult. Besides the various Sarcostemmas[4] there was the Afghan grape, the possibility of a preparation from hops as suggested by Max Müller, or from sugar-cane; or, as recently suggested by E. B. Havell[5], from rāgi, the common millet[6], from which an intoxicating drink is still made in the Eastern Himālayas.

In both Veda and Avesta the Soma plant is described as

---

[1] Madhu seldom occurs in the Avesta and then only in the sense of honey, never in that of Soma. See Hillebrandt, VM. I. 238; Oldenberg, RV. 368.

[2] Soma is *madhumān* 'honied' (IX. 96, 13), and madhu is *somya* 'Soma-like' (III. 53, 10).

[3] *Cf.* Roth PW. under *Soma;* Hillebrandt, VM. I. 68.

[4] Viminale, Intermedium, Brevistigma and Brunonianum. See Hillebrandt, VM. I. 4 *ff.*

[5] *What is Soma?* JRAS. July 1920, pp. 349-351.

[6] *Eleusine coracana.* "It is cultivated along the Himālayas up to a height of 3000 feet," *op cit.* p. 351.

having hanging branches[1], and a yellow colour[2]. Mountain-growth, yellow colour and hanging branches (?) are the two or three points in which Veda and Avesta agree in the description of the Soma-stalk[3]. It is most probable that this is a true description of the plant used for Soma during the undivided Indo-Iranian period. The technical expressions 'stalk', 'yellow', 'mountain-grown', etc. were so firmly imbedded in the Soma-Haoma ritual as to reappear in both the Ṛv. and the Younger Avesta. While in Persia there was less probability of a break in the tradition, in India, as shown above, substitutes most likely had to be found for the ancient Soma plant. Substitutes of such a nature would naturally be chosen as would best conform to the traditional description of the Soma plant and juice, and in any case the technical terms of the ritual would be retained, even if there was a lack of perfect correspondence[4]. Since the Soma sacrifice was the 'soul' of the Vedic ritual and the three daily pressings constituted the framework in which practically all of the gods were worshipped, it is clear that large quantities of the plant used for the sacred liquor must have been necessary. It is difficult to think of such quantities being brought from a distance, unless perhaps the plants could be cleansed and stored for future use, as is the custom of the modern Parsees[5]. But, as said before,

---

[1] *Naicāśākha* Ṛv. III. 53, 14 according to Hillebrandt (VM. I. 14), a name of the Soma plant as having branches that bend down, and *nāmyāsus* (*nam* to bend) 'with bending sprouts', Mill's translation of Yasna IX. 16. Unfortunately full certainty attaches to the interpretation of neither word.

[2] *Hari* 'yellow' (Ṛv. IX. 92, 1), and *zāiri* 'golden-hued' (Yasna IX. 16, 30).

[3] Vedic aṃśu, Avestan āsu.

[4] In this respect the Soma sacrament may be compared with the use of wine in the Holy Communion of the Christian Church. The liquor used is grape-juice fermented, or unfermented, or any liquid made to look like grape-juice. Here the colour is the essential thing, for it must be red like blood.

[5] Jivanji Jamshedji Modi, Art. *Haoma* ERE. VI. 506-510, says that twigs of the Soma plant, a species of Ephedra, are brought from Persia to India, where they are washed and purified and then laid aside for thirteen months and thirteen days. If properly cleansed and stored they can be used several years afterwards.

it is probable that some Indian plant or shrub growing not too far away from the Vedic settlements was used for the preparation of the sacred drink[1] perhaps as a substitute[2] for the original Iranian plant. Whatever it was, it flourished during the rainy season, swelling with milk (II. 13, 1), generated and strengthened by Parjanya, the deified raincloud (IX. 82, 3; 113, 3[3]). It had a stalk *(aṃśu)* which was ruddy (VII. 98, 1), and the whole plant was called *ándhas*[4]. According to the later ritual the Soma shoots had to be purchased from a Śūdra. This transaction was made the subject of a dramatic representation, one of the earliest anticipations of the later drama. The Śūdra was not merely a trader in Soma shoots but also an impersonation, as Hillebrandt thinks, of the Gandharva (*e. g.* Kṛiśānu) who held back the celestial Soma[5]. This would seem to indicate that the Soma shoots came from a non-Aryan tribe, such a tribe as the Kikaṭas, who apparently are mentioned in connection with the Soma plant.

---

[1] To illustrate the possibility of there being more than one plant fit to produce Soma, reference may be made to the 'cow-tree' of Brazil which yields a quantity of milk especially at sunrise, the milk after being drawn growing yellow; the *Masseraudúba*, a milk-tree also of Brazil, concerning which an observer writes: "We cut several notches in the bark of some logs of this tree that had lain on the ground for a month, and in a minute the rich milk was oozing out in great quantities, some of which we collected in a basin, *diluted* it with water, *strained* it, and used it for supper and breakfast" (W. A. Cook, *By Horse, Canoe and Float through the Wilderness of Brazil*, p. 374); "the Carnaúba Palm, which yields a white liquid like cocoanut milk" (*op. cit.* p. 375); and certain beverages used by the Creek Indians, concerning which Roosevelt wrote: "They had a cool drink made *from honey and water*, besides another made from fermented corn, which tasted much like cider, ... also the Black Drink, a bitter beverage brewed from the crushed leaves of a small shrub" (WW. I. 84, 88).

[2] According to Śāṅkhāyana III. 20, 9-11, in case the recognised Soma plant was not available, it was permitted to take as a substitute the plant most resembling the one recognised by ordinary usage, but the words of the ritual were not to be changed. Quoted by Hillerbrandt, VM. I. 23.

[3] *Cf.* Yasna X. 3: I praise the cloud and the waters that made thy body to grow upon the mountains. See Hillerbrandt, VM. I. 56-57.

[4] Etymologically the same as the Gr. ἄνθος, 'flower'.

[5] Hillebrandt, VM. I. 81; *Vedic Index*, II. 475.

Mid Kīkaṭas what do thy kine, O Indra?
That tribe nor mixture[1] pours nor heats oblation;
Bear thou to us the wealth of Pramaganda,
Give up, O Maghavan, to us the 'low-branched'. III. 53, 14.

4. The Sacramental Preparation of the Soma Juice.

Of the Soma hymns translated above, IV. 27 describes the bringing down of the heavenly Soma by an eagle, while VIII. 48 and X. 119 depict the effects which spring from the drinking of the divine intoxicant. The hymns to Soma in Book IX are addressed to Soma *Pavamāna*, that is, to Soma while in the process of passing through the filter. Two of these hymns are herewith reproduced on the basis of Griffith's translation with certain changes:—

To Soma Pavamāna, IX. 1.

1. By most exhilarating stream
   And sweetest, Soma, filter thee,
   Pressed out for Indra as his drink.
2. Fiend-slayer, present everywhere,
   He through the wooden trough has reached
   His seat, his metal-wrought abode.
3. Be thou best Vṛitra-slayer, best
   Granter of bliss, most liberal;
   Our noble patrons' wealth increase.
4. Flow onward with thy juice unto
   The banquet of the mighty gods;
   Flow unto victory and fame.
5. O Indu, we draw nigh to thee,
   This is our object, day by day;
   To thee our wishes are addressed.
6. By means of the unfailing fleece
   The daughter of the sun doth cleanse
   Thy Soma that is streaming forth.
7. Him seize and hold fast in the fight
   Ten slender maidens, sisters all,
   In the decisive day of war.

[1] The word *āśir* rendered 'mixture' means 'the milk that serves for mixing with Soma'.

8. Him send they forth, the virgin band,
They blow the bagpipe[1] musical;
Threefold protection is the juice.

9. Milch-kine inviolable anoint
The infant Soma with their milk,—
Soma for Indra as his drink.

10. In the wild raptures of this draught,
Indra slays all his enemies;
The mighty one bestoweth wealth.

To Soma Pavamana, IX. 28.

1. Sent forth by men, this mighty steed,
Lord of the mind, who knoweth all,
Runs to the woollen straining-cloth.

2. Within the filter hath he flowed.
This Soma for the gods effused,
Entering all their various worlds.

3. Resplendent is this deity,
Immortal in his dwelling place,
Foe-slayer, feaster best of gods.

4. Directed by the sisters ten,
Bellowing on his way this bull
Runs onward to the wooden vats.

5. This Pavamāna made the sun
To shine and all his various worlds,
Omniscient, present everywhere.

6. This Soma filtering himself,
Flows mighty and infallible,
Slayer of sinners, feasting gods.

The preparation of Soma was the supreme ritualistic performance of the Ṛigvedic religion. There were three distinct stages in the operation, the pressing, the filtering and the mixing, of the sacred liquor. The ceremonial was elaborate and costly. It is difficult to get a clear picture of all the details, but happily this is not necessary for the purpose in hand.

---

[1] The Soma-stalk is probably meant, which seems to have given forth a sound when struck. So Hillebrandt, LR. 32, n. 3.

a) The Pressing of the Soma. — Probably the most archaic, if not the most usual, method was by means of the mortar and pestle[1], for this is the Iranian way, both ancient and modern, of extracting the Soma[2]. In only one hymn of the Ṛv. and that probably a late one, is there a clear reference to the mortar.

To the Mortar, etc. I. 28.

1. There where the broad-based pressing-stone[3]
Stands upright to crush out the juice;
2. Where dual parts to crush the stalk
Are like the parts of man and wife[4];
3. There where a woman practises
The backward and the forward move;
4. Where as it were with reins to guide
They bind with cords the twirling-stick[5].

---

[1] *Ulūkhala*, 'mortar' I. 28, 1, 5; *ulūkhala-musala*, 'mortar and pestle', AV. IX. 6, 15; Śatapatha Brāh. I. 1, 4, 6.

[2] Yasna XXIV. 7; XXV. 2. For the modern usage see J. J. Modi, ERE. VI. (1914), article *Haoma*, according to whom *hāvana* (*hu* 'to crush') is "the utensil in which the twigs of the *haoma* plant are pounded."

[3] The broad-based *grāvan* (usually rendered 'press-stone') is clearly the mortar. In AV. III. 10, 5 there is mention of *vānaspatyā grāvāṇaḥ*, 'forest-tree pressing-stones', *i.e.* the wooden mortar and pestle. So Śat. Brāh. I. 4, 7, 10, according to which the wooden mortar and the wooden pestle are called *grāvāṇaḥ* 'press-stones'. *Cf.* Hillebrandt VM. I. 161-162. In Kashmir a similar wooden mortar and pestle are used for removing the husks from rice, and women do the pounding alternately drawing back the stick and driving it down (*cf.* v. 3). The mortar is made of the trunk of a tree sawed off into a block and hollowed out so as to have a large bowl-shaped opening.

[4] The mechanism of pestle and mortar, as of the two fire-sticks, suggests sexual analogies. In vv. 2-3 there is *double entendre*. This is furthered by the fact that the roots *su* and *sū*, originally one root mean 'to press' and 'to generate', respectively. *Cf.* Hillebrandt, VM. I. 162.

[5] The mention of *manthā* 'twirling-stick' does not fit in well with the picture of the mortar. Two explanations have been suggested. One that of Oldenberg (Ṛv. Noten, I. 24, note 2), who suggests that it may refer to the production of fire as an integral part of the Soma ritual, vv. 3-4 belonging together. The other is that of Hillebrandt (VM. I. 161), who thinks the twirling stick went with the mortar both together forming 'a kind of hand-mill' for the crushing of Soma. A

Each stanza has the following refrain:

O Indra, drink thou eagerly
Of Soma liquor mortar-pressed.

Two more stanzas of the same hymn may be quoted:

5. Whenever thou from house to house[1]
Art harnessed, mortar, for thy task,
Then utter here thy clearest sound,
Loud as the drum of conquerors.

6. Lord of the forest, once the wind
Blew all about thy summit high;
Mortar, for Indra press thou forth
The Soma juice that he may drink.

A reference to the same method of pressing Soma may possibly be found in X. 101, 10-11 (confessedly obscure stanzas):

10. Into the wood's lap pour thy tawny (object),
With stony cutters make the product ready;
Embrace and compass them with girdles tenfold,
And to both chariot poles attach the car-horse.

11. Between the car's two shafts the car-horse bulky
Goes to his place as goes the doubly wedded;
Place on the wood the sovereign of the forest.
And sink a well, although ye do not dig it.

If this interpretation is correct, the pestle is represented by the 'stony cutters', the car-horse and *Vanaspati* 'the

further suggestion may be made. May it not be that first the Soma shoots were pounded and crushed in the mortar, and then after water was added to obtain the juice, the whole was churned by the regular Indian twirling apparatus, the better to secure the juice? In the ritual of Soma-pressing as followed by Indian Parsees the priest after pounding the soma twigs in the hāvana and adding water "gives a little push to the pestle which is within the mortar and causes it to turn in a circle". "This part of the ritual", explains J. J. Modi (ERE. art. *Haoma* in a foot-note) "is a relic of the old practice, when, after being pounded, the *haoma* twigs were regularly rubbed in the mortar with the pestle to extract the juice further". This may possibly throw light on the Vedic reference.

[1] The reference to the mortar in every house (v. 5) as a means of pressing Soma suggests that Soma was a popular drink in the early Rigvedic days, or at least in the area where this hymn was produced.

sovereign of the forest', while 'the wood' and 'the wood's lap' indicate the mortar[1].

There was a second Ṛigvedic method of pressing Soma, namely by means of the *grāvāṇaḥ* or 'press-stones', the stones resting on the 'ox-hide' and, according to the later ritual, being manipulated in connection with two boards. Three hymns are addressed to the deified press-stones, X. 76, 94 and 175, from which the following quotations are made:

This very excellent oblation press ye out;
Like steed hand-guided is the Soma-pressing stone. X. 76, 2.

These speak a hundredfold, yea speak a thousandfold,
They cry aloud to us *with tawny-coloured* mouths;
The pious press-stones busied with the pious work
Get, *even before the Hotar*, taste of th' offered food. X. 94, 2.

These speak aloud, for they have found the honied juice,
Over the ripe flesh of the stalk they hum a song.
As they devour *the branch of the red-coloured tree*,
Bellow aloud the bulls that gnaw the Soma shoots[2]. X. 94, 3.

The skilful ones dance with the sisters linked with them,
Making the earth reëcho with the noise they make. X. 94, 4.

The winged ones lift up their voice unto the sky,
The dusky nimble ones dance in the *ākharā*[3]
Down, downward to *the nether stone's place* go they all,
Much juice receive they from the sun-bright Soma stalk. X. 94, 5.

With one accord the pressing stones
Over the nether ones play the lord,
Giving the bull his bull-like strength. X. 175, 3.

From these passages we get the following details: The press-stones, like steeds, are held by the hand. They gnaw the branch of the ruddy Soma tree, and so with ruddy mouths cry aloud. Like priests they busy themselves with the pious work, speaking a thousandfold, and getting a taste

[1] So Hillebrandt, VM. I. 163. Oldenberg, (Ṛv. Noten II. 317) rejects this. Macdonell and Keith (*Vedic Index* II. 476 n. 31) admit its possibility.

[2] Tentative translation of the very difficult word *sūbharva*, following Hillebrandt, VM. I. 18 n. 2. Rejected by Oldenberg, Ṛv. Noten II. 301.

[3] Difficult word. Perhaps 'hole', 'cavity', 'lair' (Lanman. AV. VI. 49, 3).

of the Soma even before the Hotar. They as skilful and nimble ones dance with the sisters (the ten fingers). As eagles they lift their voices to the sky and as bulls they crunch the Soma shoots. Among the press-stones are those called the 'nether' stones *(úparāḥ)* and over these the 'upper' stones lord it. There is nothing in this description which would not be appropriate for mortar and pestle except the multiplicity of press-stones. But as shown above, the mortar and pestle are called 'press-stones' in Śat. Brāh. I. 4, 7, 10; and in the AV. IX. 8, 15 they are metaphorically identified with the press-stones.

Two words, *camū* and *dhiṣaṇā,* apparently mean 'bowl', for they are both used in the dual, of heaven and earth, as the two great bowls which close upon each other at the horizon. Thus:

He made the two great bowls[1] that face each other,
Both of them being packed full with his treasure.

The same expression is used of *dhiṣaṇe* (dual)

He props apart *the bowls that face each other.* X. 44, 8.

The wondrous friend has propped asunder the two worlds,
He has the two bowls rolled asunder like two skins. VI. 8, 3.

And, O ye heavens and earth, grant wide dominion,
To us, ye blissful world-halves, lofty shelter;
Give ample room and freedom for our dwelling,
Ye hemispheres[2], that it may be unhindered. VI. 50, 3.

Hillebrandt (VM. I. 169, n. 4) cites five passages in which *camū* stands next to *sutā* apparently in the sense of 'pressed in the bowl' or mortar[3]. While another interpretation is possible as shown by Oldenberg[4], yet Macdonell and Keith admit the possibility of Hillebrandt's view.

Dhiṣaṇā is a difficult word. In the passages quoted above it is certainly used in synonymous parallelism with

---

[1] Bowls, *camū,* in dual *camvā.*

[2] Hemispheres, i. e. two bowls, *dhiṣaṇe.*

[3] V. 51, 4; VIII. 4, 4; 76, 10; IX. 46, 3; X. 24, 1.

[4] ZDMG. 62 (1908), 459-470.

'heaven and earth', and 'the two world-halves'. It seems to mean much the same as *camū*[1], *i. e.* 'bowl' or 'hollow', referring primarily to the mortar or similar cavity in which Soma is pressed and then to the two world-bowls, heaven and earth. *Dhiṣaṇā,* like *barhis,* the fire-sticks, the pressing-stones, etc. has received apotheosis, as a great deity[2]. Thus,

In *Dhiṣaṇā's* lap are the pair of press-stones. I. 109, 3.
What drop of thine spurts out, what shoot of Soma,
Arm-moved, from lap of *Dhiṣaṇā* down falleth,
Or what from the Adhvaryu's cleansing filter,
That offer I to thee with cry of *vaṣaṭ*. X. 17, 12.

In these passages *Dhiṣaṇā* clearly means a hollow of some sort in which the press-stones work and from which Soma drops may spout forth, or Soma twigs escape. This might either be the bowl-like mortar or the ox-hide placed in the *Vedi* or in a hollow specially prepared on the sacrificial ground, so that it would have a bowl-like shape and be able to hold the unfiltered Soma juice.

The ox-hide is frequently mentioned in connection with the Soma ritual:

The press-stones chew and crunch thee *on the ox's hide;*
Into the waters sages milk thee with their hands. IX. 79, 4.
This Soma *on the skin of cows*
Is sporting with the pressing stones. IX. 66, 29.

Effused by means of pressing-stones,
Upon the ox-hide visible. IX. 101, 11 (Griffith's trans.).

These passages indicate clearly that the Soma shoots were crushed by the press-stones on the skin of an ox (or

---

[1] *Cf.* PW. under *camū*.

[2] *Cf.* the following texts concerning the goddess *Dhiṣaṇā*:

The goddess *Dhiṣaṇā* the Soma presseth
Eagerly for your delight, O Indra, Agni. I. 109, 4.
The mighty *Dhiṣaṇā* has fired thee boundlessly,
And so thou slayest Vṛitras, breaker-down of forts. I. 102, 7.

And with reference to the exhilaration of the singer or warrior:

Ready am I, when *Dhiṣaṇā* has quickened;
Ere the decisive day will I praise Indra.

cow)[1]. According to the later ritual the hide rested on two pressing-boards[2], which were themselves laid across a sounding-hole dug beneath[3]. There is no mention of the pressing-boards in the Ṛv., but we may possibly infer the presence of a shallow bowl-like pit to which the skin was fitted as a receptacle to catch the Soma juices. This is suggested by the sounding-hole of the later ritual, as well as by the statement that the press-stones were in the lap of *Dhiṣaṇā* (I. 109, 3), which has been shown above to be probably bowl-like in shape, and by the further statement that the 'talking press-stone is *set down upon*[4] *the altar*'[5].

The Soma shoots during the pressing seem to have been moistened with water doubtless to aid in extracting the juice or to increase the yield[6].

b) The Straining of the Soma. — This was done by pouring or pressing the juice through a sieve made of wool. Numerous synonyms were used for the strainer[7]. The self-purification[8] of the sacred juice as it passed through the sieve was the supreme moment in the preparation of Soma. To Pavamāna 'the self-purifying' are addressed the hymns of a whole book of the Ṛv. References to the filtering of Soma may be seen in vv. 1 and 6 of IX. 1 and vv. 1, 2, 6 of IX. 28, hymns translated above. As further illustrations the following translations are given:

---

[1] To catch the Soma drops as the shoots were pressed, the skin of the semi-sacred cow was regarded as appropriate.

[2] *adhiṣavane phalake.*

[3] Hillebrandt, VM. I. 148.

[4] *ava bhṛi*, V. 31, 12.

[5] The most notable comment on the meaning of *dhiṣaṇā* is that of Oldenberg, SBE. 46, 120-122. He concludes that "it was a sort of *support* on which the pressing-stones rested" (p. 122). But would not the natural support of the earth, hollowed out in the form of a shallow bowl or altar answer all difficulties? Macdonell and Keith (Index II. 476) following Hillebrandt (VM. I. 179-181) hold that *dhiṣaṇā* in some passages denotes the *vedi* 'alter', as in I. 109, 3.

[6] *Cf.* the corresponding procedure in the Zoroastrian ritual, both ancient and modern: Yasna III. 3 '*haoma-water*', and Art. ERE. on *Haoma*, '*Zaothra* water'.

[7] Which may be seen in *Vedic Index* I. 508, n. 4, and Hillebrandt, VM. I. 203

[8] *pavate* 'he cleanses himself'; *pavitra* 'sieve'.

Indu, as Indra's friend, for us
Flow pure with stream of sweetness *like*
Parjanya, master of the rain. IX. 2, 9.

This one *by ancient birth* pressed out
For all the gods, himself a god,
Flows tawny to the straining cloth. IX. 3, 9.

Bellowing flow the Indu-drops,
Like cattle lowing to their young,
Forth have they run from *both the hands*[1]. IX. 13, 7.

Ye *purifiers*, purify
Soma for Indra, as his drink;
And so make us more opulent. IX. 4, 4.

Soma, while filtering himself,
Flows *thousand-streamed* across the wool,
To Indra's and to Vāyu's tryst. IX. 13, 1.

These rapid Soma drops have stirred
Themselves to motion like strong steeds,
Like cars, like armies hurried forth. IX. 22, 1 (Griffith).

Like steed urged on to battle, finder of the light,
Do thou rush to the sky-cask mothered by the stones
Strong Soma on the summit of the woolly sieve
Doth purify himself for Indra's nourishment. IX. 86, 3.

Three aspects of Soma Pavamāna are here distinguished: colour, movement and sound. In colour Soma is tawny. Its flow through the strainer is mentioned in every hymn of Bk. IX. Not less than a dozen synonyms are employed

[1] The word translated 'from both the hands' *(gabhastyoḥ)* is in the locative dual, lit. 'in the two hands'. The meaning seems to be that 'purified in the hands' (*gabhastapūta* II. 14, 8), the juice runs forth, that is to say 'from the two hands'. Compare

The *hand-cleansed* liquor bear ye to the famous,
Ye pious ones, to Indra offer Soma. II. 14, 8; and
Stone-pressed it purifies itself in both the hands. IX. 71, 3.

Whether this process was the same as that of the later ritual is uncertain. *Cf.* Geldner, VS. I. 121 n. 1; Hillebrandt, VM. I. 202-203; Vedic Index, II. 477. But note the following detail of the modern Parsee ritual: "If any particles of the twigs still remain unpounded, they are removed from the mortar and placed in the strainer, *where they are rubbed with the hand* to make all the extract pass into the cup below". *Art. Haoma*, ERE.

to describe and emphasize the wondrous movement of the sacred juice. The drops of the 'thousand-streamed' Soma, as they fall from the strainer into the reservoir below, are likened to race-horses, racing cars and armies charging forward in battle. The noise of Soma is by hyperbole compared with the bellowing of cattle and the thunder of the sky.

A heavenly bird, thou lookest down, O Soma,
Swelling the streams with toil[1] at the gods' banquet;
Enter the Soma-holding vessel, Indu,
Go thundering forward to the ray of Sūrya. IX. 97. 33.

The dripping of the 'thousand-streamed' Soma from the woolly sieve into the reservoir below is a microcosmic picture of the fall of rain from the cloud-sieve. In fact, as the kindling of Agni before the dawn is a piece of sympathetic magic to secure the rising of the sun, so the filtering of the Soma drops through the strainer serves as a similar magic device to secure the fall of rain[2]. As Agni, 'the altar-fire' is clothed upon with the attributes of the sun and lightning, in the same way, the flow of Soma through the microcosmic sieve is described in terms of such macrocosmic transactions as thunder, lightning and rain. Lastly, as Agni's theophanic[3] moment is when the ghee-fed altar-flame blazes up, so the theophanic moment of Soma is when the round drops fall from the sieve into the wooden vat below.

c) The Mixing of the Soma.—The Ṛigveda distinguishes between the unmixed[4] and the mixed Soma juice. Vāyu, Indra-Vāyu and often Indra take their Soma clear as befits their impetuous nature. The other gods partake of a mixed drink thinned, as it were, by combining the Soma juice

---

[1] *Karman* 'work' means here as usually in the Ṛv. sacrificial work. It is the same word as later denotes 'cyclic recompense', the principle of retribution.

[2] Oldenberg, RV. 459.

[3] *Theophany* is technically a manifestation of a god in terms of time and space, that is to say, in nature.

[4] *Śukra*, *śuci*, 'clear'.

with milk[1], curd or grain. These are the three celebrated 'mixed-drinks'[2] of Soma, the cow-mixture, curd-mixture and grain-mixture. Soma seems to have been mixed with honey in the libation for the Aśvins. Judging, then, from the comprehensive nature of the rite (having to do, as it did, with all the gods), the number of priests who took part, and the ceremonial complexity of it all, one is justified in asserting that the sacramental preparation of the Soma juice was the supreme ritualistic performance of Ṛigvedic religion. Nothing approached it in these respects except, perhaps, the production of Agni by means of the two fire-sticks. The celebration of the Lord's Supper among Christians presents some points of contact with the Vedic rite, — points of contact which belong to the category of 'developmental coincidences'.

5. Soma as an Offering to the Gods.

There were three daily pressings of Soma, morning, noon and night[3]. All the Ṛigvedic gods had a share in the Soma offering[4]; some of them as Indra and Vāyu a greater and more regular share, while others as Pūṣan only occasionally participated. Agni is mentioned especially in connection with the morning pressing, and the Ṛibhus in connection with that of evening. To Indra accompanied by the Maruts belongs the midday libation. The other gods find their respective places, morning or evening. The libations to the 'all-gods' provide against any one being overlooked. Some gods as *e. g.* the Aśvins were apparently not originally Soma-drinkers. Indra received the lion's share, being according to the hymns the Soma-drinker *par excellence.* He participated in all three pressings and had sole right to the midday one.

---

[1] Since the custom of mixing Soma with milk was Iranian as well as Indian (Yasna X. 13), it doubtless goes back to the undivided Indo-Iranian period.

[2] *Tryāśiraḥ.*

[3] Only two pressings are mentioned in the Avesta, Yasna X. 2.

[4] Except perhaps Rudra, *cf.* Oldenberg, RV. 452.

Lord of bay steeds, at dawn the juice thou drankest;
Thine, only thine, is the noon-day libation;
Now drink thou with the wealth-bestowing Ṛibhus,
Whom for their skill thou madest friends, O Indra. IV. 35, 7
(Griffith's translation).

Already in the Ṛv. there are traces of an order of precedence which the gods follow in receiving the offerings, the order being: Vāyu, Indra-Vāyu, Mitra-Varuṇa, Aśvins, Indra, Viśve devāḥ, Sarasvatī[1]. Vāyu ever has the precedence as the first-drinker *(agrepā)*, although Indra is the chief drinker. The combination of special gods with special priests as formally stated in the later ritual, is not unknown to the Ṛv.[2] For example:

II. 36. To Various Gods.

1. In cows[3] and waters is he clad, while sent to thee,
The men have milked him with the filters and the stones:
Drink, Indra, from the Hotar's cup—first right is thine—
The hallowed Soma poured with *vaṣaṭ* and *svāhā*.
2. With sacrifices linked, with dappled steeds and spears,
Gleaming upon your way with ornaments, O friends,
Seated upon the litter, sons of Bharata,
Drink Soma from the Potar's cup, ye men of heaven.
3. To us come near, ye ready hearers; as at home[4]
Upon the sacred straw sit down, enjoy yourselves;
And, Tvaṣṭar, gladdened, in the juice delight thyself,
Associated with the gods and goddesses.
4. Bring the gods hither, sage, and sacrifice to them,
O willing Hotar, seat thee in the three abodes;
Accept for thy delight the proffered Soma meath,
Drink from the Agnidh's cup, delight thee in thy share.
5. This Soma is the increaser of thy body's might,
Is placed within thine arms as strength and victory;
For thee is pressed, O Maghavan, for thee brought nigh;
Drink of it from the Bráhman's cup, drink thou thy fill.

---

[1] Ṛv. I. 2, 3; II. 41, etc. *cf.* Hillebrandt, VM. I. 269.

[2] See Ṛv. I. 15, 2, 3, 5; II. 36-37.

[3] Referring to the *gavāśir*, or addition of milk to Soma.

[4] Invitation to the *gnās*, 'divine wives'.

6. Accept the sacrifice, ye two, and mark my call;
The Hotar priest is seated, following ancient use.
To both kings goeth forth the homage that attracts,
From the Praśāstar's cup drink ye the Soma meath.

This is a highly ritualistic hymn, full of priestly and sacrificial technique. No less than six priests are either mentioned or implied, the *Hotar* connected preferentially with Indra, the *Potar* with the Maruts, the *Neṣtar* with Tvaṣtar and the divine wives, the *Agnīdh* with Agni, the *Brahmán*[1] with Indra, and the *Praśāstar* with Mitra-Varuṇa[2].

The Soma offering was not a fixed, but rather a free-will offering, in which the rich and noble displayed unusual liberality toward both gods and priests. Gods and priests alone partook of the Soma. Hence the ceremony was hieratic in character[3].

6. SOMA AND THE MOON.

In the post-Vedic literature Soma is identified with the moon. For example, in Chānd. Up. V. 10, 4 the moon is called 'king Soma, the food of the gods[4]. The same expression occurs still earlier in the Śat. Brāh. I. 6, 4, 5, etc.[5] In the Kauṣ. Brāh. VII. 10 the mystical identification of Soma and the moon is explained as follows: 'The visible moon is king Soma. He enters into this (plant) when bought[6]. So when one buys king Soma, it is with the

[1] Or *Brahmaṇācchaṃsin*.

[2] Hillebrandt regards this linking together of special priests with special gods as a remnant of the time when tribal and family peculiarities of worship were more pronounced than we find them in the cult of the Ṛv., which cult in his opinion, was produced by the fusion of the gods and priests of different times and of different tribes. See VM. I. 260-263.

[3] For this whole section on the Soma offering, see Oldenberg, RV. 451-461.

[4] The conception of the moon as something edible is common in folklore. In German folklore it is a 'lump of butter' and in English there is the saying. 'The moon is made of green cheese'.

[5] *Somo rājā devānām annam*.

[6] It is only when the soma plant is purchased from the hands of strangers, probably non-Aryans, that it becomes a holy thing, the earthly representative and embodiment of the heavenly Soma, the moon.

thought: 'The visible moon is king Soma, may he be pressed'[1].

Prof. Hillebrandt, who is inclined to look at most things Vedic *sub specie lunae*[2], maintains that the post-Vedic identification of Soma and the Moon holds for the Ṛv. also. His statement is: Soma has in the whole Ṛv., in its earliest as well as its latest parts, only the meaning: Soma-plant, *i. e.* Soma-juice and Moon[3]. Taking his cue from such post-Vedic passages as that in the *Kauṣ. Brāh.* quoted above, he holds that the moon is a receptacle of Soma or *amṛita* and that when the worshipper presses the Soma plant, it is with the belief that the extract is the veritable lunar ambrosia, king Soma of the sky. Confessedly the most important Ṛigvedic passage suggesting this identification is X. 85, 1-5, 19, which reads as follows:

1. Through truth the earth beneath is propped,
And through the sun the heavens above;
Through *Ṛita* stand the Ādityas fast,
And Soma in the sky is set.
2. Through Soma are the Ādityas strong,
Through Soma spacious is the earth;
And hence on high is Soma placed
Within the constellations' lap.
3. Soma they think they have imbibed,
When they have crushed the Soma plant;
The Soma that the Brāhmans know,
Of that no one doth ever taste.
4. ....garrisoned,
....O Soma, guarded well,
Hearing the press-stones standest thou,
None tastes of thee that lives on earth.
5. What time, O god, they drink thee up,
Thou fillest out thyself again;
Vāyu is Soma's guardian,
The moon distributor of the years.

---

[1] See for this whole discussion Hillebrandt, VM. I. 267-450.

[2] He identifies Varuṇa, Apāṃ Napāt, Bṛihaspati, Yama, and Soma with the moon.

[3] VM. I. 274.

19.[1] New and still new he being born becometh,
The signal of the days precedes the mornings;
Coming, he giveth to each god his portion,
The moon prolongs the years of our existence.

According to these stanzas Soma is set in the sky, in the lap of the stars, under the guardianship of Vāyu. Unlike the juice of the earthly Soma plant, no one ever tastes of the heavenly Soma which the Brāhmans know. When the ambrosia of the sky is drunk up, it swells out again. By being born it becomes new again and again. The moon is definitely mentioned as distributing (or shaping) the years and prolonging the lives of men. This testimony, although *indirect*, is sufficient evidence that in this hymn at least a difference is drawn between the heavenly and the earthly Soma and that the heavenly Soma = Moon. But, be it noted, in this most cogent of all Ṛigvedic passages the evidence is still indirect. As Oldenberg, followed by Macdonell, correctly says: There is in the whole of the Ṛv. no clear identification of Soma with the moon, no clear reference to the conception that the moon is the food of the gods[2]. The difference between the heavenly and the earthly Soma is still further indicated in the following couplet:

May heavenly drink exhilarate thee, Indra,
And also what is pressed in earthly places. X. 116, 3.

Passages like the following, while they may refer to the heavens and the moon, may be equally well related to the microcosmic heaven of the straining sieve and the sun-like Soma drop falling from it into the reservoir below:--

In aspect he is *like the sun*,
He runneth forward to the lakes,
The seven heights and lofty sky.

---

[1] v. 19 = AV. VII. 81, 2. AV. VII. 81, 3-4 contains fairly clear, though indirect, references to the moon as Soma. In AV. XI. 6, 7 there is direct identification: 'Let god Soma free me, whom they call the moon'.

[2] Oldenberg, RV. 610; Macdonell, VM. 113.

This Indu filtering himself
Stands over all the worlds aloft,
Soma the sun-like deity. IX. 54, 2-3.

There are, of course, references to the moon in various Ṛigvedic hymns, for example:—

Amid the waters runs the moon,
The well-winged (eagle) in the sky;
Ye lightnings with your golden tires,
No one doth reach and find your place.

O never may that light, ye gods,
Plunge downward from the lofty sky;
And never may we lack the juice
Of the health-giving Soma plant. I. 105, 1, 3.

Here the 'well-winged' may refer to the sun quite as well as to the moon, making in v. 1^{a-c} the series, moon sun and lightning. In v. 3^{a} the 'light' in the sky may also be the sun. The mention of the moon in v. 1^{a} and of Soma in v. 3^{d} does not necessarily mean their identification. So also with the following:

The Soma seen within the bowls
As in the flood the moon is seen,—
Drink thou of it, for 't is thy right. VIII. 71, 8.

The incontrovertible data bearing upon the problem are, accordingly, the following: (1) The heavenly origin of Soma as postulated in the earliest hymns of the Ṛv. (2) The early conception of Soma as the draught of immortality[1]. (3) The difference between the heavenly and the earthly Soma as indicated in late Ṛigvedic hymns. (4) The mystical identification of Soma with the moon, implicit[2] in

[1] Note that (1) and (2) are not merely early Vedic, but also Indo-Iranian and probably even Indo-European.

[2] The reference in X. 85, 3 to a Soma known only to Brāhmans suggests that the later view of Soma as the earthly counterpart of the moon was a Vedic 'mystery' or secret doctrine, *cf.* Macdonell, VM. 112-113. If Hillebrandt should prove to be right in his view that book IX. is dominated throughout by the synthesis of Soma and moon, it would mean that the connection between the two was purposely veiled as a sacred mystery known only to the priests. Macdonell remarks that "it is possible that amid the chaotic details of the imagery of the Soma hymns, there may occasionally lurk *a veiled identification* of ambrosia and the moon" (VM. 113).

some of the latest hymns of the Ṛv.[1], and explicit in the post-Vedic literature. The force of the above mentioned data is increased by the mystical nature of the Soma sacrament and the microcosmic character of the strainer, so suggestive of heavenly phenomena, such as cloud, thunder, lightning and rain. Then, too, the parallel between Agni and Soma is suggestive. Both gods, while dwelling on earth, are heaven-born. Agni, the deified Altar-Fire, is the earthly counterpart of the sun, the heavenly altar-fire. While dwelling on earth, Agni is still in heaven[2]. It was natural, then, to seek a heavenly form also for Soma, the deified Sacrificial Drink. There was certainly belief in a heavenly Soma before the earthly Soma was definitely[3] identified with the moon. The nectar of the sky was probably without a local habitation, except perhaps the clouds, until it was localised in the moon. The round yellow drop, as it fell shining from the strainer, would naturally be compared with the moon, as the big Drop of the sky; or the thought of the moon as a bowl full of yellow Soma would be suggested by the bowls of the sacred drink set out for the gods. And since the sun had been appropriated by Agni as his heavenly counterpart, there remained the moon for Soma. The sayings of folklore, which among various peoples represent the moon as something edible doubtless contributed also to the final synthesis of Soma and moon.

It seems, then, to the present writer that the general consensus of Vedic scholarship is right in its opposition to Hillebrandt's main contention that Somá in the Ṛv. everywhere means the moon[4]. At the same time it must not be overlooked that no Vedic scholar has done so much as Hillebrandt, and only in a less degree Bergaigne to make

[1] In books I. and X.

[2] *Cf.* John III. 13. "He that descended out of heaven, even the Son of man, who is in heaven".

[3] Or at least *publicly* identified.

[4] See especially Oldenberg, RV. 599-612.

clear the cosmic and mystical significance of Soma. The following stanzas which are addressed to Soma, although taken from the heart of an Indra hymn (VI. 44, 22-24), illustrate what is meant:

22. This god, by might, with Indra as his ally[1],
On being born brought Paṇi to a standstill;
This Indu stole away the warlike weapons,
The magic arts of his ungracious father[2].

23. This Indu made the glorious Dawns fair-mated[3],
Within the sun the light of day established;
He found in heaven, within the third light-regions,
The threefold drink of gods, the Amṛit hidden.

24. The heaven and earth he propped and held asunder,
The chariot with the sevenfold reins he harnessed;
Within the cows Soma with strength maintaineth
The ripe spring worked by mechanism tenfold.

We have here the reciprocal service of two Vedic gods, Soma and Indra, who as allies, each help the other. Soma strengthens Indra for his exploits, and so what Indra accomplishes when filled with Soma and working in the power of the sacred stimulant, is virtually Soma's work. It is because Soma is heavenly and divine that he is able to exhilarate Indra. He is the soul and strength of Indra, without whom Indra could do nothing. From this point of view Soma is as great as Indra or greater. Hillebrandt does ample justice to the cosmic and mystical aspects of these and similar stanzas, but his treatment is to some extent vitiated by his premature identification of Soma with the moon.

7. Soma and Immortality.

In a hymn already translated[4] Soma is described as himself immortal and the giver of immortality. In the

---

[1] In IV. 28, 1 Indra has Soma for an ally (*yuj*). The close relation between Indra and Soma is further indicated by texts which say that Soma is 'Indra's beloved friend' (IX. 100, 1) and 'bears the name of Indra' (IX. 109, 14).

[2] Is Tvaṣṭar the father of Soma?

[3] That is to say, gave to Dawn the sun as husband. *Cf.* VII. 75, 5.

[4] VIII. 48, 3, 12-13. p. 210 *ff.*

heavenly world Soma is 'united with the Fathers' (the blessed dead) as the ground of their immortality (VIII. 48, 13). Soma is called 'the father of the gods'[1], which seems to mean that as the life-giving drink, Soma is creative of the real abiding existence even of the gods.

Three things have already been distinguished: Soma the plant, Soma the drink, and Soma a heavenly nectar, of which the earthly Soma is a symbol and embodiment[2].

The immortal is usually connected with the ethical. Has Soma anything to do with the right? Where the word *ṛita* occurs in connection with Soma, its meaning in most cases, it is true, is ritualistic rather than ethical, 'rite' rather than 'right'. There are many allusions to 'the home of the rite'[3], clearly a reference to the altar or Soma-receptacle; and to 'the stream of the rite'[4], referring plainly to the flow of Soma through the strainer. Soma is also described as a 'lofty rite'[5], an expression probably covering the whole liturgical procedure. An ethical element, however, is manifested in the following couplet:

> Cleansing thyself resolve the knot that 's knotted,
> Discriminate 'twixt straight and crooked conduct. IX. 97, 18.

In the following stanzas of VII. 104 Soma is represented as an ally of Truth, smiting sin and punishing the sinner:

> 9. Those who the good man's speech delight to slander,
> And those whose habit is to harm the righteous,
> May Soma hand them over to the serpent;
> Or to the lap of Nirṛiti consign them.
>
> 12. Good wit is his who has discrimination,
> Real and unreal, both words oppose each other;
> Of these twain what is true and what is upright,
> That indeed Soma helps, untruth he smiteth.

---

[1] *Pitā devānām*, IX. 109, 4.

[2] Compare the three parallel Biblical conceptions of 'the Tree of Life' (Gen. III. 22, 24; Rev. II. 7, XXII. 2, 14); 'the Water of Life' (Rev. XXII. 17; John IV. 7-24; VII. 37-39); and the Holy Spirit as that to which the earthly symbols point (John IV. 24, VII. 39; Rom. VIII. 11; I Cor. XV. 44-49).

[3] *Ṛitasya yoni*, IX. 64, 11, 22, etc.

[4] *Ṛitasya dhārā*, IX. 63, 14, 21, etc.

[5] *Ṛitam bṛhat*, IX. 56, 1.

13. Never aids Soma him whose ways are crooked,
Or him who falsely claims the Kṣatriya title;
He smites the Rakṣas, smites the falsehood-speaker,
Both lie entangled in the net of Indra.

The last line indicates that Indra acts as executioner on behalf of Soma, being strengthened for his penal tasks by the sacred drink. The stanzas IX. 67, 22-27 contain prayers to Soma, Agni and Savitar for cleansing[1]. The translation is on the basis of Griffith, with certain changes.

22. This day may Pavamāna cleanse
Us with his purifying sieve,
The Potar present everywhere.

23. O Agni with thy cleansing sieve,
Which in the flame is manifest,—
With that do thou our prayer refine.

24. Thy cleansing sieve is bright with flame
With that, O Agni, purify,
Yea, cleanse us with the flow of prayer[2].

25. God Savitar by both of these,
By cleansing sieve and flow of prayer
Purify me on every side.

26. Cleanse us God Savitar with three,
O Soma, with sublimest forms,
Agni, with forms of power and might.

27. May the god's company make me clean
And Vasus make me pure by song;
Purify me, ye general gods,
O Jātavedas, make me pure.

O that we could be certain that these noble verses meant as much as we would know they meant, if they only stood in a Varuṇa hymn. At any rate, whether the meaning is much or little, the form is excellent. It is a cry for cleansing, whether ritualistic, or moral, or both, and the language is adapted to the liturgy of the Soma sacrifice. After the analogy of Soma, Agni also had a

[1] Note the terminology: *pū* to purify; *Pavamāna* 'the self-purifying'; *pavitra* sieve', 'strainer'; *potar* 'purifying' priest.

[2] Or Brahman-rite (Ludwig).

strainer[1] of glowing fire[2]. That Soma, then, has a distinct ethical quality is unmistakable. The ethical climax is reached, when Soma is assimilated to Varuṇa and the Ādityas:

Thine are King Varuṇa's eternal statutes,
Lofty and deep, O Soma, is thy nature;
All-pure art thou, like Mitra the belovéd,
Adorable, like Aryaman, O Soma. I. 91, 3 (after Griffith).

The Ṛigvedic conception of the state of the departed dead is set forth in the following prayer:

IX. 113, 7-11. To Soma Pavamāna.

7. Where radiance inexhaustible
Dwells, and the light of heaven is set,
Place me, clear-flowing one, in that
Imperishable and deathless world.
(O Indu, flow for Indra's sake).

8. Make me immortal in the place
Where dwells the king Vaivasvata[3],
Where stands the inmost *shrine* of heaven,
And where the living waters are.

9. Make me immortal in that realm,
Wherein is movement glad and free,
In the third sky, third heaven[4] of heavens,
Where are the lucid worlds of light.

---

[1] The Vedic word, *pavitra*, is the same word that is used in modern Hindi in the expression *Pavitra Ātmā*, 'Holy Spirit'. The word ātman occurs about 20 times in the Ṛv. in the sense of 'breath', 'soul', 'self', 'organism', *etc*. *Cf*. A. H. Ewing, *Hindu Conception of the Functions of Breath*, II. 10-18. Later on ātman formed one element in the great equation Bráhman = Ātman. This great word etymologically so suitable as a synonym for the O. T. *rūᵃh* and the N. T. πνεῦμα 'Spirit' has always been connected with metaphysical speculation rather than with ethical endeavour. The Indian Christian Church has attempted to fill the word ātman with an ethical content and so make it the equivalent of πνεῦμα.

[2] With the close connection between Soma the sacred drink and Agni the sacred fire compare Matt. III. 11: "He shall baptize you with the Holy Spirit and with fire". Note that the Greek πῦρ 'fire' is etymologically connected with *pū* to purify and *Pavitra* 'means of purifying', 'sieve'.

[3] Yama, the son of Vivasvant.

[4] *Cf*. 2. Cor. XII. 2 "Such a one caught up even to the third heaven" (= Paradise).

10. Make me immortal in the place
Where loves and longings are fulfilled,
The region of the ruddy (sphere),
Where food[1] and satisfaction reign.

11. Make me immortal in the place
Wherein felicity and joy,
Pleasure and bliss together dwell,
And all desire is satisfied.

Four times repeated is the prayer 'Make me immortal' addressed to Soma, the giver of immortality. Grassmann is probably right in regarding the refrain, 'O Indu, flow for Indra's sake' as a purely mechanical addition. Hence it is omitted. There is a gravity and solemnity about these stanzas, which remind one of a similar description of Paradise in Rev. VII. 14-17.

Other passages which indicate the nature of the activities of the blessed dead are the following:

The gracious Soma with his light has helped us,
Wherewith our ancient Fathers, footstep tracing,
Light finding, robbed the mountain of the cattle. IX. 97, 39.

For thou, O Soma, art the Fathers in the sky.
Who are set forth as heads of heaven and strengtheners. IX. 69, 8.

Like a dark steed adorned with pearls, the Fathers
Have decorated heaven with constellations. X. 68, 11 (Griffith).

It would seem that the blessed dead are closely associated with the gods in their cosmic activities. Stanzas IX. 69, 8 and X. 68, 11 might be interpreted as meaning that the Fathers on joining the gods in heaven become 'constellations' and 'heads of heaven', *i. e.* stars[2]. Soma is described as equivalent to the Fathers, doubtless in the sense that the continuous existence of the blessed dead was due entirely to Soma as the principle of immortality.

---

[1] *svadhā*, 'spirit-food' through the *śrāddha*, or offering to the dead.

[2] So Hillebrandt, VM. I. 397-398. We are reminded of Daniel XII. 3, "They that turn many to righteousness shall shine *as the stars* for ever and ever"; and Matt. XIII. 43. "Then shall the righteous shine forth *as the sun* in the Kingdom of their Father".

On the whole, then, as suggested above, the doctrine of Soma bears much the same relation to the religion of the Ṛv. as that of the Holy Spirit does to the religion of the Bible.

CHAPTER IX.

UṢAS AND THE AŚVINS.

1. **Uṣas.**—As the personification of one of the most radiant phenomena of nature, Uṣas is very appropriately represented as a woman, the lady Dawn. Macdonell is right in calling Uṣas 'the most graceful creation of Vedic poetry'[1]. As Indra is characterized by strength, Agni by priestly knowledge, and Varuṇa by righteous order, so Uṣas is characterized by feminine charm. Amid the throng of masculine deities of the morning—Sūrya, Savitar, Pūṣan, Viṣṇu, Agni and the Aśvins—Uṣas appears in the east in delicate feminine beauty. She has many lovers—Agni, Sūrya, Pūṣan and the Aśvins. Uṣas 'dawn' is as transparent as Agni 'fire' or Sūrya 'sun', and so the personification remains rudimentary. The Vedic poet is always conscious of the physical fact of dawn, and this helps somewhat to remove the scandal of the lady Dawn's too promiscuous love affairs. Uṣas is celebrated in 21 hymns, 14 of which are found in the family books. She is the only goddess of importance.

To Uṣas, IV. 51[2].

1. This light appearing ever here to eastward
With clearness has arisen from out the darkness;
Now may the daughters of the sky, far-shining,
The glorious Dawns, for mankind make a pathway.

2. The Dawns resplendent have arisen eastward,
Like sacred posts set up at sacrifices;
Bright, gleaming, purifying, have they opened
The double portals[3] of the pen of darkness.

3. To-day may the far-shining Dawns, the bounteous,
Inspire the liberal man to noble giving;
Amid obscurity let the niggards slumber,
All-unawakened in the midst of darkness.

---

[1] VM. 46.

[2] For the translation compare Hillebrandt LR. 3-4, and Macdonell VRS. 93-99.

[3] *Cf.* I. 48, 15, 'the twin doors of heaven'.

4. Ye Dawns, ye goddesses, is this your pathway,
To-day a recent one or is it ancient,
Whereby ye, rich, richly shone on Navagva,
Angira and Daśagva and Saptāsya?
5. For ye, O goddesses, with steeds yoked duly,
Traverse the worlds within a day, awakening
The sleeping world two-footed and four-footed,
The world of living creatures, Dawns, to motion.
6. Where was that ancient Dawn and which one was it,
At which the gods assigned tasks to the Ribhus?
When the bright Dawns their bright way go, unaging,
All have the same look, there is no distinction.
7. Auspicious have these bright Dawns been aforetime,
Splendidly helpful, true as born of *rita;*
At which with hymns the zealous sacrificer
Praising and chanting has obtained wealth quickly.
8. In self-same manner come they forth from eastward,
From one place spreading out in self-same fashion;
The goddess Dawns from Ṛita's seat awaking
Disport themselves like troops of loosened cattle.
9. These Dawns now as of old the same in nature
Come ever into view, of unchanged colour,
Concealing night's black monster with their brilliant
Forms,—they the bright, the gleaming, the resplendent.
10. Riches, ye daughters of the sky, far-shining,
Bestow on us, ye goddesses, with offspring.
From pleasant couch to you ward we awaking
Would be possessors of a host of strong sons.
11. This, daughters of the sky and Dawns far-shining,
Of you implore I, I whose sign is worship.
We would among the tribes of men be famous;
Let Dyāus and goddess Pṛithivī bestow that.

The following points may be noted:

a) The plural *uṣasaḥ* refers in some cases to successive dawns[1], in others probably to the dawngleams of the same morning[2].

[1] I. 123, 2, 8, 9, 12; 124, 2; 113, 8, 15; VII. 76, 3; 80, 3.

[2] IV. 51, 1-3, 10; VI. 64, 1-2; VII. 75, 3; 78, 1, 3; 79, 2. These passages as belonging to the family books are, on the whole, earlier than those in which the reference is to successive dawns. With the distinction between uṣasas and Uṣas compare the analogous distinction between agnis and Agni, somas and Soma.

b) The dawns are the various aspects or successive appearances of the one goddess, the Lady Dawn, who is young, good-looking, well-dressed and nobly-born (being the sister of Bhaga and the kinswoman of Varuṇa)[1]. She smiles (I. 123, 10; 124, 7), sings[2] (I. 92, 3; 123, 5), dances (I. 92, 4) and displays her charms (I. 92, 4; 123, 11; 124, 3-4, 6). If Indra is the very picture of a Kṣatriya lord, Uṣas may be taken as the 'counterfeit presentment' of a Kṣatriya lady[3].

c) Uṣas, negatively removes the black robe of night, drives away bad dreams, and wards off evil spirits and the hated darkness[4]. Positively she opens the gates of heaven, illumines the ends of the sky, and discloses the treasures concealed by darkness, distributing them bountifully[5].

d). Accordingly Usas is the goddess 'Bounty'[6]. When she begins to appear in the morning, the prayer is offered: 'Up let there spring bounteousnesses *(sunṛitāḥ)*, up plenteousnesses' (*puramdhiḥ* I. 123, 6). She is a veritable Lady Bountiful, since she spontaneously displays her charms to all, morning by morning, and distributes *(bhajate)* treasures[7], assigning to every man his fortune (*bhāga* I. 123, 3), quite after the manner of Bhaga. Thus Uṣas is a kind of female Bhaga, in fact his sister or other self. Hence when it is

---

[1] I. 92, 4; 123, 2, 3, 5, 10-11.

[2] *Cf.* 'The morning stars sang together"—Job. XXXVIII, 7.

[3] Pischel's view (VS. I. 30, 196; III. 200) that the description of Uṣas is drawn from that of a Vedic *demimondaine* is based upon her behaviour like that of a brotherless maid (I. 124, 7), her too ready display of her bosom (VI. 64, 2; I. 123, 10; 124, 4) and her numerous love affairs.

[4] I. 113, 14; VIII. 47, 14, 16; VII. 75, 1.

[5] I. 113, 4, *cf.* I. 92, 4 and IV. 51, 2; I. 92, 11; 123, 4, 6.

[6] *Sunṛitā* I. 123, 5; 124, 10. Other epithets of the same sort are *dakṣiṇā* 'honorarium' I. 123, 1; VI. 64, 1; *dāsvati* 'generous' I. 48, 1; *maghonī* 'liberal' I. 48, 8; *citramaghā* 'of splendid gifts' I. 48, 10; and *Viśvavārā* 'all-bounteous', I. 113, 19.

[7] The treasures of light rescued from the demon Darkness. or, metaphorically stated, the 'dawn-cows'.

said that the broad car of *Dakṣiṇā* has been yoked, the reference of course is to the expected priestly honorarium, but with a side glance at her who is the very embodiment of bounty, the bountiful[1] Uṣas (I. 123, 1). Through her example[2] as Lady Bountiful Uṣas stimulates the wealthy to thoughts of liberal giving to the priests (I. 48, 4; IV. 51, 3; VII. 81, 6) and stimulates every god to bountifulness (VII. 79, 5).

e) The ruddy gleams of Uṣas are thought of as cattle, 'the dawn-cows[3]. From this point of view Uṣas is called 'the mother of cows'[4]. Or to change the imagery, the multitudinous patches of colour[5] splashed against the morning sky may be each regarded as a carriage and span, and from this point of view Uṣas is a 'driver of cars' (I. 48, 3), as many as a hundred being mentioned (I. 48, 7). The car of Uṣas is well-decorated[6], and her steeds consist of ruddy horses[7] or oxen[8].

f) Like Savitar, Uṣas wakes up man, beast and bird[9].

Leader of graciousnesses, shining brightly
Is seen the one that hath unclosed the portals.
She stirring up the world, hath looked on riches;
Dawn hath awakened every living creature. I. 113, 4.

---

[1] Both Indra and Uṣas are characteristically 'bountiful' *(Maghavan* and *Maghonī),* Indra as winning the cloud-cows and Uṣas as winning the dawn-cows. Uṣas Maghonī is declared to be 'most like to Indra' (VII. 79, 3).

[2] *Cf.* Matt. V. 44-45.

[3] I. 92, 1-2; IV. 51, 8; 52, 5.

[4] IV. 52, 2-3; VII. 77, 2.

[5] The gleams of Uṣas are also likened to sacrificial posts (I. 92, 5; IV. 51, 2) which then as now were doubtless daubed with red ochre, or yellow ghee (*cf.* III. 8, 1).

[6] Like the Greek chariot in the Metropolitan Museum, New York City.

[7] III. 61, 2; IV. 51, 5, etc.

[8] I. 124, 11; V. 80, 3, etc. As contrasted with the thought-swift steeds of Indra and Sūrya, the slow-moving dawn-gleams of Uṣas are very appropriately represented by wagons drawn by bullocks.

[9] I. 48, 5-6; 49, 3; 92, 9; 113, 4-6, 8-9, 14; 124, 1, 4, 10, 12; IV. 51, 5; VI. 64, 6; 65, 1; VII. 77, 1; 79, 1.

Uṣas assigns to all their various tasks, such as lordship and glory, worship of the gods, acquisition of wealth, and toil (I. 113, 5-6, 9). She even allotted to the Ṛibhus their work (IV. 51, 6). As 'waking with Uṣas' the gods are often described as *Uṣarbudh.* Uṣas the bountiful awakens bountiful givers, but leaves niggards unawakened (I. 124, 10; IV. 51, 3). The bountiful goddess[1] loves bountiful people.

g) Uṣas is the sister of Rātri, 'Night'.

The sisters' pathway is the same, unending;
God-taught, by that alternately they travel.
Fair-formed, of different hues, and yet of one mind,
Night and Dawn clash not, neither do they tarry.
The one departeth and the other cometh,
Unlike in hue day's halves march on together.
The same in form to-day, the same to-morrow,
They follow Varuṇa's eternal statute.

I. 113, 3; 123, 7-8 (Griffith with some changes).

In the Āprī hymns Night and Dawn are forms of Agni. They constitute a dual divinity, both being daughters of Heaven (X. 70, 6) and mothers of *ṛita* (I. 142, 7). There is only one hymn addressed to *Rātri*[2] 'Night', X. 127.

1. Night drawing near has looked abroad,
In many places with her eyes;
All glories has she now assumed.
2. Pervaded has the immortal one
The depths, the heights, the ample space;
With light she drives away the gloom.
3. The goddess Night, approaching nigh,
Her sister Dawn[3] has ousted quite;
The darkness too will disappear.

---

[1] In our modern religious life the offertory is made an occasion for special prayer. It is thus introduced into the ritual and made a part of worship. In Vedic days the same general idea was expressed by saying that *Dakṣiṇā* 'contribution', 'offertory', honorarium' is a goddess (sometimes identified with Uṣas).

[2] Indebtedness is acknowledged to the translations of Hillebrandt (LR. 149) and Macdonell (VRS. 203-207, and HR. 40-41).

[3] As night covers the dark half of the day, so Dawn is here made to include the light half. Compare *ahanī* (I. 123, 7), lit. 'the two days', *i. e.* the two day-halves, and *dyāvā* (I. 113, 2) 'the two skies', *i. e.* the day-sky and the night-sky.

4. To us this day thou hast appeared,
At whose approach we seek our homes[1]
As birds their nests upon the tree.

5. Home too have gone the villagers,
Home those possessing feet and wings,
Home even the greedy hawks have gone.

6. Ward off the she-wolf and the wolf,
Ward off the thief, O brooding Night.
And so be easy to traverse.

7. The darkness has drawn nigh to me,
Black, obvious, painting mystic scenes,
O Dawn, disperse it like a debt.

8. My hymn like kine I've brought to thee,
Take it, Night, daughter of the sky,
Like song of praise to conqueror.

Rātri, as Macdonell says[2], is not conceived as the dark, but as the bright night, the stars being apparently thought of as her eyes. Night thus lighted up (vv. 1-2) stands in opposition to the 'blind darkness' (X. 89, 15)[3].

h) Uṣas, like Varuṇa, Pūṣan and other deities of the light, is a pathmaker[4]. Knowing the way, she does not miss the directions (I. 124, 3; V. 80, 4), in other words, she knows her own path. Accordingly she has opened up and left a path for Sūrya to travel (I. 113, 16). And by her shining she reveals the paths of men and makes them easy to traverse (VII. 79, 1; IV. 51, 1; V. 80, 2).

i) Uṣas is called *immortal* in a context where her unvarying appearance at dawn is emphasized.

From days eternal hath Dawn shone, the goddess,
And shows to-day this lustre, she the wealthy;

---

[1] With verses 4-5 may be compared II. 38, 4-8.

[2] VM. 124.

[3] Hillebrandt, LR. 149.

[4] *Pathyā Revatī*, 'she of the wealthy path' (V. 51, 14) is invoked as a goddess of journeying mercies and well-being. The concrete *Uṣas* and the abstract *Pathyā Revatī* are both path-goddesses, heavenly 'Girl Guides', as it were.

So shall she shine in days to come; *immortal*
She moves on, self-determined, undecaying[1]. I. 113, 13
(Griffith with a few changes).

Here the immortality of Uṣas is definitely connected with the fact that she has flushed continuously aforetime, and will flush throughout the days to come. The '*everlasting* power' of Uṣas is inferred from the observation of her invariable procedure. We say: Dawn is invariable, Nature is uniform. The Vedic Indians said: Uṣas is immortal. What the origin of the concept of immortality was as applied to the gods is thus clear. It was due to the observation of the regular recurrence of the phenomena of nature. Men are declared to be mortal on the basis of experience, but there is no known beginning or end of the Sun's rising, the appearance of dawn, the play of the lightning, etc., etc.

"Men may come and men may go
But *we go on for ever*":

as Tennyson makes the waters of the "Brook" to say. By this road of observation and experience the Vedic Aryans arrived at one valid distinction between God and man. God is *immortal*, man is mortal. The ground of the immortality of the gods may be conceived as due to the drinking of Soma (IX. 106, 8) or to the vital stimulation of Savitar (IV. 54, 2), but the fact of their immortality doubtless was inferred as stated above.

j) Uṣas is clearly connected with the duration and measurement of time, that is, with the notion of past, present and future.

She, first of endless morns to come hereafter,
Follows the path of morns that have departed.
Last of the countless mornings that have vanished,
First of bright morns to come hath dawn arisen.
I. 113, 8a-b, 15c-d (Griffith's translation).

---

[1] Or: "The goddess Dawn has flushed in former ages,
And here to-day the bounteous maiden flushes;
So also may she flush in days hereafter.
With powers her own she fares immortal, ageless".
Macdonell, HR. 39.

The thought of the Dawns that have departed gives rise to a pensive note:

Gone are the men who in the days before us
Looked on the flushing of the earlier morning. I. 113, 11
(Griffith's translation with slight change).

It reminds one of Tennyson's song in the Princess:

Tears, idle tears, I know not what they mean,
Tears from the depth of some divine despair,
Rise from the heart and gather to the eyes,
In looking on the happy autumn fields
And thinking of the days that are no more.

The dividing line between past and future is, according to the Vedic poet, not sunset but dawn. It is Dawn that wastes away the days of the life of a man, as a skilful gambler reduces the stakes of his opponent (I. 92, 10). It was at dawn that to the Vedic poet came the 'solemn thought' that he was one day nearer the end of his earthly life. Thus Dawn was called 'leader·of days' (VII. 77, 2), since she brings up the days one by one. And each Dawn, as she appears, seems to yearn eagerly to join the company of departed dawns (I. 113, 10). As regards further dawns they are thought of as simply the continuous repetition of past dawns. The analogies of nature suggest no certain progress[1], (a concept due to historical experience), but only repetition[2]. There is (at least in· the later hymns to Uṣas) no joyful anticipation of the future, but only pensive contemplation of the past, and of future days as destined soon to join the company of past days. This attitude points in the direction of the later *Pessimism*.

k) Adumbration of the idea of *Transmigration* through the repeated birth[3] of Uṣas[4]. There is in the

---

[1] Is the later doctrine of the endless repetition of the cycle of the four *yugas* due to the influence of such analogies?

[2] Compare Ecclesiastes I. 2-11.

[3] *Punaḥ punarjāyamānā* 'born again (and) again' (I. 92, 10) suggests the later *punarjanma* 'rebirth'; and *punarbhū* 're-born' (I. 123, 2) reminds one of the Brāhmaṇa term *punarmṛityu* 're-death'.

[4] Also of Agni, Sūrya and Soma.

Ṛv. no clear indication of belief in Transmigration. No passage may be quoted with certitude[1], and the whole conception of a future life with the Fathers is against it. Still certain analogies may be cited as likely to point in the direction of the later doctrine. The devas 'gods' rose out of nature. They were in general deified natural phenomena. Or, to put it in another way, they are the product of the religious instinct working on the raw material of natural phenomena. Uṣas is immortal, Sūrya is immortal, etc. But the immortality of Uṣas is made up of the twin processes of dying (implied) and of being born again at dawn. This is a most potent and pregnant analogy, sure to have had its effect in furthering the later doctrine of rebirth. For according to that doctrine man too is immortal (in a lower sense) until he attains release. Death and rebirth follow each other in endless succession, even as the sunrise follows the sunset[2].

l) Uṣas as regularly appearing in the east is an expression of *ṛita* in the sense of 'cosmic order'. She is 'born in *ṛita*' and so is a 'protectress of *ṛita*' (I. 113, 12). She does not infringe the ordinances of *ṛita* and of the gods[3], the proof being that she comes day by day to the place appointed. Being obedient to the rein of *ṛita*, she goes straight along the path thereof, never missing her way (I. 123, 13; 124, 3). The liturgical day begins with the appearance of Uṣas in the east, when she causes all

---

[1] Swāmī Dayānand Sarasvatī (*Ṛigvedādibhāṣyabhūmikā*, 211 ff.) finds in X. 59, 6-7 a proof text for transmigration in the Ṛigvedic period. A reference to the context, however, (vv. 4-5) shews that this is extremely improbable.

[2] Compare the well known lines of Milton's Lycidas:—

"Weep no more, woeful shepherds, weep no more,
For Lycidas your sorrow is not dead,
Sunk though he be beneath the watery floor;
So sinks the day-star in the ocean bed,
And yet anon repairs his drooping head,
And tricks his beams, and with new spangled ore.
Flames in the forehead of the morning sky".

[3] I. 92, 12; 123, 9; 124, 2; VII. 76, 5.

worshippers to awake and the sacrificial fires to be kindled (I. 113, 9). Thus she is an expression also of 'ritualistic order'. As preceding the gods of light, Agni, Sūrya, Savitar, etc., Uṣas is called 'the mother of the gods' (I. 113, 19)[1]. She is besought to bring all the gods to drink the Soma (I. 48, 12); and for this reason, perhaps, the gods are often described as 'waking with Uṣas. Uṣas and Agni are each called 'banner of sacrifice', since the light of each gleams at the time of the morning Soma-pressing (I. 113, 19; 96, 6). The freshness of an Indian morning (even in the hot season), the exhilaration due to the night's rest, the splendour of the dawn, and the solemnity of the time of the morning sacrifice, all combined to produce a certain exaltation of spirit. Such a mental state, since it was experienced in the early morning, would naturally be attributed to the grace of the morning gods, Uṣas and Savitar[2].

m) Uṣas is closely connected with the sun. She generated Sūrya and was produced for the production of Savitar[3]. Thus as preceding the rising of the sun, Uṣas is thought of as his mother. But Sūrya follows Uṣas as a young man a maiden (I. 115, 2), and from this point of view Uṣas (=Sūryā) is conceived as the wife or mistress of Sūrya[4]. The soul of the dead man goes to the sun and to Uṣas (X. 58, 8)[5].

n) Comparisons.—The knowledge possessed by Uṣas is not stressed. She has wit enough to do her own proper work and not to lose her way when she comes through the dark. She is chiefly expert in displaying her beauty

---

[1] From this point of view also she is said to have 'generated Sun, sacrifice and Agni' (VII. 78, 3).

[2] With the prayer to Uṣas, 'Place in us excellent mental force (*kratu* I. 123, 13), compare the Gāyatrī, 'May he stimulate our thoughts' (III. 62, 10).

[3] VII. 78, 3; I. 113, 1; *cf.* Macdonell, VM. 48.

[4] *Cf.* Macdonell, VM. 48.

[5] Savitar and Pūṣan as sun-gods are represented as conductors of the dead to the place of the Fathers.

and in winning admiration. If we compare together Agni, Indra and Uṣas, we find that Agni, the priestly god, is *par excellence* the *wise* god bearing the epithet *jātavedas* 'knowing all generations', Indra is the *strong* god exhilarated with Soma and slaying the demons, and Uṣas the Maiden Dawn is the *fair* goddess. Indra is manifested in the lightning and thunderbolt. The theophany of Uṣas is the ruddy flush spread over the east at dawn.

She is as distinctly delicate and feminine as Indra is rough and masculine. As there are masculine[1] hymns and feminine[2] hymns, so there are masculine phenomena of nature and feminine phenomena of nature. Had lightning been conceived as feminine and dawn as masculine, the whole nature and poetry of things would have been reversed. Since the strength and rude impetuosity of Indra are bound up with the drinking of Soma, it is altogether fitting that Soma is not an offering to Uṣas[3]. Agni is a Vedic priest; Indra, a Vedic warrior; and Uṣas a Vedic lady. For a warrior not knowledge but strength is the requisite. From the description of Uṣas we may infer that Vedic ladies were not careless in the matter of personal adornment, and were expert in feminine arts and wiles. Uṣas is a woman. Grace and attractiveness belong to her. Knowledge belongs to Agni and power to Indra. Yet each as a deva shares to a greater or less degree in the divine attributes of wisdom and power. Indirectly then through a study of the gods who were made after their likeness, one may get light upon the ways and aptitudes of the priests, warriors and women of the Vedic age.

2. AŚVINS.--These twin deities are celebrated in about

---

[1] *E. g.* "When I survey the wondrous Cross" and "Onward Christian soldier", etc.

[2] *E. g.* "Let me come closer to thee, Jesus." This distinction between masculine and feminine hymns may be further illustrated by the difference between *Śaiva* poetry and the relatively more soft and sensuous *Vaiṣṇava* poetry.

[3] Oldenberg (RV. 354) refers to the tendency to offer to each individual god the kind of food or drink corresponding to his special nature.

54 entire hymns, over half of which are found in books I and VIII. Judged by the statistical standard the Aśvins rank in popularity next to Indra, Agni and Soma. The twin Nāsatyā(u)[1] are among the most 'opaque' of all the Ṛigvedic gods, in this respect being like Indra and Varuṇa. The result is that in the endeavour to determine their original physical basis there are wide differences of opinion among scholars[2]. For example, the twin horsemen have been identified with heaven and earth[3], day and night[3], sun and moon[4], two royal succouring saints[5], morning and evening star[6], the twin stars in the constellation Gemini[7], the twin lights before dawn, half dark, half light[8], morning and evening[9], fire of heaven and fire of the altar[10], rain-giving and dew-giving[11], and morning and evening wind[12]. One reason for this uncertainty doubtless is that the Aśvins are pre-historic gods, and so in the course of their development have suffered so many transformations that their original physical significance has been almost or quite lost sight of.

a) The Pre-Vedic Aśvins.—In the Boghaz-Köi tablets (1400 B. C.) the name Nāsatya[13] occurs together with Mitra, Varuṇa and Indra. The form of the word Nāsatya

---

[1] *Nāsatyā(u)* of uncertain meaning, possibly 'not-untrue'.

[2] Hillebrandt, VM. III. 379-396, subjects the principal theories to a searching criticism.

[3] Yāska, Nir. XII. 1, 1. Yāska simply quotes the varying opinions known to him.

[4] Yāska, *op. cit.* and Ludwig, RV. III. 334. Regarded by Hillebrandt as the least objectionable of all the theories.

[5] *Yāska, op. cit.* and Geldner, VS. 31.

[6] Oldenberg, RV. 207-215; and, with much less confidence, Macdonell, VM. 53-54; and Bloomfield, Rv. 113-114.

[7] Weber, IS. V. 234, 266.

[8] Myriantheus, Goldstücker, Hopkins, Ragozin.

[9] Max Müller, *Origin and Growth of Religion,* 205.

[10] Bergaigne.

[11] Vodskov.

[12] Brunnhofer, IT. 99.

[13] *ilāni na-ša-at-ti-ia* = 'gods Nāsatya', *i. e.* more than one.

shows that the consonantal shift from *s* to *h* had not yet taken place: therefore the period represented must be Indo-Iranian, or early Iranian[1]. In the Younger Avesta we meet with the demon *Nāonhaithya,* clearly the degraded representative of the earlier Nāsatya. The Nāsatyā(u) belong almost certainly, then, to the early Indo-Iranian or proto-Iranian deities. May they be traced back still further to the Indo-European period? There are distinct points of contact between the Indian Aśvins, on the one hand, and the Greek sons of Zeus[2] and the Lettic god-sons, on the other. They are all horsemen, and each pair of deities has either a sister or a common sweetheart, the daughter of the sun. The resemblances are so striking that such scholars as Oldenberg, Macdonell, Hillebrandt and Bloomfield all agree in postulating some sort of connection[3]. Since a common name is lacking, it is possible that the myth existed only in germ before the Indo-European clans separated, the observation of the same physical phenomenon in each case leading to 'developmental coincidences' in the course of time. The similar nature and functions ascribed to the Indian Aśvins, the Greek Dioscuri, and the Lettic god-sons, are very significant even though their names differ.

b) The identification of the Aśvins.—Of all the guesses concerning the original physical nature of the Aśvins, as set forth above, 'the twilight and the morning star theories seem the most probable'[4]. The twilight[5]

---

[1] *Vedic Index:* I. VIII-IX. But see Giles, CHI. I. 72, for the hypothesis that the Boghaz-köi tablets reveal the presence of "Aryans on the move towards the East.

[2] Διοσκοῦροι as represented, for example, on the coins of the Graeco-Bactrian King Eucratides.

[3] Oldenberg, RV. 213; Macdonell, VM. 53-54; Hillebrandt, VM. III. 379-380; Bloomfield, RV. 113-115.

[4] Macdonell, VM. 54.

[5] The very term 'twilight', *i. e. twinlight,* indicates the analysis into two separate lights, of the gray light preceding the dawn. Twilight, then, may be

consists of twin-lights half-dark and half-light. These two lights fuse together and so correspond well with the description of the Aśvins as inseparable twins[1]. The twilight is a true harbinger of the day, preceding, as it does, the appearance of both the dawn and the sun. If it be objected that the twin-lights of the morning twilight are hardly conspicuous enough to stand alongside of Agni, Uṣas and Sūrya as deities of the morning, it may be answered that the *Aśvinā(u)*, as 'dual divinities', practically fuse into one[2]. The morning twilight, though gray[3], is almost as distinct an object of perception as the dawn or the rising of the sun; and the fact that it is the harbinger of dawn gives it a very definite significance for the sacrificial day.

If we consider the concomitants[4] of the morning twilight, we notice that in the midst of it there often appears the morning star or the waning moon, or both; and further that the morning twilight is confronted by the evening twilight. It is possible, then that the original duality of the twin-lights of morning may have been replaced, here and there, by the duality of morning and evening twilight or of morning and evening star. Such a shifting among closely associated phenomena is entirely comprehensible.

Illustrations of these possible developments may now be noted. The morning star appears at the same time with Agni, Uṣas and Sūrya. It suits all the conditions

interpreted as either one light made from the fusion of two separate lights, or two lights which have coalesced into one. The twilight has a distinct character of its own, separate from that of night, day, dawn or sunrise.

[1] In II. 39 the union of the Aśvins is compared with that of two eyes, two hands, two feet, two lips, two breasts, two nostrils, two worlds, etc.

[2] So Mitra and Varuṇa, interpreted as the light that fills the sky and the sky that is filled with light, fuse into one inseparable unity in the compound Mitra-Varuṇa.

[3] Compare the well-known lines from Milton's Lycidas:

'So sang the uncouth swain to the oaks and rills,
While the still morn went out with sandals *gray*'.

[4] At Landour, Mussoorie, during the summer of 1921 the author made a careful study of the phenomena of the early morning sky.

except the duality of the Aśvins. Analogy, however, may help us here. Uṣas, the morning flush followed by the day is preceded by the evening flush followed by the night, hence *Uṣasā*, 'the two Dawns' (I. 188, 6; V. 1, 4). Ahan 'day' is preceded by an equal length of time, hence *ahanī*, 'the two days', *i. e.* night and day (1. 123, 7). Rodasī 'world' (earthly or heavenly) is confronted by its opposite, hence *Rodasī* 'the two worlds', heaven and earth. In like manner Nāsatya[1] (once in sing. IV. 3, 6), interpreted as the morning star, is confronted by an evening star, therefore, *Nāsatyā, Aśvinā* 'the two horsemen'[2], the morning and evening stars[3]. The dual in each case links together two things which, while akin, are by no means the same or even closely associated. If the morning glow and the evening glow, though differing in the time of their appearance, are called *Uṣasā* 'the two Dawns', why may not *Aśvinā* 'the two horsemen' be, in like manner, a name for the morning star and evening star, or if preferred, a name for morning twilight and evening twilight? Or possibly each includes the other, the morning twilight and morning star going together, and the evening twilight and evening star.

There are, indeed, a few Ṛigvedic texts which seem to indicate the connection of the Aśvins with both morning and evening, since they are referred to as 'born separately' (V. 73, 4), 'born here and there' (I. 181, 4), as having ruddy

---

[1] The Younger Avesta demon Nāonhaithya (=earlier Nāsatya) is in the singular.

[2] The connection with the horses, as suggested by the name *Aśvins* 'horsemen' (*aśva* 'horse') comes out also in the conception of the Greek *Dioscuri* and the Latin *Castor and Pollux* as mounted horsemen. *Cf.* the reverse of the Eucratides coins. So Bloomfield RV. 114.

[3] The 'two-star' theory of the Aśvins is supported by the Lettic myth of th god-sons who are called respectively the morning and the evening star, and by the Greek myth that the Dioscuri were rewarded by being placed in the sky as two stars. Bloomfield, RV. 114.

paths[1] at evening and morning (VIII. 22, 14), and as invoked on both occasions (X. 39, 1; 40, 4). It is probable, however, that even when the Aśvin hymns were written, there was no very clear consciousness of their original physical basis, for by the time of Yāska (fifth century B. C.), as shown above, most diverse opinions were held. Indo-European comparative mythology lends some support to the identification of the Aśvins with the morning and evening stars. The Dioscuri were placed as twin stars in the heavens, and in Lettic mythology the morning star peers at Saule[2], the daughter of the sun.

c) The Aśvins are closely associated with Uṣas, the Dawn, for the three appear in the morning about the same time. It is clearly the twilight hour, for the appearance of Agni, Uṣas and Sūrya is represented as roughly synchronizing with that of the Aśvins (I. 157, 1). The daughter of the sun mounts the three-seated[3] car of the Aśvins (I. 34, 5, etc.), a way of expressing the similarity of function and simultaneity of appearance that holds between the morning dawn and the morning twilight (or the morning star). Such contiguity between Uṣas (=Sūryā) and the Aśvin brothers led also to a romance. The Lady Dawn chose the two Horsemen to be her husbands, a bit of mythological polyandry (IV. 43, 6; I. 119, 5). The situation is complicated by the fact that the Sun Maiden is represented also as the sister of the Aśvins (I. 180, 2), as well as their wife[4]. Another 'affair' of the Lady Sūryā

[1] *Rudravartani* 'ruddy-pathed' is an exclusive epithet of the Aśvins. An alternative epithet is *hiraṇyavartani*, 'golden-pathed'.

[2] *Saule* = Sūryā 'sun-maiden'. Bloomfield (RV. 114-115) and Hillebrandt (VM. II. 41. ff; III. 386) have made it practically certain that Sūryā is to be identified with Uṣas.

[3] 'Three-seated', either to provide seats for Uṣas and the two Aśvins (Vedic Index, *Vandhura*), or to bring the parts of the chariot into correspondence with the three daily sacrifices (Macdonell, VM. 50). Note the continuous play on the word 'three' in I. 34.

[4] As the two Aśvins have a sister Sūryā (Uṣas), so the two Dioscuri have a sister Helena. And as the two Aśvins wed the one Sūryā, so the two Lettic god-sons

is related in X. 85 9, where Soma (the Moon)[1] is the wooer and the two Aśvin brothers are groomsmen[2].

The steeds of the Aśvins are not only horses, but are also frequently described as birds[3] and their car as honey-bearing. They have a honey-whip[4] with which they besprinkle their worshippers. They are ruddy (*rudra*), their bird-steeds are red, and their path is red or golden. We are reminded of Savitar, whose golden arms are probably the morning and evening glow. It is accordingly natural to think of the Aśvins, their bird-steeds, and their paths, as sharing in the ruddiness of the ruddy dawn.

d) As an illustration of the Aśvin hymns there is here reproduced VII. 71[5]:—

1. Away from Dawn her sister Night departeth,
The black one leaves the ruddy god a pathway.
We would invoke you rich in kine and horses;
By day and night from us ward off the arrow.

2. Unto the mortal worshipper approach ye,
Upon your chariot bringing wealth, O Aśvins.

---

wed the one daughter of the sun. These embarrassing connections represent the mythological rendering of the phenomena of the morning sky in terms of human relationships.

[1] Compare the Lithuanian folk-song (Bloomfield RV. 114), according to which the Moon 'wedded the Maiden Sun' and afterward 'wandered by himself afar, and coquetted with the morning star'. The waning moon is often seen in conjunction with the morning star.

[2] This seems to reflect the connection of the new moon with the evening flush or of the old moon with the morning flush. As Sūryā (Uṣas) has a double 'affair' with both the two Aśvins and the Moon, so has the Lettic Daughter of the Sun. Uṣas, the Dawn, appears as the only lady amid the throng of masculine deities of the morning. Are her numerous love affairs with Agni, Pūṣan, Aśvins, Sūryā and Soma (Moon) the reflection of similar experiences in Vedic life, when the brotherless maiden was in danger, and too close proximity between the sexes was apt to lead to intrigue?

[3] At any rate, the time of the appearance of the Aśvins is the time of the singing of birds.

[4] The 'honey-whip' (I. 157, 4) is regarded by Oldenberg (RV. 209) as the morning dew; by Griffith as the stimulating and life-giving breeze' of the early dawn.

[5] Compare Hillebrandt, LR. 7-8; Macdonell, VRS. 130 ff. and HR. 42-43.

Ward off from us unhealthiness and ailment;
Lovers of honey, day and night protect us.
3. At this the latest daybreak may your stallions,
The kindly ones, whirl hitherward your chariot;
Bring it wealth-laden, thong-drawn, O ye Aśvins,
Hither with horses yoked by sacred order.
4. The car, twin lords of men, by which ye travel,
Three-seated, filled with riches, matutinal;
With that to us come hither, ye Nāsatyas,
On your behalf may it approach, food-laden.
5. Ye heroes twain from old age freed Cyavāna,
Brought a swift horse for Pedu, serpent-killing[1],
Delivered Atri from distress and darkness,
And placed the son of Jahuṣa in freedom.
6. This is my thought, O Aśvins, this my praise-song,
Gladly accept this well-wrought hymn, ye mighty;
These prayers addressed to you have been sent forward,
Do ye protect us evermore with blessings.

e) Whatever may have been the original physical basis of the Aśvins, it is clear that as early morning deities of light they were regarded as heralds of the dawn and harbingers of day. As such they may well have been conceived as 'finding and restoring or rescuing the vanished light of the sun'[2]. As a further development of the same point of view, the Aśvins are regarded in the Ṛv. as typically succouring and miracle-working gods. The heavenly myth has been translated into the terms of human life. The Aśvins are 'a very present help in time of trouble'. They are divine physicians, who cure whatever is diseased, restore sight, and heal the maimed[3]. They ward off the arrow[4] of 'unhealthiness and ailment' (VII. 71, 1-2). They are 'rich in kine and horses', and their car is wealth-bringing and food-laden. Four instances of the succouring power of the Aśvins are referred to in VII. 71, 5. They

[1] This epithet of Pedu's swift horse is derived from other cognate passages.
[2] Macdonell, VM. 51.
[3] VIII. 18, 8; 22, 10; I. 116, 16; X. 39, 3.
[4] It may be the 'arrow' of Rudra. In later Hindu mythology the Aśvini Kumāras are medical gods.

restored youthful vigour to the aged sage Cyavāna, prolonged his life, and made him the husband of maidens. They gave a swift, white, dragon-slaying horse to Pedu. They delivered Atri from a burning pit. They rescued Jāhuṣa at night and bore him away to freedom. It is uncertain how many of these stories are to be interpreted mythically as referring to the release of the sun from darkness, and how many are to be regarded as the experiences of actual persons, whose remarkable deliverances from peril or disease would easily be attributed to the Aśvins in view of their character as divine deliverers and healers.

f) The genealogy of the Aśvins is variously expressed. They are several times called children of Dyāus (or the sky)[1]. Once they are said to have the ocean as their mother[2]. They are also once called the twin sons of Vivasvant 'the luminous' and Tvaṣṭar's daughter Saraṇyū, 'the swift'[3]. These various ways of putting the matter probably reduce to much the same thing.

g) The Aśvins are closely connected with love, courtship, marriage, virility and offspring. They acted as groomsmen or 'best men' at the marriage of Soma (Moon) and Sūryā (X. 85, 8-9). They received Sūryā upon their chariot, hence they are besought to conduct the bride home in the same way (X. 85, 26). They are invoked to bestow fertility (X. 184, 2). Among their wonder-working deeds of grace may be mentioned the restoration of youth and virility to the aged sage Cyavāna, so that he became the husband of maidens, the making a barren cow to yield

---

[1] I. 182, 1; 184, 1; X. 61, 4.

[2] I. 46, 2, *sindhumātarā*. The *sindhu* is doubtless the heavenly ocean, hence 'ocean-mothered' probably means the same as 'sons of the sky'.

[3] Vivasvant and Saraṇyū may possibly be interpreted as the luminous day-sky and the dark night-sky, the 'twilight' theory of the Aśvins being thus supported. See Myriantheus, *Die Açvins oder Arischen Dioskuren* (1876) p. 57, and Ragozin. Vedic India, 252-256.

milk and the giving of a child to the wife of a eunuch[1]. They also gave a husband to the old maid *Ghoṣā*[2].

h) The Aśvins may be compared with Indra. Both the Aśvins and Indra are represented as great helpers and deliverers. With this difference, however, that the deliverances wrought by the Aśvins are a peaceful manifestation of divine grace, not as in the case of Indra, a deliverance from foes in battle. Again, both the Aśvins and Indra are connected with the waters, but with a difference. The Aśvins conduct across the ocean *(sindhu),* but Indra conducts across the rivers as *e. g.* the Vipāś and Śutudrī (III. 33). For the way in which the Aśvins deliver from the perils of the ocean, see especially the story of Bhujyu, son of Tugra, which Hillebrandt regards as the only saga of the Ṛv. that refers to the literal and earthly ocean[3]. If the account is to be taken literally, it looks as if Bhujyu had suffered shipwreck in the *samudra,* that is to say, either the Indus after the junction of its tributaries, or the ocean beyond. It is even possible to interpret the whole adventure of Bhujyu mythologically, as is done by Myriantheus and Bergaigne. On the whole, however, it is better to follow the hint furnished by IE. comparative mythology, and take the narrative literally. For as Hillebrandt suggestively remarks[4]: The connection of the Aśvins with Sūryā, that of the Dioscuri with Helena, and the relation of both the Aśvins and the Dioscuri to the sea, points to a common background. Here, as in the case of Indra, myths that had their original home in the sky, have been brought down to earth. It may be that the Aśvins' deliverance of the sun, who seemed likely to perish in the

---

[1] VII. 71, 5; I. 112, 3; 116, 13.

[2] I. 117, 7; X. 40, 5. Note that hymns X. 39, 40 are ascribed to the lady *Ghoṣā*, as a female Ṛiṣi.

[3] VM. III. 18. More or less fully in agreement with Hillebrandt are Oldenberg, RV. 214, n. 2; Pischel und Geldner, VM. XXIII; and *Vedic Index*, II. 432, Art. *samudra*.

[4] VM. III. 18; *cf.* Oldenberg, RV. 214.

ocean of the sky, was made to cover, by analogy, all similar deliverances from earthly waters, and then was extended to embrace every kind of rescue without exception. Thus the Aśvins finally came to be regarded as typical succouring and miracle-working gods.

CHAPTER X.

THE MINOR GODS OF THE VEDIC PANTHEON.

The distinction between major and minor gods, as between older and younger gods is already recognised in the Ṛv.

> Obeisance to the gods, both great and little;
> Obeisance to the younger and the older. I. 27, 13.

Varuṇa, Indra, Agni and Soma are the 'major' gods. From the point of view of ethical greatness Varuṇa deserves to stand first, although judged by the number of hymns composed in his honour, he occupies only the sixth place. Indra is first in importance, if judged by the statistical test. He was clearly the most popular of all the Vedic deities, for as the slayer of both atmospheric and human foes he was the warrior god *par excellence,* and as such appealed not only to the ruling and military Kṣatriyas, but also to the people in general[1]. Indra, the warrior god, and the two ritualistic gods, Agni and Soma, are the three most popular deities of the Ṛv., since approximately three-fifths of its hymns were composed in their honour[2]. Much space has already been given to the treatment of the four great gods, Varuṇa, Indra, Agni and Soma. The minor gods must be satisfied with much less attention. The order of treatment will be *A.* Celestial, *B.* Atmospheric, and *C.* Terrestrial Gods.

A. Celestial Gods.

Varuṇa and the Ādityas, and also Dyāus, have already been considered[3], and the dawn-gods Uṣas and the Aśvins

---

[1] Yahweh, the national god of the Hebrews, combined in himself both the austere ethical character of Varuṇa and the militant qualities of Indra. He was at once the god who 'cannot look upon iniquity' (Habakkuk 1. 13) and 'the lord of hosts', 'mighty in battle' (Ps. XXIV. 8).

[2] Macdonell, VM. 20.

[3] pp. 111 ff.; 98 ff.

have been the subject of a special chapter (IX). There remain only the sun-gods Sūrya, Savitar, Pūṣan and Viṣṇu.

1. SŪRYA[1]. — Only ten or twelve hymns are addressed to this god, most of them being found in the first and tenth books. Sūrya as the designation of the round red orb of the sun is as concrete and transparent as *Agni* 'fire', or *Uṣas* 'dawn'.

VII. 63, 1-6. To Sūrya[2].

1. Common to all mankind, the genial Sūrya,
He who beholdeth all, is mounting upward;
The god, the eye of Varuṇa and Mitra,
Who rolls up darkness like a piece of leather[3].

2. Sūrya's great ensign, restless as the billow,
That urges men to action mounteth upward;
Onward he still would roll the wheel unchanging,
Which Etaśa moveth, harnessed to the car-pole.

3. Refulgent from the bosom of the Mornings,
He riseth up saluted by the singers;
As the god Savitar to me he seemeth,
Who violateth not the law unchanging.

4. The gold-gem of the sky, far-seeing rises,
Whose goal is distant, speeding onward, shining;
Now may mankind by Sūrya stirred to action
Attain their goals and do the tasks assigned them.

5. Where the immortals have prepared his pathway,
He followeth his course like flying eagle;
With homage and oblations would we worship
You, Mitra-Varuṇa, when the sun has risen.

6. Now Mitra, Varuṇa, Aryaman vouchsafe us
Freedom and room, for us and for our children:
May we find paths all fair and good to travel
Preserve us evermore, ye gods, with blessings.

---

[1] Derived from *svar* 'light' and cognate with the Avestan *hvare* 'sun', who has like Sūrya swift horses and is called the eye of Ahura Mazda (Yasna I. 35).

[2] After Griffith with some changes. *Cf.* Hillebrandt, LR. 8-9; Macdonell, VRS. 124 ff.

[3] As a man on rising in the morning, rolls up the skin on which he has slept, so the rising sun rolls up the darkness. So Grassmann, *Uebersetzung*. The custom still survives in India of rolling up one's bedding into a bundle, and leaving it thus until evening.

Sūrya's theophanic moment is when he rises above the horizon. He reveals the glory[1] of the gods, being called the *face*[2] of the gods in general (I. 115, 1) and especially that of Agni (X. 7, 3); also the *eye*[3] of the gods (VII. 77, 3), and especially the eye[4] of Mitra and Varuṇa[5] (VI. 51, 1; VII. 61, 1; 63, 1, etc.) as well as that of Agni (I. 115, 1). Since the sun is the eye of Mitra and Varuṇa, the rising of the sun is the theophanic moment of the two great Ādityas also, when they are especially to be worshipped (VII. 63, 5-6).

The affinity between the eye and the sun is recognised, each, as it were, being made for the other. In the funeral hymn, X. 16, 3, the eye of the dead man is conceived as going to Sūrya: 'Thine eye go sun-ward and thy spirit wind-ward'. So in the great cosmogonic hymn X. 90, 13, the sun is thought of as born from the eye of the world-giant Puruṣa:

> The moon was gendered from his mind,
> And from his eye the sun was born.

---

[1] *Cf.* Milton's Paradise Lost IV. 32-35:

> "O thou that with surpassing glory crowned.
> Look'st from thy sole dominion like the god
> Of this new world: at whose sight all the stars
> Hide their diminished heads".

Cf. for the same imagery Ṛv. I. 50, 2 (after Griffith with changes):

> The constellations slink away,
> Like thieves, together with the night,
> Before the all-beholding sun.

[2] *Cf.* Rev. I. 16: "His countenance was as the sun shineth in his strength".

[3] *Cf.* Rev. I. 14: 'His eyes were as a flame of fire'.

[4] Macdonell (VM. 23) pertinently remarks that the fact that the sun as the eye of Mitra and Varuṇa is always mentioned in the first verse of a hymn suggests that it is one of the first ideas that occur when these two gods are thought of. It is doubtless as 'the eye of Mitra and Varuṇa' that Sūrya in a few passages is called an Āditya (I. 50, 13; 191, 9; VIII. 90, 11).

[5] *Cf.* I. 50, 6:

> With that same eye wherewith thou seest,
> O purifying Varuṇa,
> The unquiet one among mankind.

In what is probably one of the latest hymns to Sūrya in the Ṛv. (X. 158, 3-5) there is a prayer for sight[1]:

3. May Savitar the god, and may
Parvata also give us sight;
May the creator give us sight.

4. Give sight unto our eye, give thou
Our bodies sight that they may see;
May we survey, discern this world.

5. Thus, Sūrya, may we look on thee,
On thee most lovely to behold,
See clearly with the eyes of men. (Griffith's translation.)

The sun is naturally described as far-seeing and all-beholding (VII. 63, 1, 4). He is the spy *(spaś)* of the whole world (IV. 13, 3). Especially is he a witness of the good and evil deeds[2] of men (VI. 51, 2; VII. 60, 2). As such he is besought, when rising, to declare men sinless to the Ādityas and Agni (VII. 62, 2). There are also the prayers:

This day, ye gods, while Sūrya mounteth upward,
Deliver us from trouble and dishonour. I. 115, 6.

4. O Sūrya, with the light whereby thou scatterest gloom,
And with thy ray impellest every moving thing,
Keep far from us all feeble, worthless sacrifice,
And drive away disease and every evil dream.

7. Cheerful in spirit, evermore, and keen of sight,
With store of children, free from sickness *and from guilt*,
Long-living, may we look, O Sūrya, upon thee
Uprising day by day, as great as Mitra thou.

9. Thou by whose lustre all the world of life comes forth,
And at the evening turns again unto its rest,
O Sūrya with the yellow hair, rise up for us
Day after day, *still bringing purer innocence.* X. 37, 4, 7, 9
(Griffith, with some changes).

According to the earlier hymn (VII. 62, 2) the function of Sūrya is to declare men guiltless, but here he seems to be

[1] As the Vedic Aryans penetrated farther and farther into India, blindness must have become more and more common among them, even as to-day. This fact gives the prayer a pathetic interest.

[2] There is here suggested the affinity of the sun with purity and truth, and his hostility to the opposite. *Cf.* John III. 19-21.

thought of as making them guiltless[1]. There is also a reference to the healing activity[2] of Sūrya, who drives away disease[3].

Sūrya has a car variously described as drawn by a horse called *Etaśa* (VII. 63, 2) or by many horses or mares, or by seven bay mares (*haritaḥ* I. 50, 8-9). Sūrya's car and steeds seem to represent his rays of light, for both his steeds and his rays are said to *carry* him (*vah*. I. 50, 1, 8). Sūrya is poetically conceived as both animate and inanimate. As animate he is an eagle, a bull and a steed[4]; as inanimate, a wheel, the gold-gem of the sky, a variegated stone set in the midst of heaven, a brilliant weapon concealed by Mitra-Varuṇa with cloud and rain[5], etc.

Surya's relationships are confused. As appearing after dawn in time he is described as the child of Dawn[6]; but again he is pictured as following Dawn 'as a young man follows a maiden' (I. 115, 2), the lady Dawn being here represented as the wife of Sūrya (VII. 75, 5)[7]. Sūrya is the son of Dyaus (X. 37, 1), but many gods are said to have generated him or caused him to ascend the sky.

Sūrya as the heavenly form of Agni dispels darkness (VII. 63, 1), smites the denizens thereof such as witches (I. 191, 8-9), and shines for all the world (VII. 63, 1). Sūrya measures[8] the days (I. 50, 7) and prolongs them (VIII. 48, 7).

---

[1] *Anāgas* 'guiltless'; *anāgāstva* 'guiltlessness' X. 37, 7, 9.

[2] Is the healing function of Sūrya based upon the hygienic value of sunlight? *Cf.* Malachi IV. 2, "The sun of righteousness shall arise *with healing in his wings*".

[3] In I. 50, 11-12 there is a reference to jaundice, *hariman*, 'the yellow disease', which is of the colour of the sun, and for this reason, perhaps, may have been conceived as caused by the sun and to be healed by the sun. Compare the probably similar relation of Varuṇa to dropsy according to VII. 89 (Zimmer, AL. 392), and also that of Sūrya to blindness.

[4] VII. 63, 5; V. 47, 3; VII. 77, 3.

[5] VII. 63, 2, 4; V. 47, 3; 63, 4.

[6] VII. 63, 3; 78, 3. On the principle of *post hoc ergo propter hoc*.

[7] This illustrates how plastic and free Vedic thought was in dealing with its mythology. The personification of the sun was very slight.

[8] In V. 85, 5 the sun is represented as a measuring line with which Varuṇa measures off the earth.

He is once called 'the divine priest of the gods'[1], and the epithet *viśvakarman* 'all-creating' is once applied to him (X. 170, 4). Sūrya's pathway was prepared for him by the immortals in general (VII. 63, 5), more especially by Varuṇa (I. 24, 8; VII. 87, 1) and the Ādityas (VII. 60, 4). The question is raised, why the sun does not fall from the sky:

How is it that without being held or fastened,
He does not fall, although directed downward?
By what power does he move? Who has discerned that?
Erect as prop of heaven he guards the zenith. IV. 13, 5; 14, 5.

The answer is that Sūrya protects the law of the universe[2]. His uniform[3] wheel follows a uniform, unchanging, universal law. In his obedience to law Sūrya is like Savitar. So central is the sun in the economy of things that he is once called the soul (*ātmā*) of all that moves or is stationary.

2. SAVITAR.[4] — Reference has already been made to the view of Usener, followed by Schrader[5], that the primitive IE. world was characterised by the formation of 'special gods'. It has also been pointed out that the different Vedic sun-gods, Sūrya, Savitar, Viṣṇu, Pūṣan, Vivasvant, and perhaps Mitra, illustrate such formations[6], since each god represents a special aspect of the sun. An alternative view would be that each special sun-god was, in origin, the creation of a different Vedic tribe, all of these being finally brought together within the Ṛigvedic pantheon as 'parallel forms' of the sun-god. Savitar, like Sūrya, is mentioned in ten or twelve hymns, at least eight of these belonging to the 'family books'. The following is a specimen hymn[7]:

---

[1] *asuryaḥ purohitaḥ*, VIII. 90, 12.

[2] *viśvasya vratam*, X. 37, 5.

[3] *Samāna*, VII. 63, 2-3.

[4] From *sū* 'to stimulate' (in Ṛv. only of Savitar); akin to *su* 'to press (from which comes *Soma* and *sū* 'to generate', from which is derived *sūnu* 'son'. The close mutual relations of these three roots or meanings may have helped the development of both Savitar and Soma.

[5] p. 82.

[6] p. 83.

[7] Indebtedness is acknowledged to the translations of Macdonell, VRS. 10 ff; Hillebrandt, LR. 90 ff.; and Hopkins, RI. 48 ff.

To Savitar, I. 35.

1. I call on Agni first of all for health and weal,
I call on Mitra-Varuṇa to aid me here;
I call on Night that brings the busy world to rest,
I call on Savitar the god for needed help.

2. Rolling along the way through space of darkness,
Laying to rest th' immortal and the mortal,
God Savitar on golden chariot seated
Comes hither all existent things beholding.

3. The god goes by a downward, by an upward path,
Adorable he goes with two bright horses.
From the far distance cometh Savitar, the god,
Driving off every kind of pain and hardship.

4. His chariot omniform, pearl-decked[1] and lofty,
With yoke-pins golden, Savitar hath mounted,—
He the adorable and brightly beaming
Who clothes himself with might and spaces darksome.

5. Drawing his car with golden pole, the dusky
White-footed coursers have surveyed the peoples.
For ever do the settlers and all creatures
Rest in the lap of Savitar the godlike.

6. God Savitar's laps form two of the three heavens,
One is the world of Yama, man-restraining.
As on an axle-end, all things immortal
On him repose; let him who knoweth tell this.

7. The sky-bird hath surveyed the realms of mid-air,
The Asura, of wisdom deep, well-guiding.
Where is the sun now found? Who understands it?
To which of all skies hath his ray extended?

8. He hath surveyed the earth's eight summits lofty,
The three waste lands, the leagues, the seven rivers.
Savitar god has come, whose eyes are golden,
Choice gifts upon the worshipper bestowing.

9. The golden-handed Savitar, the active god,
Between the heavens and earth proceedeth on his way.
He drives diseases far away, impels the sun,
And reaches through the darksome space the light of heaven.

10. Let th' Asura, well-guiding, golden-handed,
Go forward, aiding well, whose thoughts are kindly;

[1] The pearls are most probably stars as in X. 68. 11.

Chasing off sorcerers and evil spirits,
The god at eventide arises lauded.

11. Thine ancient paths, O Savitar, are dustless,
Thy paths well-fashioned in the middle region;
By those paths easy to traverse protect us,
This day on our behalf be intercessor.

The following aspects of Savitar may be noted :—

a) Savitar is connected with both evening and morning[1]. He goes by a downward and an upward path (v. 3). He goes around the night on both sides, *i. e.* at evening and morning (V. 81, 4). He regularly precedes the 'two days' *i. e.* night and day (V. 82, 8). Savitar has 'two laps', apparently the lap of mid-air whence he seems to sink at evening, and the lap of the horizon from which he seems to rise at dawn (I. 35, 6). It would seem then that Savitar's theophanic moment is found at evening and dawn, at the time of the setting and the rising of the sun.

b) Savitar seems to have charge of the sun during the interval between evening and morning[2]. He clothes himself with the dark space, rolling along through it, impelling the sun[3], and finally reaching the light of heaven (vv. 2, 4, 9). It is apparently with reference to this period of mystery between sunset and sunrise that the singer asks:

---

[1] Compare Hopkins, RI. 46; Macdonell, VM. 33-34.

[2] It looks as if Savitar in I. 35 where conceived as the power which impels and guides the sun from the place of his setting back to the place of his rising, the sun being apparently thought of as turning back and returning overhead in a reverse direction during the night. In v. 1 the night work is distributed between Rātri and Savitar. Rātri puts men to sleep, while Savitar gives them all needed help during the hours of darkness, banishing distress, driving away the demons of the night, and, as he escorts Sūrya through the darkness back to his place of rising, incidentally surveying all creatures (vv. 2, 5, 7, 8). This view is supported by the similar conception found in the *Aitareya Brāhmaṇa* III. 44. *Cf.* Bergaigne, RV. III. 56; Macdonell, VM. 10; Wallis, CR. 115 ff. According to Sāyaṇa Savitar is the sun before rising.

[3] Savitar, the motive power of the sun, is identified in V. 81, 3 with Etaśa, the steed who draws the car of the sun. *Cf.* VII. 63, 2. So Bergaigne, RV. II. 333. It is from this point of view, doubtless, that Savitar is represented as conducting the departed to where the righteous dwell (X. 17, 4).

Where is the sun now found? Who understands it?
To which of all skies hath his ray extended [1]? (v. 7.)

c) Savitar has two arms, which he raises up [2]. A characteristic trait found in the family books, hence early. His hands and his fingers are mentioned. His two arms are probably the evening and morning glow [3].

d) Savitar is pre-eminently *a golden deity*. He has golden arms (VI. 71, 1, 5; VII. 45, 2) and a golden car with golden yoke-pins and golden pole (I. 35, 2, 4, 5). He is golden-handed (I. 35, 9-10), golden-eyed (I. 35, 8) and golden-tongued (VI. 71, 3). Lustre or 'mighty splendour' *(amáti)* is characteristic of Savitar, and golden lustre is ascribed to him alone (III. 38, 8; VII. 38, 1). His golden arms are beautiful (VI. 71, 5) and he is 'fair-fingered' (*svanguri*). This last epithet reminds us of the Homeric ῥοδοδάκτυλος 'rosy-fingered' as applied to Ἠώς 'Dawn'. Savitar's two golden arms seem to mean the same thing as his golden lustre [4]. In view of all the facts the inference seems justified that Savitar's theophanic moments were the evening and morning glow, the ruddy flush which often covers the evening sky and the morning sky at sunset and sunrise. So far as the dawn is concerned, Savitar is a 'mythological synonym' of Uṣas.

e) With the evening flush Savitar impels all creatures to 'turn in' and go to sleep, and with the morning flush stirs them to awake and go to work [5]. The goddess Night (*Rātrī*) also 'brings the busy world to rest' (I. 35, 1); and

[1] A similar question is asked in I. 24, 10 with reference to the stars.

[2] II. 38, 2; IV. 53, 4; VI. 71, 1, 5; VII. 45, 2.

[3] So Barth, RI. 20: "Savitṛi, the quickener, who, as he raises his long arms of gold, rouses all beings from their slumber in the morning and buries them in sleep again in the evening". Also Grassmann, *Uebersetzung*, I. No. 229.

[4] The epithet *ayohanu* 'metal-jawed' or 'golden-jawed' (Sāyaṇa), VI. 71, 4, doubtless refers to the same golden glow at evening and morning, hence to be rendered 'bronze-jawed' rather than 'iron-jawed'.

[5] IV. 53, 3; VI. 71, 2; VII. 45, 1. Note the stereotyped expression *niveśayan prasuvan*. In IV. 53, 3 both processes—the putting to sleep and the awakening—are accomplished *aktubhiḥ*, *i. e.* by Savitar's beams, the evening and the morning flush.

impelled by Sūrya the impeller (*prasavitar*) men awake in the morning to pursue their ends and do their work (VII, 63, 2-4). Thus there is an overlapping of function between Savitar and Rātri in the evening, and between Savitar and Sūrya in the morning. As a specimen of an evening hymn to Savitar the following stanzas are given from II. 38:

4. The one who weaveth folds her work together,
The artizan lays down his task half-finished;
Savitar mounteth up, the time dividing,
He has approached in likeness of Devotion[1].

5. Through various dwellings, through entire existence,
Spreads manifold the household flame of Agni;
The mother gives her son the choicest portion,
Quite as he wished, by Savitar excited.

6. Now he returns who had gone forth for profit,
All who have fared abroad yearn for their fire-side;
And each, his task half-finished, homeward journeys,
According to god Savitar's commandment.[2]

7. The fishes find their portion in the waters,
The wild beasts spread abroad through desert places;
The woods are given to the birds. These statutes
Of Savitar the god no one infringeth.

8. Even the restless Varuṇa at sunset
Seeks, as he may, a refuge in the waters;
His nest the egg-born seeks, their stall the cattle,
Each in his place god Savitar appoints them.

These stanzas present a delightful picture of the Vedic home-coming at the close of the day, when not only man but also fish, beast and bird seek, each, their place of rest. Half-finished tasks are laid down, and the genial hearth-fire is seen glowing far and wide. The evening meal is prepared, and a mother gives a choice bit to her hungry son. Certain lines remind one of Gray's Elegy. The

---

[1] Twice a day Savitar comes and arises, or lifts up his arms, at evening and at morning. The glow at the time of the evening sacrifice is the very picture of *Aramati 'Devotion'*. The evening glow divides between day and night.

[2] It is doubtless with reference to the home-coming at evening that Agni's epithet damūnas, '*domestic*', is applied to Savitar. (I. 123, 3; VI. 71, 4.)

following is a morning litany in which Savitar along with other dawn deities is invoked:

Agni, the gracious, has upon the breaking
Of radiant mornings looked, on wealth's bestowal.
Come, Aśvins, to the dwelling of the pious,
Sūrya, the god, is rising with his splendour.

God Savitar hath spread on high his lustre,
Waving his flag like a spoil-seeking hero.
Varuṇa-Mitra follow stablished order,
What time they make the sun ascend the heaven.

IV. 13, 1-2 (after Griffith with some changes).

f) Savitar is the lord of 'stimulation' (*prasava* V. 81, 5). As such he assumes all forms[1]. The different forms of life, fish, beast, and fowl, together with their abodes and forms of sustenance, are due to the ordinance of Savitar (II. 38, 7). He is once called *prajāpati*[2] 'lord of offspring' (IV. 53, 2). He bestows on men length of life or 'life succeeding life' (IV. 64, 2)[3]. Upon the gods in general and the Ṛibhus in particular, he bestowed immortality (IV. 54, 2: I. 110, 3)[4], in this respect resembling Soma.

The word *savitar* 'stimulator', 'vivifier' is twice used as an epithet of Tvaṣṭar[5]:—

Tvaṣṭar the god, omniform, vivifier[6],
Offspring begets and feeds in various fashion. III. 55, 19.

---

[1] *Viśvā rūpāṇi* V. 81, 2. Savitar's car is once called *viśvarūpa* 'omniform' I. 35, 4.

[2] Prajāpati is here an epithet of Savitar, 'the supporter of heaven and *prajāpati* of the world'. In IX. 5, 9 prajāpati is mentioned in connection with Soma and Tvaṣṭar, being identified with Soma. From these uses as an epithet Prajāpati finally attained an independent position as the supreme god, according to X. 121, 10.

[3] Either long life for the individual or for the race, probably the latter, 'racial immortality' for men, to correspond with personal immortality for the gods.

[4] The conception of Savitar as a 'quickener', who bestows immortality, may be compared with the similar conception of 'the last Adam' who was made a 'quickening' or life-giving Spirit (πνεῦμα ζωοποιοῦν) I. Cor. XV. 45.

[5] *Tvaṣṭṛi* 'fashioner', 'creator', from *tvakṣ* (= common root *takṣ* 'to fashion', Avestan *thwakṣ*.

[6] Both couplets contain the words *devas Tvaṣṭā savitā viśvarūpaḥ*. *Viśvarūpa* is used in a pregnant sense 'shaping all forms', as well as 'possessing all forms'. In both couplets 'the generative or creative faculty of the deity is referred to' Macdonell, VM. 117.

Even in the womb god Tvaṣṭar, generator,
Omniform, vivifier, made us consorts. X. 10, 5.

This would seem to indicate that Tvaṣṭar is the more ancient deity, and that Savitar has fallen heir to some of the functions of Tvaṣṭar. Tvaṣṭar, the craftsman deity and the artificer of the gods, seems to have been the apotheosis of the creative activity manifest in nature. Perhaps he may be regarded as a 'mythological synonym'[1] of Dyāus; for, as paternity is the leading characteristic of Dyāus, so the adorning of all things with form, the shaping of the fœtus in the womb, is the work of Tvaṣṭar[2]. The conception of heaven as creative must have been quite natural in view also of the multitudinous transformations that take place in the sky[3]. As the creator of all living forms, both human and animal, Tvaṣṭar is the energy manifested in generation and birth (I. 188, 9; III. 4, 9). Thus he is a universal father. He is the ancestor of the human race, in so far as his daughter *Saranyu* was the mother of Yama, the first man (X. 17, 1). Vāyu is his son-in-law (VIII. 26, 21); Agni (I. 95, 2) and (by inference) Indra, (VI. 59, 2; II. 17, 6) his sons. The 'omniform' Tvaṣṭar has also a son called *Viśvarūpa* 'Omniform'.

It would seem probable, then, that Savitar was first a descriptive epithet of Tvaṣṭar and afterwards attained to

---

[1] If a 'mythological synonym', then Tvaṣṭar may have been originally an epithet of Dyāus, just as in two passages Savitar is an epithet of Tvaṣṭar.

[2] X. 110, 9; I. 188, 9; X. 184, 1; III. 4, 9, etc.

[3] As the theatre of ever-changing colours and forms *(rūpāṇi)*, cloud and sunshine, night and day, the sky might very well be called *viśvarūpa*. In fact the epithet *viśvarūpa* 'omniform' is once applied to the night-car of Savitar which is adorned with pearls, *i. e.* stars. I. 35, 4.

[4] Thus Tvaṣṭar forged the thunderbolt of Indra, sharpened the axe of Brahmaṇaspati, and fashioned a wonderful bowl, the chalice of the gods—a kind of Vedic 'Holy Grail'—which the Ṛibhus made into four, this last being probably, as Hillebrandt thinks, the moon and its four phases. I. 32, 2; X. 53, 9; I. 20 6; 161, 5.

definite personification as a 'special god' in charge of the general work of 'stimulation', the most marked example of Savitar's energy of impulsion being that of the sun. Savitar conducts the sun through the darkness from west to east[1], and has to do especially with the evening and morning glow. During the day he is united with the rays of the sun (V. 81, 4), the epithet *sūryaraśmi* 'sun-rayed' being applied in the Ṛv. to him alone (X. 139, 1). While Savitar is sometimes identified with Mitra, Pūṣan and Bhaga, light-deities of the day, yet his most characteristic domain is probably that of the night, the time of 'the sun before rising' (V. 81, 4-5; 82, 1, 3)[2]. Savitar impels the car of the Aśvins before dawn (I. 34, 10). In his own department Savitar is supreme. Here not even Indra, Rudra or the Ādityas can violate his independence (II. 38, 7, 9; V. 82, 2).

g) The 'golden text'[3] of the whole Ṛv. is the famous *Savitrī* or *Gāyatrī*[4] stanza, the most sacred of all Vedic stanzas:

That longed-for glow of Savitar,
The heavenly one, may we obtain;
So may he stimulate our thoughts[5]. III. 62, 10.

Or as Macdonell (HR. 33) translates:

May we attain that excellent
Glory of Savitar the god,
That he may stimulate our thoughts.

Here Savitar's power of stimulation is transferred to the spiritual world, and he becomes the inspirer and

---

[1] In like manner Savitar is besought to convey the departed spirit to where the righteous dwell (X. 17, 4).

[2] So Sāyaṇa on V. 81, 4.

[3] Compare John III. 16 in the Bible, the *Kalima* in Islam, and the threefold refuge of the Buddhist creed.

[4] Called *Sāvitrī* because addressed to Savitar and *Gāyatrī* because composed in the gāyatrī metre.

[5] *Tat Savitur vareṇyam*
Bhargo devasya dhīmahi,
Dhiyo yo naḥ pracodayāt.

quickener of thought. As Savitar awakens the world to do its work, so he awakens the spirit of man. The morning glow is an emblem of the inward illumination which the earnest worshipper or student desires for himself at the beginning of the day, or in the post-Vedic period at the beginning of Vedic study. As Soma exhilarates to holy thought and prayer, so Savitar stimulates.

h) Finally, Savitar through his quickening and inner illumination makes men sinless:

> If we have done aught 'gainst the gods through thoughtlessness,
> Weakness of will, or insolence, men as we are,
> Whether we've sinned against the gods or mortal men,
> Make[1] thou us free from sin and guilt[2], O Savitar. IV. 54, 3.

And so he is able to declare them sinless to the sun and Aditi (I. 123, 3; V. 82, 6).

Savitar with his morning glow drives away the sorrows of the night and all bad dreams (V. 82, 4-5).

3. PŪṢAN.—A unique figure in the Vedic pantheon, his car being drawn by goats, his hairbraided, his weapon a goad, and his food mush. He seems to have been a pastoral[3] deity originating perhaps in a single Vedic tribe[4]. Accordingly he is represented in the following hymn as a shepherd or herdsman god:

---

[1] *Suvatāt,* from sū, to 'constitute' sinless through the process of inward quickening and illumination (*sava* V. 82. 6). There is here the suggestion possibly of a dynamic working in the human spirit, something akin to the thought of Ps. LI., 'Create in me a clean heart'.

[2] *anāgasaḥ,* 'guiltless'.

[3] The derivation from *puṣ* 'to thrive' would seem to indicate that Pūṣan was a Vedic '*Sondergott*', the personification of the idea of 'thrift' or 'prosperity', the 'prosperer'.

[4] Since of the ten hymns addressed to Pūṣan either singly or conjointly with Indra or Soma, six belong to the sixth book, it is a plausible conjecture that the worship of Pūṣan originated in the Bharadvāja clan.

To Pūṣan, VI. 54[1].

1. Pūṣan, provide us with a guide,
Who shall at once direct us right,
And who shall say: 'it is just here'.
2. With Pūṣan we would join ourselves,
Who shall us to the houses guide,
And say to us; 'it is just these'.
3. The wheel of Pūṣan is not hurt,
Never falls down his chariot-box,
Nor does his felly quake and creak.
4. Who with oblation worships him,
Him Pūṣan never overlooks;
That man is first to find him wealth.
5. After our cows let Pūṣan go;
May he protect and guard our steeds;
May Pūṣan for us booty win.
6. O Pūṣan, follow thou the kine
Of Soma-pressing worshipper,
And of ourselves who laud thee well.
7. Let none be lost, let none be hurt,
Nor suffer fracture in a pit;
Come back with all the cows unharmed.
8. The watchful Pūṣan, him who hears,
Whose property is never lost,
The lord of wealth, we supplicate.
9. O Pūṣan, in thy service may
We never suffer injury;
We laud and praise thee in this place.
10. From far away may Pūṣan place
His right hand round us to protect;
May he drive back to us the lost.

The following characteristics of Pūṣan may be noted:

a) He shepherds domestic animals. Prosperity for a pastoral tribe means good pasture (I. 42, 8) for cattle and their careful shepherding, so that none may fall into a pit, break a limb, be seized by thieves, be devoured by

[1] For the translation compare Hillebrandt, LR. 71 ff. and Macdonell, VRS. 111 ff.

wild beasts or stray away and become lost[1] (VI. 54, 5-10; I. 42, 2-3). In the hymn translated above Pūṣan is represented as a divine herdsman[2], a 'good shepherd'[3], who guards and guides his own and ever seeks and finds the 'lost'. By analogy the activity of Pūṣan is extended, so that he makes all hidden treasures manifest and easy to find (VI. 48, 15), such as the hidden Agni and the hidden Soma (X. 5, 5; I. 23, 13). His exclusive epithets *anaṣṭapaśu* 'losing no cattle', and *anaṣṭavedas* 'losing no goods', emphasize this trait of his character.

b) Pūṣan is a 'path-lord (*pathaspati* VI. 53, 1). As such he guards every path, delivers from the dangers of the road, such as the wolf and highwayman, grants auspicious paths, and makes them lead to booty[4]. His goad is *paśusadhanī*[5], that is, it directs cattle straight, in the morning on the road to pasture and in the evening on the road home (VI. 53, 9). As path-lord Pūṣan also escorts the bride on the way to her new home (X. 85, 37), and along with Agni and Savitar conducts the dead on the far path to the gods and the fathers (X. 17, 3-5)[6]. The pertinent stanzas from the great funeral hymn are worth quoting in this connection:—

3. May Pūṣan bear thee hence, for he hath knowledge,
Guard of the world, whose cattle ne'er are injured;
May he consign thee to these Fathers' keeping,
And to the gracious gods let Agni give thee.

---

[1] Compare the following Biblical passages: Gen. XXXI. 39; 1 Sam. XVII. 34-36; John X. 1, 12; Matt. XII. 11; Luke XV. 3-7.

[2] *paśupā*, 'cattle-protector', is referred directly only to Pūṣan (VI. 58, 2).

[3] *Cf.* Ps. XXIII. 1; John X. 11, 14.

[4] VI. 49, 8; I. 42, 1-3; X. 59, 7; VI. 53, 4.

[5] Pūṣan's goad is a bucolic weapon and its function to keep cattle in the straight path is apparently the link of connection between Pūṣan's work as cattle-protector and that of path-hord. Pūṣan's second weapon, the awl, is describrd as 'prayer-inspiring' (*brahmacodanī* VI. 53, 8). The gracious light and impulses of the morning sun constitute an awl by which Pūṣan produces a devotional spirit in the close-fisted and so brings them to the employment of the priestly singer.

[6] Pūṣan's goat serves the same purpose in conducting the sacrificial horse to the world of the gods (I. 162, 2-4).

4. May Āyu, giver of all life, protect thee;
May Pūṣan guard thee on thy pathway forward;
Thither let Savitar the god transport thee,
Where dwell the pious who have passed before thee.

5. Pūṣan knows all these realms; may he conduct us
By ways that are most free from fear and danger;
Giver of blessings, glowing, all-heroic,
May he the wise and watchful go before us.

6. Pūṣan was born to move on distant pathways,
On the far path of earth, far path of heaven;
To both most wonted places of assembly
He travels and returns with perfect knowledge. X. 17, 3-6.
(Griffith with some changes.)

c) Pūṣan's birth, habitat and connections are in the heavens. He was born on the far path of earth and sky, and so knows all the routes. He moves back and forth between heaven and earth, and his car never breaks down. *Āghṛiṇi* 'glowing' is his exclusive epithet. He is the heavenly herdsman (*gopā*)[1]; or, to change the figure, he sails his golden ships through the aerial ocean, acting as the messenger of Sūrya (VI. 58, 3). These descriptions point clearly to the sun. The personification of Pūṣan as the sun was so faint that apparently the moral sense of the Vedic age was not scandalized by his being called the paramour of his sister (the Dawn) and the wooer of his mother (the Night)[2]. The whole mythical transaction was thoroughly transparent. Pūṣan and Savitar are closely related[3]. Pūṣan moves in the energy (*prasava* X. 139, 1) of Savitar, and both conduct the dead to the place of the 'fathers'. Savitar is the sun as 'the great stimulator of life and motion', making the world to awake in the morning and sending it to rest in the evening; while Pūṣan is the

[1] X. 17, 3; 139, 1.

[2] VI. 55, 4-5. The incestuous love affairs ascribed to Pūṣan may be the survival of an earlier conception of him as a goat-god.

[3] Pūṣan is also called the brother of Indra (VI. 55, 5), and the epithet *Narāśaṁsa* 'praised of men', otherwise exclusively limited to Agni, is twice applied to him (I. 106, 4; X. 64, 3).

sun as the heavenly herdsman, pathmaker[1], and traveller, who moves through the sky from sunrise to sunset[2].

The question arises as to which was primary and which secondary in Pūṣan, his earthly function as a bucolic god or his heavenly function as the sun. Macdonell thinks that 'the beneficent power of the sun manifested chiefly as a pastoral deity' underlies the character of Pūṣan (VM. 37), while Oldenberg takes Pūṣan's character as a path-god to be primary (RV. 230 ff.). Where such great authorities disagree the solution is difficult. If, however, Pūṣan is really derived from *puṣ* 'to thrive'[3], then he most probably was in origin an abstract *Sondergott,* 'he of thrift', 'prosperer'. Concrete content would be secured by a very early identification of Pūṣan with the sun as the best realizer of the notion of a herdsman god, since the sun shepherds the literal cows of earth as well as the cloud-kine and light-kine of the skies[4]. Thus in all probability 'Pūṣan was originally the countryman's deity, somewhat as were Pan and Faunus[5]. As Agni and Soma were Brāhman gods and Indra a Kṣatriya god, so Pūṣan was probably a Vaiśya god.

4. VIṢṆU.—A god of minor significance[6] in the Ṛv., but of primary importance in the later history of India in view of his inclusion in the great triad, Brahmā, Viṣṇu

---

[1] *Cf.* Ps. XIX. 5-6.

[2] Pūṣan's team of mountain-climbing goats fits in well with his climb up the steep of heaven to the zenith and then down to the place of sunset. It is even possible that Pūṣan himself was originally a goat-god, his goat-team being the survival of an earlier theriomorphic stage. *Cf.* Oldenberg, RV. 74-75.

[3] Denied by Pischel and Geldner, VS. I. 193.

[4] We may compare the local *Baalīm* of Palestine, concerning whom Morris Jastrow writes: "For the Canaanites the old Semitic deities became protectors of the soil, presiding over vegetation. In general these protectors were viewed as *personifications of the sun*".—Hebrew and Babylonian Traditions, 1914, p. 28.

[5] Drisler, *Notes on the Vedic Deity Pūṣan* in Classical Studies in honour of Henry Drisler, 1894, p. 242.

[6] Of the five or six Ṛigveda hymns addressed to Viṣṇu three belong to Book I, and the rest stand late in Books VI. and VII. Hopkins may, therefore, be correct in regarding the Viṣṇu hymns as late.

and Śiva. The following hymn (I. 154)[1] illustrates Viṣṇu's chief activity :—

1. Let me tell forth the mighty deeds of Viṣṇu,
He who has measured out the earthly regions;
And has the upper gathering-place established,
Having strode out, the wide-paced one, with three strides.
2. Through his heroic deed is Viṣṇu lauded,
He who like wild beast haunts the lofty mountains,
Wandering at will, in whose three ample footsteps
All worlds abide, all creatures have their dwelling.
3. Let my inspiring hymn go forth to Viṣṇu,
The bull, the mountain-dweller, the wide-pacing,
He who alone has measured out with three steps
This long and far-extended place of gathering.
4. Whose three steps filled with honey-mead, unfailing
In heavenly joys, delight themselves in amṛit;
He who in threefold manner earth and heaven
Alone supports, even all the world of being.
5. I would attain to that dear realm of Viṣṇu,
Where men devoted to the gods delight them;
For dear and most akin to the wide-strider
Is in his highest step the well of honey.
6. To your realms would we go, O Indra-Viṣṇu,
Where are the many-horned and nimble cattle;
There shineth brightly down the highest footstep,
The footstep of the bull, the widely pacing.

The 'three steps' of Viṣṇu constitute his chief characteristic. These are either the three stations, sunrise, zenith and sunset, or the three levels, sunrise, mid-air and zenith, most probably the latter[2]. For the highest step[3] of Viṣṇu is described in language which clearly identifies it with the position of the sun in the zenith[4].

---

[1] For the translation *cf.* Griffith, HR. I. 207; Hillebrandt, LR. 89; Macdonell VRS. 30 ff. and HR. 35.

[2] So Macdonell, VM. 38, and Bloomfield, RV. 169. Agni's characteristic epithet *triṣadhastha* 'three-seated', *i. e.* found in earth, mid-air and sky, is once applied to Viṣṇu. I. 156, 5.

[3] *Paramam padam*, I. 154, 5-6.

[4] The highest step of Viṣṇu is in X. 1, 3 identified with the highest, *i. e.* the third place of Agni. Yāska calls the zenith *Viṣṇupada* 'the step of Viṣṇu'.

The highest step of Viṣṇu is connected with the ideas of the Viṣṇu-worshippers of that time concerning *life after death.* There the pious are happy in the dear abode of Viṣṇu (I. 154, 5). There is the well of honey, and there are found the many-horned and nimble cattle (I. 154, 6)[1]. The situation of Viṣṇu's 'highest step' is not easily described. It is beyond the flight of birds[2]. It is seen by the liberal like an eye fixed in heaven (I. 22, 20). It shines down brightly (I. 154, 6). The note of yearning for the heavenly home, the elysium of Viṣṇu (I. 154, 5-6)[3] is clearly sounded.

Viṣṇu's highest step is represented as his distinctive abode (I. 154, 5). Hence his theophanic moment is after he has taken his three steps and climbed the mountain[4] of the sky, in other words, when the sun is in the zenith. Viṣṇu's epithet 'mountain-dwelling' and 'mountain-abiding' (I. 154, 2-3) are probably connected with the same order of ideas unless Viṣṇu was originally a mountain-god in the literal sense.

Viṣṇu took his three steps for a gracious purpose, namely to deliver man from distress (VI. 49, 13) and to provide him with the earth[5] as a dwelling[6]. In all this Viṣṇu acted as a protector or preserver[7], an interesting anticipation of his later function as Preserver. In one passage (VII. 100, 6) there is a reference to different forms

---

[1] A bucolic heaven 'flowing with milk and honey'.

[2] I. 155, 5. *cf.* I. 24, 6 of Varuṇa.

[3] With 'the sun-home of souls' in the Ṛv. compare the sun-clad glory of the redeemed in the Bible: "They that are wise shall shine *as the brightness of the firmament;* and they that turn many to righteousness *as the stars for ever and ever*", Dan. XII. 3; and "Then shall the righteous shine forth *as the sun* in the kingdom of their Father". Matt. XIII, 43.

[4] Compare the representation of the Semitic *Shamash* (sun) on very early Babylonian seals as a mountain climber.

[5] Viṣṇu (VII. 99, 3) made fast the earth round about with pegs. The vault of the sky is conceived as a tent, which is fastened down at the horizon on all sides with tent-pegs, as it were.

[6] VI. 69, 5-6; VII. 100, 4.

[7] *Trātṛ* I. 155, 4.

of Viṣṇu: 'Do not conceal from us this form, since thou didst assume another form in battle'. The various *avatāras* of Viṣṇu depend upon this power of changing his form.

Viṣṇu and Indra are closely associated[1], forming in one hymn (VI. 69) the dual divinity Indra-Viṣṇu. Here there is mutual assimilation, Indra, becoming a wide-strider and Viṣṇu a Soma-drinker and fighter. Both do 'heroic deeds'[2] which are praised in almost identical language in their characteristic hymns (I. 32, 1; 154, 1).

The name Viṣṇu is not transparent like Agni and Uṣas, its derivation[3] being uncertain. Oldenberg (RV. 228) thinks that Viṣṇu was originally an abstract deity—'he of wide space', having nothing concrete corresponding to his three steps[4]. According to Macdonell, however, Viṣṇu is the sun conceived as 'the personified swiftly moving luminary' which with vast strides traverses the whole universe (VM. 39). It is possible that Viṣṇu began as an abstract 'Sondergott' and later found concrete content in the sun.

B. Atmospheric Gods.

The Maruts have been described in connection with Indra their chief[5] and Parjanya in connection with Mitra-Varuṇa[6]. Hence there remain only Vāyu-Vāta, Rudra, Trita Āptya, Apām Napāt, Mātariśvan, Aja Ekapād and Āpaḥ.

---

[1] Is this because their natural basis was similar—sun and lightning—, Indra as the lightning slaying Vṛitra and Viṣṇu as the sun striding through the worlds? Or was there conceivably a historical ground in the union of the Viṣṇu-worshippers and the Indra-worshippers, as suggested by Hillebrandt (VM. III. 348)?

[2] *viryāṇi.*

[3] *Viṣ* 'to be active', hence 'the active one' (Macdonell VM. 39); *vi-ṣnu (sānu* '*summit*') 'over the summit', hence 'he who climbs over the summit' (Bloomfield RV. 168); preposition *vi* with ending *snu* 'the wide-striving' (Oldenberg RV. 292, n. 1).

[4] The three steps correspond in later Hindu mythology to the three worlds, heaven, earth and hell.

[5] p. 202 ff.

[6] p. 141 ff.

1. VĀYU-VĀTA[1].—Each of these names for wind expresses both the physical element and its divine personification, but Vāyu more commonly refers to the god and Vāta to the element of wind[2]. There is only one complete hymn to Vāyu (I. 134) and two to Vāta (X. 168, 186), these hymns belonging to the latest portions of the Ṛv. The following stanzas of I. 134 in the unusual Atyaṣṭi metre are reproduced after Griffith with some changes:

3. Two bay steeds Vāyu yokes, Vāyu two ruddy steeds,
Swift-footed to the chariot, to the pole to draw,
Best coursers, to the pole to draw.
Awaken Bounteousness, as when
A lover wakes his sleeping love.
Illumine heaven and earth, make thou the dawns to shine;
For glory make the dawns to shine.

4. For thee the radiant Dawns in the far-distant sky
Stretch out bright garments wondrously in beams of light,
Bright-coloured in their newest beams.
For thee the nectar-yielding cow
Pours all rich treasures forth as milk.
The Marut-host hast thou engendered from the womb,
The Maruts from the womb of heaven.

Also the hymn to Vāta,[3] X. 168:—

1. Of Vāta's car I now will tell the greatness:
Shattering, thundering, its roar advances;
It moves sky-touching, lurid hues producing,
Fares too along the earth, the dust up-whirling.

2. The hosts of Vāta follow close thereafter,
And haste to him as women to their trysting.
With them united, on the self-same chariot,
The god, the King of all this world, speeds onward.

3. Proceeding on the pathways through the mid-air,
Never on any day halts he his chariot,

[1] From *vā* 'to blow', possibly connected with Lat. *Ventus* and Teut. *Woden*. Vāyu is referred to in the Avesta (Farg. XIX. 13) as 'the powerful wind made by Mazda'.

[2] Macdonell, VM. 81.

[3] *Cf.* the translations of Griffith, HR. II. 600; and Macdonell, VRS. 216 ff and HR. 62.

The first-born, friend of waters, order-loving[1],—
Where was he born and whence obtained he being?

4. As breath of gods[2] and germ of all creation,
Wanders this god according to his pleasure.
His sound is heard, but no one sees his likeness;
That Vāta let us worship with oblation.

The following comments may be made:—

a) Of all the forces of nature wind is the most restless. It never halts (X. 168, 3). The constant movement of the air is more palpable than that of any other element. Hence *niyutvat* 'drawn by a team' is a characteristic epithet of Vāyu, for he is always travelling about, of course, with carriage and span. Besides the gentle breeze, there are found to-day three types of wind in the Vedic area, wind accompanying dust-storms, wind that blows up the monsoon, and wind that accompanies the rain-storm. It may be that all are referred to in the hymn to Vāta. There is mention of the wind that whirls up the dust, and Vāta as 'the order-loving friend of waters' may be, as suggested by Hopkins, the wind that "brings the monsoon-clouds in due season"[3]. The wind whose sound is thunder, which touches the sky and produces the lurid lightning hues, is clearly the wind that accompanies thunder and lightning. Vāyu, as the gentle morning zephyr, breathes upon Uṣas, the Lady Bountiful, and awakens her, as 'a lover wakes his sleeping love'.

b) To wake up Uṣas is to make the dawns to shine and illumine heaven and earth. Close connection between the morning breeze and the morning dawn; and hence for Vedic thought a causal relation between the two. The morning breeze, as starting up first, is naturally conceived as the cause of the dawn. Since then Vāyu wakes up Uṣas, it is for him, *i. e.* on his behalf, that the radiant dawns in

---

[1] *ṛilāvan.* cf. *ṛilaspati* lord of *ṛita,* VIII. 26, 21.

[2] In VII. 87, 2 Vāta is called the breath *(ātman)* of Varuṇa.

[3] ION. 47.

the far distance 'broaden out goodly garments in wondrous beams'[1].

c) Vāyu in six or seven hymns is joined with Indra as a dual divinity in the form *Indra-Vāyu.* This close connection with Vāyu 'Wind' helps to determine the place and function of Indra, one of the most 'opaque' of all the gods. As Lightning and Wind co-operate in the thunder-storm, so Indra and Vāyu ride on the same car[2], a mythological expression for united function. This union of Indra and Vāyu explains why either of them may represent the deities of the atmosphere in the later Vedic triad[3].

d) The first draught of Soma is Vāyu's share[4]. Is this a merely ritualistic detail, or the reflexion of the fact that the monsoon-wind regularly precedes the monsoon and a blast of wind usually initiates a thunder-storm? If Vāyu becomes active before Indra, then he must have had the prior Soma-draught. The violence of both must have seemed to the Vedic Indians to indicate exhilaration with Soma.

e) The difference between collective wind and individual gusts or blasts of wind seems to be suggested by the varying number of the cars and teams of Vāyu. In one place Vāyu is said to have two horses (I. 134, 3) and a shining, wide-gleaming, heaven-touching car; in other places, 99, 100 or 1000 horses, and 1000 cars[5]. As Agni is related to the agnis, Soma to the soma-drops, and Indra to the Maruts, so would it be natural for Vāyu 'Wind' to be related to the winds (cf. II. 11, 14 for *vāyavaḥ*). The difficult word *viṣṭaḥ*[6] 'expansions', developments', 'divisions', must refer either to the individual

---

[1] Note literal *beams* and figurative *garments.*

[2] Vāyu has Indra as his charioteer (*Indra-sārathi* IV. 46, 2; 48, 2).

[3] p. 151.

[4] I. 134, 1. 6; 135, 1; IV. 46, 1, *etc.*

[5] IV. 46, 3; 48, 4; II. 41, 1.

[6] X. 168, 2 (only here in Ṛv.). The meanings are derived theoretically from those of the verbal form *vi-sthā*.

blasts which form the host of Vāyu[1], or to the natural concomitants of wind such as the waters[2], etc. or to both.

f) The wind presents itself as a mysterious element[3]. It wanders where it listeth. Its sound is heard, but no one sees its form[4]. That is to say, its theophany is in terms of sound, not in terms of sight. Its origin is uncertain. Once it is called the child of heaven and earth (VII. 90, 3), and again it is said to have sprung from the breath (*prāṇa*) of the world-giant (X. 90, 13). Hence in the late hymn (X. 168, 3) the question is raised: 'Where was he born, and whence obtained he being?'

g) The hygienic and vital aspects of wind were well known to the Vedic Indians. They knew that air is the condition of life and air in motion the condition of health. If there were terrible activities of Vāta, in which he 'generated the Maruts from the wombs of heaven', that is, sent forth his brood of winds to accompany the thunder-storm, shattering trees and whirling up dust, there were also gracious[5] and remedial activities. Vāta wafts healing and prolongs life, for in his house is the treasure of immortality (X. 186)[6]. It is from this point of view that Vāta is called the source of the world and the father of men, yea the very 'breath[7] of the gods. If then the Greek

---

[1] So Muir, OST. 'gusts' (?); Hopkins, ION. 47 'forms of Vāta'; Bloomfield, RV. 155. 'blasts of Vāta'.

[2] So Hillebrandt, LR. 61, 'Vātas Scharen'; and Macdonell, VRS. 217, 'hosts of Vāta'.

[3] *Cf.* John III. 8; "The wind bloweth where it will, and thou hearest the voice thereof, but knowest not whence it cometh, and whither it goeth: so is every one that is born of the Spirit". Note that both 'wind' and 'Spirit' translate the same Greek word πνεῦμα.

[4] *Cf.* I. 164, 44: 'The pull (or drag, *dhrāji*) of Vāyu is perceived, not his form'.

[5] In VIII. 26, 23 Vāyu has the epithet *Śiva*; *cf.* VIII. 18, 9.

[6] Macdonell, VM. 82.

[7] *ātman* X. 186, 4. Vāyu-Vāta would seem, accordingly, to be connected with the Hindu doctrine of the *Prāṇas* or 'Vital Breaths?

word for wind furnishes in the New Testament a name for the Holy Spirit, we need not wonder that the Vedic Indians also found in Vāyu-Vāta the symbol of a transcendent reality.

2. ĀPAḤ.—The Waters are praised in four entire hymns [1]. Their personification is very slight, not more than that of Pṛthivī 'Earth'. The following is Professor Macdonell's metrical translation of VII. 49 [2]:—

1. With ocean for their chief they flow unresting;
From the aerial flood they hasten cleansing;
For whom the mighty Indra's bolt cut channels,
Here may those Waters, goddesses, preserve me.
2. Waters that come from heaven or run in channels
Dug out, or flow spontaneously by nature,
That, clear and pure, have as their goal the ocean:
Here may those Waters, goddesses, preserve me.
3. In midst of whom King Varuṇa is moving,
And, looking down, surveys men's truth and falsehood;
Who clear and purifying, drip with sweetness;
Here may those Waters, goddesses, preserve me.
4. In whom King Varuṇa, in whom, too, Soma,
In whom the All-gods drink exalted vigour;
Into whom Agni, friend of all, has entered;
Here may those Waters, goddesses, preserve me.

The following comments may be made:—

a) It is the heavenly waters that are celebrated in this hymn, but not perhaps to the exclusion of the earthly [3]. Their place is beside the sun. King Varuṇa moves in their midst. Indra with his bolt dug out their channels [4], and Apām Napāt, 'Child of the Waters', the lightning form

[1] VII. 47, 49; X. 9, 30.

[2] HR. 63, *cf.* Hillebrandt, LR. 70.

[3] The distinction between the waters 'above the firmament' and the waters 'under the firmament' is not very clearly drawn, so that in the *Naighaṇṭuka* (V. 3) the waters are reckoned as terrestrial deities only.

[4] The reference in VII. 47, 4 and 49, 1 to Indra's digging with his bolt the channels of the waters may be best interpreted as alluding to the heavenly waters. It is an extension by analogy, when Indra is represented as hollowing out the channels of the Vipāś and Śutudrī (III. 33, 6).

of Agni, 'without fuel shines among them'[1]. At the same time the waters are represented as flowing in channels, natural or artificial, and as having the ocean for their goal[2].

b) The waters are naturally conceived as feminine[3]. They are mothers, young women (or wives), and goddesses. As mothers they generate Agni in his lightning form as the 'Child of Waters' (X. 91, 6) as well as in his earthly form. They have most auspicious fluid, which they are besought as loving mothers to give. They are most motherly, the sources of everything both fixed and moving. In their union with the Soma juice, in order to provide the Indra-drink[4], the waters are compared with young women:

> Those in whom Soma joys and is delighted,
> As a young man with fair and pleasant damsels.
>
> . . . .
>
> So maidens bow before the youthful gallant,
> Who comes with love to them who yearn to meet him[5].
>
> X. 30, 5-6 (Griffith's translation).

c) The waters are wealthy, that is, in a pregnant sense, wealth-giving[6]. They are mistresses of boons, and come bringing ghee, milk and honey (X. 9, 5; 30, 13). The waters may be called wealth-giving either as fertilizing the earth and causing abundant harvests, or, more probably, as a constituent of the Soma drink, delighting Indra and the other gods and so inciting them to give boons. It is not the waters as such, but the waters as mixed with Soma that are praised in VII. 49, 4 and X. 30.

---

[1] I. 23, 17; VII. 49, 1, 3, 4; X. 30, 4.

[2] Even here the reference may be to the heavenly waters as either dug out by the bolt of Indra, or falling spontaneously without the accompaniment of thunder and lightning.

[3] With *Āpah* 'Waters' we may compare *Usasah*, the successive Dawns or simultaneous dawn-gleams.

[4] *Indra-pāna* VII. 47, 1; X. 30, 9.

[5] Note the fondness for sexual analogies in the Ṛv.

[6] *revati* X. 30, 8, 12, 14. This epithet is also applied to Usas, as the bountiful goddess of the Dawn.

d) The waters are nourishing, strengthening, life-giving. Theirs is the 'wave of nourishment' (VII. 47, 1). They furnish drink to men and are a constituent of the drink of Indra (X. 9, 4; VII. 47, 1). It is only an extension of the same idea, when the waters are called medicinal, and are conceived as the source of healing and immortality.

Amṛit[1] is in the waters, in them medicine. I. 23, 19.
The floods are all-medicinal. I. 23, 20.

Ye waters, teem with medicine,
To keep my body safe from harm,
So that I long may see the sun. I. 23, 21.

Ye waters are most motherly physicians[2]. VI. 50, 7.

e) The waters cleanse and purify:—

Hundredfold-cleansing, in their nature joyful,
To paths of gods the goddesses move forward;
Never infringe they Indra's ordinances. VII. 47, 3.

Let the floods motherly, the waters, cleanse us,
Purify us with oil[3], the oil-refiners;
For they bear off all stain, the goddess waters.
Up from them come I purified and brightened. X. 17, 10.

It is the extension by analogy from physical cleansing to moral cleansing that explains the following prayer:—

Whatever evil is in me,
If I 'gainst any have done wrong,
Or told a lie and sworn to it,
Ye waters, bear it far from me. I. 23, 22 = X. 9, 8.

The waters are associated with Varuṇa who distinguishes between truth and falsehood (VII. 49, 3). Hence they bear away[4] not only the defilement of the flesh (X. 17, 10), but also such spirit-defiling sins as violence and lying.

---

[1] With the *Amṛit* that has its home in the waters compare the 'living water' and 'the water of life' of John IV. 10 and Revelation XXII. 17.

[2] Doubtless the starting point in all these conceptions was the experience of the vital need of water and of its well-known hygienic value.

[3] The custom of rubbing the whole body with oil for remedial, cleansing and sacramental purposes is common in India to this day.

[4] *pra vah* X. 9, 8; 17, 10. *Cf.* "Behold the Lamb of God, that *taketh away* the sins of the world" —John I. 29. Note the conception, however feebly held, of a "fountain opened .... for sin and for uncleanness" (Zech. XIII. 1).

3. Rudra. — Distinctly a subordinate god, being celebrated in only three entire hymns[1], but important as being the Vedic anticipation of Śiva, the third person of the Hindu Trimūrti. As the later Śiva with his phallic symbol is more like a Dravidian demon than an Aryan deva, so the Ṛigvedic Rudra[2] is the most demonic of all the early gods. He may have absorbed aboriginal elements from the very beginning. With Pūṣan alone he wears his hair braided[3], possibly a sign of Dāsa or Śūdra influence. Men so dreaded the fearsome Rudra that the adjective *Śiva*[4] 'auspicious' was attached to him as a euphemistic epithet.

To Rudra, II. 33[5].

1. Let thy goodwill, sire of the Maruts, reach us;
From the sun's sight remove us not, O Rudra.
In mercy may the hero spare our horses;
May we with offspring, Rudra, be prolific.

2. Through those most wholesome remedies by thee given,
Rudra, I would attain a hundred winters.
Drive far away from us distress and hatred,
Diseases drive away in all directions.

3. Of what is born thou art the best in glory,
Bolt-wielding Rudra, mightiest of the mighty.
Across distresses ferry us in safety,
Repel thou from us all attacks of mischief.

4. May we not anger thee, O mighty Rudra,
With worship poor, ill-praise, joint-invocation.
By remedies do thou raise up our heroes,
I hear thou art the best of all physicians.

5. Rudra invoked with gifts and invocations
I would propitiate with hymns and praises.

---

[1] II. 33; VII. 46; I. 114.

[2] Derived either from *rud* 'to cry', hence 'Howler' (Sāyana), or according to Pischel (VS. I. 57) from the hypothetical root *rud* 'to be ruddy'. Both meanings are suitable.

[3] *Kapardin* I. 114, 1, 5; VI. 55, 2; IX. 67, 11. *Cf. Vedic Index* I. 135.

[4] *Cf.* the similar Dravidian root *se, sev, siva* 'red, 'ruddy'. See A. C. Clayton. *The Ṛigveda and Vedic Religion*, 1913, pp. 76-78.

[5] Acknowledgment is made of special indebtedness to the translations of Hillebrandt, LR. 95-97, and Macdonell, VRS. 56-67 and HR. 55-56.

Gracious, fair-lipped, accessible, and ruddy,
May he subject us not to his fierce anger.

6. Me begging succour has the bull made happy,
By his puissant strength, he girt with Maruts.
Shade in the heat, as 'twere, I would attain to,
Would fain, uninjured, win the grace of Rudra.

7. Where is that gracious hand of thine, O Rudra,
Which is for us medicinal and cooling?
Bearer away of harm by gods inflicted,
Be thou, O Bull, compassionate to *me* ward.

8. I for the bull, the ruddy-brown and whitish,
Mightily voice a mighty panegyric.
Adore the radiant one with lowly worship,
We praise the name, the terrible name of Rudra.

9. With firm limbs, multiform, the strong, the ruddy,
Has decked himself with jewels bright and golden.
From Rudra, this great universe's ruler,
Let not divine dominion ever vanish.

10. Worthy art thou that bearest bow and arrows,
And thine adorable all-coloured necklace.
Worthy art thou that wieldest all this terror;
There's nothing mightier than thou, O Rudra.

11. Praise him the famous, youthful, and car-seated,
Like dread beast pouncing on his prey, the mighty.
Be kind, when lauded, to the singer, Rudra;
Than us some other may thy missiles lay low.

12. Even as a son bows down in reverence lowly
What time his sire draws nigh with kindly greeting,
So praise I the true lord, who giveth richly;
To us thou grantest remedies when lauded.

13. Your remedies, O Maruts, that are cleansing,
That are most wholesome, mighty ones, and helpful,
Those that our father Manu hath selected,
Those I desire, yea Rudra's balm and healing.

14. May Rudra's missile turn aside and pass us,
May the vast ill-will of the fierce one spare us;
Relax thy bow-string for our liberal patrons,
O bounteous one, be kind to our descendants.

15. So, bull, that here art ruddy-brown and far-famed,
Since thou, O god, art neither wroth nor slayest,
To this our invocation be attentive.
We would with strong sons speak aloud at worship.

Comments: —

a) Rudra is the father of the group of gods known variously as Rudras, Rudriyas and Maruts. The Maruts in the Ṛv. are clearly storm-gods, compounded of storm-winds, lightning-flashes and showers of rain. As such they are closely associated with Indra[1]. There is a family resemblance between Rudra and the Maruts in that both father and sons wear ornaments of gold (the lightning flashes?), are armed with weapons especially with bow and arrow, are besought to avert their cow- and man-slaying stroke[2], and are rich in healing remedies[3]. The original conception of Rudra would, then, seem to have covered "not the storm pure and simple, but rather its baleful side in the destructive agency of lightning"[4].

b) Rudra is not described in the same terms as Indra. He is never represented as slaying Vṛitra, nor is the characteristic epithet of Indra, *vajrabāhu,* 'bolt-armed' applied to Rudra more than once[5]. There are in fact three kinds of lightning mentioned in the Ṛv. as judged by its effects. Indra with his bolt slays the cloud-demon Vṛitra and releases the waters. So whenever peals of thunder and flashes of lightning are followed by a downpour of rain, it is Indra's work. Secondly, whenever there is lightning, thunder, hailstorm or mist[6], without rain or with only a few drops of rain, then it is the work of Vṛitra[7], for Vṛitra clothes himself in the habiliments of Indra, and would appear as 'an angel of light'. Thirdly,

---

[1] See p. 202 ff.

[2] I. 114, 10; VII. 56, 17.

[3] II. 33, 13. The remedies appear to be the waters, for the Maruts 'rain down waters........ medicine' (V. 53, 14).

[4] Macdonell, VM. 77.

[5] II. 33, 3.

[6] As so often occurs in connection with dust storms in the Punjab from March to June.

[7] *Cf.* I. 32, 13.

whenever the lightning strikes man or beast[1], it is the work of Rudra. Indra's bolt is beneficent, since he smites only the foes, demonic or human of his worshippers, but the arrow of Rudra is maleficent. Rudra thus partakes of the nature of both Indra and Vṛitra, being both divine and demonic.

c) While 'the destructive agency of lightning' is to be regarded as Rudra's original sphere and function, there is no ground for limiting it to this. There probably was a very early extension by analogy. If Rudra was at first the one who hurls the destructive lightning-dart, later, as the Aryans advanced further into the Punjab, he may have been thought of as hurling the dart of sunstroke[2] — that very real peril in India — or as hurling the darts of illness and disease in general[3]. Such an extension of function would be congruous with Rudra's original activity, and in the light of Rudra's character as depicted in the literature of the Yajurveda period must have taken place sooner or later. The numerous references in II. 33 to diseases and remedies would seem to indicate that such an extension of Rudra's functions may have occurred well within the Ṛigvedic period.

d) Some one has said that the gods are the first philosophy. It is equally true that they are the first and earliest science. For the mythical conceptions which early mankind formed concerning them "represent the conjectural science of a primitive mental condition"[4]. The Vedic Indians knew from experience that certain things in nature

---

[1] Near the author's home in the U. S. A. both men and cattle have been killed by lightning.

[2] Suggested, perhaps, by the use of *ghṛṇi* in II. 33, 6 and VI. 16, 38.

[3] Both Oldenberg (RV. 216-224) and Hillebrandt (VM. II. 192 ff.) emphasize Rudra's connection with disease, Oldenberg regarding him as a god of mountain and forest, whence the shafts of disease attack mankind, and Hillebrandt making him responsible for the sickly season immediately following the rains, when almost every one is stricken down with fever.

[4] Macdonell, VM. 1.

were wholesome, vitalizing, remedial, *e. g.* water, wind and storm. A storm accompanied by lightning, wind and rain clears the murky dust-laden air of the Punjab and gives a new sense of freshness and vitality. So the Vedic singer said: 'Vāta wafts healing'; 'the Maruts have pure, wholesome, vitalizing remedies'; Rudra, the father of the Maruts, is 'the greatest physician of physicians'; Soma, the drink of immortality, is 'medicine for a sick man'; Soma-Rudra together 'drive away illness'; the Aśvins (so mysterious to us) are 'physicians with remedies'; and Varuṇa, the august Deity, has 'a hundred, a thousand medicines'.

In the long list of Vedic gods of healing, namely Rudra, the Maruts, Vāta, Waters, Soma, Soma-Rudra, Aśvins and Varuṇa, it is probable that in nearly every case we have to do with water. It is an ingredient of the Soma-liquor, and the honey of the Aśvins may have been the morning dew. It is possible, however, that the remedies that are contained in the waters refer in part at least to the plants and herbs which owe their existence to the waters; and which are used for either medicines, or charms or for both[1]. The gods of healing are 'departmental gods', and yet in the matter of healing ministry there is overlapping of function. Each of seven or eight Vedic gods is a *healer*. In this way were expressed the hygienic experience and judgments of the time. Thus natural phenomena of hygienic value transfigured and personalized as gods are conceived after the manner of human physicians with their remedies. Indirectly, then, we may learn through these pictures of divine physicians something about human physicians in the Vedic age.

It may be that Rudra, who is fairly 'opaque', represents the coalescence of more than one god[2]. In fact, when the

---

[1] We may compare the great symbol in Revelation of "a river of water of life", on both sides of which grew the "tree of life," the leaves of which were "for the healing of the nations" (Rev. XXII. 1-2).

[2] So Hopkins (ION. 118) who regards Śiva as 'the combination of a Vedic storm-god and a local aboriginal disease-god'.

pantheon was in such unstable equilibrium as it was in the Vedic age, there were constantly functioning the contrasted processes of separation and combination. A god (like Agni) might cast off an epithet (like rudra[1]), which would become a separate god. But the epithet in order to find a 'local habitation' may be thought of as attaching itself to another god or godling. Hence it is altogether possible that diverse elements have been brought under the name of Rudra. This is suggested by the differing views as to his nature that are held by such scholars as Weber, Schrœder, Oldenberg, Hillebrandt and Macdonell.

e) Notwithstanding Rudra's maleficent character, he is appealed to as a god of grace. As 'the bearer away of harm by gods inflicted' (II. 33, 7) he is besought to avert the anger of the gods (I. 114, 4)[2]. This is the Ṛigvedic analogue of the grace of Śiva as expressed in the famous lines of the *Tiruvāsagam:*

> "Thou mad'st me thine; didst fiery poison eat, pitying poor souls,
> That I might thine ambrosia taste, — I, meanest one"[3].

4. Apām Napāt, Trita Āptya, Mātariśvan, Ahibudhnya and Aja Ekapād may be dismissed with few words. They are in general to be regarded as 'mythological synonyms' of Indra and Rudra, interpreted as the lightning[4]. Apām Napāt and Trita Āptya go back to the Indo-Iranian period. These two with Mātariśvan are sometimes identified with Agni, especially in his aerial form. All are invoked only incidentally in scattered verses, except Apām Napāt who is celebrated in one whole hymn, of which a few stanzas are here reproduced: —

---

1 Rudra occurs as an attribute of both Agni and the Aśvins.

2 Doubtless through the healing of diseases inflicted by the gods.

3 Macnicol, IT. 175.

4 *Cf.* Macdonell, VM. 67-74.

To Apām Napāt[1], *II. 35.*

4. Him the young man the youthful maiden waters
Unsmiling circle round, make bright and shining.
He with clear flames shines bountifully upon us,
Ghee-mantled, without fuel, in the waters.

8. Who in the waters with his heavenly splendour
Shines widely forth, eternal, order-loving;
The plants and other beings as his branches
Do propagate themselves with all their offspring.

9. Son of the waters, he the lap hath mounted
Of (waters) prone, erect he, clad in lightning.
Bearing his lofty and transcendent greatness
The golden-hued and swift streams flow around him.

10. He is of golden form, of golden aspect;
The golden-hued is he, the son of waters;
To him born from a golden womb, when seated,
The givers of gold-gifts present oblation.

13. In them the bull a germ has generated;
He as a child sucks them, in turn they kiss him.
He son of waters of unfading colour,
Works here on earth as with another's body.

14. Him stationed in this highest place and shining
For aye with undimmed rays, the waters bringing
Ghee to their son as food,—the nimble waters
Themselves with all their garments fly around him.

Here the cloud-born lightning is represented as surrounded by the lady waters, very much as the youth Soma sports[2] with the maiden waters. We are reminded also that the Maruts are born of *Pṛiśni,* the mottled storm-cloud, and that Parjanya is the personification of the rain-cloud.

C. Terrestrial Gods.

Pṛithivī, Agni, Bṛihaspati and *Soma* have already been considered. There remains only the treatment of Sarasvatī

[1] Compare the translations of Macdonell, VRS. 68-78 and HR. 64-66.

[2] This reminds us of Śrī *Kṛiṣṇa* and the Gopis. Is it possible that these early representations influenced the course of the *Kṛiṣṇa* legend?

and the Rivers with some reference to deified mountains, forests, trees and plants.

1. **Sarasvatī and the Rivers.** — The heavenly and the earthly waters are not shut off from each other in water-tight compartments: each class involves the other. The heavenly waters fall in the form of rain, and run in the rivers to the sea, while the earthly waters owe their origin to the heavenly. In the famous *'Nadīstuti'* hymn (X. 75) there is the following interesting catalogue of the rivers: —

5. Favour ye this my laud, O Gangā, Yamunā,
Sarasvatī and Śutudri and Paruṣṇi;
Marudvṛidhā with Asikni and Vitastā,
O Ārjikiyā with Suṣoma hear my cry.

6. First with Tṛiṣṭāmā thou, united to flow forth,
With Rasā and Susartu and with Śvetyā here,
O Sindhu, with Kubhā and with Mehatnu joined,
Thou seekest in thy course Krumu and Gomati.

The list begins with the Gangā on the east and ends with the Sindhu and its tributaries on the west[1]. In view of this order it would be most natural to think of the composition of the hymn as having taken place at the eastern end of the Ṛigvedic world[2], perhaps on the Sarasvatī or even in the region lying between the Gangā and the Yamunā, the present Sahāranpur District. The Sarasvatī is clearly distinguished from the Sindhu, and its situation between the Yamunā and the Śutudrī identifies it beyond question with the modern Sarsūti near Thānesar. The Sindhu as the chief of the great river system of the Punjab is singled out for special praises as follows:

3. To heaven ascends her roar on high above the earth,
With shimmer she displays her endless vehemence;

---

[1] *Cf.* Sir A. Stein, *Some River Names in the Ṛigveda,* JRAS. Jan. 1917: "The analysis of the river names given in our Ṛigveda verse has proved that leaving aside the still uncertain Ārjikīyā, they follow each other in strict order from east to west".

[2] *Cf.* Vedic Index under *Vitastā:* "The rareness of the name in the Ṛigveda points to the Punjab not having been the seat of the activity of the greater part of the Vedic Indians".

As showers of rain that break forth thundering from a cloud,
So[1] Sindhu rushes onward bellowing like a bull.
4. Like mothers to their calves, like milch-kine with their milk,
So, Sindhu, unto thee the roaring rivers run.
Ev'n as a warrior monarch leads his army's wings,
So leadest thou the rivers, moving at their head.
7-8. Most active of the active, Sindhu, undeceived,
Like a mare splendid, like a woman fair to see.
Good steeds has Sindhu, goodly cars and goodly robes,
Golden is she, well-fashioned, rich in ample wealth[2].

These stanzas furnish a commentary on the sixth stanza, which describes the relation which exists between Sindhu and her tributary streams. There is the description of a mighty river which is fed by branches on both sides, the Sindhu controlling them, just as a warrior king commands the two wings of his army.

To be compared with 'the hymn in praise of the Rivers' (X. 75) is 'Viśvāmitra's conversation with the Rivers', *Vipāś* and *Śutudrī* (III. 33)[3]. As Varuṇa dug the bed of the Sindhu, the chief of the rivers, so Indra dug the beds of the sister streams Vipāś and Śutudrī. In both hymns the rivers are compared with racing mares and mother cows. The personification of the deified rivers is slight, being held in check by their obvious physical character.

Sarasvatī is invoked in three entire hymns of the Ṛv.[4] She is regarded as the most worshipful of all the rivers, being described as 'most mother-like, most river-like, most goddess-like'[5] and as the *asuryā* or divine one among the streams (VII. 96, 1). She is depicted in grandiloquent terms as a rushing, powerful flood, that surpasses all other waters in greatness, with her mighty waves tearing away the heights of the mountains as she moves roaring

[1] Lit. *when*.

[2] Griffith's translation with changes.

[3] p. 187 ff.

[4] VI. 61; VII. 95, 96.

[5] Or 'Best of mothers, of rivers, of goddesses', II. 41, 16 (Macdonell, VM. 86).

along[1]. In view of the fact that the eastern Sarasvatī (modern *Sarsūti*) must always have been one of the minor rivers of the Punjab, some scholars hold that the Sarasvatī in most passages is to be identified with the Sindhu (Indus)[2]. But this, as already shown, is not probable. The basin of the Sarasvatī was the last halting place of the Vedic Indians before they left the land of the seven rivers[3] and entered the Jumna-Ganges area. There is evidence that the Aryan tribes were held back for a considerable time by the dense aboriginal population which occupied the banks of the Jumna[4]. As in this protracted struggle the broad waters of the Jumna must have been a bulwark for the aborigines against the Aryans[5], so must the Sarasvatī have been for the Aryans against the aborigines. Sarasvatī is described as a 'metal fort' protecting the Aryan tribes and chieftains that dwell upon her banks, smiter of foes, slaying the *Pārāvatas*[6], and besought by her worshippers not to let them go into captivity to strange and distant fields[7]. The Sarasvatī, as the region where the 'five tribes' tarried longest, was doubtless the centre of gravity of the Ṛigvedic world. Its banks would be hallowed by the composition of hymns and the performance of sacrificial rites. In fact, the river Sarasvatī and its area were in sacredness the Vedic analogue of the later Gaṅgā and Madhyadeśa. The religious significance of that sacred stream is indicated by the fact that on its banks two 'special' goddesses apparently had their origin, *Sarasvatī* 'she of the Sarasvatī river', and *Bhāratī*, the personified

---

[1] VI. 61, 2, 8; VII. 95, 1.

[2] In VII. 95, 1 *Sarasvatī* .... *Sindhu* must mean either the water-abounding Sindhu or the stream Sarasvatī, most probably the later.

[3] Probably Sarasvatī, Śutudrī, Vipāś, Paruṣṇī, Asiknī, Vitastā and Sindhu.

[4] Chap. II. p. 45 ff.

[5] See Ṛv. VII. 18, 19 for the victory of Sudās and the Tritsus over their foes on the Yamunā.

[6] Probably a people on the Yamunā. See Vedic Index, *Pārāvata*.

[7] VI. 61, 2, 7, 12, 14; VII. 1, 2; VIII. 21, 18.

offering of the Bharatas[1]. These two goddesses appear in conjunction in the Āprī hymns[2]. Since the area of the Sarasvatī river was so important in connection with the composition of hymns, the goddess Sarasvatī, as the apotheosis of that river, came to be regarded as the inspirer[3] of fair hymns and as the stimulator of good thoughts. The transition to the post-Vedic meaning of Sarasvatī as goddess of eloquence and wisdom presents no difficulty[4].

In relation to the other rivers of the Punjab Sarasvatī is called 'seven-sistered', 'seven-fold', and 'one of seven'[5]. These terms link her up so closely to the whole river system of the Punjab, that while she is the genius of the Sarasvatī river, she is so in no exclusive sense. She might almost be called the one river-genius as manifested in each of the seven rivers. This explains the paradox created by the insignificance of the river Sarasvatī as set over against the grandeur of her description. As the Greek artist in creating the ideal human figure levied upon the physical excellences of all mankind, so Sarasvatī is clothed upon with everything that is gracious, striking and terrible in any of the Punjab rivers. This tendency to idealization was doubtless helped by the fact that Sarasvatī was a name that had come down from the Aryan past freighted with ancient memories[6].

Sarasvatī, while an earthly stream, has a heavenly origin. She flows from the mountains, the (celestial) ocean. She has the celestial *Sindhu* for her mother. She is called

---

[1] Oldenberg, RV. 243.

[2] I. 188, 8; II. 3, 8; III. 4, 8, etc.

[3] *codayitrī* I. 3, 10. Cf. *pracodayāt* in the *Gāyatrī* formula.

[4] Vedic wisdom flourished within the river system of the Punjab, just as Egyptian wisdom was nourished by the Nile and Babylonian wisdom by the Euphrates and Tigris.

[5] VI. 61, 10, 12; VII. 36, 6.

[6] The earliest Sarasvatī was the Iranian *Haraqaiti* (the modern Helmand) beyond Kābul. Possibly, as some scholars think, Sarasvatī was also applied as a sacred name to the Sindhu. If so, there were three Sarasvatīs, as AV. VI. 100 might be interpreted to mean.

pāvīravī, probably 'daughter of lightning'[1], and is besought to descend to the sacrifice from the great mountain of the sky[2]. The celestial origin of Sarasvatī is an anticipation of the later doctrine of the celestial origin of Gaṅgā.

Finally, Sarasvatī grants progeny and assists in procreation. Divodāsa was her gift to Vadhryasva[3]. Is this a reference to the fact that man's seed is *watery* in nature, or does the function assigned to Sarasvatī reveal the consciousness of the need of a larger population on the part of the Aryan tribes settled on the Sarasvatī, in order to meet in battle the vast multitudes of the aborigines who were blocking their way to the fertile territory between the Jumna and the Ganges[4]?

2. MOUNTAINS.—As rivers are conceived as divinely animate, so are the mountains. In various passages the mountains are mentioned along with other deified natural objects, such as waters, plants, trees, etc., and also with gods like Savitar, Ahibudhnya and others[5]. Once they are described as manly, firm-set and rejoicing in food (III. 54, 20). *Parvata,* 'he of the mountain', is thrice conjoined with Indra to form the dual divinity, Indra-Parvata[6], who are invoked as 'van-fighters', who smite with their bolt, drive on a great car, and bring pleasant food. Parvata sometimes means 'cloud-mountain' as in II. 11, 7-8:—

7. Indra, thy bay steeds showing forth their vigour
Have sent a loud cry out that droppeth fatness.
At once the broad earth spread herself to take it;
Even the cloudy moving mountain rested.

8. Down, never ceasing, has the mountain settled;
Bellowing has it wandered with the mothers[7].

---

[1] The descent of water as well as of fire and soma is connected with the lightning.

[2] VII. 36, 6; 95, 2; VI. 49, 7; V. 43, 11.

[3] II. 41, 17; X. 184, 2.

[4] For Sarasvatī see Macdonell, VM. 86-88, and *Vedic Index*, Art. *Sarasvatī.*

[5] VII. 34. 23; VI. 49, 14, etc.

[6] I. 122, 3; 132, 6; III. 53, 1.

[7] The celestial waters.

Swelling the roar in the far-distant regions,
They[1] have spread wide the blast sent forth by Indra.
(Griffith's translation with changes.)

Here the moving, bellowing mountain refers clearly to the cloud-mountain of the sky. In view of this ambiguity, Parvata in the compound Indra-Parvata may refer both to terrestrial and to celestial mountains. Each meaning might be an extension by analogy of the other. The Himālayas being visible from so large a part of the Ṛigvedic habitat of the Aryans must certainly be covered by the term *Parvata.* If the cloud-mountain and the lightning are joined together in the drama of the thunder-storm, hardly less is it true of the Himālayas and the lightning. The monsoon storms often begin in the Himālayas and work backward to the plains. While all waters have their ultimate source in the celestial mountains, the rivers of the Punjab spring immediately from the Himālayas. Thus according to either interpretation Parvata[2] alone or Indra-Parvata are very properly described as 'rejoicing in food'[3]. It is quite in harmony with the Ṛigvedic conception of the mountains as divine that according to later Hindu thought the high peaks of the Himālayas are regarded, like Sinai and Olympus, as the seat of the gods.

3. Forests, Plants and Trees. — *Araṇyānī* 'she of the wild-wood', a jungle goddess, is celebrated in X. 146[4]: —

1. O Jungle maid, O Jungle maid,
Methinks that thou hast lost thy way;
Dost not ask for the village? Why?
Alarm has seized thee, has it not?

2. When to the *Vṛiṣārava's*[5] call
The *ciccika*[5] makes answering cry
With cymbals dancing, as it were,
Then does the wildwood maiden thrill.

---

[1] Maruts.

[2] In the plural *parvatāsaḥ*, III. 54. 20.

[3] *Cf.* Oldenberg, RV. 255.

[4] *Cf.* the translations of Hillebrandt, LR. 150-151, and Macdonell, HR. 81-82.

[5] Not identified. Possibly owl and parrot.

3. Yonder, the cattle graze, methinks,
And what seems like a house appears;
And then at eve the Jungle maid
Seemeth to start the creaking wains[1].

4. Here some one calls his cow to him,
Another there has felled a tree;
At eve the dweller in the wood
Thinks to himself, some one has screamed.

5. The Jungle maiden never harms,
Unless another is too bold;
So after eating of sweet fruit
A man at will may safely rest.

6. Sweet-scented, redolent of balm,
Apart from tillage, full of food,
Of all wild beasts the mother, too[2],
Her have I praised, the Jungle maid.

The personification of Aranyāṇi is very slight, for in v. 4 the same word means simply 'jungle'. The Jungle maid as the spirit of forest solitude is addressed in a chaffing bantering manner as one who is shy and fearful, having lost her way in the mazes of the forest. She is harmless, unless one becomes too intimate with her gloomy recesses or encounters her children the wild beasts. The thousand and one eerie sounds that are heard at night in a forest are vividly described. Our thoughts go forward to the *Āranyakas* or 'Forest treatises' of a later time, when the forests were the home of hermits.

Plants (*oṣadhi*), as divine, are invoked in one whole hymn (X. 97), where they are described as mothers and goddesses, with Soma as their King. It is uncertain how far the healing virtues of plants are celebrated in this hymn, and how far their uses in connection with magic. The hymn itself looks like a charm for the purpose of exorcising a disease-demon. Of course, the medicinal use of plants receives due recognition[3]:

---

[1] Carts often travel by night in India, to avoid the heat of the day.

[2] The point of view from which Aranyāṇi 'forest' is called the mother of the beasts is obvious.

[3] Oldenberg, RV. 256, n. 3.

He who hath store of herbs at hand,
Like kings amid a crowd of men,—
Physician is that sage's name,
Fiend-slayer, chaser of disease. (Griffith's translation.)

Large trees[1] were sometimes invoked as gods especially in connection with the deified Mountains and Waters[2]. Such were the *Asvattha* and the *Parṇa*[3], from which sacrificial vessels were made. The wood work of a chariot is frequently called *vanaspati*[4]; so also is *yūpa*, the 'post' to which the sacrificial victim is tied[5]. In the Âprī hymns Vanaspati is regularly invoked in the verse next to the last, and in the same verse *Śamitar* 'divine butcher' is mentioned[6]. In III. 8, 1, 3, 6, 11 the Yūpa is expressly referred to under the name of *vanaspati*, 'tree'[7]. In this hymn Vanaspati is described as hewn out with an axe (vv. 6, 11), erected (1-3, 6), purified (5), anointed (1), and well-robed with a cord or garland (4). The deified sacrificial Post[8] represents the apotheosis of an accessory of the divine. As Agni, the sacrificial fire, received apotheosis because of his connection with the worship of the gods, so is it with Vanaspati, the sacrificial post. Hence Vanaspati as divine is implored in the same hymn to grant wealth (1, 6) with children (2, 6), to drive away poverty (2), and to give splendour (3) and good fortune (2, 11).

---

[1] *Vanaspati* 'forest-lord'.

[2] VII. 34, 23; X. 64, 8; Vāl. VI. 4.

[3] X. 97, 5. From the *Kiṁśuka* and Śalmali chariot wheels were made, X. 85, 20.

[4] II. 37, 3; III. 53, 20, etc.

[5] Oldenberg, RV. 91, 255-257, and SBE. XLVI. 12, 252-255.

[6] II. 3, 10; III. 4, 10; VII. 2, 10.

[7] We may compare the N. T. use of 'tree' (Gal. III. 13; 1 Peter II. 24) for Cross.

[8] In the same way the Cross of Christ is sometimes referred to as if it had received a kind of semi-apotheosis:

"In the Cross of Christ I glory,
Tow'ring o'er the wrecks of time;
All the light of ancient story
Gathers round its head sublime".

CHAPTER XI.

THE ESCHATOLOGY OF THF RIGVEDA.

1. As an introduction to the subject there is here presented a translation of the great Funeral Hymn[1] X. 14, addressed to Yama:

1. Him who has passed away along the mighty steeps,
And has spied out the path for many mortals,
Vivasvant's son, convener of the peoples,
Yama the King, present thou with oblation.

2. Yama was first to find for us the pathway,
A way that from us never can be taken[2],
Whereon have gone away our former fathers
Along their several paths—they who were born here.

4. Upon this strewn grass, Yama, pray be seated,
Joining thyself with Aṅgirasas, Fathers.
Let spells seer-uttered bring thee to us hither,
Do thou, O King, rejoice in this oblation.

5. Come hither with th' adorable Aṅgirasas,
Here with Virūpa's sons delight thee, Yama.
Thy sire Vivasvant call I; (may he revel),
When seated on the litter at this worship.

6. As for Aṅgirasas, our Sires, Navagvas,
Atharvans, Bhṛigus, lovers of the Soma,
We would continue in the loving-kindness
Of them the worshipful, and in their favour.

To the dead:—

7. Go forth, go forth upon those ancient pathways,
By which our former fathers have departed.
Thou shalt behold god Varuṇa, and Yama,
Both kings, in funeral offerings rejoicing.

8. Unite thou with the Fathers and with Yama,
With *iṣṭapūrta* in the highest heaven.

---

[1] Indebtedness is acknowledged especially to Hillebrandt, LR. 118-119, and Macdonell, VRS. 164-175 and HR. 85-86.

[2] Or: From us this *pasture* never can be taken. So Hillebrandt, LR. 118, and Macdonell, VRS. 165.

Leaving behind all blemish homeward hie thee,
And all-resplendent[1] join thee with a body.

To the demons:—

9. Begone, disperse, slink off from here, ye demons;
For him the Fathers have prepared this dwelling.
To him a resting place King Yama giveth,
By days distinguished, and by nights and waters.

To the dead:—

10. Past the two sons of Saramā, the two dogs,
Four-eyed and brindled, hasten thou by pathway straight;
Draw near thou to the Fathers rich in bounty,
Who at a common feast with Yama revel.

To Yama:—

11. Thy two dogs, Yama, guardians are and four-eyed,
Mankind-beholding, watchers of the pathway;
Commit him to the care of these, King Yama,
Welfare on him bestow and health abiding.

To the living:—

12. Broad-nosed, brown-coloured (?) and hunters of living men
The two as Yama's envoys wander 'mongst the tribes.
May these give back to us a life auspicious,
That we may here and now behold the sunlight.

To the priests:—

13. For Yama press the Soma-juice,
Th' oblation pour; the sacrifice
Being well prepared to Yama goes,
With Agni as its messenger.

14. Step forward and to Yama King
Pour the oblation rich in ghee;
May he direct us to the gods,
That we may live a life prolonged.

15. To Yama King th' oblation pour
Most rich in honied sweetness. This
Our hymn of praise is for the Riṣis, ancient-born,
The ancient makers of the path.

2. In the Ṛigvedic period the dead were disposed of by both burial and cremation[2]. Burial is probably referred

---

[1] *suvarcas* translated by Hillebrandt 'in voller kraft' (LR. 118) and by Macdonell 'full of vigour' (VRS. 170).

[2] *Cf.* Ṛv. X. 15, 14 'Those cremated and those not cremated'. Both methods are practised in modern India at the present time.

to in the expression 'house of clay' (VII. 89, 1), and also in X. 18, 10-11 as translated by Macdonell[1]:—

10. Approach the bosom of the earth, the mother,
This earth, the far-extending, most propitious:
Young, soft as wool to bounteous givers, may she
Preserve thee from the lap of dissolution.

11. Wide open, Earth, O press not heavily on him;
Be easy of approach to him, a refuge safe;
As with a robe a mother hides
Her son, so shroud this man, O earth[2].

It is probable, as Oldenberg holds[3], that burial was the older method being connected with the conception of the dead as going down into the underworld. But cremation was clearly the usual way. As the fire-sacrifice went up in smoke and flame to the heavenly world of the gods, so also did the dead man when burned upon the funeral pyre[4]. Thus cremation was closely bound up with the Ṛigvedic ideas of the future life. Ṛv. X. 16 is a cremation hymn, of which the following stanzas are reproduced (after Griffith with some changes):

1. Consume him not, nor injure him by burning;
Agni, cast not away his skin and body.
O Jātavedas, when thou hast refined[5] him,
Then send him on his way unto the Fathers.

2 c-d, 4 c-d. When he attains unto the world of spirits[6],
Then may he win the deities' high favour.
With thine auspicious forms, O Jātavedas,
Bear this man to the region of the pious.

---

[1] HR. 88.

[2] It is barely possible that these verses may refer to the disposition of the bones and ashes after cremation, as Oldenberg, (RV. 571) and Hillebrandt (LV. 122) seem to think. But see *Vedic Index* I. 8.

[3] RV. 543-548.

[4] Compare the dying utterance of a modern martyr in Tibet: "I thank you for throwing me into this fire, for the flames of this fire lift me up high so that I may reach heaven soon". Streeter and Appasami, *The Sadhu* 80.

[5] Lit. 'cooked' him.

[6] *Asunīti* lit. 'spirit-guidance', *i. e.* Agni's guidance of the souls of the dead from this to the other world. *Cf.* Oldenberg, RV. 528.

6. What wound soe'er the dark bird hath inflicted,
The ant, wild animal, or deadly serpent,
May Agni heal it, he the all-devouring,
And Soma who has passed into the Brāhmans.

9. Far hence send I the raw-flesh-eating[1] Agni,
Stain-bearing may he go to Yama's subjects;
But may the other Jātavedas carry
Oblation to the gods, for he is skilful.

It looks as if only the gross material body were consumed in the flames, the immaterial or spiritual part being carried heavenward when refined or 'cooked' in the fire. It is true, verses 1 and 6 read as if the whole body with its members intact were translated to the skies, but doubtless this way of putting things may be accounted for on the hypothesis of a belief in a body so refined and purified by fire as to be free from all imperfections[2], something like the 'subtile' body of later Indian thought. It will be noticed that, as Agni is invoked at cremation not to injure or destroy the dead, that is, the immortal part that survives death, so mother Earth is besought at burial not to press too heavily upon the departed, but to preserve him from the lap of dissolution[3].

It is practically certain, as already pointed out[4], that in the IE. period gifts to the dead were buried or burned with the corpse—gifts of such things as food, weapons, clothes and domestic animals, and sometimes slaves or even wife[5]. It is to the credit of Ṛigvedic morality that the primeval IE. custom of *Satī* was not continued, the only reference to it being in the form of a ritualistic substitute therefor, as described in X. 18, 8-9:—

8. Arise, come to the world of life, O woman;
Thou liest here by one whose breath has left him.

---

[1] *Kravyād*, an epithet also of the demon Kimidin, VII. 104, 2.

[2] *Cf*. X. 14, 8; 16, 6.

[3] X. 16, 1; 18, 10-11.

[4] Chap. I., p. 11.

[5] Oldenberg, RV. 587; Hillebrandt, VM. II. 8.

Come: thou hast entered now upon the wifehood
Of this thy lord who takes thy hand and woos thee[1].

9. From the dead hand I take the bow he wielded,
To win for us dominion, might and glory.
Thou there, we here, rich in heroic offspring,
Will vanquish all assaults of every foeman[2].

Here we have the ritualistic survival of what is called in AV. XVIII. 3, 1 'the ancient custom' of burning with the dead man his widow[3], as well as his weapons.

The following stanzas of X. 16 refer to the burning of a he-goat and perhaps also of the flesh of a cow along with that of the corpse:

4 a-b. The he-goat is thy part; with fire consume him;
Let thy fierce flame, thy glowing heat devour him.

7. Shield thee with cows[4] against the flames of Agni,
Be wholly covered with their fat and richness;
So may the bold one eager to attack thee
With fierce glow, fail to girdle and consume thee[5].

It looks as if we had here the idea of *substitution*[6], the fire doing its worst upon the enveloping cover of goat's

---

[1] Possibly v. 8^{c-d} refers to the dead husband, as interpreted by Griffith:
'Wifehood with this thy husband was thy portion,
Who took thy hand and wooed thee as a lover'.

[2] Macdonell's translation, HR. 87.

[3] The custom of '*sati*', or widow-burning, was revived in later days, but perhaps, as Oldenberg remarks (RV. 587), it may never have altogether ceased, in spite of the authority of the Ṛv., just as now-a-days there is an occasional case of '*sati*' in India in spite of the authority of Government. Compare the following account as reported in the Calcutta *Statesman* of June 19, 1921:—

A case of *sati* has been reported in village Sarajpur near Katni on July 3. The husband, aged 35, was a carpenter in the employ of the Katni Cement Factory, and died of fever. His young wife, who was richly adorned and dressed, remained at home when the body was taken to the cremation ground, and when the people returned, she went out without speaking to them. Some of her friends went in search of her later, and on returning to the cremation ground found both bodies burning together.

[4] That is, the product (ghee) or the flesh of cows.

[5] Griffith's translation with changes.

[6] Oldenberg, RV. 587-588.

flesh and cow's flesh (or ghee), and so (in theory at least) sparing the dead man thus enveloped.

As has already been pointed out in Chap. I, it is practically certain that the service and worship of the dead was practised during the IE. period. The offering to the Manes of food and drink undoubtedly existed during the Ṛigvedic period, but the detailed account of the *Śrāddha* ceremonies is found only in the later literature[1]. The service of the dead is of immemorial antiquity, and bears witness to the belief in a future life.

3. The most important technical terms of Ṛigvedic psychology are *asu*[2] 'spirit', 'breath', expressive of physical vitality, and *manas* 'soul', the seat of thought and emotion. Upon the presence of *asu* and *manas* life depends. For example, *gatāsu*[2] in X. 18, 8 means 'he whose breath has gone', hence dead; and reference has already been made to *asunīti*, Agni's leading of the spirit of a dead man from this world to the next (X. 16, 2). The Ṛigvedic conception of *manas* 'soul' as imperishable is probably based upon the early belief that the soul is capable of separation from the body during the dream-state or even during unconsciousness. For example, in Ṛv. X. 58 the *manas* or 'soul' of a man who is lying unconscious and apparently dead is thought of as having gone away to Yama, or to heaven and earth, the four quarters, the ocean, the motes in the sunbeams, waters and plants, sun and dawn, the lofty mountains, etc. and is besought to return from the distant place wherever he may be. This is doubtless a spell to bring back a sick man to life and health. In the following two passages there may perhaps be found the germ of the later doctrine of metempsychosis, since the soul (*manas*) is thought of as going to the waters or the plants[3]:—

---

[1] Oldenberg, RV. 548-554. The Śrāddha mantras are at the present time mostly Vedic, although they may contain later additions.

[2] *Cf. gatamanas* 'he whose soul is gone forth'. *Taitt. Saṃh.* VI. 6, 7, 2.

[3] Macdonell, VM. 166.

The sun receive thine eye, the wind thy *spirit*[1],
Go, as thy nature is, unto the sky and earth.
Or to the *waters* go thou, if it be thy lot;
Go make thy home in *plants* with all thy members[2] (X. 16, 3).

Thy *spirit*[3], that went far away,
Unto the *waters* and the *plants*,
We cause that to return again,
That thou mayst live and sojourn here[4]. X. 58, 7.

As already indicated, the body has a part in the future life[5]. The *asu* and *manas* remain united there as here, which is a guarantee that all the functions of the mental life remain intact. Thus the full personality of the departed, consisting of body *(śarīra),* soul *(asu)* and spirit *(manas),* is preserved. Having a body, the departed drink Soma[6], eat the funeral offerings or 'spirit-food' (IX. 113, 10) and hear the sound of the flute and of song (X. 135, 7)[7].

4. The Ṛigvedic Paradise is variously described as situated in the midst of the sky (X. 15, 14), in the highest heaven (X. 14, 8), in the third heaven[8], the inmost recess of the sky (IX. 113, 8-9), in the lap of the ruddy (dawns) (X. 15, 7), and in the highest step of Viṣṇu (I. 154, 5; X. 15, 3), that is the place of the sun at the zenith. We may note in passing the bright sunny character of the Ṛigvedic paradise, so different from the (probably earlier) conception of a dark 'underworld' as the abode of the dead[9].

---

[1] *ātman.*

[2] Griffith's translation with some changes.

[3] *manas.*

[4] Griffith's translation with some changes.

[5] X. 14, 8; 16, 5.

[6] The Fathers are often called *Somyāsaḥ* 'lovers of Soma', X. 14, 6, etc.

[7] According to AV. IV. 34, 2 the departed have abundance of sexual gratification. It is only fair to say that this detail in the joy of the blessed dead is not found in the Ṛv. The providing of the great gods with wives furnished a starting point for the notion of this kind of bliss. We are reminded of the Houris of the Qurān.

[8] *Cf.* 2 Cor. XII. 2.

[9] Oldenberg, RV. 548, thinks that the transition from the idea of an underground Hades to that of a heavenly Paradise was mediated by the fact that both

The blessed dead are furnished with bodies suitable to the new environment, as the following passages indicate:

Leaving behind all blemish homeward hie thee,
And all-resplendent join thee with a body. (X. 14, 8.)

They that, consumed or not consumed by Agni,
Amid the sky in spirit-food do revel,—
Along with these prepare, O sovereign ruler,
A passage to the skies, a heavenly body[1]. (X. 15, 14.)

Back to the Fathers, Agni, do thou send him,
Who, to thee offered[2], goes with spirit-viands.
Endued with life may he attain to offspring;
May he rejoin a body, Jātavedas. (X. 16, 5.)

Here is one light for thee, another yonder;
Enter the third and be therewith united.
Uniting with a body be thou welcome,
Dear to the gods in their sublimest birthplace.
(X. 56, 1 Griffith's translation.)

As there is an earthly and a heavenly life, so there is an earthly and a heavenly body. The earthly body at death either suffers dissolution in the earth or is consumed on the funeral pyre. When thus 'cooked' or refined by Agni, the dead man ascends by the 'ancient paths' to the realm of Yama, Agni conducting his soul to the sun-home of the Fathers, where he is united with another body. The new body is congruous with the new environment, and so is a luminous or glorified body (X. 14, 8; 56, 1). When the soul of the dead man returns hither, he is said

---

the heavenly Gods and the earthly Fathers received similar worship. It was logical, then, to think of the Fathers as associated with the Gods in the highest place of bliss.

[1] More literally: Along with these prepare according to thy power as sovereign ruler this spirit-guidance (to heaven) and a body. In X. 59, 5-6 Asunīti is apparently 'he of spirit-guidance'. The prayer addressed to Asunīti is clearly for either restoration of health in this life or for restoration of the body and faculties in the heavenly world. To find transmigration here (Swāmī Dayānand Sarasvatī, *Ṛigvedādibhāṣyabhūmikā*, 211-212) is to read later views into the text, and is not in harmony with Ṛigvedic eschatology.

[2] Note how the corpse when cremated is represented here as an offering to Agni. *Cf.* Oldenberg, RV. 585, n. 2.

to go back home[1]—to his 'true home', as it were. Naturally, then, in putting on a heavenly body the dead man puts off all the imperfections of earth (X. 14, 8); or, as the AV[2]. has it, 'sickness is left behind and limbs are not lame or crooked'. Old age is overcome (X. 27, 21). On reaching the realms of light, the sainted dead are welcomed by the gods and are beloved of them (X. 56, 1). This fair picture is rendered even fairer by certain details contributed by the AV., according to which the blessed dead see father, mother and sons, and unite with wives and children (AV. VI. 120, 3; XII, 3, 17).

We may now describe more particularly the felicity of the blessed dead. They see Varuṇa and Yama (X. 14, 7), revel with Yama in the heavenly paradise, partake of the funeral offerings (*svadhā*), and share in the feasts of the gods (X. 14, 10; 15, 14). The most detailed account is found in IX. 113, 7-11[3]. According to this striking passage, the Ṛigvedic Heaven is a place of radiance inexhaustible and of living waters, of spirit-food and complete satisfaction, of movement glad and free,—a place where King Yama has his seat, where felicity and joy, pleasure and bliss abound, and where loves and longings are fulfilled and all desires are satisfied. The grave and solemn tone of this Ṛigvedic hymn of Paradise reminds one of the similar utterance in Rev. VII. 16-17:

> They shall hunger no more, neither thirst any more;
> Neither shall the sun smite them any more, nor any heat:
> For the Lamb that is in the midst of the throne shall be their shepherd
> And shall guide them unto the fountains of the waters of life;
> And God shall wipe away all tears from their eyes[4].

---

[1] *punah* 'back' 'again' (X. 16, 5), and *astam* 'home' (X. 14, 8). So Bloomfield, RV. 251 "returning to their true home".

[2] III. 28, 5.

[3] Translated in Chap. VIII. pp. 241-242.

[4] Charles, *The Revelation of St. John*, New York, 1920, I. 216-217, II. 406.

We are reminded also of the following lines in Tennyson's *Passing of Arthur*, concerning which Taine[1] remarks that "nothing calmer and more imposing has been seen since Goethe":

> .... the island-valley of Avilion,
> Where falls not hail, or rain, or any snow,
> Nor ever wind blows loudly; but it lies
> Deep-meadowed, happy, fair with orchard lawns
> And bowery hollows crown'd with summer sea. (377-381.)

All three passages describe the future life and environment in terms of the present life. This is inevitable. Each passage is capable of either a material or a spiritual interpretation. In view of the Atharva-Veda emphasis[2] on completeness of body and limbs, streams flowing with milk, honey and wine, the presence of many-coloured cows that yield all desires, and abundance of sexual gratification, as distinctive marks of the heaven of the blest, one is naturally inclined to read Ṛv. IX. 113, 7-11 in the same light[3]. But if the AV. and the Brāhmaṇas had been marked by progress toward the spiritual rather than by reaction toward the material and carnal, it would have been equally natural to have interpreted IX. 113, 7-11 in the light of their spirituality.

The blessed dead are represented as having fellowship with the gods and Yama in the realms of light. When they arrive, they are dear and welcome to the gods (X. 56, 1). They behold both Yama and Varuṇa (X. 14, 7). Here we have the conception of heaven as a fellowship of the immortal heavenly gods with those sainted souls that have come from the earth.

Heaven is depicted as a reward for those that risk their lives in battle, bestow liberal sacrificial fees, practise rigorous austerity *(tapas*[4]*)* and lay up merit for themselves

[1] History of English Literature.

[2] AV. IV. 6, 1; 34, 2, 5, 6, 8.

[3] So Oldenberg, RV. 531-532. *Cf.* Macdonell, VM. 168.

[4] X. 154, 2-5.

through their offerings and pious gifts (X. 14, 8). Thus the departed are represented as united in paradise not only with the Fathers and with Yama, with the rays of the sun (I. 109, 7), and with glorified bodies, but also with what they have sacrificed and given *(iṣṭapūrta)* while on earth. Such 'treasure'[1] laid up in heaven will be theirs on their arrival. We have here possibly the germ of the later doctrine of *Karma,* a word which means in the Ṛv. 'work' in general, or specifically 'sacrificial work'. Such works constitute the merit which wins the bliss of heaven for the departed soul. It is only necessary to universalize the notion of 'work', making it apply to everything in the universe, both animate and inanimate, in order to get the full-fledged doctrine of *Karma,* as held in later times[2].

The most important references to the future life as shown above are found in the later portions of the Ṛv., in the tenth and first books. Just as eschatology received emphasis among the Hebrews only in the exilic and post-exilic periods (B. C. 586 and onward), so it looks as if Ṛigvedic eschatology belonged in the main to the later period of the Ṛigveda hymns, say about B. C. 1000-800. Ṛigvedic ideas concerning the future life are connected especially with Viṣṇu (I. 154, 5-6), Soma (IX. 113, 7-11) and Yama. Soma grants the draught of immortality; Yama discovered the path by which the blessed dead travel from earth to heaven; and in the highest step of Viṣṇu there is a well of honey. It may be that each group of ideas was elaborated originally in a particular tribal or priestly circle.

5. If the righteousness of the righteous[3] seemed to the Ṛigvedic seers to require a heavenly abode as a place of reward, then naturally and logically the wickedness of the

[1] *Cf.* St. Matthew VI. 20.

[2] *Cf.* Bloomfield, RV. 195.

[3] *Sukṛitaḥ* 'well doers' (X. 16, 4): *devayavaḥ, devayantaḥ*, 'god-devoted' 'god-serving' I. 154, 5.

wicked would demand a separate abode as a prison or place of punishment. The passages are confessedly few which may be quoted from the Ṛv. in support of a doctrine of hell[1]; but, though few, their evidence is clear enough. Consider the following:—

Roaming about, like brotherless young women,
Of evil ways, like dames that trick their husbands,
As such being full of sin, untrue, unfaithful[2],—
They for themselves this deep place have created. IV. 5, 5.

O Indra-Soma, dash the evil-doers[2] down
Into the pit, the gloom profound and bottomless,
So that not one of them may ever thence emerge;
Such be your wrathful might to overpower them. VII. 104, 3.

In these two passages the emphasis is upon the casting of the wicked into a 'deep place' *(padam gabhīram*[3]*)* or 'pit' (*vavra*). Similarly the wish is expressed that the thief and robber may lie under the three earths, and that the demoness in the form of an owl may plunge down into the endless (*i. e.* bottomless) pits (VII. 104, 11, 17). These references show that the prison-house of the wicked was conceived as a deep or bottomless pit of darkness,

'As far removed from God and light of heaven
As from the centre thrice to the utmost pole'[4].

When one has been cast into this pit, no exit is possible. Every sinner creates for himself 'this deep place' through the evil deeds which he has committed (IV. 5, 5)[5].

In general, then, we may say that the conception of hell seems to have been forced upon the Ṛigvedic seers by the facts of the moral life.

6. Two hymns of the Ṛv. are devoted to the praise of the *Pitṛis* or Fathers[6]. Certain stanzas of X. 15 are here reproduced:—

[1] Oldenberg RV. 536-542; Macdonell, VM. 169.

[2] Note the word for wicked: *duskṛitaḥ* 'evil-doers', *pāpāsaḥ* 'sinners', *anṛitāḥ* 'untrue', *asatyāḥ* 'unfaithful'.

[3] *Narakasthānam* 'hell'—Sāyana.

[4] Paradise Lost, I. lines 73-74.

[5] *Cf.*Acts I. 25, "Judas fell away, that he might go to his *own place*".

[6] X. 15 and 56.

1. Let them rise up, the lower, up the higher,
Yea up the midmost Soma-loving Fathers.
May they who have attained to life eternal,
Kind, order-knowing, aid us when we call them.

2. To-day be this our homage to the Fathers,
Who passed beyond, the earlier and the later;
Those who are seated in the space terrestrial,
Or now sojourn amid the clans fair-settled.

4. Fathers, come hither with your aid, grass-seated;
These offerings have we made to you: enjoy them.
So come to us with your most wholesome succour,
And grant us health and welfare without blemish.

5. Invited are the Soma-loving Fathers
Unto the dear deposits on the litter
Of sacred grass; may they draw nigh and hearken,
Yea intercede for us and grant us succour.

6. Southward being seated and the knee inclining,
Welcome unitedly this our oblation.
O Fathers, hurt us not for any trespass
That we through human frailty have committed.

8. Vasiṣṭhas, our forefathers, Soma-loving,
Who are considered meet for Soma-drinking,—
Sharing in gifts with these let Yama eager
With eager ones at will eat our oblations.

10. Come, Agni, with the thousand god-adoring
Forefathers seated at the heating-vessel,
All eaters, drinkers of oblations, truthful,
Who journey with the deities and Indra.

11. Ye Agni-tasted Fathers, come ye nigh to us,
Sit each upon his seat, ye that good guidance give.
Eat the oblations that are proffered on the grass,
And then grant wealth to us and hosts of hero sons.

12. Of Fathers who are here and who are absent,
Of Fathers whom we know and whom we know not,
Thou, Jātavedas, knowest well the number;
With spirit-food prepared accept our offering[1].

We are here introduced to Ṛigvedic ancestor-worship[2]. The Fathers thus adored have passed through death and

[1] Indebtedness is acknowledged to Macdonell, VRS. 176-186; Hillebrandt LR. 119-120; and Griffith.

[2] *Cf.* Chap. I. pp. 11-12.

attained to life[1], the implication being that it is life immortal[2], since the Fathers are associated with the Devas in their activities and in the worship they receive. This conception of the sainted dead seems logically to shut out transmigration. The Soma-loving Fathers are invited to the earthly sacrifices, where they sit along with the Devas on the *barhis* or litter of sacred grass. They come in thousands and take their proper places on the sacrificial ground, being seated to the south, the region of the dead. Here they receive their portion of the libations[3] for which they yearn.

The Fathers receive adoration, and are invoked to hear, intercede for and protect their descendants, granting unto them perfect health and welfare[4]. They are also besought not to injure their descendants for any sin which they may have committed against them. They are also represented as givers of wealth and offspring[5].

Cosmic activities are sometimes ascribed to the Fathers, such as adorning the sky with stars, placing darkness in the night and light in the day, finding the hidden light, and generating the dawn[6]. Being assimilated to the gods and leading the same kind of life, the Fathers receive almost divine honours[7], and in one passage (X. 56, 4) are apparently called gods. They constitute a special group of deities or at least of demi-gods.

The Fathers are distinguished as earlier and later, as

---

[1] *Asu* 'spirit', 'life' (X. 15, 1), the context showing that it refers to the heavenly life, conceived of course after the analogy of the earthly *asu* 'breath'.

[2] The Fathers are actually called immortal in AV. VI. 41, 3.

[3] As the Devas are nourished and strengthened by offerings, so are the Fathers. *Svadhā* means 'inherent power', and in X. 14, 3; 15, 14; IX. 113, 10, it seems to mean the 'spirit-food' or drink which confers this power. Oldenberg. RV. 531 n. 2; SBE. XLVI. 162.

[4] X. 15, 2, 4, 5. Note the practice of 'prayers to the dead'.

[5] X. 15, 6, 11; 16, 5; 18, 9.

[6] X. 68, 11; VII. 76, 4.

[7] Macdonell, VM. 170.

lower, higher and middle[1], and as known or unknown, even those who are unknown to their descendants being known to Agni[2]. In general the term *pitṛis* refers to the early forefathers, who travelled from earth to heaven by the ancient paths which Yama discovered. These paths they, the ancient-born, helped to make for their descendants, the recent dead, who go to join them (X. 14, 2, 7, 15). Certain ancient clans are mentioned as represented by the Fathers, especially the Aṅgirasas, Navagvas, Atharvans, Vairūpas, Bhṛigus and Vasiṣṭhas (X. 14, 4-6; 15, 8). These ancient path-makers are called in one place Ṛiṣhis (X. 14, 15)[3].

7. Yama, the chief of the blessed dead, is never explicitly called a god, but only a King. Still it is everywhere implied that he is a god, for he is closely associated with Varuṇa, Bṛihaspati, Agni and Mātariśvan, and is mentioned in the lists of 'the gods[4]. Yama is celebrated in only three whole hymns[5] besides the one containing the famous dialogue between Yama and his sister Yamī (X. 10). Most of the references to Yama are found in the tenth and first books.

a) The ancestry and relationships of Yama are uncertain and perplexing. According to one account (X. 17, 1-2) Yama and (by implication) his twin sister Yamī are the children of Vivasvant and Saraṇyu, the daughter of Tvaṣṭar. Vivasvant[6] 'the luminous' is clearly a deity of light. Whether he be interpreted as the rising sun[7], the luminous sky[8], or simply the sun[9] makes very little difference,

---

[1] As belonging to earth, sky and mid-air.

[2] X. 15, 1, 2, 13.

[3] We are reminded of the distinction drawn in RV. I. 1, 2 between ancient and recent *Ṛiṣis*.

[4] X. 14, 7; 13, 4; I. 164, 46; X. 64. 3; 92, 11.

[5] X. 14, 135, 154.

[6] vi+vas 'to shine forth', 'be resplendent'; *cf.* Avestan *Vīvanhvant*.

[7] Roth, PW.; Macdonell, VM. 43.

[8] Ludwig, RV., III. 333, V. 392; Ehni, Yama 19, 24.

[9] Hillebrandt, VM. I. 488; Hopkins, RI. 128, 130; Bloomfield, RV. 141, *et al.*

since each involves the other. Saraṇyu 'the swift' may be taken as a synonym of Sūryā or Uṣas the Dawn[1], or perhaps better with Myriantheus[2] as the night which, of course, ends with the dawn. Vivasvant and Saraṇyu were responsible for two pairs of twins, Yama and Yamī and the two Aśvins. If the Aśvins are taken to be the twin-lights of the morning twilight, half-dark and half-light, then Vivasvant and Saraṇyu, interpreted as the day-sky and the night-sky, would furnish a very suitable parentage for them, for the twilight shares in the colour of both parents. In like manner Yama and Yamī may perhaps be interpreted as moon and Dawn[3], both sharing in the qualities of day and night, and represented as having a love-affair which ended in a wedding (X. 85, 8-9). The physical basis of the heavenly romance may then be seen when the waning Moon draws near to, and finally fuses with, the Dawn, otherwise called Sūryā, the Sun-maiden.

Compare the following stanza of a Lithuanian folk-song[4].

> "The Moon did wed the Maiden Sun,
> In an early day of spring-tide;
> The Maiden Sun arose betimes,
> The Moon just then did slink away".

Hillebrandt thinks that the two wives of Vivasvant (X. 17, 2) are Night and Dawn, Night vanishing and Dawn taking Night's place in the affections of the Sun. But these references are so occasional and fugitive that, as Hillebrandt says, they explain nothing, but stand in need of explanation themselves[5].

From an entirely different circle of mythical ideas comes the statement that Yama and Yamī are children of

---

[1] So Bloomfield JAOS. 15, 172-188, and Macdonell, VM. 125.

[2] AAD. 57. So Hillebrandt, VM. I. 503, n. 1.

[3] Unless, as some think, Yamī is a later creation, like Indrāṇī and Varuṇānī. So Hillebrandt, VM. I. 495. But perhaps Yama and Yamī may be taken as Heaven and Earth, the primeval parents of all things. *Cf.* X. 10, 9.

[4] Quoted by Bloomfield (RV. 114) from Prof. Chase's version, with alterations.

[5] VM. I. 503.

the Gandharva in the waters and of the water nymph[1], although these two are possibly to be identified with Vivasvant and Saraṇyu[2].

Yama, the son of Vivasvant, clearly belongs to the Indo-Iranian period, because identical with Yima, the son of Vivanhvant. The twins Yama and Yamī correspond with Yima and Yimeh, Yamī belonging to a late Ṛv. hymn (X. 10) and Yimeh to the Bundahiṣ, a part of the younger Avesta. Yama Vaivasvata (X. 14, 1) has an interesting doublet in the person of Manu Vivasvant (Vāl. 4, 1) called later also Manu Vaivasvata (AV. VIII. 10, 24). Doubtless the two originated in different mythical circles. They introduce us to the problem of the origin and the future life of mankind.

b) At the head of the human race stands, according to Ṛigvedic conception, a first man, either Manu[3] the first sacrificer (X. 63, 7), or Yama the first to discover the pathway from earth to heaven (X. 14, 1-2), because the first to die. Manu is definitely called 'our father' (I. 80, 16; II. 33, 13) as also is Yama (X. 135, 1). The twins Yama and Yamī may be taken as the progenitors of the human race, as it were the Indian Adam and Eve. The motive of the strange dialogue (X. 10) between the twin brother and sister turns upon the ethics of such a relationship. Yamī presses for it on the ground that Yama is the 'only mortal' (v. 3) and that progeny is necessary in order to people the world (vv. 1, 3). Yama on the other hand draws attention to the fact that

Great is the law of Varuṇa and Mitra (v. 6).
The hero sons of Asura the mighty,
Upholders of the sky, look round them widely (v. 2).
They stand not still, nor ever close their eyelids,
Spies of the gods, that here about us wander (v. 8).

---

[1] *apyā yoṣā* X. 10, 4.

[2] So Sāyaṇa and Max Müller.

[3] Manu (or Manus) 'man' from *man* 'to think'. *Cf.* the Hebrew *Adam* 'man'.

The ethical difficulty of the origin of the human race from the union of a primeval brother and sister reminds one of the similar trouble one finds in discovering where Cain and Abel got their wives (if not from among their own sisters)[1]. It looks as if Yama and Yamī were originally anthropomorphised natural phenomena, such as Moon and Dawn, or Heaven and Earth[2]. The name Yama 'twin' seems to indicate that there was such a pair of natural phenomena. When Yama became anthropomorphised, the name Manu (Manus) 'man' was altogether suitable. To say that Yama and Manu are doublets is to say that they are practically identical[3].

Beyond the first man the roots of humanity run back into the world of the gods[4], to Vivasvant (the Sun)[5], the father of Manu[6] and the father of Yama and Yamī, the last two being identical, probably, with Heaven and Earth, the parents of all that is.

Sacrifice is carried back to primeval man. Manu presented the first offering to the gods (X. 63, 7), and hence Manu's original sacrifice is a prototype of the Ṛigvedic sacrifice. For the Ṛigvedic priest is often said to perform the ritual of sacrifice *Manuṣvat,* 'as Manus did' (I. 44, 11, etc.). The priest also thinks of himself as functioning in the 'home of Manu' or the 'seat of Vivasvant', expressions to be explained as the place of sacrifice. The Iranian

---

[1] Of course in both instances we are dealing with the realm of conceptions.

[2] Heaven and earth as natural twins might very well be called Yama and Yamī. They are also the parents of all that is. As Vivasvant and Saraṇyu, Day and Night, are the parents of the Aśvins, conceived as the twilight, so might they well be the parents (or revealers) of Yama and Yamī conceived as Heaven and Earth.

[3] Their practical identity is symbolized by their both being made sons of Vivasvant.

[4] Oldenberg, RV. 276. *Cf.* Luke III. 38, "Which was the son of Adam, which was the son of God".

[5] The sun-source of the soul becomes finally, as we have seen, the 'sun-home' of the soul.

[6] Manu seems to be Indo-European, because it corresponds with Mannus (Tacitus, *Germania* Cap. II), Germ. *Mann,* and English man.

Vivanhvant was the first to prepare the Haoma, and the Ṛigvedic Vivasvant performed similar functions (Vāl. IV. 1). Thus Manu-Yama was the first man, the first sacrificer, the first ruler, the first one to see death, the first to blaze a pathway from earth to heaven, and the first to become the king of the blessed dead in the realms of light.

c) The Ṛigvedic Heaven as the abode of the Fathers has already been described. Yama is the king thereof. His dwelling is in the 'remote recess' of the sky. There he gathers the people together, gives the dead man a resting place, prepares an abode for him, and under the well-leaved tree of Paradise drinks[1] the draught of immortality with the gods, while at the same time, as their clan-lord and father, he attends lovingly to the ancient ones[2]. The seat of Yama, which is the abode of the gods[3], is a place of music and song. Yama as the first and 'sole mortal' (X. 10, 3) on earth is represented as choosing death and abandoning his body on behalf of gods and men, in order to open up for them a path between earth and heaven (X. 13, 4; 14, 1). If this is the correct interpretation[4], then there is ascribed to Yama a love for the human race which bore fruit in sacrifice.

Yama's regular messengers are two dogs, 'hounds of heaven' as it were, the sons of Saramā. They are described in X. 14, 10-12 as four-eyed, broad-nosed, and brindled or brown[5]. The two dogs of Yama are clearly as closely associated together as are the Aśvin pair or the twins Yama and Yamī. If Yama and Yamī be taken as Heaven and Earth, then it would seem natural, with Bloomfield, to

---

[1] *Cf.* Mark XIV. 25; Luke XXII. 18.

[2] IX. 113, 8: X. 14, 1, 7, 9; 18, 13; 135, 1.

[3] *devamāna* X. 135, 7.

[4] Interpretation uncertain. *Cf.* Oldenberg, Ṛv. Noten II. 210-211: and Macdonell, VM. 172.

[5] In the AV. VIII. 1, 9 the two dogs are distinguished as 'brindled' *Śabalas* (possibly to be identified with the Gr. Κέρβερος. Bloomfield RV. 106) and *Śyāma* 'dark', an interpretation of the difficult word *udumbala* 'brown' (?).

think of the two heavenly dogs as originally the sun and moon. But this is very uncertain. In view of the fact that in both the Greek and the Iranian mythology of the dead only one dog plays a part, it is possible that the Indian love of correspondence and symmetry has led to the creation of two dogs. But whatever these dogs originally represented, their business is described as guarding, Cerberus-like, the way from earth to heaven[1], as selecting the candidates for death, and as entrusted with their care as they journey heavenward (X. 14, 10-12).

[1] In modern stories these dogs guard the doors leading to heaven and hell.

PART C.

THE SIGNIFICANCE AND VALUE OF THE ṚIGVEDA

CHAPTER XII.

THE ṚIGVEDA AND LATER HINDU DEVELOPMENTS.

The Ṛigveda is the fountain-head[1] of Hindu religion, philosophy, law, art and social institutions. It is no more possible to understand later Hinduism without a knowledge of the Ṛv. than it would be to understand the New Testament or the Qurān without a knowledge of the Old Testament. The Ṛv. has fulfilled itself in the thought, institutions and history of India. To show how this is so, is to write at once the last chapter on the religious contents of the Ṛv. and the first chapter on the significance and value thereof.

1. The Ṛigveda and Hindu Art.

a) Poetry. — The contents of the Ṛv. are entirely metrical, which agrees with the fact that the beginnings of literature are, as a rule, in the form of poetry. There are about fifteen metres, of which ten are represented by the translations made in this book. The verse-line forms the metrical unit, and generally has eight, eleven or twelve syllables. Stanzas consist usually of four lines, but also of three, five and seven. Some hymns are composed of strophes either of three stanzas *(trica)* in the same simple metre, or of two stanzas in different mixed metres *(pragātha)*. The *(Triṣṭubh)* stanza consists of four eleven-syllable lines. It is the most 'common metre' in the Ṛv. For example:

---

[1] "The Vedas furnish the only sure foundation on which a knowledge of ancient and modern India can be built up".

Whitney, JAOS. V. 291.

With mine own self I meditate this question,
When shall I have with Varuna communion?
What gift of mine will he enjoy unangered?
When shall I happy-hearted see his mercy? VII. 86, 2.

The *Gāyatrī* stanza has three eight-syllable lines, and is illustrated by the famous Gāyatrī text, as translated by Macdonell (HR. 33):

May we obtain that excellent
Glory of Savitar the god,
That he may stimulate our thoughts. III. 62, 10.

The *Jagatī* has four twelve-syllable lines:

Whatsoever wrong against the heavenly race we do,
Being but men, O Varuṇa, whatever law,
Of thine we may have broken through thoughtlessness,
For that transgression do not injure us, O God. VII. 89, 5.

As the *Triṣṭubh* ends in a trochaic rhythm (– ⏑ – ⏑), so the *Jagatī* ends in an iambic rhythm (⏑ – ⏑ –). The *Anuṣṭubh* contains four eight-syllable lines, as in the hymn to *Aranyāṇi*, X. 146: —

O Jungle maid, O Jungle maid,
Methinks that thou hast lost thy way;
Dost not ask for the village? why?
Alarm has seized thee, has it not?

The Vedic Anuṣṭubh developed later into the Śloka of classical Sanskrit. About 180 Ṛigvedic passages have been translated in this book, ranging from a single line to a complete hymn. Of these the number of passages in the four principal metres are as follows[1]: Triṣṭubh 100, Gāyatrī 36, Jagatī 29, and Anuṣṭubh 13. Only ten passages are in the unusual metres. Among these are the following: *Paṅkti*, with five eight-syllable lines, as in IX. 113, 7,

Where radiance inexhaustible
Dwells, and the light of heaven is set,

[1] Max Müller, following Śaunaka, divides the 10,409 Ṛigvedic stanzas among the different metres as follows: Triṣṭubh, 4,253; Gāyatrī, 2, 451; Jagatī, 1, 348; Anuṣṭubh 855, etc. (*Ancient Sanskrit Literature*, p. 22).

Place me, clear-flowing one, in that
Imperishable and deathless world.
O Indu, flow for Indra's sake.

Prastārapaṅkti, with four lines, a Triṣṭubh, a Jagatī and two Gāyatrī, as in X. 18, 11 (Macdonell's translation),

Wide open, earth, O press not heavily on him;
Be easy of approach to him, a refuge safe;
As with a robe a mother hides
Her son, so shroud this man, O earth.

Bṛihatī, with four lines, first, second and fourth Gāyatrī, and the third Jagatī.

To Yama king th' oblation pour
Most rich in honied sweetness. This
Our hymn of praise is for the Riṣhis, ancient-born,
The ancient makers of the path. X. 14, 15.

Purastādbṛihatī, with a Triṣṭubh and three Gāyatrī lines, as follows:

Against us is the riteless, shameless Dasyu,
Inhuman, keeping alien laws;
Do thou, O slayer of the foe,
This Dasyu's weapon circumvent. X. 22, 8.

Dvipadā, two lines, Jagatī and Gāyatrī:

Another brandisheth a bolt placed in his hand;
With that he smites and kills his foes. VIII. 29, 4.

Atyaṣṭi, a complicated stanza of seven lines, three Jagatī and four Gāyatrī as follows:

Two bay steeds Vāyu yokes, Vāyu two ruddy steeds,
Swift-footed to the chariot, to the pole to draw,
Best coursers, to the pole to draw.
Awaken Bounteousness, as when
A lover wakes his sleeping love.
Illumine heaven and earth, make thou the dawns to shine,
For glory make the dawns to shine. I. 134, 3.

Thus it will be seen that while the stanzas of the more common metres are made up of lines of the same type, the rarer stanzas are formed by combining lines of different length. The rhythm of only the last four or five syllables is rigidly determined. Thus the metres of the Ṛv. stand midway between the archaic metres of the Avesta, which are governed only by the number of syllables, and the more polished measures of Classical Sanskrit in which, as a rule, the quantity of every single syllable is fixed. The Vedic metres are the foundation of all the classical Sanskrit metres except two[1].

The hymns of the Ṛv. are nearly all religious, only a few being semi-religious or didactic in quality, for example, the Gambler's lament in X. 34, of which certain stanzas are here reproduced from Professor Macdonell's excellent translation[2].

2. She[3] wrangles not with me nor is she angry:
To me and comrades she was ever kindly.
For dice that only luckless throws effected
I've driven away from home a wife devoted.

3. Her mother hates me, she herself rejects me:
For one in such distress there is no pity.
I find a gambling man is no more useful
Than is an aged horse that's in the market.

4. Others embrace the wife of him whose chattles
The eager dice have striven hard to capture;
And father, mother, brothers say about him:
"We know him not, lead him away a captive."

5. When to myself I think, "I'll not go with them
I'll stay behind my friends that go to gamble;"
And those brown nuts, thrown down, have raised their voices,
I go, like wench, straight to the place of meeting.

6. To the assembly hall the gambler sallies,
And asking, 'Shall I win?' he quakes and trembles.
And then the dice run counter to his wishes,
Giving the lucky throw to his opponent.

10. Grieved is the gambler's wife by him abandoned,
Grieved, too, his mother as he aimless wanders.
Indebted, fearing, he desiring money,
At night approaches other people's houses.

---

[1] Macdonell, ERE. VII., article *Hymns (Vedic)*; VRS. XVII-XVIII., and HR. 9-10.

[2] HR. 88-90.

[3] The wife of the gambler.

13. 'Play not with dice, but cultivate thy tillage,
Enjoy thy riches deeming them abundant.
There are thy cows, there is thy wife, O gambler':
This counsel Savitar the noble gives me.

14. Make friends with us, we pray, to us be gracious,
Do not bewitch us forcibly with magic;
Let now your enmity, your anger slumber,
Let others be in brownies' toils entangled.

There is here a distinct anticipation of the proverbial and sententious poetry of later days.

We have to distinguish between two types of religious poetry in the Ṛv., on the higher side, consisting 'in praises of the gods and generally accompanying the sacrifices offered to them', and on the lower side consisting 'in spells or charms directed against hostile powers, and accompanying some domestic practice of a magical character'[1]. There are about a dozen such hymns, which deal unmistakably with magic practices[2].

We may also trace in the Ṛv. the beginnings of Hindu lyric, dramatic and epic poetry. The whole Ṛigvedic collection is fundamentally lyric, special hymns, of course, having a lyric-dramatic or a lyric-epic setting. The most poetical hymns in the Ṛv. are those addressed to Dawn, which Macdonell pronounces 'equal, if not superior, in beauty to the religious lyrics of any other literature[3].' The dialogue between Viśvāmitra and the Rivers (III. 33) is essentially dramatic. Notable storm and battle lyrics are found among the hymns addressed to Indra, Parjanya and the Maruts.

---

[1] Macdonell, ERE. Art. *Hymns (Vedic).*

[2] Confined largely to the tenth book. *E. g.* compare the following stanza from an incantation in the form of a song of triumph over rival wives as translated by Macdonell (in MS.):

Vanquished have I these rival wives,
Rising superior to them all,
That over this heroic man
And all his people I may rule. X. 159, 6.

[3] VRS. XXVIII. *Cf.* also Hopkins' *Early Lyric Poetry of India* in ION. 36-66.

There are several colloquies in which the speakers are divine beings[1]; also two in which the agents may be human, *viz.* the dialogue between Yama and Yamī (X. 10) and between Purūravas and Urvaśī (X. 95). These hymns foreshadow the dramatic works of a later age[2]. There is Epic material in the Battle of the Ten Kings (VII. 18), in which the great Sudās overcame his allied foes. Among the multitudes of personal names[3] found in the Ṛv., especially in the *Dānastuti* hymns, many doubtless have epic significance, if we only knew the facts. On the whole, the average of literary merit in the Ṛigvedic hymns must be pronounced 'remarkably high'[4], especially if one takes into consideration the early date at which they were composed. The poetic endowment revealed in the hymns of the Ṛv. has continued in India down to the present time, for India is a land of poetry and song.

b) Music.—Certain musical instruments are mentioned—the drum, flute and lute—as used by the Vedic Indians. The Maruts and the Aṅgirasas are represented as heavenly singers, after the analogy of the earthly. The hymns used in the Soma sacrifice were certainly chanted by the priests[5]. Thus Indian musical theory undoubtedly had a religious origin. The love of the people of modern India for music[6] and song is clearly connected with the musical tastes and aptitudes of the earliest times. The fact that the whole Ṛigvedic collection is *lyric* is significant.

---

[1] IV. 26; X. 51, 52, 86, 108.

[2] Macdonell, VRS. XXV.

[3] See *Vedic Index*.

[4] Macdonell, VRS. XXVIII.

[5] "These various priests fall clearly into three divisions, according as their main business was the recitation of hymns to accompany the offering, or the actual manual acts of sacrifice, *or the singing of songs*".—Keith, Art. *Priest, Priesthood (Hindu)*, ERE. X. 312. The Soma hymns are still chanted to-day by Sāmaveda Brāhmans, but without the accompaniment of sacrifice. See Fox Strangways, *Music of Hindustan*.

[6] See H. A. Popley, *The Music of India*, Calcutta. 1921.

c) Painting and Sculpture.—The representation of the human or animal form clearly began in the Buddhistic period, if not earlier[1]. There are two artistic methods. One is to copy faithfully from nature, making only such changes as the ideal seems to require. Such is the Greek method, which kept close to nature. The other is to express symbolically certain ideas. Here in the interests of symbolism there is often a wide departure from nature. Such in general is the Hindu method, especially in the later period. The Trimūrti figure in the Elephanta Caves has a threefold head. Kālī has four arms. Ganeśa has the head of an elephant and the body of a man. The artistic aim in all these instances is not to copy nature, but symbolically to express ideas[2]. So far as definitely known, there was no painting or sculpture in the Ṛigvedic period. But there were plenty of ideas scattered through the hymns—ideas which challenged artistic expression. Thus Agni, the fire-god, is 'hundred-eyed' or 'thousand-eyed' (I. 128, 3; 79, 12), the reference being clearly to his multitudinous points of flame. Puruṣa, the cosmic man, a pantheistic name for the totality of things, is represented (X. 90, 1) as having 'a thousand heads, a thousand eyes, a thousand feet'. Indra, in order to keep up his strength for the Vṛitra-fight, eats three hundred buffaloes and drinks three lakes of Soma, the thought being that vast accomplishments presuppose vast eating and drinking. As the strong one *par excellence* Indra is called *sahasramuṣka*, 'thousand-testicled'. Such symbolical numbers determine the character of Hindu art, which is not imitative but symbolical,

---

[1] "The existence of idols in Vedic times has been asserted in the cases of a painted image of Rudra, of Varuṇa with a golden coat of mail, and in the distinction drawn between the Maruts and their images".—W. Crooke, *Images and Idols (Indian)*. ERE. VII. But this is very doubtful. A use of fetish symbols, probably not in the form of images, may however be admitted. *Cf.* Oldenberg, RV. 87-89.

[2] A similar kind of religious symbolism is found in the book of Revelation, *e. g.* I. 20, V. 6, etc. as well as in Ezekiel.

for when the numbers are not too large, they may be expressed on canvas or in stone. A thousand heads cannot be so expressed, but the four heads of Brahmā can. Thus the most characteristic quality of Hindu religious art is in deepest harmony with the symbolical representations of the Ṛv.[1]

2. The Ṛigveda and Hindu Society and History.

a) Historical names. — A considerable number of words are found in the Ṛv. which became later the names of historical or semi-historical personages in Hindu story. A few instances may be given: *Sītā*[2] and *Rāma*[3], *Rādhā*[4] and *Kṛiṣṇa*[5]; and *Arjuna*[6]. Also the words *Śarman* 'protection' (III. 15, 5, etc.) and *Varman* 'mail', caste designations of Brāhman and Kṣatriya respectively; and the word Sūri 'wealthy patron', a caste surname among Jains. Of later divine names which already appear in the Ṛv. may be mentioned *Viṣṇu, Śiva* ('gracious', an epithet of Rudra and other gods), *Gaṇapati* (an epithet of Bṛihaspati II. 23, 1), and *Bhagavān,* 'the blessed one', a later name for god. Many other words of literary or historical interest might be mentioned as occurring in the Ṛv. such as *vraja* 'cow-stall' (origin of the regional name *Braj), Mātariśvan,* a later name for 'wind', *dāsa* 'slave' *varṇa* 'colour', 'caste', *Kāśī* 'clenched fist' (name of Benares), etc., etc.

b) Caste. — The sources of Hindu caste have already been traced[7]. It was undoubtedly the sharp antithesis in

---

[1] Such representations often involve ugliness, but "it should be remembered that all this ugliness is symbolical; the supernatural powers of the deity are intended to be expressed by these unnatural forms"—Moore, HR. I. 345. But see Macdonell, JRAS. 1916, pp. 125 ff., who finds the motive for the representation of Śiva with four arms, in the necessity of his identification.

[2] Furrow IV. 57, 6-7.

[3] From *ram* 'to rest'; proper name X. 93, 14.

[4] Which might be formed from *rādha* (Masc. and neut.) '*gift*' I. 30, 5.

[5] 'Black' as epithet (of the dark half) of day VI. 9, 1; also as a proper name.

[6] 'White', as applied to the light half of day VI. 9, 1.

[7] Chapter II. See also Ketkar's *History of Caste in India,* Ithaca, 1909.

colour, race and religion — especially *colour*[1] — between Aryan and Dasyu that led to the extreme rigidity of the Hindu caste system. In this way the Aryan sought to guard the purity of his blood. The movement in the direction of caste rigidity began during the Ṛigvedic period, for in one of the latest hymns (X. 90, 12) the four fundamental orders are mentioned. Caste forms the very warp and woof of Hindu society down to the present time, and more than anything else marks off Hindu social organization from that of other nations.

c) Pessimism[2]. — There are practically no traces of a pessimistic attitude toward life in the Ṛv. There is indeed a pensive note sounded in the hymn to Uṣas (I. 113, 10-11) which, while in no sense abnormal, may perhaps be regarded as pointing in the direction of the later pessimism. It looks as if the roots of Hindu pessimism were to be found partly in the trying climate of India and the gradual fusion of the Aryans with the aborigines, and partly in the doctrines of karma and transmigration, which, while lauded by some as the acme of philosophic insight, tend to produce in others a spirit of hopelessness. The fact that pessimism is not found in the Ṛv. is proof enough that its hymns — even the latest of them — were composed prior to the rise of the Brāhmaṇa and Upaniṣad doctrines of Karma and Transmigration and before their outcome in a pessimistic view of life. Thus considered, the hymns of the Ṛv. are the purest expression on the soil of India of the Aryan spirit[3].

3. The Ṛigveda and Hindu Popular Religion.

a) Ritual. — The ritual of the Brāhmaṇas was clearly continuous with that of the Ṛv. The modern ritual of Hinduism is the result of the fusion of two streams, — the

---

[1] The name for caste is *varṇa* 'colour'.

[2] Oldenberg, RV. 2; Bloomfield, RV. 212, 263-265; Griswold, ERE. Art. *Pessimism (Indian).*

[3] *Cf.* Chapter II. 53; Farquhar, ORLI. 82.

Aryan going back to the Ṛv. and the Dravidian representing primitive indigenous custom. It is difficult to distinguish between the two, since they have become so completely fused. It looks, however, as if temple and image[1] were Dravidian in origin, since neither is definitely and unmistakably mentioned in the Ṛv. Ṛigvedic religion was essentially open-air religion — a thing of the grass-strewn sward and of the sunken fire-pit. Its temple was the open sky. The theophany of its deities took place not through the appearance of images, but in connection with the blazing up of fire, the rosy flush of dawn, the rising of the sun, and the flash and glitter of lightning. The Ṛigvedic ritual undoubtedly contributed its part to the formation of the complex modern ritual.

b) Magic. — Religion and magic have always been more or less intermingled — religion that persuades the gods and magic that compels them. Magic is present to-day in every religion, the formula 'In a good day be it spoken', the injunction 'touch wood', and the thought of passing beneath a ladder as unlucky being twentieth century examples in the West. The whole galaxy of lucky and unlucky times, actions and objects is shot through with the view-point of magic. When the emphasis is upon the ritually exact rather than the ethically correct, then the tendency is enevitably toward a magical conception of religion. Such was increasingly the tendency during the transition from the Ṛigveda to the Brāhmaṇas. At last the sacrifice became greater than the gods, and the priests who manipulated the sacrifice greater than all. The large magical element in the popular religion of India is derived undoubtedly from Aryan as well as from Dravidian sources. The tendency of recent scholarship has been to emphasize somewhat the place of magic in the Ṛv.

---

[1] Farquhar, ORLI. 51 n. 1.

c) Priesthood.—As pointed out above, the priesthood in the Brāhmaṇa period became the depository of the inherent powers of the gods and the sacrifice. Later on came the great philosophical and religious awakening of the Upaniṣads. The doctrine of Bráhman-Ātman added, indeed, a new element to the old, but did not supersede it, at least for the great mass of the people. The Brāhman priest would officiate at the popular ceremonies, while being not infrequently himself a devotee of the new doctrine of the Ātman. The temple-priests of later Hinduism are probably not in all cases Brāhmans. As temples and images are probably Dravidian in origin, so are at least many of the priests that minister in connection with them[1]. But the priesthood of modern India, whether Brāhman or non-Brāhman, may be regarded, so far as it ministers to an Aryan cult, as derived from the original Vedic priesthood.

d) Austerity[2].—This practice which has always played so large a part in Hindu religion has left distinct traces in the Ṛv., especially in X. 136 (after Griffith with some changes):

To the Muni[3].

1. The hairy one supports the fire,
The poison-fluid, and heaven and earth;
He is all sky to look upon,
The hairy one is called this light.

2. The Munis, girdled with the wind,
Wear garments soiled, of yellow hue:
After the wind's course follow they,
When once the gods have entered them.

3. Transported with the ecstasy
Of Munihood we mount the winds;
Ye, mortal men, are able now
To see our bodies and no more.

---

[1] Temple-priests *(pūjārī)* are usually illiterate, and are despised by learned Brāhmans.

[2] *Tapas*, lit. 'heat'.

[3] Perhaps from *man* 'to think', 'rave'. *Cf.* vipra, from vip to 'shake', 'quake'.

4. He flies through regions of the air,
Beholding all the various forms,—
The Muni, who was made a friend
Of every god for ministry.
5. The steed of Vāta, Vāyu's friend,
The Muni, by the gods impelled,
In both the oceans hath his home,
In eastern and in western seas.
6. Treading the path of sylvan beasts,
Gandharvas and Apsarasas,
The hairy one knows every thought,
Sweet and most stimulating friend.
7. Vāyu has twirled for him; for him
He breaketh things most hard to bend;
When he, the hairy one, has drunk
With Rudra from the poison-cup.

The Munis, who thus practiced austerity in Vedic days, are like the ascetics of modern times in having long hair, wearing yellow garments, drinking poison-liquids that produce ecstasy, and being taken possession of by the gods. The sun as the long-haired one, the yellow-clothed, the heavenly ascetic wandering through the sky, and the supreme performer of *tapas,* is the architype of the earthly ascetic[1].

4. The Ṛigveda and Hindu Philosophical and Religious Thought.

a) Philosophical Conceptions.—The most fundamental of the philosophical concepts of India are ***bráhman, ātman, māyā, karman*** and ***punarjanman.*** ***Bráhman*** (nom. neut. ***bráhma***) occurs often in the Ṛv. in the sense of 'sacred formula', 'prayer', 'spell'. It was the inherent potency of the sacred formula, due to a magical[2] conception thereof, which led finally to the supreme conception of ***bráhman*** as identical with ***ātman***[3], the 'soul' of the universe.

---

[1] Vv. 1, 4-6. *Cf.* Oldenberg, RV. 404, 406; Hillebrandt, LR. 150.
[2] See Hillebrandt, *Brahman* ERE., and Griswold, *Brahman.*
[3] Ātman occurs in the Ṛv. in the sense of breath, wind, soul.

'*Bráhman* is the greatest word in the whole history of Indian philosophy"[1], for 'there is contained in it the religious development of India during thirty centuries'. Māyā often occurs in the sense of 'mysterious power', the source of the magic transformations that take place in nature. The transition to the later philosophical meaning of 'magic power', 'illusion', 'non-reality', was easy. *Karman* (nom. neut. karma), as already pointed out, means in the Ṛv. simply 'work' in general, or more specifically 'liturgical work'. The development of the later meaning of 'fruit of work', 'recompense', was not difficult[2]. In fact, there is a distinct suggestion of this doctrine in the expression *iṣṭapūrta* (X. 14, 8), the gain which accrues in the life to come from the sacrifices and gifts made in this life. *Punarjanman*, 'transmigration' does not occur in the Ṛv., but the participles *punaḥ punarjayamānā* 'being born again, again', as applied to *Uṣas* (I. 92, 10), and *navonavo jayamanaḥ* 'being born anew, anew', as applied to the Moon (X. 85, 19) point in the direction of the later technical term. In the thought too, of the *manas* or soul of a dead man as going to the waters or plants (X. 16, 3; 58, 7) there may perhaps be found the germ of the later doctrine of metempsychosis[3]. At any rate, 're-birth' is not postulated of living beings in the Ṛv., but only of the recurring phenomena of nature anthropomorphically conceived. Thus the roots of the fundamental concepts of Hinduism together with the technical names thereof already appear in the Ṛv. As the most pregnant conceptions of the Ṛv. are impersonal, *ṛita* 'order', *karman* 'work', *brahman* 'word' and *maya* 'power'; so is it later on in the period of the Vedānta, when the whole realm of being is pre-empted by the two great impersonalities[4], *bráhman* 'reality' and *maya* 'non-reality'.

---

[1] Griswold. Brahman 1.

[2] *Karman* occurs about 40 times in the Ṛv., but never in the later sense of 'the fruit of work'.

[3] Chap. XI. p. 313.

[4] Bráhman may perhaps be better described as super-personal than as impersonal.

b) Ethics.—The ethical conceptions of the Ṛv. are essentially tribal[1], as is natural in an early stage of society. It was Aryan *versus* Dasyu. And yet there are hints of a larger sense of duty. For example, the following prayer is addressed to Varuṇa:

> Against a friend, companion, or a brother,
> A fellow-tribesman, *or against a stranger*,
> Whatever trespass we have perpetrated,
> Do thou, O Varuṇa, from that release us. V. 85, 7.

The supreme ethical concept of the Ṛv. is that of *ṛita* 'order'. Ethical antitheses are expressed by such contrasted terms as *ṛita* (or *satya*) and *anṛita* 'true and false' *sādhu* and *vṛijina* 'straight and crooked'. The term *ṛita,* notwithstanding its greatness as an ethical concept, finally dropped out of use—a commentary on the direction taken by ethical thinking—and its connotation was taken up in the later notions of *karma* and *dharma.* This change was not for the better. Ṛita as embodied in the will of Varuṇa was connected with a god of grace, who could pardon sin and restore the sinner to his fellowship. Karma, on the contrary, was the merely mechanical working of the principle of retribution.

c) The Forgiveness of Sin.—He who is *par excellence* the ethical god of the Ṛv. is the one who is supremely concerned with the forgiveness of sin; for, as Macdonell says, 'there is no hymn to Varuṇa, in which the prayer for forgiveness of guilt does not occur'[2]. Other gods also are represented as forgiving sin, but the references to forgiveness are only incidental and fugitive, whereas this function is central with Varuṇa, and, as we have seen, practically every hymn composed in his honour is shot through with the thought of it. Later on Varuṇa, like all the other gods, was swallowed up in the conception of an impersonal and non-moral world-ground, just as *ṛita* was

[1] Even up to the present time the world has hardly transcended the stage of tribal morality.

[2] VM. 27.

absorbed in the notion of Karma. From the point of view of the later orthodoxy, Brāhmanical and Vedantic, the forgiveness of sin is impossible. The Ṛigvedic belief in 'the forgiveness of sins' was conserved only in connection with the later heterodox and sectarian cults[1], and even then imperfectly, as a rule, since they have all been more or less influenced by the dominant orthodoxy, which found no place for forgiveness. The doctrine of Karma has ever stood in the way of a belief in the free exercise of the divine grace.

d) Polytheism.—The Ṛigveda is as frankly polytheistic as Homer's Iliad or Virgil's Æneid. Animism, or polytheistic nature worship, lies at the foundation of all of the Indo-European mythologies, Indian and Iranian as well as Greek, Roman and Teutonic. The hymns to the All-gods *(Viśve Devāḥ)* present the clearest proof (if any further proof were needed) of the Ṛigvedic polytheism. For example, VIII. 29[2]:—

1. Brown is one, bountiful, of varied form, and young;
He wears a golden ornament. (Soma)
2. Another has, resplendent, occupied his seat,
The intelligent among the gods. (Agni)
3. Another beareth in his hand a metal axe,
The strenuous among the gods. (Tvaṣṭar)
4. Another brandisheth a bolt placed in his hand;
With that he smites and kills his foes. (Indra)
5. Bright, fierce, with cooling remedies, another bears
Within his hand a weapon sharp. (Rudra)
6. Another makes the paths to prosper; like a thief
He knows the place of hidden wealth. (Pūṣan)
7. Another, the wide-pacer, makes three mighty strides
To where the gods delight themselves. (Viṣṇu)
8. Two fare with birds, together with a female friend,
Like travellers they both go forth. (Aśvins)

[1] Such as the Vaiṣṇava and Śaiva sects and those founded by Kabir, Nānak, Keshab Chander Sen, *et. al.*

[2] Acknowledgment of indebtedness to Hillebrandt LR. 98-99, and to Macdonell VRS. 147-152.

9. The twain on high have made themselves a seat in heaven,
The sovereign kings, whose drink is ghee. (Mitra-Varuṇa)

10. Of a great chant some singers have bethought themselves;
By it they caused the sun to shine. (Aṅg [illegible]asas)

This hymn is in the form of a series of riddles. Each god is described without being named, it being left to the cleverness of the reader correctly to identify each. There are described seven individual gods, two dual divinities, and one group of semi-divine beings. The Ṛigvedic pantheon probably represents the gods of different Aryan tribes. Political federation was doubtless followed by religious federation, according to the usual custom in ancient times[1]. Had the O. T. Psalter been constructed after the fashion of the Ṛv., it would have contained hymns addressed to the gods of many Semitic tribes[2]—to the various Baalim and to Ashtoreth, Molech, Chemosh, Tammuz, *et al.*, as well as to Yahweh. Polytheism and idolatry, it is true, were not uncommon in ancient Israel down to the time of the Babylonian Exile, 586 B.C.[3] But the authors of the O. T. books were prophets and prophetic historians, who were loyal to the exclusive worship of Yahweh. In the chapter on the Vedic World of Gods and Demons[4] it was pointed out how we can watch one god, say Prajāpati, just rising above the horizon, another like Indra at the zenith, and still another at the sunset time, 'the twilight of the gods', *e.g.* Trita Āptya. The birth and death of gods has gone on from the Ṛigvedic period down to the present time. One can watch the process of apotheosis in India to-day. Polytheism inevitably means the waxing and waning of gods, a conception so detrimental to the idea of an Eternal God. And this aspect of modern Hinduism goes back by unbroken sequence to the Ṛv.

---

[1] Compare the procedure of Solomon, king of Israel, in introducing foreign gods along with foreign wives. 1 Kings XI. 1-8.

[2] *Cf.* Griswold, GVR. 32.

[3] *Cf.* Jeremiah VII. 17-18, Ezekiel VI & VIII.

[4] p. 87 ff.

Another defect connected with polytheism is the opportunity it offers for the squabbling of the gods. There is, indeed, less of this among the Ṛigvedic gods than among the Olympic deities. Still it is present to some extent, especially in connection with Indra, who fell out with his own father, was at odds with Sūrya, and attacked the wain of Uṣas[1]. Such squabbling is inevitable in every promiscuous polytheism; and, as might be expected, the gods of Hinduism down to the present time are not free from it.

e) Pantheism.—During the latter part of the Ṛigvedic period there was a steady movement toward unity. This movement assumed two forms, one looking toward monotheism and the other toward pantheism. The clearest expression of the pantheistic point of view is found in the celebrated hymn to *Puruṣa*[2], X. 90, which in the words of Macdonell constitutes 'the starting-point of the pantheistic philosophy of India'[3].

1. A thousand heads has Puruṣa,
A thousand eyes, a thousand feet;
He holding earth enclosed about,
Extends beyond, ten fingers length.

2. Whatever is, is Puruṣa,
Both what has been and what shall be;
He ruleth the immortal world,
Which he transcends through sacred food.

3. As great as this is Puruṣa,
Yet greater still his greatness is;
All creatures are one-fourth of him,
Three-fourths th' immortal in the heaven.

4. Three-fourths ascended up on high,
One-fourth came into being here;

---

[1] This squabbling may be only the mythological rendering of natural happenings, such as the thunderstorm's darkening of the sky, blotting out of the sun, and spoiling of the dawn. But the language of primitive myth is sooner or later taken seriously and then the mischief is done, for through the myth is promulgated an unethical conception of God.

[2] Indebtedness is due to the translations of Macdonell, Hillebrandt, Griffith, Scherman (PH. 11-23) and Deussen (AGP. 150-158).

[3] VRS. 195.

Thence he developed into what
Is animate and inanimate.

5. From Puruṣa was born Virāj,
And from Virāj sprang Puruṣa;
When born he reached beyond the earth,
Forward and backward everywhere.

6. When gods performed a sacrifice
With Puruṣa as their offering,
Spring was its oil and Summer-heat
Its fuel, its oblation Fall.

7. As sacrifice upon the straw
They sprinkled Puruṣa ancient-born;
With him the Devas sacrificed,
The Sādhyas and the Riṣis too.

8. From that completely-offered rite
Was gathered up the clotted oil;
It formed the creatures of the air,
And animals both wild and tame.

9. From that completely-offered rite
Ṛicas and Sāma-chants were born;
The metręs too were born from that,
And all the Yajus-formulæ.

10. From that were horses born and all
The beasts that have two rows of teeth;
Cattle were also born from that,
And from that sprang the goats and sheep.

11. Then they dismembered Puruṣa:
How many portions did they make?
What was his mouth called, what his arms,
What his two thighs, and what his feet?

12. His mouth became the *Brāhmaṇa*,
And his two arms the *Kṣatriya;*
His thighs became the *Vaiśya*-class,
And from his feet the *Śūdra* sprang.

13. The Moon was gendered from his mind,
And from his eye the Sun was born;
Indra and Agni from his mouth,
And Vāyu from his breath was born.

14. Forth from his navel came the air,
And from his head evolved the sky;
Earth from his feet and from his ear
The quarters: thus they framed the worlds.

15. Seven sticks confined the altar-fire,
Thrice-seven sticks as fuel served,
When gods performing sacrifice
Bound as their victim Puruṣa.

16. With sacrifice the gods made sacrifices,
These sacred usages were thus primeval;
These mighty powers attained unto the heavens,
Where are the Deities, the ancient Sādhyas.

The *Puruṣa-Sūkta* is one of the latest hymns of the Ṛv. It alone mentions the four orders or castes (v. 12) and the three Vedas, if not all four (v. 9). At the same time its fundamental conception, namely the genesis of the world through the sacrificial dismemberment of the world-giant Puruṣa, is very archaic[1]. Puruṣa, 'Man', is declared to be whatever is, has been, or shall be (v. 2), the clearest statement of pantheism in the Ṛv. The unity of the world, then, is found in the conception of a Cosmic Man, and its multiplicity is traced to the sacrificial dismemberment of the same. The gods performed the sacrifice (vv. 6-7, 15), although it looks as if they at the same time were regarded (rather inconsistently) as the result of the sacrifice (v. 13). The *motif* is the primeval custom of human sacrifice, while the central place of sacrifice in the cosmic order and the subordinate position assigned to the *devas* approximates to the point of view of the Brāhmaṇas. Both monism and polytheism exist side by side, as in later Hinduism — the monism of the all-embracing Puruṣa and the polytheism of the devas. The key to the solution of the mystery of things is found in the conception of the whole of nature as a living organism, the body of an original Puruṣa 'Man' or 'Spirit', involving therefore a spiritual interpretation of the universe. The line of thought found in this hymn is prophetic of the great monistic doctrine of *Bráhman-Ātman,* the central doctrine of the Upaniṣads and of the later Vedānta philosophy.

---

[1] Compare the similar myth of the world-giant *Ymir* in Scandinavian mythology.

f) Monotheism[1]. — A true and consistent theism ever presents itself as an ethical monotheism. Varuṇa represented the nearest approach in Vedic India to the doctrine of monotheism, and Varuṇa was *par excellence* the ethical god of the Ṛv. This is no accident but a principle that widely rules. For example, the Zoroastrian reform was at once monotheistic and ethical. The Gāthās put no greater emphasis upon the uniqueness of Ahura Mazda than upon the supremacy of the moral law. The monotheism of the O. T. Prophets was set in a context of stern ethical teaching. And the distinct ethical advance[2] of the New Testament accompanied the enrichment of the O. T. doctrine of God. Even the derivative[3] monotheism of Muhammad was closely bound up with the fierce proclamation of such morality as he understood and appreciated. But while there can be no true theism that is not ethical, there may, of course, be important ethical developments, which are more or less divorced from the thought of God[4].

The development of an ethical monotheism presupposes the work of a prophet or prophets[5]. It was so in ancient Israel as well as in ancient Irān; it also proved true in the rise of Muhammadanism. In each of these monotheisms the uniqueness of God is emphasized. Yahweh is the 'one' God of Israel[6]. Ahura Mazda, the 'Wise Lord' of Zoroaster, is a unity, although his nature is explicated by the Amesha Spentas, his six or seven attributes or functions[7]. The Allāh of Muhammad is *lā-sharīk* 'without associate'. There were priests and hymn-writers in the Ṛigvedic period, but no moralists of the type of Zoroaster and Buddha. If we

---

[1] See Macnicol, *Indian Theism*.

[2] *Cf.* the Sermon on the Mount, Matt. V-VII.

[3] Essentially Judaic and Rabbinical.

[4] *E. g.* those connected with the names of Confucius, Buddha and Socrates.

[5] This holds true also of certain theistic societies of modern India, such as the Brāhma Samāj founded by Keshab Chander Sen, and the Ārya Samāj founded by Dayānand Sarasvatī.

[6] Deut. VI. 4.

[7] See Moulton, TM. 21-35; v. Schroeder, AR. 282.

say (as we must) that the penitential hymns addressed to Varuṇa are the work of men who had something of the spiritual insight of true prophets, we are also compelled to say that the prophetic succession soon ceased. Varuṇa from being almost a Ṛigvedic Yahweh and an ethical counterpart of Ahura Mazda gradually dwindled into a godling of lakes and pools; and at the same time the sublime conception of *Ṛita,* 'Moral Order', vanished or was swallowed up in the notion of *Karma.* The spiritual tragedy of the waning of Varuṇa and of the collapse of Vedic monotheism must not, however, blind us to the significance of the appearance in the Ṛigvedic age of the conception of a holy god. The Varuṇa hymns, so Hebraic and penitential in quality, bear witness to the theistic capacity of the Vedic Indians[1].

We must distinguish between an ethical and a speculative monotheism. Varuṇa came very near being the god of an ethical monotheism. As an example of a speculative monotheism, one may cite the *Hiraṇyagarbha-Prajāpati* Hymn[2].

To the Unknown God. X. 121.

1. The Golden Germ arose in the beginning,
Born the sole lord of everything existing;
He fixed and holdeth up this earth and heaven,—
Who is the god to worship with oblation?[3]

2. He who gives breath and strength, he whose commandment
All beings follow, yea the gods acknowledge;
Whose shadow immortality and death is,—
Who is the god to worship with oblation?

3. He who through greatness hath become sole monarch
Of all the moving world that breathes and slumbers;

---

[1] Macnicol, IT. 24.

[2] For the translation compare Hillebrandt, LR. 132-133; Deussen, AGP. 128-134; Scherman, PH. 24-29; Griffith, HR. 566-567, and Griswold, *Brahman* 25-26.

[3] Or, according to the later interpretation '*Ka*' (i. e. 'Who') is the god to worship with oblation; in other words, Let us worship with oblation the god 'Who', i. e. the unknown god.

Who ruleth over quadrupeds and bipeds,—
Who is the god to worship with oblation?

4. The one to whom through might these snowy mountains
Belong, the sea with Rasā, as men tell us;
To whom belong these quarters and the two arms,—
Who is the god to worship with oblation?

5. He through whom sky is firm and earth is steady,
Through whom sun's light and heaven's vault are supported;
Who in mid-air is measurer of the spaces,—
Who is the god to worship with oblation?

6. He to whom look the rival hosts in battle,
Sustained by his support and anxious-hearted,
When over them the risen sun is shining,—
Who is the god to worship with oblation?

7. What time the mighty waters came containing
Everything germinal, producing Agni,
Thence there arose of all the gods the one life,—
Who is the god to worship with oblation?

8. He who in might surveyed the floods containing
Creative force, the sacrifice producing;
Who 'mid all gods has been and is alone god,—
Who is the god to worship with oblation?

9. Ne'er may he harm us, he earth's generator,
He who with order true begat the heaven,
And gendered, too, the bright and mighty waters,—
Who is the god to worship with oblation?

10. Prajāpati, apart from thee no other
Hath all these things embraced and comprehended;
May that be ours which we desire when off'ring
Worship to thee; may we be lords of riches.

Hiraṇyagarbha means 'the golden germ'. It is described as having generated the waters which contain creative force and everything germinal and which produce fire and sacrifice (vv. 7-9). In vv. 6-7 Sūrya and Agni are mentioned, and the whole hymn is rightly regarded as composed in imitation of the *Sajanāsa* hymn[1] to Indra (II. 12). Thus the reference is apparently to fire in its different forms as constituting the one life (*asu* v. 7) of the gods. There

[1] So Deussen, AGP. 128; and Oldenberg, Ṛv. Noten II. 341.

is emphasis upon the *uniqueness*[1] of the one who alone is worthy of adoration. He is described as the one god above the gods, as the one life of the gods, and as the one creator and ruler of all that is; and finally he is identified with *Prajāpati*[2], the personification of the creative activity of nature. In X. 121, 10 Prajāpati, as Macdonell says[3] is clearly 'the name of the supreme god'. But Prajāpati is simply the apotheosis of the notion of creative activity and seems to be identical with the generative Agni. His cosmic significance is set forth in noble terms, but in no passage of the Ṛv. is Prajāpati connected with the ethical. Thus the ethical monotheism of Varuṇa is succeeded by a speculative monism, which halts between monotheism and pantheism. Prajāpati fits into a pantheistic scheme almost as well as Puruṣa; and with neither Puruṣa nor Prajāpati is polytheism[4] inconsistent. That is to say, in the Ṛv. polytheism, pantheism and monotheism exist side by side in unstable equilibrium, a condition of things which is reproduced through the whole history of Hinduism[5].

---

[1] *Eka* 'one', 'sole', vv. 1, 3, 7, 8, 10. We are reminded of the uniqueness of Indra as expressed so often by the same word *eka*.

[2] Prajāpati 'lord of creatures' appears twice in the Ṛv. as an epithet of Savitar (IV. 53, 2) and of Soma (IX. 5, 9); and in the tenth book, four times as a distinct deity, who became the chief god of the Brāhmaṇa period.

[3] VM. 118.

[4] *Cf.* X. 90, 6, 13, 16; 121, 7.

[5] There are, it is true, certain theistic sects in modern India which reject polytheism and pantheism, such as the Brāhma, Ārya and Prārthanā Samājas. These, however, do not represent the dominant tendency of Hindu thinking, nor is it certain that they will permanently resist the tremendous pull of orthodox Hinduism. It is to be remembered that Hinduism assimilated Indian Buddhism to itself.

CHAPTER XIII.

THE FULFILMENT OF THE RELIGION OF THE ṚIGVEDA

1. Ṛigvedic religion, as we have seen, belongs most probably to the period B. C. 1500-500[1]. The proper comparison, then, is between Vedic religion and Hebrew religion as roughly contemporary. The origins of both are similar. Vedic religion is rooted in the polytheistic nature-worship of the pre-historic IE. world, and Hebrew religion is likewise preceded by the polytheistic customs and institutions of the pre-historic Semitic world[2]. A truly ethical—which is also a truly spiritual—conception of God is difficult to attain, and even when attained, is difficult to maintain. Something of the struggle and agony involved can be seen by reading the Gāthās of Zoroaster, the prophets of the Old Testament, the Apostolic writings of the New Testament, and the Qurān of Muhammad. Ethical monotheism ever began as an unpalatable doctrine, and the prophets and teachers thereof have had to suffer. The tendency has been stubborn toward reaction. Nominal monotheism has not infrequently been made really polytheistic, for example in Zoroastrianism through the counter-reformation of the Younger Avesta which restored so many of the old daēvas, and in Roman Christianity as well as in Islām through the adoration of saints. The great catastrophe of the Babylonian Exile (B. C. 586) alone cured Israel of polytheism and idolatry; for only those returned from the exile who were really loyal to the prophetic doctrine of the one holy God.

2. During the period of early Hebrew history (up to B. C. 586) the monotheism of the prophets was in unstable equilibrium. Its advocates were nearly always in the

---

[1] Or reducing the time-limit by 500, B. C. 1300 to 800. Macdonell, HR. 7.

[2] *Cf.* Robertson Smith's *Fundamental Religious Institutions of the Semites*; also Gen. XXXI. 19, XXXV. 2, Joshua XXIV. 2.

minority, fighting against heavy odds. Besides this, the early Hebrew theism itself was more henotheistic than monotheistic, in the sense that the reality of the gods of other peoples was apparently recognised. As already pointed out, an impartial collection of religious lyrics during the pre-exile period would doubtless have contained almost as miscellaneous and polytheistic a collection as is found in the Ṛv. Yahweh, like Varuṇa, might have stood in the midst of a multitude of other gods. These considerations help to place early Vedic religion more on an equality with early Hebrew religion. As the prophetic doctrine of Yahweh, the one holy god of Israel, was the ethical and spiritual kernel of Hebrew religion, so the doctrine of Varuṇa held the same place in Ṛigvedic religion. Some fundamental elements of true religion may, indeed, be taught by the coarsest polytheism, for example, the existence, power, manifestation and wonder-working of God; His grace and helpfulness and care for His own; His working in nature and in history; communion with Him in this life and in the life to come. There is much raw material on all these points, found throughout the Ṛv. in hymns to the most varied gods. The same thing holds true of the polytheism of the Semitic world. Every deity even of the most chaotic polytheism is, as it were, an organization of the idea of God. But as already remarked (p. 87), only the god of an ethical and exclusive monotheism possesses personality in the fullest sense, that is a personality worthy of the infinite and eternal God.

We have in the Ṛigvedic pantheon a chaos of deities imperfectly personalized, shading into one another, indefinite in outline, and tending to fusion. If the process of fusion had been brought to a climax, all the gods would have been amalgamated together into one God. Against this process was the fact that as soon as one god disappeared, another took his place. The waxing and waning of the gods ever went on, the processes counterbalancing each other, so that the pantheon was always full. It is true, some of the chief gods such as Varuṇa and Indra greatly excel others in completeness of personification; nevertheless, not even these are fully personalized. For if we define perfect personality as an infinite and exclusive personality, in other words, such a personality as is to be found only on monotheistic premisses[1], then it is clear that not even Varuṇa can be pronounced completely personalized, since he is confronted with other gods.

Then, too, as stated above, the ethical character even more than the exclusive character of a monotheism is what contributes supremely to the personality of deity. Of all the Ṛigvedic gods ethical quality belongs supremely to Varuṇa. There is a distinct lack of the ethical except in the Varuṇa hymns, not of course that it is altogether absent elsewhere but that no adequate place is given to it. It is not a central conception in the Ṛv. as a whole. The truth of this is supported by the testimony of Deussen, himself, an ardent admirer of things Indian, to the effect that the ethical element, in which the real worth of a religion lies, falls in the Ṛigveda surprisingly into the shade[2].

This contrast between Varuṇa and the other Ṛigvedic gods is highly significant. It means that in the earliest period of the Ṛv. there was present a worthy candidate for the honours of an ethical and exclusive monotheism. Such a monotheism in ancient Israel was the result of a stern struggle on the part of the prophets against the Baalīm and all the other gods of the kindred Semitic tribes. The Gāthās of Zoroaster reveal the ethical stress and strain which he passed through before the daēvas were cast out of heaven and Ahura Mazda exalted to the supreme place. Muhammad had something of the same experience during the Mecca period, when, with his back to the wall, he battled heroically against the adversaries of Allāh most high. But

[1] See p. 87.

[2] AGP. 82.

a similarly strenuous ethical temper seems to have been lacking during the Ṛigvedic period, or at least to have come to large fruition only in the circles that produced the Varuṇa hymns. Varuṇa[1] had nearly all the righteousness and the other *devas* had what was left. So Varuṇa ought to have been exalted, and the other devas, as in Irān, ought to have been dethroned.

3. In Chapter XII the Ṛigveda was brought into relation with later Hindu developments. It was there shown that there are many things in the Ṛv.—literary, artistic, social, philosophical and religious—that are fulfilled in the later history of Hinduism. The question arises: Is there anything in the Ṛv. in the way of ideal or aspiration that is not thus taken up in Hinduism (that is, adequately), but rather still awaits satisfaction and fulfilment? To answer this question we must turn our attention again to the majestic figure of Varuṇa. Here we meet with a series of truly ethical ideas—the conception of the holy will of Varuṇa and of sin as a transgression of his law; the conception of morality as of the inmost nature of things[2] and of Varuṇa as the august witness of the deeds of men; the sense of sin gained through the pressure of disease and affliction, and the consciousness that fellowship with Varuṇa can be broken; confession of sin to Varuṇa and prayer for deliverance; and the experience of Varuṇa's mercy and grace as followed by 'slave-like devotion'[3] on the part of the sinner. It is, of course, not easy, when interpreting these ancient records, to avoid falling into 'the psychologist's fallacy'[4], for one is doubtless often tempted to press unduly

---

[1] Including, of course, the Ādityas, who simply explicated his many-sided personality.

[2] "Avestan Ahura Mazda and Vedic Varuṇa are the guardians-in-chief of the *ṛta*, the cosmic and moral order of the universe and man".—Bloomfield. RV. 232.

[3] *Cf.* Chapter V. Varuṇa the Ethical God.

[4] That is, "reading one's own mind into that of another man without making due allowance for differences of innate capacity and of acquired outlook". R. R. Marett, *Psychology and Folklore*, London, 1919, p. 228.

such resemblances in phraseology as seem to connect Ṛigvedic penitential experiences with analogous Hebrew and Christian experiences. Nevertheless, the consensus of the best modern scholarship definitely confirms the view that Varuṇa and the Ādityas, whatever the reasons may be, stand in an ethical group by themselves. For example, the late Prof. Oldenberg was so impressed with the ethical tone of the hymns to Varuṇa and the Ādityas that he, for this and other reasons, regarded them as a group of loan-gods derived from the Semitic world[1]. Macdonell[2] asserts that 'there is no hymn to Varuṇa (and the Ādityas) in which the prayer for forgiveness of guilt does not occur'. And according to Bloomfield[3] 'Vedic Varuṇa in his ethical strength has a Hebraic flavour'. To realize the full justice of these statements it is necessary only to read the Varuṇa hymns translated in Chap. V above, and to compare them with such Psalms as XXXII and LI, and with such passages of the New Testament as the incident of the Sinful Woman, and the parable of the Lost Son and of the Pharisee and Publican[4]. From these comparisons we see how near Varuṇa came to being a Ṛigvedic Yahweh, 'full of compassion and gracious, slow to anger and plenteous in mercy'[5]. It is not too much to say with Bloomfield[6] that "by the side of even the loftiest figure and the loftiest traits of the Hellenic or Teutonic Pantheon[7] Varuṇa stands like a Jewish prophet by the side of a priest of Dagon". "And yet," as Bloomfield asks, "what permanent moral strength have the Hindus derived from Varuṇa[8]? Very little *as yet,* it must be admitted. The lofty conception of Varuṇa may have

---

[1] RV. 195.
[2] VM. 27.
[3] RV. 232.
[4] Luke VII. 36-50; XV. 11-32; XVIII. 9-14.
[5] Exodus XXXIV. 6.
[6] RV. 232.
[7] One might also add: and of the other Ṛigvedic gods.
[8] RV. 232.

influenced the formation or development of the various local and shifting theisms[1] of India; but, on the whole, it is true that Varuṇa "has left no really lasting impression on India's religions[2]". He has been able neither to furnish the germ and starting point of a truly catholic Indian monotheism, nor even himself to survive in any worthwhile fashion. The pantheistic monism[3] of the later Ṛigvedic period continued to wax stronger and stronger, while the figure of Varuṇa went on waning, until there was nothing left of him, but a godling of lakes and pools, a kind of second-rate Neptune, de-ethicised and almost depersonalized. In the struggle between the notion of a personal and holy God and that of an impersonal and non-moral world-ground, the victory lay decidedly with the latter. *Brahma* mounted up into the splendour, while Varuṇa sank into 'the twilight of the gods'. "If Varuṇa had prevailed, India would have become monotheistic and theocratic, which it never did"[4]. So much for past history, but what of the future? That in the past the impersonal and non-moral *brahma* has gained the pre-eminence over the personal and moral Varuṇa proves nothing certain for the future. The odds will doubtless finally be on the side of the truer conception, whichever that may be.

One may assume that the truer conception is represented by Varuṇa, for there is set forth in him a lofty monotheistic and ethical ideal,—an ideal, too, which though sorely needed, has up to the present time never been adequately realized in India, but still awaits satisfaction and fulfilment. What if the conception of the Ṛigvedic Varuṇa, whose 'Hebraic flavour' is so generally recognised

[1] As an instance of a 'local and shifting' theism the *Deva Samāj* may be mentioned. The founder began as a Brāhma Samāj theist, continued in this attitude for some years after leaving the Brāhma Samāj, and finally abandoned theism altogether. See Farquhar, MRMI. 173 ff.

[2] Bloomfield, RV. 200.

[3] Pantheistic for the literati, polytheistic for the multitude.

[4] Bloomfield, RV. 200.

by scholars, should finally be completed and fulfilled by that of 'the God of Abraham, Isaac and Jacob', 'the God and Father of the Lord Jesus Christ'?

Nor is this all of ancient ideal and aspiration that still challenges and awaits fulfilment. Bound up with the conception of Varuṇa is that of *Ṛita,* 'eternal order'. Over against the later speculative idea of the world as the result of *karman* and as essentially *māyā,* there is here presented, at least occasionally, the notion of the 'course' and 'order' of things as the product of the will (*vrata*) of Varuṇa. Thus the Ṛigvedic conception of the holy will of Varuṇa points forward to, and stands ready to coalesce with, the New Testament conception of the holy will of God.

Still another ancient conception is profoundly significant, that of the group of Ādityas and Amesha Spentas. As the (sevenfold) Amesha Spentas simply explicate the nature of Ahura Mazda, so do the (sevenfold) Ādityas the nature of Varuṇa. This unity in sevenfold diversity[1] on the part of both Amesha Spentas and Ādityas is suggestive of the difference between underlying essence and hypostatic division. Aditi, the mother of the Ādityas, seems to express the common nature of the Āditya-group.

Along with this must be mentioned the triad of Sūrya in heaven, Agni on earth, and Vāyu or Indra in the mid-air, corresponding to the threefold Vedic division of the universe. According to this scheme the 33 or 33,000,000 gods all reduce to three. These three have a common fiery nature, Sūrya 'sun', Indra 'lightning' and Agni 'fire'. Agni is a 'descent' (*avatāra*), having been brought from heaven to earth by the lightning and wind. Sūrya is the 'eye' or theophany of Varuṇa and Agni is his earthly counterpart and representative. If Varuṇa occupies ethically the highest place in Ṛigvedic religion, Agni

[1] "The seven Spirits" before the throne of God in Rev. I. 4 seem, in like manner, simply to explicate the unity of the one Spirit after the analogy of Isa. XI. 2.

stands next to him. Agni, while heavenly in origin, is a dweller among men. He is represented as a messenger between earth and heaven, as a mediator between gods and men, as a great high priest, the divine and heavenly counterpart of the earthly priesthood, as the one who intercedes with Varuṇa on behalf of sinners—a thing rendered possible because of his close connection with Varuṇa, and as the one who himself forgives sin and makes men guiltless before Aditi[1]. We cannot but recall the New Testament description of the Lord Jesus Christ[2]. Thus the two most ethical gods of the Ṛv., Varuṇa in heaven and Agni his counterpart and in a sense his *avatāra* on earth, are both represented not only as righteous[3] themselves, but also as making men righteous through the putting away of their sin and guilt. Other Ṛigvedic gods, it is true, are represented as forgiving sin, but only incidentally and casually, whereas this is the essential function of Varuṇa and (to a lesser degree) of Agni. It is a striking fact that the most ethical gods of the Ṛv. are just the ones who are most concerned with the forgiveness of sin. When ultimate reality came to be conceived later as an impersonal and non-moral world-ground, then there was no place for forgiveness, but only for the mechanical working of the principle of retribution.

Soma represents another 'descent' from heaven, coming

---

[1] See Chapter VI. Agni the Priestly God.

[2] Christ is described as:—

(a) The Son of God. Matt. XVI. 16; Acts IX. 20, etc.

(b) Heavenly in origin and nature, John III. 13; 1 Cor. XV. 47.

(c) Dwelling among men. John I. 14.

(d) Messenger between heaven and earth. John I. 51.

(e) A great High Priest. Heb. III. 1; V. 1-10, etc.

(f) Mediator between God and man. Heb. XII. 24; 1 Tim. II. 5.

(g) Intercessor with God for men. Luke XXIII. 34 (text not quite certain); Rom. VIII. 34.

(h) One who was manifested to take away sin, and Himself forgives sin. Mark II. 10; Luke VII. 47-49.

[3] *ṛitāvan*, 'orderly', 'order-loving'.

down in the form of rain, entering the Soma plant, and becoming the Soma juice, the drink of immortality. Thus, like Agni, Soma is heavenly in origin, but earthly in habitat. Certain points of contact between the ritual of the Soma sacrifice and the Christian ritual of Holy Communion[1] might have been indicated. Both Agni and Soma, the two Ṛigvedic 'descents' were originally the personification and apotheosis of the natural elements 'fire' and 'soma juice'. Before long they were conceived anthropomorphically as gods in the likeness of men. As such they were thought of as descending from heaven in order to dwell in the midst of humanity.

The triple character of Agni as celestial, terrestrial, and atmospheric, constitutes the earliest Indian triad. This is the basis of the post-Vedic resolution of all the gods into forms of only three gods, which constitute a kind of spatial trinity, Sūrya, the fire of the sky, Agni, the fire of earth, and Indra the fire of the mid-air. Vāyu, 'Wind', is associated with Indra or even made alternative with him. Soma, the *amṛit* of the skies, descends to earth in connection with the lightning and wind. Both Vāyu and Soma have points of contact with the Christian doctrine of the Holy Spirit. On the day of Pentecost (Acts II. 1-4) the descent of the Holy Spirit was marked by the rushing of a mighty wind, by flames of fire, and by a strange and supernatural exhilaration, in Ṛigvedic parlance by a manifestation of Vāyu, Indra and Soma. The two early triads[2], the Ṛigvedic triad of the three forms of Agni, and the more explicit

---

[1] Chap. VIII. 231.

[2] Compare the following triads in Egypt and Babylonia:

1. *Egypt.*

a. Thebes:	*Amon*	'father',	*Mut*	'mother',	*Montu*	'Son'.
b. Memphis:	*Ptah*	,,	*Sekhet*	,,	*Imhotep*	,,
c. Abydos:	*Osiris*	,,	*Isis*	,,	*Horus*	,,

2. *Babylonia.*

a. *Anu*	'sky'	*Enlil*	'earth and atmosphere',	*Ea*	'waters on and below earth'.
b. *Sin*	'moon',	*Shamash*	'sun',	*Ishtar*	'goddess of love.'

post-Vedic triad of Sūrya, Agni and Indra (or Vāyu), were anticipations of the later Hindu doctrine of the *Trimūrti,* Brahmā, Śiva and Viṣṇu. One is reminded of the Christian Trinity. In all of these triads alike the Hegelian law of the three stages seems to hold good—the law of thesis, antithesis and synthesis. Thus the two early triads consist of a heavenly fire as thesis, an earthly fire as antithesis, and the atmospheric fire of the lightning as the union or synthesis of the two. Brahmā as creator is the thesis, Śiva as destroyer is the antithesis, and Viṣṇu as preserver (at once creating and destroying) is the synthesis. In like manner, as regards the Christian Trinity, God the Father is the thesis, the Son is the antithesis and the Holy Spirit belonging to and proceeding from both the Father and the Son is the synthesis. We may find a real anticipation of, and a preparation for, the Christian doctrine of the Trinity in the Ṛigvedic conception of Varuṇa, Agni and Soma, since Varuṇa, like God the Father, is heavenly, while Agni and Soma, like the Son and the Holy Spirit, are 'descents' from heaven to earth. Such points of contact must not be over-emphasized. Nevertheless the real fulfilment of the Ṛigvedic conception of the holy and sin-pardoning Varuṇa, of the sacrificial and high-priestly Agni and of Soma the divine exhilaration and draught of immortality, is to be found in the Christian doctrine of the Father, Son and Holy Spirit, rather than in the later Hindu conception of Brahmā, Śiva and Viṣṇu.[1] But even the Trimūrti may be made to yield something worth comparing with the Christian Trinity. Brahmā, like God the Father, is conceived as Creator. Śiva is the Sannyāsi and ascetic god. We are reminded of Him who "emptied Himself, taking the form of a servant"[2], who "though he

---

[1] It looks as if the *Trimūrti* simply gathered up the chief Hindu cult-objects, Brahmā representing the earlier Vedic worship, and Viṣṇu and Śiva the two 'great sectarian cults' of the later age.

[2] Phil. II. 7.

was rich, yet for our sakes became poor"[1], and who "had not where to lay His head"[2]. Thus the fulness of creative activity and the emptiness of renunciation are expressed both by the Hindu Brahmā and Śiva and by the Christian Father and Son. The Vaiṣṇava cult has ever expressed itself in joy and ecstasy, in dance and song. We are reminded that "the fruit of the Spirit is.........joy"[3], and that those that are "filled with the Spirit" speak one to another "in psalms and hymns and spiritual songs.[4]

In the Tiruvāśagam[5] even a vicarious activity is ascribed to Śiva, as set forth in the well-known lines:

> "Thou mad'st me thine; did'st fiery poison eat, pitying poor souls,
> That I might thine ambrosia taste,—I, meanest one".

This is suggestive of the Cross and passion of the Lord Jesus Christ, who became poor that we through His poverty might become rich[6], who died that we through His death might be made alive for evermore[7]. The question arises whether there is any conception in the Ṛv. of suffering for mankind on the part of deity. There is, indeed, the sacrifice of *Puruṣa*[8], the cosmic man, from whom the whole creation is said to have sprung. Rev. K. M. Banerjea[9] makes much of this as having affinity with the Christian doctrine of the sacrifice of the Lord Jesus Christ. But, while the Lord Jesus went to His sacrificial death with full consciousness and definite purpose, it is difficult to think of Puruṣa as more than a symbol of pantheistic unity without personal consciousness or power

[1] 2 Cor. VIII. 9.

[2] Luke IX. 58.

[3] Gal. V. 22.

[4] Eph. V. 19.

[5] Of Mānikka Vāśagar, Pope's ed., p. 195. See Macnicol, IT. 175.

[6] 2 Cor. VIII. 9.

[7] Heb. II. 9.

[8] X. 90.

[9] AW. 10.

of choice. Thus conscious self-sacrifice on behalf of another has a profoundly ethical quality[1] which can hardly be ascribed to the sacrifice of Puruṣa, unless that be regarded as a voluntary act of self-emptying for the sake of the universe, Puruṣa dying, as it were, in order that the whole world might come into being. While, then, the *Puruṣa-sūkta* might suggest the sacrifice of some one having the central cosmic significance of *Puruṣa,* there is nevertheless no adequate reason for taking Puruṣa to be more than a symbol covering all that is, and so essentially pantheistic. At most the term Puruṣa 'man' and the thought of an eternal sacrifice might be regarded as pointing dimly in the direction of "the Lamb slain from the foundation of the world"[2].

In X. 13, 4 occurs a passage[3] which may possibly be translated as follows:

> He, for Gods' sake chose death to be his portion:
> He chose not, for men's sake a life eternal.
> ....
> Yama delivered up his own dear body.
> (Griffith after Ludwig and Grassmann.)

If this is a correct translation, the reference may be to a voluntary and sacrificial death on the part of Yama, in order to open up for gods and men a path to heaven. Yama might have had a life eternal upon earth, but he chose death and gave up his body for the sake of others. We are reminded of the Lord Jesus Christ, who laid down His life for His own[4], rose again from the dead[5], became 'the first fruits of them that are asleep'[6], and thus 'opened the kingdom of heaven to all believers'.

Animal sacrifices were offered in connection with the

---

[1] John XV. 13.

[2] Rev. XIII. 8.

[3] See Chap. XI. 326.

[4] John X. 15-18.

[5] 1 Cor. XV. 3-8.

[6] 1 Cor. XV. 20.

Ṛigvedic ritual[1]. Besides the sacrifice of bulls[2], buffaloes[3] and goats[4] there was the horse-sacrifice[5] and possibly even human sacrifice[6]. If in the Levitical legislation the blood of 'goats and bulls' (Heb. IX. 13) may be regarded as pointing forward to 'the blood of Christ' (id. v. 14), is it too much to take the bloody offerings of the Ṛigveda as having the same reference and fulfilment? Thus both Hebraic and Ṛigvedic sacrifices may be regarded as 'a shadow of the good things to come' (Heb. X. 1), as types and symbols of the sacrifice of 'the Lamb of God that taketh away the sin of the world' (John I. 29)[7].

In connection with the animal sacrifices of the Ṛv. mention must be made of the *yūpa* or *vanaspati,* the sacrificial 'post' or 'tree'[8]. This is the post to which the animal designated for sacrifice was tied. The sacrifice communicated its sanctity to the post, which also like fire-sticks, press-stones, and other accessories of the divine, received a kind of apotheosis. With the praise of the *Sacrificial Post* to which the animal victim was bound, we may compare the praise of the *Cross,* often called 'the Tree':

'In the Cross of Christ I glory'.
'When I survey the wondrous Cross,
On which the Prince of glory died!'

Again, as the sacrificial post carried with it (in the thought of the Vedic Indians) the gift of wealth, children, splendour, blessing, victory (Ṛv. III. 8), so the Cross of Christ (in the experience of the ages) has meant health, wealth, knowledge

---

[1] See Oldenberg, RV. 355-366.

[2] X. 28, 3; 27, 2; 86, 14.

[3] V. 29, 7; VI. 17, 11.

[4] I. 162, 2-4.

[5] I. 162-163; IV. 38, 39, 40.

[6] *Cf.* the legend of *Śunahśepa* I. 24, 12-13.

[7] *Cf.* Phillips, TV. 225.

[8] Ṛv. III. 8 is addressed to the deified Sacrificial Post (*Yūpa*); and its synonym *Vanaspati*, 'Sacrificial Tree', occurs in each of the ten *Āprī* hymns.

efficiency, the freeing of the slave, the prohibition of the drink curse, etc., for these things are found wherever God in Christ is best known. And in addition to these temporal by-products of the sacrificial death of the Lord Jesus Christ, there is the supreme experience of 'the forgiveness of sin' and 'the peace of God which passeth all understanding'.

4. The most striking points of contact between Ṛigvedic doctrine and Hebrew and Christian doctrine are undoubtedly to be found in the field of *eschatology*[1]. There is drawn in the Ṛv. the ethical distinction between the righteous and the wicked both in character and in destiny. The righteous at death go to the heaven of Yama, a place of blessedness unspeakable, while the wicked are cast into a dark and bottomless pit. So in the Bible Heaven is described as a place of 'fulness of joy' and of 'pleasures for evermore'; a place of 'glory', a state of 'eternal life', a 'kingdom prepared from the foundation of the world'; a place prepared for the redeemed in the 'many mansions' of the 'Father's house', where they will be received by Christ, and will enjoy His fellowship for ever[2]. Similarly Hell is described in the Bible as a condition of 'shame and everlasting contempt'; a state of punishment consisting of 'outer darkness', of 'the eternal fire prepared for the devil and his angels', and of 'the weeping and the gnashing of teeth', the state of those 'for whom the blackness of darkness hath been reserved for ever.'[3].

Both the Ṛigveda and the Bible set forth the luminous nature and environment of the life of the blessed dead. The Vedic paradise or 'sun-home of the soul' is situated in the lap of the ruddy dawns, or in the highest step of Viṣṇu, the place of the sun at the zenith. There the blessed dead have bodies which are congruous with their

[1] pp. 314 ff. and 319 ff.

[2] Ps. XVI. 11; LXXIII. 24; Dan. XII. 2; Matt. XXV. 34, 46; John XIV. 2-3.

[3] Dan. XII. 2; Matt. XXV. 30, 41, 46; Jude 13.

environment. Likewise both in the O. T. and the N. T. the 'righteous' and 'they that turn many to righteousness' are described as 'shining forth as the sun in the Kingdom of their Father', 'shining as the brightness of the firmament', and 'as the stars for ever and ever'[1].

According to both the Ṛv. and the N. T. the blessed dead are furnished in the heavenly world with bodies suitable to their new environment. As the Vedic saint put on a heavenly body, by implication luminous and glorified, so he put off all the blemishes and imperfections of the earthly body[2]. According to the New Testament the transfigured Christ, His face shining like the sun and His garments being white as the light, was the pledge and pattern of the glorified state of the believer. The promises of Scripture all point to this, 'the body of our humiliation' being destined to be 'conformed to the body of His glory'. It was the conviction of the Apostle Paul that 'as we have borne the image of the earthly, we shall also bear the image of the heavenly', and that 'if the earthly house of our tabernacle (*i. e.* our bodily frame) be dissolved, we have a building from God, a house not made with hands, eternal in the heavens'; and the normal Christian attitude was defined by him as 'waiting for our adoption, to wit, the redemption of the body'[3].

Finally, in both the *Ṛigveda* and the Bible there is set forth the blessedness of the Divine presence and fellowship. According to the Ṛv. the sainted dead behold Yama and Varuṇa and commune with the heavenly ones in the realms of light[4]. The O. T. pictures the state of the blessed dead as one in which they shall behold God's face in righteousness and shall be satisfied, He being the strength of their

---

[1] Dan. XII. 3; Matt. XIII. 43.

[2] p. 314 *ff.*

[3] Matt. XVII. 2; Phil. III. 21; 1 Cor. XV. 49; 2 Cor. V. 1; Rom. VIII. 23.

[4] X. 14, 7, 10; 56, 1. See p. 314 ff.

heart and their portion for ever[1]. The N.T. picture is essentially the same. The blessed dead are to be where Christ is, in the place which He has prepared for them. They shall see Him even as He is and be like Him.[2]. A note of yearning is heard in Paul's desire 'to depart and be with Christ'[3].

The points of contact between the Ṛigvedic and the Biblical eschatology are thus very striking. We note in the Vedic doctrine of the future life a further 'Hebraic flavour' in addition to that of the penitential hymns. In proportion as the description of the Ṛigvedic paradise approximate to that of the Biblical picture of the future state of the redeemed, it is clear that it diverges from the doctrine of transmigration as held in the later Hindu eschatology.

5. As already remarked, the early religion of the Vedic Indians, like that of each of the other Indo-European peoples, Iranians, Greeks, Romans, Celts, Teutons and Slavs, was polytheistic. What hints or suggestions of truth did such a polytheism furnish? In the first place, the Ṛv. polytheism, so essentially animistic in character, emphasized one fundamental doctrine of true religion, namely the omnipresence and immanence of Deity. Nature, especially in its striking phenomena, such as heaven, sun, moon, lightning, wind, rain, etc., was regarded as an apocalypse of the Divine. We may compare Ps. XIX. 1:—

> The heavens declare the glory of God
> And the firmament showeth His handiwork.

Then too the fact has already been pointed out in connection with the description of each deity, that there is much raw material in the Ṛv. on such important topics as the following: the existence, manifestation, power, wonder-working, justice, grace and helpfulness of God (or

---

[1] Ps. XVII. 15; LXXIII. 26.

[2] John XIV. 3; 1 John III. 2.

[3] Phil. I. 23. *Cf.* the similar note in Ṛv. I. 154, 5.

gods); God as the lord of nature and of battles; the correlation of grace and faith; repentance, confession, and the forgiveness of sin; communion with God, God's care for His own, and the future life. Thus even in connection with a polytheistic and not fully ethicised conception of Deity, it is clear that the Vedic Indians had some light, the Eternal God not having left Himself without witness among them. We may thankfully acknowledge every gleam of spiritual illumination which the hymns of the Ṛv. reveal, in particular the picture of the gracious and sin-pardoning Varuṇa.

The Ṛigvedic polytheism, as we have seen, was in unstable equilibrium, with a tendency toward monotheism on the one side, toward Pantheism, on the other. Early Iranian polytheism through the influence of the Zoroastrian reform issued in something very similar to an ethical monotheism, while early Vedic polytheism, in the absence of a prophetic personality like Zoroaster, issued finally in pantheism. The pantheism thus chosen did not altogether negate either polytheism or monotheism, but suffered them to remain as unripe views suitable for those regarded as immature.

6. We may glance finally at a notable modern attempt to find a strict and consistent monotheism in the Ṛv. Swāmī Dayānand Sarasvatī[1] (1824-1883) looked out on the religious life of India and saw two foreign monotheisms, both of Semitic origin, namely Christianity and Islam, which were growing relatively faster than Hinduism[2]. He noticed that each had a compact and definite creed, so

[1] Lajpat Rai, *Ārya Samāj*, 250 ff.; Griswold, Art. *Ārya Samāj*, ERE. II.

[2] This still continues. According to the Census of 1921 the increases in population in the Indian Empire during the decade 1911-1921 together with their percentages for Hindus, Muhammadans, Buddhists and Christians respectively are as follows:—

Hindus	— 852,306	that is	·39% decrease
Muhammadans	+2,087,934	" "	3·13% increase
Buddhists	+ 849,815	" "	7·92% "
Christians	+ 877,876	" "	22·64% "

different from the chaotic condition of things in Hinduism[1]. It was obviously only a question of time for these foreign creeds to win the day in India, unless the adverse tide were checked. In order to effect this, he saw clearly that an indigenous monotheism having the same virility and militant character as Islām and Christianity must either be discovered or created. He felt that it must be a distinctly Indian monotheism, not like the Brāhma Samāj with its striving after an international platform and an all-embracing creed. The many gods of the Ṛv. were, accordingly, interpreted as different names for the one God and the unity of Hindu pantheism[2] was conceived monotheistically. He observed that both Islām and Christianity permit widow-remarriage and that as a result the ratio of their increase is superior to that of Hinduism. Without interfering with the Hindu prejudice against the remarriage of widows, he provided a plan against the loss of population thereby entailed, *viz.*, the doctrine of *niyoga*, by which widows could be utilized apart from marriage for the propagation of offspring[3]. A brief creed in the form of 'ten principles' was elaborated to serve for purposes of religious propaganda[4]. An Indian theism was thus produced with a short and definite creed (or more exactly with a creed within a creed), to oppose the foreign theisms, Christianity and Islām. It left almost everything intact in Hinduism except polytheism and idolatry. These things were not found in the foreign theisms, nor in the

---

[1] Lajpat Rai, *op. cit.* 113.

[2] The unity affirmed in the quotations on p. 117 of Lajpat Rai's *Ārya Samāj* is the unity of the impersonal *brahma*, *ekamevādvitīyam* 'one only without a second', not that of God construed personally and monotheistically.

[3] Lajpat Rai, *op. cit.* 89, 147 ff. Niyoga, it is true, is sanctioned in Manu V. 158-160. See also Deut. XXV. 5-10, Gen. XXXVIII. 8.

[4] This creed (*op. cit.* p. 101 ff.) is so colourless and general that almost any theist on the face of the earth might subscribe to it, if he were allowed to put his own interpretation on article 3. It looks as if this creed were primarily intended for the purpose of foreign propaganda, the real working creed of the Ārya Samāj consisting of the fifty-one teachings of Dayānanda (*op. cit.* 81 ff.).

Vedas as interpreted by Swāmī Dayānand, hence must not be found in the new-born Indian theism. Swāmī Dayānand guessed correctly that for a time at least the average educated Hindu would prefer to join such a theism as the Ārya Samāj rather than one or the other of the foreign theisms. In doctrine and polity Swāmī Dayānand kept so close to orthodox Hinduism that there was no violent break in passing over from the Sanātan Dharma to the Ārya Samāj. This all represents an extremely clever attempt on the part of Swāmī Dayānand.

It would have been possible for the founder of the Ārya Samāj to have constructed a distinctively Indian theism on the basis of Varuṇa, the most ethical and theistic of all the Vedic gods, thus linking up Indian with Iranian theism[1] and providing a possible line of approach to the Parsee Community. But this would not have promised the immediate results which he desired, and besides would have required a type of scholarship and a critical acumen which he did not possess. There are so few references in the *Ṛigvedādibhāṣyabhūmikā* to the Varuṇa hymns that, in view of their lofty spiritual quality, one cannot but feel that Swāmī Dayānand did not find the 'Hebraic flavour' of these hymns quite to his taste[2]. To overlook the theistic and ethical significance of Varuṇa is as if one were to pass by the prophecy of Isaiah and concentrate one's attention upon Esther and Ecclesiastes.

Notwithstanding these and other defects which might be pointed out, Swāmī Dayānand succeeded in founding an indigenous Indian theism non-polytheistic and non-idolatrous, right in the very home of pantheism, polytheism and idolatry. This was certainly a notable achievement. If in reducing the multiplicity of Ṛigvedic gods to one God, he committed a sin against the critical conscience,

---

[1] Varuṇa originally the same as Ahura Mazda.

[2] In the Vedic stanzas quoted by Lajpat Rai (*op. cit.* 117 ff.) as furnishing a basis for a monotheism "of the highest, most exclusive and most exalted kind", there is not a single quotation from any hymn to Varuṇa and the Ādityas.

this much may be said on his behalf that the logical goal of polytheism is monotheism[1]; and further that a modern political and religious reformer, while even granting that for the consciousness of the Vedic Indians there were 'gods many and lords many', might yet be permitted for nationalistic purposes to hold that 'instead of issuing in pantheism[2] Vedism ought to have issued in a clear-cut and definite monotheism'[3], and hence for all practical purposes did so issue. The Society founded by Swāmī Dayānand has drawn a large number of educated Hindus out from the influence of pantheism, polytheism and idolatry, has set before them the worship of one God, and has instilled into them a strenuous and optimistic spirit. In these respects the Ārya Samāj is akin to Christianity and Islām, and is to be reckoṇed among the important theisms of the world. One may cherish the hope that with the increasing knowledge of sound methods of research the Ārya Samāj may be led to make a more searching and critical examination of the foundations of its faith as laid in the ancient literature. It is reassuring to be told that 'the Ārya Samāj does not claim infallibility'[4] for the Vedic translations, commentaries and (by implication) theology of its founder Swāmī Dayānand Sarasvatī. This apparently leaves the way open for profound changes to be made in the future.

7. Conclusion.—To sum up in brief. While certain aspects and teachings of the Ṛigveda, such as its dominant polytheism, its incipient pantheism, and its increasing tendency toward an abstract and non-ethical intellectualism find their fulfilment in the later Hinduism, there are other aspects of Ṛigvedic teaching which point rather in the direction of Christianity, such as the monotheistic and ethical Varuṇa, the high-priestly and mediatory Agni, the

[1] p. 87 n. 2.

[2] Pantheism for the *literati*, polytheism or at most an unstable monotheism for the multitude.

[3] p. 110.

[4] Lajpat Rai, *op. cit.* 97.

emphasis on the forgiveness of sin in connection with Varuṇa and the Ādityas, and the doctrine of the last things—heavenly home, luminous body, beatific vision, etc., etc.—so different from the later doctrine of transmigration. In view of this latter group of conceptions and aspirations, which have had no adequate fulfilment in Hinduism, but have such obvious points of contact with Biblical religion, Farquhar is justified in saying that "this early faith stands much nearer to Christianity than it does to Hinduism", and that "the religion of Christ is the spiritual crown of the religion of the *Rigveda*[1]. For the same reason K. M. Banerjea[2] writes that "if the authors of the Vedas could by any possibility now return to the world, they would at once recognize the Indian Christians far more complacently as their own descendants than any other body of educated Indians".

It is a fundamental truth that God has never left Himself without witness in any age or among any people, for the things that are seen attest the *existence* of the unseen God, the 'rains and fruitful seasons' bear witness to His *beneficence,* and to some extent the operations of conscience reflect His *will* and make manifest His *Law*[3]. Thus there is a light that lighteth every man that cometh into the world[4], the light of intelligence and reason, the light of conscience, the light that springs from the fact that we are made for God and that our hearts are restless until they rest in Him[5]. As 'by divers portions and in divers manners' God spake to the Hebrews through their prophets[6], so He spake, though less clearly, to the Vedic

---

[1] CH. 75, 77.

[2] Arian Witness, 10.

[3] Acts XIV. 17; Rom. I. 20; II. 14-15.

[4] John I. 9.

[5] Augustine.

[6] For the Christian attitude to the Old Testament see the following excellent statement by Dr. Farquhar, CH. 51-52: "Jesus acknowledged that the faith of Israel was from God, yet declared that He had been sent to transform it into a

Indians through their *Riṣis* and *Munis*, giving to both peoples more or less clear intimations of His nature and will, and making the very light which they received, however broken and partial, prophetic of a perfect illumination yet to come. For to both peoples alike, yea to all peoples, God's final revelation is in and through His Son[1], the Light in whom all lesser lights are gathered up and made complete. Thus we of the twentieth century possess much more light than did the people of the earlier ages. We shall do well to take heed lest the very abundance of the light we enjoy be our condemnation, if we fail to use it as we ought, and lest the men of the Ṛigvedic days rise up in the judgment with this our generation and condemn it[2]; for the Vedic people had at most a vague conception of God, a sense that He is immanent in all the

---

new religion. This was possible, because He knew that God's method of revelation is not the presentation, once for all, of a complete system of truth expressed in a book from all eternity, but a gradual and historical process. The simple beginnings of the faith of Israel are laid before us in the Book of Genesis; they grow before our eyes in the narratives of the other books of Moses; and they find still richer development in the Prophets and the Psalms. But even in them God's will is not completely revealed. Hence, to Jesus, the religion of Israel was given by God, but not given in permanency. It was God's instrument for the training of Israel. He came to crown it by transforming it into the religion for all men, and to crown its knowledge of God by revealing Him as the father of men......

Thus the principle of living growth, of progress and development, is set before us in visible form in the Christian Scriptures. The Old Testament is the bud; the New Testament is the flower. But, though the whole of the Jewish Scriptures are contained in the Christian Bible, they are not used by the Christian as they were used by the Jew. The whole of the Old Testament is retained, but it is read through Christ. For the Jew the whole is binding; for the Christian it is binding only in so far as it is in consonance with the Spirit of Christ. The Christian does not obey the Laws of Moses, though these are all contained in his sacred book. He does not offer animal sacrifice, nor abstain from the unclean foods of the law, nor circumcise his male children. The institutions of the old law were necessary for the childhood of the world. They are pictures, symbols prophecies, but the reality is Christ."

[1] Heb. I. 1-2.

[2] Luke XI. 31-32; Matt. XI. 21-24.

operations of nature and of life, but, dim as was the light they had, they nevertheless sought after God, if haply they might feel after Him and find Him[1]; and behold a greater light[2] has shined upon us than ever illumined the sages of the Vedic age, even the light of Him who is 'the light of the world''[3].

Like the gleaming of the Himalayan snows to the traveller on the plains is the morning beauty of the Ṛigveda, more attractive, if possible, to our hearts than the dazzling splendour of the Homeric poems. It is the whole of the picture—the people, the poetry and the faith reflected in it—that captivates our hearts.

But there is a tragedy in the Ṛigveda. Every student recognizes that the noblest element in the Ṛik is Varuṇa: creator, sovereign, all-knowing, all-seeing mind, source of order both cosmic and moral, from whose holy will spring the ordinances that govern all the powers of nature and also the moral and religious life of man, God of righteousness, mercy and grace, who punishes the stubborn sinner, releases the sinner who repents and seeks a nobler life, and holds happy and loving communion, in personal friendship, with the righteous man. There is nothing else in the Ṛigveda comparable with *that.* Yet, before the end of the Vedic period, Varuṇa had become a petty godling, lord of the waters; and all the priceless promise of that early faith had been completely lost to India. We need not ask what caused his fall. Every serious mind must recognize that we have here a religious tragedy of the utmost gloom and disaster.

But the tragedy is not the end of the story. A few centuries after the close of the Vedic age, there appeared in Palestine a religious leader worthy to be recognized at once as the Heir and the Consummator of the heritage of

[1] Acts. XVII. 27.
[2] John III. 19-21.
[3] John VIII. 12.

Varuṇa. Born a Jew, he drank from his parents and from the Old Testament the noblest elements of the religion of Israel. He learned to know God, the eternal One, creator and sovereign, all-seeing and all-knowing Lord, whose holy character and will form the source of Man's moral and spiritual nature. Too pure to tolerate iniquity, He punishes the rebellious, yet He calls the sinner to repentance, and welcomes the penitent to His grace, His love and His friendship. He had nourished and cherished the people of Israel with infinite patience and tenderness, and had trained them to be His witnesses and preachers among all the races of the world. Here is the teaching of Varuna carried a step further.

From His boyhood Jesus knew God in his own experience as his Father; and the foundation of all his teaching was this, that God is the loving Father of every human being. He went far beyond the Old Testament. His teaching is for all men, and is in such form as to suit men of every race and temperament and clime. He spoke of the love of God as infinitely faithful and tender to every child of the race; and in his own life and death he shewed forth all the active love, tenderness, invincible patience and willingness to suffer for others, which he knew characterized his Father. The gospels, which bring us his life and teaching, reveal to us the holiest, tenderest, loftiest character ever seen on earth. His death on the Cross — a death which Jesus voluntarily accepted as being his Father's will — exhibits, in one unforgettable scene, the holy one dying to wean men from sin to repentance and God, immeasurable love giving up all for the sake of those who in loving sin do not love God, the Son expressing, in his sufferings and death, the anguish of the Father over His erring children. Here the grace and forgiveness of Varuṇa find their clearest exposition and an immense and glorious extension. If the hymns to Varuṇa proclaim real truth, then the teaching and the death of Jesus exhibit to the whole world the full truth on those mighty themes. In the light of the Cross, in the most touching scene in the whole world's history, we may repair the disaster of the tragedy of Varuṇa.—Can India, then, afford to do without the crucified Jesus?

INDEX OF RIGVEDA PASSAGES QUOTED

Maṇḍala I.

Maṇḍala II.

INDEX OF TOPICS

R

S

T